Voice over IP Technologies: Building the Converged Network

Mark A. Miller, P.E.

M&T Books

An imprint of Hungry Minds, Inc.

Best-Selling Books • Digital Downloads • e-Books • Answer Networks
e-Newsletters • Branded Web Sites • e-Learning

New York, NY • Cleveland, OH • Indianapolis, IN

Voice over IP Technologies: Building the Converged Network

Published by
M&T Books
An imprint of Hungry Minds, Inc.
909 Third Avenue
New York, NY 10022
www.hungryminds.com

Library of Congress Control Number: 2002100190

ISBN: 0-7645-4907-3

Printed in the United States of America

10 9 8 7 6 5 4 3 2 1

1B/RR/QT/QS/IN

Distributed in the United States by Hungry Minds, Inc.

Distributed by CDG Books Canada Inc. for Canada; by Transworld Publishers Limited in the United Kingdom; by IDG Norge Books for Norway; by IDG Sweden Books for Sweden; by IDG Books Australia Publishing Corporation Pty. Ltd. for Australia and New Zealand; by TransQuest Publishers Pte Ltd. for Singapore, Malaysia, Thailand, Indonesia, and Hong Kong; by Gotop Information Inc. for Taiwan; by ICG Muse, Inc. for Japan; by Intersoft for South Africa; by Eyrolles for France; by International Thomson Publishing for Germany, Austria, and Switzerland; by Distribuidora Cuspide for Argentina; by LR International for Brazil; by Galileo Libros for Chile; by Ediciones ZETA S.C.R. Ltda. f or Peru; by WS Computer Publishing Corporation, Inc., for the Philippines; by Contemporanea de Ediciones for Venezuela; by Express Computer Distributors for the Caribbean and West Indies; by Micronesia Media Distributor, Inc. for Micronesia; by Chips Computadoras S.A. de C.V. for Mexico; by Editorial Norma de Panama S.A. for Panama; by American Bookshops for Finland.

For general information on Hungry Minds' products and services please contact our Customer Care department within the U.S. at 800-762-2974, outside the U.S. at 317-572-3993 or fax 317-572-4002.

For sales inquiries and reseller information, including discounts, premium and bulk quantity sales, and foreign-language translations, please contact our Customer Care department at 800-434-3422, fax 317-572-4002, or write to Hungry Minds, Inc., Attn: Customer Care Department, 10475 Crosspoint Boulevard, Indianapolis, IN 46256.

For information on licensing foreign or domestic rights, please contact our Sub-Rights Customer Care department at 212-884-5000.

For information on using Hungry Minds' products and services in the classroom or for ordering examination copies, please contact our Educational Sales department at 800-434-2086 or fax 317-572-4005.

For press review copies, author interviews, or other publicity information, please contact our Public Relations department at 317-572-3168 or fax 317-572-4168.

About the Author

Mark A. Miller, P.E., is the President of DigiNet Corporation, a Denver-based data communications engineering firm specializing in the design of local area and wide area networks. He is the author of numerous texts published by M&T Books, including *LAN Troubleshooting Handbook,* 2nd Edition; *LAN Protocol Handbook; Internetworking,* 2nd Edition; *Troubleshooting Internetworks; Troubleshooting TCP/IP,* 3rd Edition; *Managing Internetworks with SNMP,* 3rd Edition; and *Implementing IPv6,* 2nd Edition. Mr. Miller is a frequent speaker at industry events, and has taught many tutorials on internetwork design and analysis at ComNet, Comdex, Networld+Interop, Next Generation Networks, and other conferences. He is a member of the IEEE and NSPE and a registered professional engineer in four states. For information on his many tutorials, including one that is based upon this text, contact him via mark@diginet.com, or visit www.diginet.com.

Credits

ACQUISITIONS EDITOR
Greg Croy

PROJECT EDITOR
Kevin Kent

TECHNICAL EDITOR
Dr. John Thompson

COPY EDITOR
Annette S. Devlin

EDITORIAL MANAGER
Ami Frank Sullivan

**SENIOR VICE PRESIDENT,
TECHNICAL PUBLISHING**
Richard Swadley

VICE PRESIDENT AND PUBLISHER
Mary Bednarek

PROJECT COORDINATOR
Maridee Ennis

**GRAPHICS AND PRODUCTION
SPECIALISTS**
Beth Brooks
Jeremey Unger
Erin Zeltner

QUALITY CONTROL TECHNICIAN
Laura Albert
Andy Hollandbeck
Carl Pierce

PERMISSIONS EDITORS
Carmen Krikorian
Laura Moss

MEDIA DEVELOPMENT SPECIALIST
Megan Decraene

BOOK DESIGNER
Jim Donahoe

ILLUSTRATOR
Donna Mullen

PROOFREADING AND INDEXING
TECHBOOKS Production Services

COVER IMAGE
© Noma/Images.com

To Brutus, our good little dog
1991-2001

Preface

Technology (and for that matter, life in general) seems to be moving at an ever-increasing pace. The classic technical example is the Internet, where terms such as *multimedia* and *electronic commerce* were not widely used just a few years ago. (I will leave the classic *life* example up to your own research!) While we used to debate whether IBM's SNA, Digital Equipment Corporation's (now part of Compaq Computer Corporation) DECnet, or Novell's NetWare was the strongest networking architecture, there is now a clear and indisputable winner – the Internet Protocol or IP – which is supported in virtually all network operating systems, including SNA, DECnet, and NetWare. And of the various elements of the Internet protocol suite, the Hypertext Transport Protocol, or HTTP, which is used to transfer information on the World Wide Web, is now the most frequently used application on many networks.

Part of the buzz surrounding IP, and its emergence as the primary networking alternative of choice, is the term *network convergence*. Simply put, *convergence* means that all networking applications – voice, data, fax, image, or various combinations – should employ a single, cohesive networking infrastructure.

However, *convergence* is one of those terms that differs in theory and practice. In theory, voice traffic, which can be converted into a digital format, can coexist along with LAN traffic on a packet network. In practice, however, a voice application is quite unique, *primarily because the voice application must occur in real time*. And that challenge – the transport of real-time information via an IP-based network infrastructure – is the topic of this text.

Who Should Read This Book

This book is written for network designers, managers, and engineers who are exploring converged network technologies and thinking about combining their voice, data, video, or other information into a single system. It is assumed that readers have some degree of experience with both voice and data communication systems, such as Private Branch Exchanges (PBXs) and routers, respectively. It is also assumed that readers have had some exposure to both local and wide area networks, and to how TCP/IP and other Internet protocols operate on these networks. Readers needing details regarding TCP/IP may find two other volumes helpful: *Troubleshooting TCP/IP*, 3rd Edition, and *Implementing IPv6*, 2nd Edition.

How This Book Is Organized

This book is organized into three major sections: text chapters, reference appendixes, and a CD-ROM.

The text chapters fall into four main categories: converged network principles and applications (Chapters 1 and 2); converged network business issues (Chapter 3); converged network technologies for protocols, wide area transport, signaling, and component systems (Chapters 4, 5, 6, and 7); and converged network implementation and analysis (Chapters 8 and 9).

The appendixes provide a number of ready references for the reader, including lists of relevant standards, contact information for standards organizations, trade organizations, and IETF working groups, acronyms, abbreviations, and more.

The CD contains three main categories: Request for Comments (RFC) documents from the Internet Engineering Task Force (IETF) that relate to converged network technologies, a sample voice over IP client implementation, and some sample traffic analysis calculators.

I trust that the information in this book will assist you in converging your networks for the next networking millennium!

mark@diginet.com
March 2002

Acknowledgments

Many individuals made contributions to this work. My technical editor, Dr. John Thompson, made numerous suggestions for improvement, and my copy editor, Annette Devlin, made sure that no grammatical rules were violated. Donna Mullen did most of the research on the appendixes and produced all of the figures.

A number of individuals assisted with the case studies, examples, and figures given in this text. In alphabetical order, they are: Rod Anderson, Dane Andon, Jason Bach, Yasmin Ben-Dror, Woody Bode, David Bonner, Bill Casey, Jon Carville, Kevin Cripps, Oscar DeLeon, Eileen Eastman, John Gallant, Glen Gerhard, Ed Gustafson, Carla Hall, Carol Heller, Larry Hengehold, Joel Hughes, Ted Jackson, David James, Rakesh Joshi, Ali Kafel, Michael Kloberdans, Marty Lowrey, Eldon Mast, Michelle McAdams, Carol Meier, Greg Meyer, Hilary Mine, Ed Morgan, Frank Ohrtman, Ann Palermo, David Russell, K.K. Singh, Atul Sinha, Holly Stanton, and Chris Ward.

Tom Howard and Luc St-Arnaud provided the client software that is included on the CD-ROM that accompanies this text.

Contents at a Glance

Contents

Table of Illustrations

Chapter 1

Principles of Converged Networks

The concepts of network convergence – using one network to transmit both voice and data information – are not new. You can trace the evolution of this technology back several decades to the birth of the Integrated Services Digital Network (ISDN). This work, which was standardized by the International Telecommunication Union – Telecommunications Standards Sector (ITU-T), formerly known as the Consultative Committee for International Telephony and Telegraphy (CCITT), was the subject of much discussion and interest in the 1980s. This book begins with a brief look at the history of the topic.

1.1 The Promise of Network Convergence

In the 1980s, the term *convergence* was rarely used. Instead, telephone providers and subscribers used the term *integrated* to describe their vision of using a single telephone line to their home or business as a multifunction line for a variety of applications. These included voice communications (one or possibly two conversations over that single line), data applications for remote host access (stay-at-home shopping, remote electric meter reading, and so on), and even video applications (*à la* the famed Picturephone developed by Bell Telephone Laboratories in the 1950s). At that time, ISDN proponents imagined that these new technologies would displace the currently deployed analog Public Switched Telephone Network (PSTN) within a few years.

Unfortunately, the implementation of ISDN was more of a challenge than the architects of the technology envisioned. When the telephone companies began to deploy ISDN, it was discovered that a large number of the local loops – the physical circuits from the telephone company central office to the end-users' premises (home or small business) – would not support this high-speed data transmission. Some of the loops were too long, and some included systems that optimized the network for voice transmission and would not support the transmission of high-speed data.

As a result, ISDN deployments were focused on the requirements for new construction. For example, if a new housing development required new telephone

service, then making that new service compatible with ISDN technology made
sense. On the other hand, retrofitting existing outside plant systems to support
ISDN was much more expensive and was often not undertaken. As a result, large
parts of the United States still do not have ISDN service available. We could say
that the promise of converged networks based on ISDN technologies met with limited success. Research from the North American ISDN Users' Forum (NIUF) is a good
resource for those interested in ISDN technologies [1-1].

But before dismissing converged voice and data networks as just one more vendor architecture or carrier offering, we need to look at another significant trend,
this time coming from the data side of telecommunications — the emerging ubiquity
of the Internet Protocol, or IP. This protocol was originally designed in support of
U.S. military and higher education data networks and was migrated into general
business usage in the 1990s. The predecessor network to the current Internet was
named the ARPANET, an acronym for the Advanced Research Projects Agency
Network, which was funded in part by the U.S. government. The ARPA architecture
divided the computer communication functions into four different layers as shown
in Figure 1-1: the Network Interface or Local Network Layer, the Internet Layer, the
Host-to-Host Layer, and the Process/Application Layer.

OSI Layer	ARPA Architecture
Application	Process / Application Layer
Presentation	Process / Application Layer
Session	Process / Application Layer
Transport	Host-to-Host Layer
Network	Internet Layer
Data Link	Network Interface or Local Network Layer
Physical	Network Interface or Local Network Layer

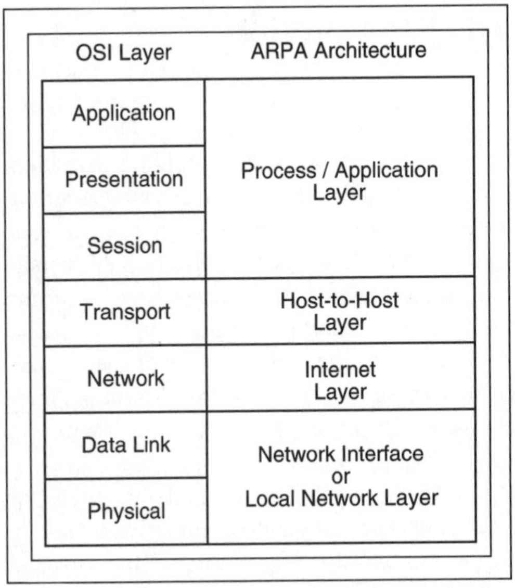

Figure 1-1: Comparing OSI and ARPA Models

Figure 1-1 also compares the ARPA architecture, originally developed in 1969,
with the more familiar Open Systems Interconnection (OSI) Reference Model,
originally published by the International Organization for Standardization (ISO) in
1978 [1-2].

The ARPA Network Interface or Local Network Layer corresponds with the OSI Physical and Data Link Layers and comprises the hardware elements of the networking infrastructure. The ARPA Internet Layer corresponds with the OSI Network Layer and is responsible for routing and switching the information (typically divided into packets) through that networking infrastructure; it must deal with issues such as packet delivery, routing tables, and addressing schemes. The Internet Protocol (IP) resides at the ARPA Internet Layer. The ARPA Host-to-Host Layer corresponds with the OSI Transport Layer and is responsible for the reliable end-to-end delivery of those packets. The Transmission Control Protocol (TCP) resides at the ARPA Host-to-Host Layer. Finally, the ARPA Process/Application Layer deals with the functions in support of the end-user's application, such as the logical connection (OSI Session Layer), data formats (OSI Presentation Layer), and application-specific support (OSI Application Layer).

At the present time, it would be very difficult to find any type of computing platform, from the smallest cell phone or personal digital assistant (PDA) to the largest mainframe computer, that does not support IP. In most cases, IP is used in conjunction with other protocols, such as the Transmission Control Protocol, or TCP. The term TCP/IP actually refers to a suite of protocols, which in most cases are incorporated into the host's operating system. A companion text, *Troubleshooting TCP/IP* [1-3], provides details on this widespread support for TCP/IP.

Two trends have emerged thus far. If you look at the voice networking side first, you find the idea of some type of combined voice/data network is not new. Unfortunately, the early implementations, such as ISDN, were somewhat problematic; as a result, most of the voice networking infrastructure within the PSTN of today is much like it was several decades ago (allowing for improvements in network technologies and capacities, such as when the PSTN became an all-digital transmission medium around 1990). Consultant James Cavanagh describes this evolution of the telephony system as three distinct markets: the First Wave, that of traditional, highly reliable yet legacy telephone systems; the Second Wave, which introduces Internet Telephony services; and the Third Wave, with its converged voice/data/video systems [1-4].

If you look at the data networking side next, you see that IP has become the common denominator infrastructure of choice and is widely implemented around the world. Thus, addressing the needs for combined voice/data networks, with technologies that are now more implementable than those of decades past, has definite appeal. A number of parties are interested in the success of such developments, including end users, network managers, equipment vendors, and networking carriers. Internetworking between the existing legacy networks and the IP networks, carrying voice, data, video, or other media, will require some careful planning, as Reference [1-5] describes.

This study of Voice over IP systems (VoIP) begins with a look at the principles of network convergence—the concepts that allow voice, data, fax, and video signals to share a common networking infrastructure. I start this journey with a look at some of the principles—and caveats—that are driving this area of technology, as discussed in References [1-6] through [1-12].

1.2 Connectionless vs. Connection-Oriented Network Architectures

In general, communications networks can provide one of two different types of network services: connectionless (CON) network service or connection-oriented (CO) network service. More specifically, an individual layer within a network architecture can be defined by the service it provides to the adjacent layer above: either CO or CON service. Taken as a whole, the communication architecture may incorporate some combination of these services in support of a particular application.

The typical model for a connection-oriented network service is the Public Switched Telephone Network (PSTN). When the end user takes the telephone off-hook, they notify the network that service is requested. The network then returns dial tone, and the end user dials the destination number. When the destination party answers, the end-to-end connection is confirmed through the various switching offices along that path. A conversation (or more typically a voice mail message) can then ensue, and when the conversation is completed, the parties say goodbye and hang up. The network then disconnects the call, terminates the billing process, and makes the network resources available for another conversation.

For the duration of the connection (or conversation), the communication path may be modeled like a very long pipeline: information is inserted into one end of the pipeline and taken out at the other end of the pipeline (Figure 1-2a). During the time the connection is active, certain statements can be made about that pipeline. For example, the data will arrive in the order in which it was sent (*sequentially*). The data will follow the same path (either a physical or logical path, depending on the network architecture in use) from the source to the destination. Finally, the relative delay of the data will be constant along that path. That is, if there is a 20 millisecond delay on the first word that is transmitted through the telephone network, there should be the same relative delay for the second word, the third word, and so on. Since these characteristics, such as sequentiality, delay, and so on, positively impact the quality and reliability of the transmission, a connection-oriented network is often referred to as a *reliable* network. The Transmission Control Protocol (TCP) is an example of a connection-oriented protocol.

In contrast, a connectionless network could be modeled by the postal system. A full source and destination address is attached to the packet (or envelope), and then that information is dropped into the network (or post office box). Each of these packets is routed independently through the network, and through the miracles of packet delivery protocols, delivery to the ultimate destination occurs — we hope, as shown in Figure 1-2b. But, like the postal system, connectionless network delivery is on a "best efforts" basis. This means they will do all they can to get your information through the network, but there are no guarantees of packet sequentiality, delay, or, for that matter, delivery at all. (At least, no guarantees for the price of a first class stamp. If you want more reliable package delivery, you can call FedEx, but it will cost you considerably more. Similarly, if a connectionless network does not meet your needs, you can always go with a CO system, but the overhead will invariably be higher.) The Internet Protocol (IP) and the User Datagram Protocol (UDP) are examples of connectionless protocols.

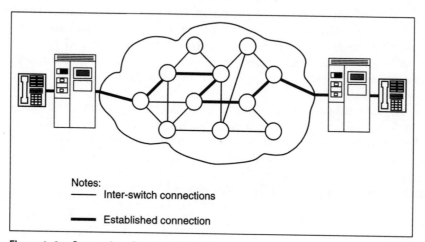

Figure 1–2a: Connection–Oriented Network

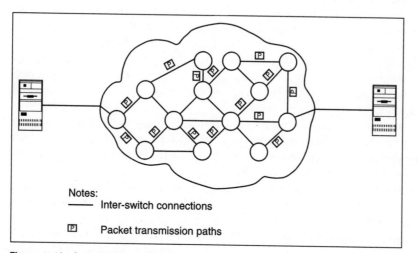

Figure 1–2b: Connectionless Network

1.3 Voice and Data Network Characteristics

Most enterprise networks are really a "network of networks," with distinct infra-structures that address specific requirements. For example, there may be a separate network for circuit-switched voice and fax; a private tie-line network for intra-company voice and fax; a centralized processing data network, such as one based on IBM's System Network Architecture (SNA); a distributed processing data net-work supporting client/server applications; a private internet or intranet for com-munication between employees; a public internet or extranet for communication with customers and/or suppliers; and systems and networks supporting other remote access configurations.

In general, voice networking infrastructures are connection-oriented, while data networking infrastructures are connectionless. But in order to determine which net-work type will be most prevalent in the years to come, consider some specifics of each technology.

1.3.1 Voice Network Characteristics

Traditional voice networks, such as the PSTN, are connection-oriented. To initiate a call, the end user takes their telephone off-hook, which signals the telephone com-pany Central Office (C.O.) that service is requested (Figure 1-3). The end user then enters the destination telephone number via the numeric keypad (or rotary dial, if you are into antiques!). The destination telephone number becomes input to the signaling system among the various C.O. switches to set up the call along the path from the source to the destination. The last C.O. in the chain signals the destination user's telephone that an incoming call is in process by sending ringing current through the line, thus creating an audible signal. When the end user (or that per-son's answering machine) takes the phone off-hook, the circuit is completed and communication can proceed.

One of the key elements that makes the PSTN so effective is its ubiquity, or uni-versal service – the premise that states that basic telephone service should be an affordable commodity to anyone who wants it. As a result, reaching (almost) any end user via the PSTN should be possible.

The current PSTN creates circuits that provide a bandwidth of 64 Kbps, an ele-ment known as a Digital Signal Level 0 (or DS0) channel. The characteristics of DS0 channels are explored in greater detail in subsequent chapters. For now, suffice it to say that the 64 Kbps of bandwidth that is provided with a DS0 (which dates back several decades) is much more than is required by current voice and fax technolo-gies. For example, a fax transmission uses only 9.6 or 14.4 Kbps of bandwidth, while the balance goes unused. Chapter 3 discusses in more detail how this "leftover" bandwidth can be used for other conversations with voice compression technologies, thus providing some of the economies of scale that help justify the investment in VoIP and FoIP equipment.

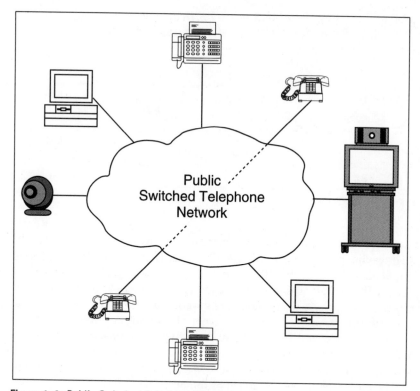

Figure 1–3: Public Switched Telephone Network

In some cases, switched network connections, which provide 64 Kbps per channel, are not adequate for the amount of information that needs to traverse the connection. For example, two PBXs may have a required number of simultaneous connections between two locations. For those applications, a private voice network can be configured, with trunk circuits provisioned according to the bandwidth requirements (Figure 1-4). As an example, if a dozen or so simultaneous conversations were expected between two locations, a Digital Signal Level 1 (or DS1) circuit would likely be employed, which provides 24 of the DS0 (64 Kbps) channels. As one might expect, the bandwidth of the trunk circuit is primarily limited by the depth of your checkbook – the carrier is quite content to provide more bandwidth as long as you are willing to pay for it. For example, the next step in the digital multiplexing hierarchy is known as DS3, which operates at 44.736 Mbps and provides the equivalent of 672 DS0 channels between two locations. Not too many organizations need this amount of bandwidth just for voice, but when other media such as data, fax, and video are considered, that amount of bandwidth is much easier to justify.

For the duration of a particular call, however, resources along the path of the circuit have been reserved on behalf of the communicating parties; as a result, the parties pay for the network services for the time that these resources have been reserved. The reservation of resources provides some predictable characteristics of that connection, including a constant delay for that unique path and sequential delivery of the information (the first word that I speak is the first word that you hear, and so on).

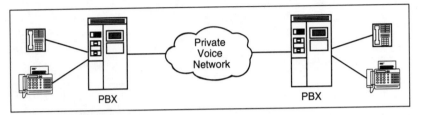

Figure 1-4: Private Voice Network

But if we were to summarize the characteristics of the telephone network, the term *reliable* would have to be used. Since the PSTN is considered a national resource, regulatory bodies such as the Federal Communications Commission (FCC) and state Public Utility Commissions (PUCs) monitor a number of PSTN operational characteristics. These include the number and duration of service outages, the time it takes to repair and restore service in the event of an outage, prices the carriers charge for their services, and so on. The phrase "five nines of reliability" comes from an industry standard for central office switches, which are designed for two hours of downtime in a period of 40 years of service. If all goes according to design, the network downtime would be calculated as follows:

2 hours of downtime/40 years * 365 days/year * 24 hours/day = 2/350,400 or 0.00000571

If this number is converted to availability (or uptime) by subtracting it from 1, you have the following:

Network availability = 1 - 0.00000571 = 0.99999429

Converting this to a percentage yields

99.999429 percent availability (or reliability)

Hence, the phrase "five nines of reliability."

As we explore throughout this book, the ultrareliable performance of the PSTN can be both a blessing and a curse. It is a blessing in that it rarely fails. (For example, when was the last time you went to a pay phone to make a call, and the pay phone was out of order? In contrast, when was the last time your PC locked up? It has been said that the good thing about conventional telephone service is that you don't have to reboot the end-user equipment!) It is a curse in that the end users know how reliable the telephone network is and expect that same level of service from a VoIP network.

1.3.2 Data Network Characteristics

In contrast to voice networks, which are generally connection-oriented, data network infrastructures are typically connectionless. Note that a distinction needs to be made between the networking infrastructure and the applications that run over that infrastructure. The applications may require a connection orientation, which would typically be handled by the ARPA Host-to-Host Layer (or OSI Transport Layer). For example, the File Transfer Protocol requires some degree of reliability and synchronization between the sending and receiving file transfer processes. Those functions are handled by TCP, which runs at the ARPA Host-to-Host Layer. IP, which is a connectionless protocol and runs at the (next lower) ARPA Internet Layer, would be considered the defining infrastructure protocol.

The origins of data networking are frequently traced to the development of packet switching and the X.25 protocol in the late 1960s. Packet switching technologies were developed, in part, in response to U.S. government requirements for secure and survivable military communication. The premise was to divide a large message into a number of smaller elements (called *packets*) and to then send these packets via different routes. The diverse routing made it much harder for an adversary to eavesdrop on the message when that message was broken up into smaller pieces and transmitted via different paths (thus yielding some degree of network security). In addition, routing around network failures was also possible, which made the network more robust or survivable. Other benefits were derived from packet switching, such as load balancing between different routes.

Early data networks relied heavily on leased line and packet switched (using X.25) connections, migrating to Internet connections as that transmission medium became more prevalent (Figure 1-5). From the host-to-host applications that were prevalent in the 1960s and 1970s, local area networks (LANs) became the data network of choice in the 1980s. Private data networks that comprised both the local network infrastructure (such as Ethernet LANs) and the wide area connections became the next step in the evolutionary process (Figure 1-6).

Figure 1-5: Public Data Network

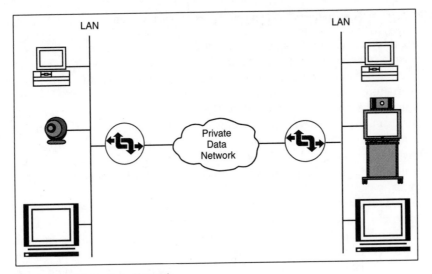

Figure 1-6: Private Data Network

In contrast to the ultrareliable, ubiquitous PSTN, data networks offer what is called "best-efforts" service. In other words, if your transmission on the Ethernet collides with mine, both are destroyed, and the retransmission mechanism built into Ethernet must be employed for subsequent transmission attempts. But that's the way it goes – the Ethernet undertook its "best efforts" to get the transmission through. At best, both transmissions will be delayed. Packet switching networks are another example of best-efforts service, because packets that arrive in error or too late may be discarded, requiring the upper layer protocol to request a retransmission. These multiple attempts yield overall network reliability that is quite a bit less than the 99.999 percent reliability provided on the PSTN. (If you doubt this, ask your end users if they can remember the last time a pay phone failed. Then ask them if they can remember the last time their local network failed. Compare the results, and I think you get the point.) But when the transmission is successful, you have access to a huge amount of network bandwidth – perhaps megabits per second of bandwidth – and are not limited to the 64 Kbps channels that are typically provisioned in voice networks.

Data networks are typically priced based on consumption. If you migrate from 10 Mbps Ethernet to Fast Ethernet to Gigabit Ethernet, you pay more per port. Similarly, if your WAN connections migrate from a DS1 circuit to a DS3, you also pay more. In contrast, PSTN pricing tends to be relatively flat, because the bandwidth consumed is a consistent 64 Kbps. For example, your PSTN rate may be $0.05 per minute any time of the day, to any destination in the United States.

Finally, there is a big difference in the speed at which innovation is required within data networks. These technologies move very quickly. The sales, marketing, engineering, customer support, and other departments within data networking organizations must be prepared to move quickly as well, as the end users of this service demand higher and higher data transmission rates, amounts of memory and information storage, and so on. Contrast this with the innovation that is required in the PSTN. The process of making a telephone call today is about the same as making one several decades ago. The PSTN infrastructure, such as the internal signaling systems, has markedly improved. However, since many of these improvements are not readily visible to the end user, the service presented to those end users may appear to be quiescent.

This brings us back to the subject of network convergence, and the implementation of an integrated voice/data network, such as that shown in Figure 1-7. Note that elements from both public and private voice and data networks are present. Our objective, however, is to take the most favorable characteristics of each network type and to design the new system to optimally handle both voice and data transport with equal facility. Our network infrastructure of choice is based on IP.

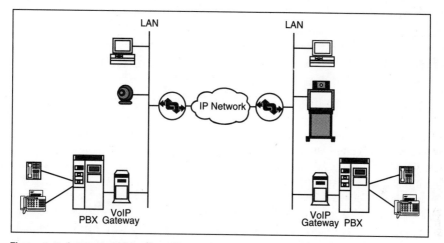

Figure 1–7: Integrated Voice/Data Network

1.4 Voice and Data Network Growth Factors

This section presents market growth and sizing information that relates to the Internet and other IP-based networks. It also contrasts traffic characteristics of voice and data networks. As with most research of this nature, the observations of the general *trends* become much more important than the finite *details* of the projections themselves, as it is unlikely that any of us can claim a high degree of success in predicting the future. Keep that premise in mind as you study this section, and look for the information that can guide you toward an informed decision regarding network convergence plans for your infrastructure.

In most organizations, the *growth* of voice traffic has been relatively flat in the past few years, while the *growth* of data traffic has increased much more aggressively, as shown in Figure 1-8. Note that at this point in our discussion we are considering growth patterns, not actual traffic volumes. Also notice that the exact point of crossover on the time axis has been omitted, as this would be a network-specific characteristic that varies from enterprise to enterprise. For example, a high-technology research center with an ATM switched infrastructure and fiber optic trunk connections may have seen its growth in data traffic exceed that of voice traffic some time ago. In contrast, a call center or service operations center may continue to have more voice than data and may not have an equivalent amount of voice and data traffic growth (the crossover point) for some time to come. And when you consider that most voice traffic today is still 64 Kbps traffic – not compressed, as the technologies of this text discuss – then the amount of traffic (measured in bits per second) that leaves your office may be greater in the voice case (today) than in the data case. In any event, however, consider that your data traffic growth should exceed that of your voice network at some time in the future, hence your interest in a converged network infrastructure.

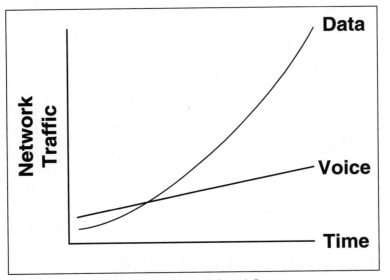

Figure 1-8: Typical Voice and Data Network Growth Patterns

To evaluate this premise, consider the following generalizations. The aggregate voice network (considering the PSTN, private networks, and so on) supports one primary application (voice) and a few data applications (such as modem traffic) that consume relatively small amounts of bandwidth (typically 64 Kbps per channel or less). The aggregate data network (including the Internet, private internetworks, virtual private networks, and application-specific networks, such as SNA backbones) supports many data applications. Much of this is heavily influenced by the large growth in the number of users attached to the Internet. The most prominent of this Internet traffic is World Wide Web information, which is clearly growing at exponential rates, fueled by electronic commerce and other interactive applications. (For an interesting look at how fast the number of Internet-connected hosts is growing on a daily basis, consult Reference [1-13].) It would not be an exaggeration to depict the generalized growth in voice traffic as being relatively flat (or linear), while the growth in data traffic has some positive slope (and possibly an exponential slope), as depicted in Figure 1-8.

The Yankee Group (Boston, Massachusetts) estimated the annual growth rate of traffic over a three-year period, and reached some of the same conclusions [1-14].

Traditional (PSTN) voice traffic is projected to decrease in North America and to increase slightly in Europe (Figure 1-9a). Trends for traditional data traffic are similar, but with larger variations (Figure 1-9b). The Internet/IP traffic projections tell a different story, however, as their increase is more than double that of the other two media types (Figure 1-9c). Therefore, these results in Figures 1-9a, b, and c quantify the intuitive hypothesis illustrated in Figure 1-8, supporting the idea that traffic will migrate from traditional networks, such as the PSTN, to IP and converged network infrastructures.

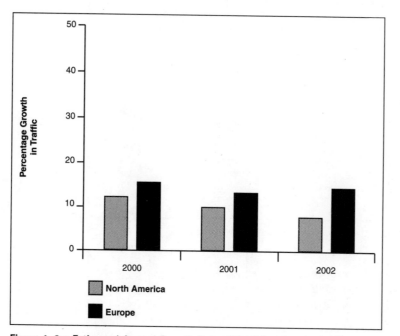

Figure 1-9a: Estimated Annual Growth Rate of Traditional Voice Traffic

(Copyright 2001, The Yankee Group)

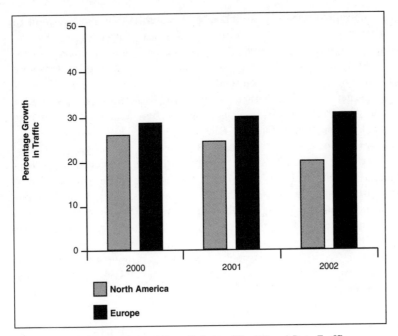

Figure 1-9b: Estimated Annual Growth Rate of Traditional Data Traffic

(Copyright 2001, The Yankee Group)

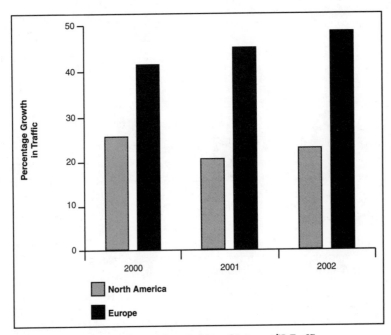

Figure 1-9c: Estimated Annual Growth Rate of Internet/IP Traffic

(Copyright 2001, The Yankee Group)

An interesting paradigm shift is occurring. In the last several decades, data has been treated as a special application to be sent over voice circuits, with dial-up modem traffic the most prevalent example. In today's environment, with packet-oriented data traffic being the area of highest growth, treating the voice traffic as a special application of data transport garners some appeal.

This can also be illustrated when the mix of global network traffic is segmented by both public (PSTN) and packet/private networks (Figure 1-10). As discussed earlier in the chapter, the PSTN voice traffic has relatively flat growth (the lower portion of Figure 1-10). When packet and private voice traffic is considered, network traffic is only slightly higher (the next highest, or second portion of Figure 1-10). PSTN data traffic has a higher rate of growth than either of the voice cases (the next highest, or third portion of Figure 1-10), while the packet and private data traffic has the highest growth of all (the top portion of Figure 1-10), once again supporting the hypothesis that traffic is migrating from the PSTN to packet-based networks that include a mix of both voice and data traffic.

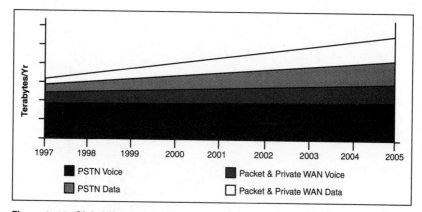

Figure 1-10: Global Network Traffic

(Courtesy of Probe Research, Inc.)

New public network infrastructures are being designed and built to handle these consolidated networks, by companies such as Quest Communications International, Inc., and Level 3 Communications, Inc. In building these new infrastructures, these firms are leveraging some of the significant increases in technology that have occurred in the last few years, such as high-capacity fiber optic backbones and routers that can handle aggregate throughputs in the gigabit per second range. These increases in technology provide one key ingredient necessary for the success of converged networks – favorable economies of scale that promise to reduce the overall costs of the enterprise infrastructure.

But determining the sources of this growth is essential for understanding the rate at which this growth will occur. Probe Research has identified five different market drivers for the Voice over IP (VoIP) and Fax over IP (FoIP) market, along with projected time frames when these market drivers will become significant (Figure 1-11). The Hobbyist phase (1996–1997) allowed two PC users equipped with compatible software and sound cards to send voice over the Internet. The Tariff Arbitrage phase (1998–1999) afforded the end user an opportunity to lower long-distance telephone costs, which became especially important for international connections. Parity with existing public and private voice systems will drive the market in the next phase (which began in 2000). For example, IP telephony gateways must provide interoperable, not proprietary, solutions, and compatibility with existing voice switching systems, such as private branch exchanges (PBXs) and central office (C.O.) switches, has become a higher priority of the vendor community. New applications have driven the market during the following phase (2001–2002), as both end users and network managers realize the benefits of unified messaging, multimedia conferencing, enhanced call centers, and other key applications. The final phase (2003–2005) will provide cost parity between packet-based voice services and the existing circuit-switched voice services.

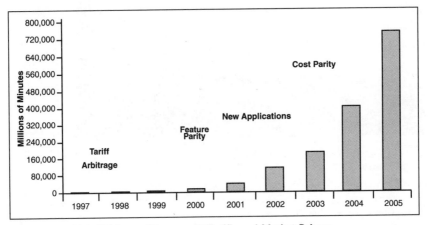

Figure 1-11: Global Voice and Fax over IP Traffic and Market Drivers

(Courtesy of Probe Research, Inc.)

In other words, the costs of the new technologies must present some advantage over the existing, well-established technologies in order to convince network managers of the long-term viability of voice and fax over IP solutions.

During these five phases, the end users of this technology can be segmented into several categories. Probe Research divides the IP telephony market into three general areas: wholesalers of telephony services, consumer/small business users, and enterprise/institutional customers (Figure 1-12). The wholesalers are those who are reselling telephone service via calling cards purchased at discount stores, convenience stores, gas stations, and so on—a market that appears to be growing at a very rapid pace, based on the number of retail displays for these products seen in stores. The calling card purchaser (or end user) is interested in low-cost telephone service, and the more technical issues regarding quality of that service, delays, and so on are of less concern (assuming, of course, that some minimum threshold of acceptable service has been met or exceeded). The consumers and small business users are possibly the most price sensitive, but are also the earliest adopters (note their presence in the 1997–1999 time frame). Enterprise and institutional customers are slower to adopt this technology (the 2000–2001 time frame), but after that have a high rate of growth as the technology is further implemented and tested. One might speculate that concerns over quality make for a more cautious entry into this technology for these organizations.

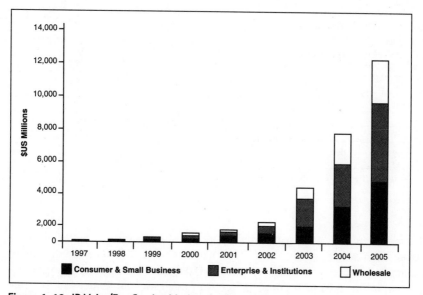

Figure 1–12: IP Voice/Fax Service Markets by Segment

(Courtesy of Probe Research, Inc.)

Financial research firm U.S. Bancorp Piper Jaffray, Inc. (Minneapolis, Minnesota) has looked at the voice and fax over IP market from the perspective of equity investments and has published a very comprehensive guide to these technologies: *IP Telephony: Driving the Open Communications Revolution* [1-15].

For the purposes of their research, Piper Jaffray segments the IP telephony market into five different categories. The Core Enabling Technology Platforms are the hardware and software components that enable IP telephony functions, and include various network interfaces, call processing and digital signal processing capabilities, switching systems, and so on. The Enterprise Solutions category includes voice gateways, client software, and other telephony functions. Applications would enable new end-user features and functions. The Carrier-Class Solutions are systems that are implemented within a carrier's network to include large-scale servers and routers, gatekeepers, billing systems, and so on. End-to-End Services are those organizations that are integrating voice and data equipment sales, installation, and other consulting-related services to other organizations.

Piper Jaffray estimates that, by the year 2003, the aggregate IP telephony market will total $14.7 billion in revenues. This is segmented somewhat differently and is broken down as follows: 6 percent from the core enabling platforms, 27 percent from gateway equipment, 8 percent from applications, and 59 percent from services. Specifics regarding the growth divided by the five segments noted above is shown in Figure 1-13.

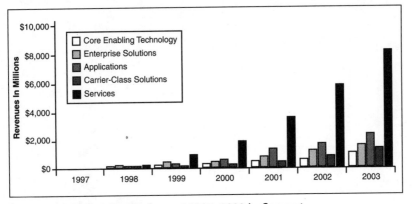

Figure 1-13: Market Growth Forecast 1997–2003 by Segment

(Courtesy of U.S. Bancorp Piper Jaffray, Inc.)

This market can be further segmented by geography, detailing the mix of product revenues that will come from international or domestic (U.S.) sources (Figure 1-14a). Note the shift from the 1997 conditions (20 percent domestic and 80 percent international) to the 2003 projections (55 percent domestic and 45 percent international), as more domestic carriers and firms adopt these technologies.

A similar change is noted in Figure 1-14b, which shows the mix of service revenues from the 1997 conditions (5 percent domestic-to-domestic, 20 percent international-to-international, and 75 percent domestic-to-international) to the 2003 projections (30 percent domestic-to-domestic, 28 percent international-to-international, and 42 percent domestic-to-international). As with the previous case, the domestic traffic will increase at the expense of the international traffic.

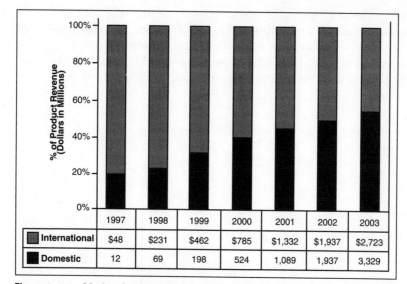

International	1997	1998	1999	2000	2001	2002	2003
International	$48	$231	$462	$785	$1,332	$1,937	$2,723
Domestic	12	69	198	524	1,089	1,937	3,329

Figure 1–14a: Market Growth Forecast 1997–2003 by Geography (Percent of Product Revenue)

(Courtesy of U.S. Bancorp Piper Jaffray, Inc.)

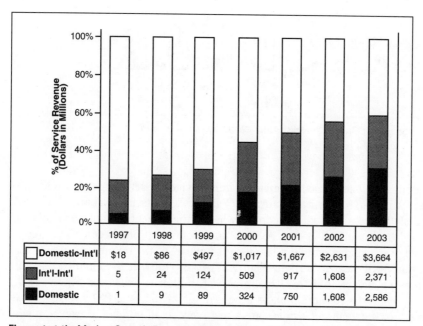

	1997	1998	1999	2000	2001	2002	2003
Domestic-Int'l	$18	$86	$497	$1,017	$1,667	$2,631	$3,664
Int'l-Int'l	5	24	124	509	917	1,608	2,371
Domestic	1	9	89	324	750	1,608	2,586

Figure 1–14b: Market Growth Forecast 1997–2003 by Geography (Percent of Service Revenue)

(Courtesy of U.S. Bancorp Piper Jaffray, Inc.)

The market growth by number of minutes of use for VoIP and FoIP services is also a key indicator of the anticipated popularity of the service (Figure 1-15). IP telephony traffic in 1998 was estimated at 476 million minutes, with 57 percent for VoIP and 43 percent for FoIP. By 2003 the total is projected to be 81.7 billion minutes, with 77 percent from VoIP, 17 percent from FoIP, and 6 percent from video over IP services.

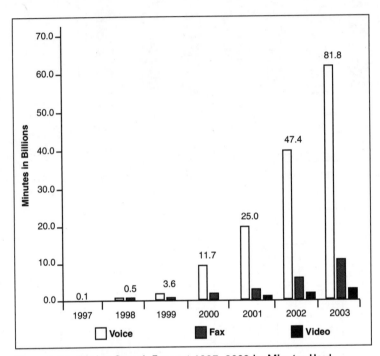

Figure 1-15: Market Growth Forecast 1997–2003 by Minutes Used

(Courtesy of U.S. Bancorp Piper Jaffray, Inc.)

The current market for telecommunication services is very large, dominated by carriers such as AT&T (United States), NTT (Japan), Deutsche Telekom (Germany), and British Telecom (United Kingdom), which primarily offer traditional dial-up and leased line solutions [1-15]. As VoIP and FoIP solutions become more commonplace, it is anticipated that a significant number of the minutes of use (MOUs) will migrate to IP-centric carriers (Figure 1-16). By 2003, it is estimated that this will represent over 81 billion MOUs, and $8.6 billion in revenues (Figure 1-17). Reviewing Figure 1-16, note that, as a percentage of the total PSTN MOUs, those that represent IP telephony services are a relatively small number. However, 6 percent of the total aggregate of worldwide telephony usage still produces some very large revenue numbers! This may be one reason that the more traditional carriers (such as AT&T) are developing IP-centric services to compete with the start-up Internet Telephony Service Providers (ITSPs) such as Level 3 and Qwest. Reviewing

Figure 1-15, note that, in the 2002–2003 time frame, video over IP services will become significant market factors as well.

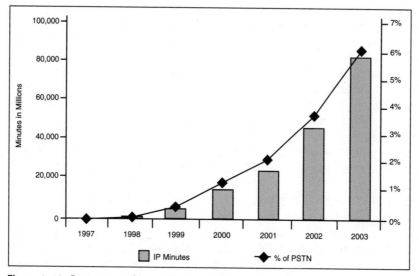

Figure 1-16: Percentage of Long-Distance Minutes Moving to IP Networks

(Courtesy of U.S. Bancorp Piper Jaffray, Inc.)

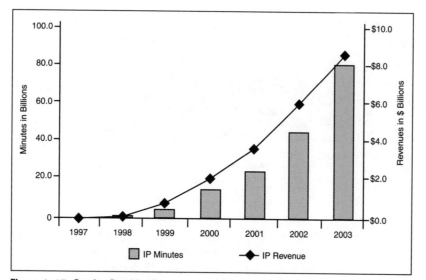

Figure 1-17: Service Provider Revenue and Minute Growth

(Courtesy of U.S. Bancorp Piper Jaffray, Inc.)

1.5 The New Market: Voice over Packet Transport

Thus far, this discussion has focused on Voice over IP technologies, assuming that hardware, software, and communication systems involved in the process are somehow connected to, or derived from, Internet research. However, there is a more general technology sector, known as Voice over Packet, or VoP, which may have a bearing on your converged network infrastructure. The VoP marketplace includes a number of broadband technologies that could be used as an alternative to conventional systems, such as the Public Switched Telephone Network (PSTN) to transport digitally encoded voice information. Examples of these transport options include Asynchronous Transfer Mode (ATM), frame relay, residential broadband (cable television systems), and Packet over SONET (the Synchronous Optical Network), abbreviated PoS.

The significance of the VoP technologies is in the amount of market share that they are projected to take away from conventional PSTN technologies in the next few years. Market researchers Probe Research, Inc., project that VoP will penetrate 14 percent of the traffic on the PSTN by 2006, as shown in Figure 1-18, taken from Reference [1-16]. While the magnitude of this number (14 percent) is not that large, it nevertheless represents a significant amount of revenues to traditional carriers such as AT&T, MCI Worldcom, and Sprint in an era of ever-decreasing profit margins.

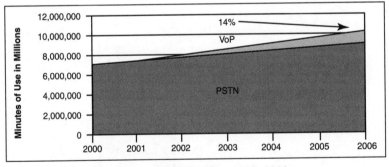

Figure 1-18: Worldwide PSTN and VoP Traffic — 2000–2006

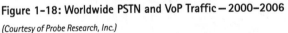

(Courtesy of Probe Research, Inc.)

Voice traffic is measured in *minutes of use*, with voice over packet minutes, as projected by Probe Research, to be any of these call minutes that are packetized for at least a portion of the call along its path from source to destination. Thus, a call that originates on the PSTN and then traverses an IP network would count as a VoP call. Likewise, a call that is packetized at the customer premises, and carried over a public network to its destination, would also be considered a VoP call. This VoP traffic can be segmented into three different markets: international, domestic long distance, and local traffic, as shown in Figure 1-19. Note that international traffic made up the majority of the VoP traffic until 2000, but domestic long distance is projected to dominate the subsequent years. Local traffic has the smallest initial market share, but grows to almost equal the domestic long-distance market in later years. Probe's research concludes that growth in the local VoP segment has been thwarted by the recent industry tumult from both the regulatory and business perspectives, but that growth should occur as those issues are resolved.

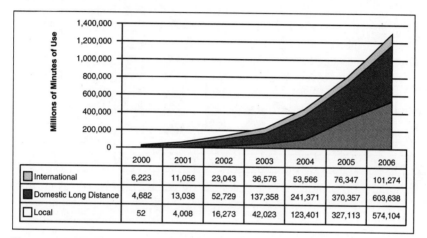

	2000	2001	2002	2003	2004	2005	2006
International	6,223	11,056	23,043	36,576	53,566	76,347	101,274
Domestic Long Distance	4,682	13,038	52,729	137,358	241,371	370,357	603,638
Local	52	4,008	16,273	42,023	123,401	327,113	574,104

Figure 1-19: Worldwide VoP Traffic by Call Segment — 2000–2006

(Courtesy of Probe Research, Inc.)

When considered individually, these three markets project very positive growth numbers. The worldwide local VoP traffic and revenues are projected to reach over 574,000 million minutes of use and almost $6 billion in revenues by 2006 (Figure 1-20).

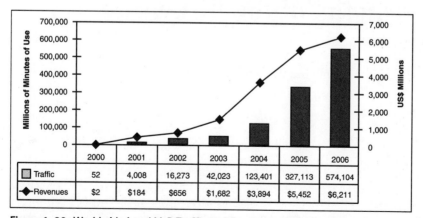

	2000	2001	2002	2003	2004	2005	2006
Traffic	52	4,008	16,273	42,023	123,401	327,113	574,104
Revenues	$2	$184	$656	$1,682	$3,894	$5,452	$6,211

Figure 1-20: Worldwide Local VoP Traffic and Revenues — 2000–2006

(Courtesy of Probe Research, Inc.)

The worldwide domestic long-distance VoP market is projected to reach over 600,000 minutes of use and over $18 billion in revenues by 2006 (Figure 1-21).

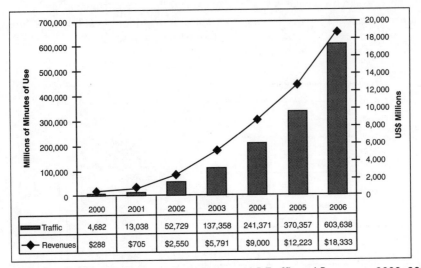

	2000	2001	2002	2003	2004	2005	2006
Traffic	4,682	13,038	52,729	137,358	241,371	370,357	603,638
Revenues	$288	$705	$2,550	$5,791	$9,000	$12,223	$18,333

Figure 1–21: Worldwide Domestic Long-Distance VoP Traffic and Revenues — 2000–2006

(Courtesy of Probe Research, Inc.)

Finally, the worldwide international VoP market is projected to reach over 93,000 minutes of use and over $12 billion in revenues by 2006 (Figure 1-22). In summary, the potential for these converged markets is so large that a number of organizations, from incumbent carriers to equipment vendors, are all vying for a piece of that revenue.

1.6 Benefits of the IP-Centric Network

These are the major hypotheses that have been presented in this chapter thus far:

◆ The idea of converging voice and data traffic into a single network is not new.

◆ The Internet Protocol, and IP-related technologies, are well understood and widely implemented (near-ubiquity) within the telecommunications industry.

◆ For many reasons, data networks, which incorporate packet switching technologies, are generally more efficient than voice networks, which use circuit-switching technologies.

♦ The growth of traffic from voice networks is relatively flat, in sharp contrast to the growth of traffic from data networks, which is very steep.

♦ Given the large number of voice communication, data communication, and Internet communication users, plus the large volumes of revenues from these industries, the total market potential for the voice, fax, and video over IP technologies is very large.

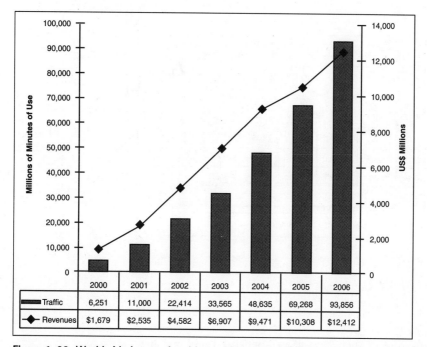

Figure 1-22: Worldwide International Long-Distance VoP Traffic and Revenues — 2000–2006
(Courtesy of Probe Research, Inc.)

With these hypotheses in mind, consider the following:

Given the current environment, does it still make sense to enhance the capabilities of the voice network to transport data, or, instead, to enhance the capabilities of an IP-centric data network to carry additional applications (voice, fax, and/or video)?

Assuming that such an IP-centric network is deployed, it is important to define the services that it can support. Nortel Networks' document, "Enhancing IP Network Performance" [1-17], divides IP services into three categories: application services, enabling services, and internetworking services. Figure 1-23, which is modeled after the seven-layer reference model, employs an IP-centric system to tie the networking infrastructure at the lower layers to the applications at the higher layers. The three key application services include mission-critical applications, such as human resources, finance, customer support, and so on; voice and fax over IP; and multimedia over IP, such as video conferences, distance learning, and so on. The enabling services enhance the capabilities of IP-based networks, dealing with issues such as traffic management, security, directory services, policy-based networking, and virtual private networks (VPNs) with remote access and extranet support. Internetworking services provide access to the IP-based network from non-IP-centric networks (such as SNA or X.25 WANs). Note that the core of this technology is the Internet Protocol.

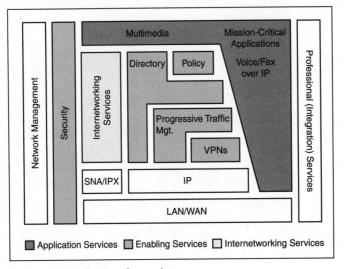

Figure 1–23: IP Services Categories

(Courtesy of Nortel Networks)

The benefits of such a converged network could include:

◆ A reduction in the overall complexity of the networking infrastructure: fewer protocols, operating systems, and so on.

◆ Synergies between carrier circuits supporting voice and data, and possible elimination of circuit redundancy.

◆ Possible reduction in carrier circuit charges.

◆ Integrated management systems and strategies that can support both the voice and data networks, instead of separate management systems.

◆ More consistent user interfaces, such as integrated fax and e-mail.

◆ Access to enhanced applications, such as integrated messaging, voice-enabled Web sites, desktop video conferencing, and others.

The next section considers how the converged network can be deployed.

1.7 Provisioning the Converged Network

Thus, the IP telephony network would include a number of elements – some from traditional voice networks, such as telephones, fax machines, and PBXs; some from traditional data networks, such as terminals, hosts, and servers; and some from new systems, such as gateways and gatekeepers, that are designed as the glue to hold all of these disparate systems together. Figure 1-24 illustrates some of these elements, which could incorporate many different subsystems, including the PSTN, dedicated WAN connections, IP routers, wiring hubs and end stations, and many others.

A call over an IP network could start with a local PSTN connection and the conversion of the analog voice signal to a digital pulse stream at the client end station, PBX, or gateway. That pulse stream will likely undergo some signal processing, including silence suppression and echo cancellation. The gateway may consult with a gatekeeper and/or Domain Name Service (DNS) server to obtain information about the desired destination, such as its transmission capabilities and IP address. The voice signal is then converted into packets, transmitted over the IP-based network to a destination gateway, and the digital pulse stream is reconstructed. As a final step, the digital pulse stream is then converted into an analog signal and delivered to the desired destination.

1.8 Challenges of the Converged Network

Despite the very positive projections for the converged network marketplace, the path from theory and concept to implementation and reality can have a few obstacles and detours along the way. In the case of voice, fax, and video over IP systems, the challenges come in several areas, as discovered by Sage Research, Inc., and illustrated in Figure 1-25 [1-18]. Respondents from large enterprise organizations that currently implement or plan to implement VoIP were asked, "Which of the following are/were challenges to deploying VoIP? Please check all that apply." Almost two-thirds of the respondents indicated that the maturity of the technology (or perceived lack thereof) presented a major challenge to their plans. Other key challenges included convincing executive management of the need for the converged technology, compatibility concerns, and cost issues. (Note that multiple responses were allowed, making the total on the graph exceed 100 percent.)

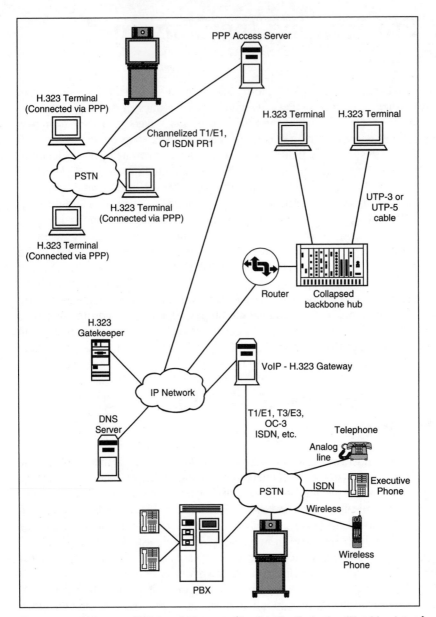

Figure 1-24: Voice over IP Network Elements (Possible Configuration, Not Mandatory)

(Source: Voice over IP Forum)

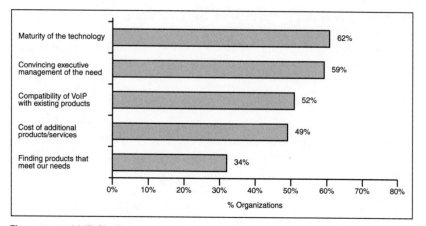

Figure 1-25: VoIP Challenges

(Courtesy of Sage Research, Inc., Natick, Massachusetts)

Those respondents from large organizations that *did not* plan to implement VoIP were asked, "Please indicate the single most important reason your organization is not deploying VoIP at this time." As illustrated in Figure 1-26, slightly more than one-third of the respondents (36 percent) felt that the technology was not mature enough to be deployed, while over one-fourth of the respondents (26 percent) felt that they did not have a need to deploy the technology at this time.

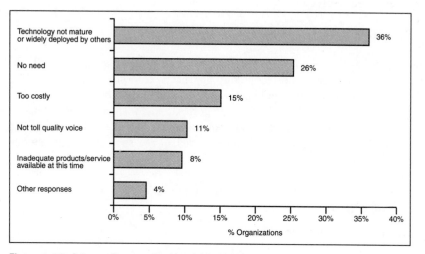

Figure 1-26: Primary Reasons for Not Adopting VoIP

(Courtesy of Sage Research, Inc., Natick, Massachusetts)

Thus, the existing mindsets of the networking constituents, the large number of players in the marketplace, and the technical difficulties afforded by the marriage of voice and data systems all contribute to the challenges of converged networks. The next sections look at these three areas individually.

1.8.1 Voice and Data Networking Mindsets

As was discussed earlier in the chapter, voice and data networks have been designed to address different challenges and, as a result, those who design, configure, and manage these two types of networks approach their respective challenges from different viewpoints. For example, in many organizations, voice telephone service is treated as a utility, much like the electric or water utilities (and possibly taken for granted). As such, it is not always afforded the high-technology moniker that is given to the computing side of the house.

Data networking requirements are often driven by the applications they support, such as a customer database. Thus, the data network is more likely to be associated with the success (or lack of success) of the entire enterprise. (If you doubt this, pick up a networking journal and look at a testimonial advertisement. The typical message is: "We installed XYZ networking products, our downtime decreased, our throughput increased, and we all lived happily ever after. If you buy XYZ products, you will become successful as well.")

Thus, when one considers implementing an integrated network, which will comprise elements from both the voice and data networks, key issues, such as who will fund, who will manage, and who will be ultimately responsible for the converged network, need to be resolved.

1.8.2 VoIP Market Players

Reviewing Figure 1-13, we note that there are five categories of segments to the IP telephony marketplace: enabling technology platforms, enterprise solutions, applications, carrier-class solutions, and end-to-end systems integrators.

Noting the wide diversity in these five categories, and considering the extensive growth factors that were discussed in Sections 1.4 and 1.5, it is not hard to realize that a number of different organizations have entered, or will soon enter, this marketplace. Examples include:

◆ Traditional carriers: both Inter-Exchange Carriers (IXCs) and Local Exchange Carriers (LECs)

◆ Internet service providers (ISPs)

◆ Internet Telephony Service Providers (ITSPs)

◆ Fax service bureaus

- PBX equipment manufacturers

- Networking equipment manufacturers

- Application developers

For completeness, we would need to add the standards organizations, such as the Internet Engineering Task Force (IETF), the International Telecommunications Union (ITU), and the Institute of Electrical and Electronics Engineers (IEEE); plus special interest groups, including the Voice over IP Forum and the International Multimedia Teleconferencing Consortium (IMTC), and others, which produce work that crosses many of the above technology segments.

1.8.3 VoIP Implementation Challenges

As we have discussed in this chapter, integrating the significant differences between voice and data networks into a single, cohesive system, and then integrating those systems, can be challenging. To identify some of the topics that are considered in subsequent chapters of this book, as well as to provide some food for thought, consider the following (Figure 1-27):

- Numerous standards exist in support of voice and data networks. How will these standards be applied to a converged network?

- Voice networks are ultrareliable. How will this reliability be translated into the converged network?

- The convergence industry is at its early stages. Will the products and services that you select from different vendors be interoperable?

- Network transmission characteristics, such as latency or delay, are more predictable with voice networks than data networks. How might these differences affect the end-user applications?

- How will the converged network integrate with any existing systems, such as a PBX or voice mail network?

- Does your network infrastructure have enough excess bandwidth to support voice, fax, and/or video applications?

- How will the converged network be managed – from the perspective of voice transmission, from the perspective of data transmission, or as an integrated system?

- Will regulatory bodies, such as the FCC, impact voice transmission over IP-centric networks, such as the global Internet?

◆ How will the existing levels of Quality of Service (QoS) be maintained? This challenge needs to be addressed from two perspectives: the perspective of the end user who is concerned about the quality of their voice call, and the perspective of the recipient of that call, perceiving whether or not the caller is understandable. This issue is especially important for emergency service agencies, such as police and fire departments, and the reliability of their E911 services.

◆ How should the user interface into the converged network be considered?

◆ How much will the converged network cost, and which department will foot the bill?

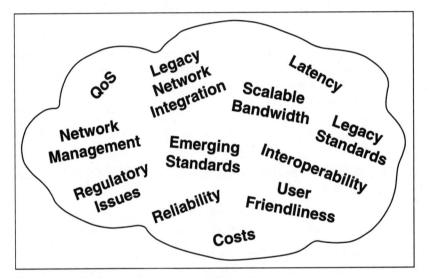

Figure 1-27: Challenges of the Converged Network

1.9 Looking Ahead

In this chapter, we have considered the principles of network convergence, the differences between voice and data networking infrastructures, the projections for growth in these respective areas, and the various players in this marketplace. Independent of these growth factors and which market research you choose to embrace, a general direction in today's networking environments points toward a convergence of the voice and data worlds—a trend that would be difficult to ignore.

The next and subsequent chapters drill down into these issues in greater detail, beginning in Chapter 2 with a discussion of the new applications that require a converged network infrastructure.

1.10 References

[1-1] The North American ISDN Users' Forum (NIUF) may be contacted at `http://www.niuf.nist.gov`.

[1-2] International Organization for Standardization. *Information Processing Systems – Open Systems Interconnection – Basic Reference Model*, ISO 7498-1984.

[1-3] Miller, Mark A. *Troubleshooting TCP/IP, 3rd Edition.* Foster City, CA: IDG Books Worldwide, Inc., 1999.

[1-4] Cavanagh, James P. "Defining the Three Markets of Telephony." Available from `www.mbird.com/pdfs/wp_three_mkts.pdf`, January 29, 2000.

[1-5] Fredj, Amy. "Interworking Between Next Generation IP and Legacy Networks." Available from `www.commatch.com/data/websotefo;es/WP-Interworking Between NG IP and Legacy Networks.pdf`, August 2000.

[1-6] Voice 2000: BCR's Guide to Emerging Voice Technologies. *Business Communications Review Supplement*, October 1998.

[1-7] Nicoll, Chris. "Multiservice Integration – Networks Converge on the Data Infrastructure." *Business Communications Review Supplement* (February 1999): 1–4.

[1-8] Miller, Mark A. "Voice, Video, and Fax over Internet Protocol: Possibilities for Converged Networks." *Decision Resources Spectrum Report*, April 15, 1999.

[1-9] Hu, Howard, and Houman Modarres. "IP Telephony – Paving the Way for Enhanced Services." Available from `www.3com.com/other/pdfs/infra/corpinfo/en_us/50304601.pdf`, Document number 503046-001, May 1999.

[1-10] Dickey, Clinton. "Voice and Data Convergence – Migration to an IP Telephony Network." Available from `www.cirilium.com/gfx/news/ip_telephony_white_paper.doc`, April 30, 2000.

[1-11] Covell, Andy. "Digital Convergence." *Network Computing* (December 11, 2000): 91–100.

[1-12] Richardson, Robert. "Unified Communications: Wireless, ASP, CPE Strategies." *Communications Convergence* (July 2001): 47–57.

[1-13] The number of Hosts and Servers on the Internet at any given time is calculated by Telcordia Technologies (formerly Bellcore) at `http://www.netsizer.com/daily.html`.

[1-14] The Yankee Group. "Global Network Strategies: The End User Speaks." 2001.

[1-15] Jackson, Edward R., and Andrew M. Schroepfer. *IP Telephony: Driving the Open Communications Revolution.* Piper Jaffray Equity Research Report, February 1999.

[1-16] Probe Research, Inc. *VoP Basic Services: Market Segmentation and Forecast.* CISS Bulletin, Volume 2, Number 4, 2001. For details, see www.proberesearch.com.

[1-17] Anderson, Rod. "Enhancing IP Network Performance: A Sensible Solution for Mission-Critical Applications." Nortel Networks Whitepaper WP503-2953EC-A, January 1998.

[1-18] Sage Research, Inc. *Primary Research Conducted in 2000.* For further information, see www.sageresearch.com.

Chapter 2

Applications for Converged Networks

The previous chapter considered the principles of converged voice and data networks, as well as the challenges that occur when one considers the integration of those different systems. This chapter brings those principles closer to reality by examining case studies of real networks that implement these concepts. In doing so, we look at a number of applications, taken from real networks, that consider voice, fax, video, and various multimedia signals that can be transported over IP-based infrastructures.

This chapter presents a number of case studies that illustrate the breadth of applications that converged networks can support, including voice, fax, video, and Web-based implementations. Some of these applications, however, may meet your networking goals more appropriately than others. Therefore, you might want to quickly scan the chapter and pick out the case studies that are most applicable to your networking objectives and environment. You can return to the other case studies as time constraints and applications dictate.

In each example, we consider the technical challenges and the enabling technologies that were deployed to solve those challenges. In addition, we introduce some of the functional components, such as gateways and gatekeepers, that are the building blocks of a converged network. Further discussion regarding the operational characteristics of these building blocks is deferred until Chapter 7.

2.1 Telephone-to-PC Communication via the Internet

Many Internet users have one telephone line into their residence or small business. Therefore, when those users connect to the Internet using a modem and a single telephone line, the telephone line is busy and other telephone calls cannot be received.

There are several solutions to this "busy signal" problem: a second telephone line, a cable or satellite hook-up, ISDN or DSL service, and so on. However, all of these solutions require additional installation and monthly costs for the Internet user. In some locations, the time required to order and install that additional service may exceed the patience of the end user.

A software-based solution to this problem has been developed by eRing Solutions, Inc. (Montreal, Quebec, Canada). The eRing product, called itRings!, allows an Internet user to receive telephone calls directly at his or her computer connected to the Internet without having to interrupt the Internet session. With itRings!, anyone using an ordinary telephone can now talk to an Internet user.

The itRings! service consists of three elements: client software, gateways, and a gatekeeper. The client software is installed on the computer of the Internet user. (This software can be downloaded without charge from the itRings! Web site, www. itRings.com.) The itRings! Client Software runs on Microsoft Windows 95, 98, Me, 2000, and NT 4.0, and requires a sound card with microphone and speakers attached. The itRings! Gateway is an Internet telephony server that links the Public Switched Telephone Network (PSTN) with IP networks. This gateway enables an Internet user to receive telephone calls directly at the PC from anyone using an ordinary telephone. The itRings! Gatekeeper is a server connected to the Internet. It manages access to the itRings! service for all itRings! Gateways and itRings! Client Software (end users) around the world.

To use itRings!, someone trying to reach the Internet user simply calls the Net Number (a toll-free telephone number) assigned by itRings! to the user (Figure 2-1a). The itRings! Client Software pops up on the screen of the Internet user (Figure 2-1b) and enables an exchange of voice messages between the person who is calling (with an ordinary telephone) and the Internet user at the PC (through the microphone and speakers). Note that the itRings! service doesn't try to emulate a second phone line and support a real-time full-duplex voice conversation over the Internet connection. Instead, itRings! allows an Internet user to be reachable at all times, with no additional costs for a second telephone line. The person calling and the Internet user exchange a few voice messages in half-duplex mode. If the conversation gets too long to be held through itRings!, the Internet user can log off the Internet modem connection and call back using the telephone.

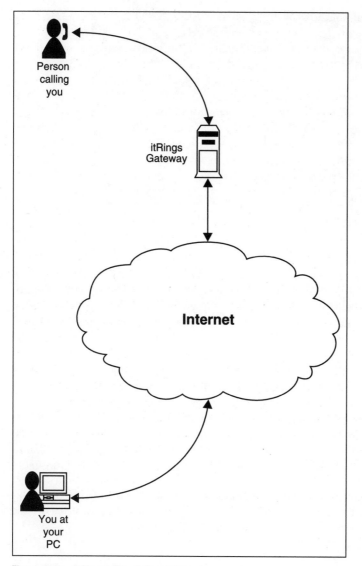

Figure 2-1a: itRings! Client Operation

(Courtesy of eRing Solutions, Inc.)

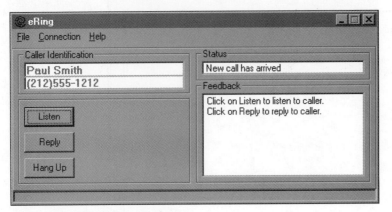

Figure 2-1b: itRings! User Interface

(Courtesy of eRing Solutions, Inc.)

Two primary services are supported by itRings!: Phone-to-PC communication and Voice Mail. With the Phone-to-PC service, the caller dials the Net Number of the Internet user. The itRings! Gateway sends a request to the itRings! Gatekeeper, which replies with the IP address of the Internet user (Figure 2-1c). The itRings! Gateway then enables an exchange of unidirectional voice messages between the person who is calling from an ordinary telephone and the Internet user at the PC. If the Internet user is not reachable when the call is placed, the itRings! Gateway offers the caller the option of leaving a voice message, which will be delivered via e-mail to the Internet user the next time he or she connects to the Internet.

Client-to-gatekeeper and gatekeeper-to-gateway communications use the User Datagram Protocol (UDP). Client-to-gateway communications, which carry the actual conversation, use the Transmission Control Protocol (TCP) for greater reliability and communication efficiency. (UDP and TCP operation will be explored in detail in Chapter 4.)

The itRings! service offers many additional features. These enhanced features include:

♦ A log of the calls received

♦ The ability to play a prerecorded message to the caller for users who do not have a microphone to answer an incoming call

♦ A message center, which can take a message from the caller if the Internet user is not online or has declined to accept the call

♦ The ability to receive calls from abroad (for example, someone calls the itRings! Gateway in Manila to reach an Internet user in the United States)

♦ The ability to receive calls from a user via a toll-free number of the itRings! service (for callers who don't have a local itRings! Gateway in their calling area)

Further information on the itRings! service is available in Reference [2-1].

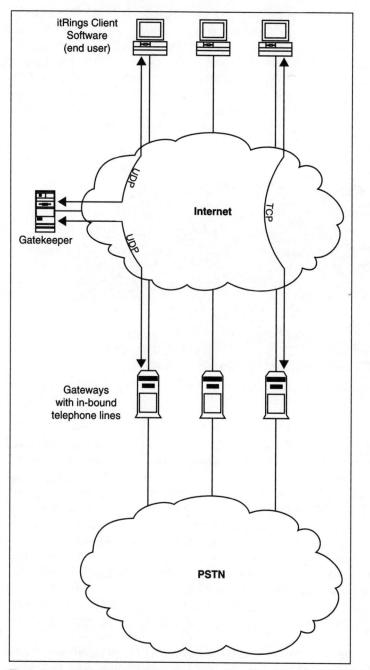

Figure 2-1c: itRings! Network Components

(Courtesy of eRing Solutions, Inc.)

2.2 VoIP Transport for PTTs

iBasis, Inc. (Burlington, Massachusetts), is a provider of wholesale international long distance services, also known as a "carrier's carrier." iBasis maintains the world's largest IP-based international Cisco Powered Network for voice over IP, with network facilities in more than 70 countries, and a network that carries international voice and fax traffic for some 120 carriers around the world (Figure 2-2). This network serves international voice and fax traffic for most of the world's largest carriers, including AT&T, Worldcom, Sprint, Qwest, Cable & Wireless, Telstra, Teleglobe, and others, plus many of the world's Post Telephone and Telegraphs (PTTs).

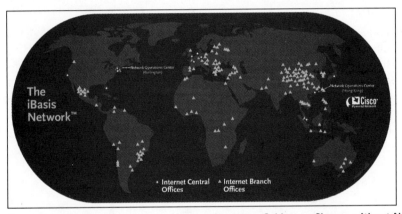

Figure 2–2: The iBasis Network as of November 2001. Subject to Change without Notice.

(Courtesy of iBasis, Inc.)

iBasis connects their Internet Central Offices directly to very large backbones, which enables them to bypass many of the points of congestion that are normally associated with the Internet. They have also developed proprietary software and methodology for least-cost routing, quality monitoring, and dynamic rerouting that has enabled iBasis to achieve very high call completion and voice quality results. The company also offers its customers service level agreements (SLAs).

An example of a PTT that has turned their international long-distance traffic over to an established Internet telephony network is the Communications Authority of Thailand (CAT), a wholly owned state enterprise of the government of Thailand. It is solely responsible for carrying all incoming and outgoing telecommunications traffic to and from Thailand, except for traffic to and from its bordering countries, which is carried by the Telephone Organization of Thailand, a government-owned domestic carrier.

In 1998, CAT recognized that Internet telephony would play a significant role in international telecommunications, and invited local Thai companies to submit proposals for a TCP/IP-based network compliant with ITU standards. CAT stipulated that the system must provide Internet telephony services to all designated countries around the world. Further, it must provide services with completion rates comparable to those of PSTN service.

In August 1999, after considering several proposals, CAT entered into agreement with the Thai company Hatari Technology Co., Ltd., whereby the latter agreed to provide and install an Internet telephony network for CAT's phone-to-phone international service. Hatari signed a service level agreement with CAT and then contracted with iBasis, Inc., for use of its global VoIP network.

Shortly after this service deployment and implementation, CAT and Hatari contracted for iBasis' IP CallCard service, branding it as PhoneNet, now a widely established Hatari-marketed service in Thailand. Because of its high quality and substantially lower caller costs when compared to international direct dial (IDD) service, PhoneNet has become a great success.

Since connecting with iBasis, CAT and Hatari have experienced significant growth in Internet telephony traffic, necessitating a doubling of capacity of Hatari's connection to The iBasis Network in early 2001. As a result of this successful three-way relationship, CAT has enabled lower-cost international telecommunications for the people of Thailand without making a substantial capital investment in new infrastructure, nor managing complex telecommunications clearinghouse arrangements.

Further information on The iBasis Network is available in Reference [2-2].

2.3 Replacing International Leased Lines

OpenTel Communications, Inc., is an international long-distance carrier based in San Francisco, California, which focuses on traffic between the United States and Asia. The voice traffic passes through an OpenTel Central Office switch and then is routed to voice gateways provided by Nuera Communications, Inc., of San Diego, California, for compression and transmission to the destination city. The voice gateways compress the traffic to between 4.8 Kbps and 9.6 Kbps, depending on the route. To ensure voice quality, OpenTel uses leased lines operating between 256 and 1,544 Kbps to interconnect their points of presence (POPs) between the United States and Asia (Figure 2-3).

Due to increased competition in the marketplace, OpenTel was under pressure to reduce the rates it charged to serve the Pacific Rim region. This required OpenTel to investigate new methods to reduce its own monthly costs for providing these services, much of which revolved around the leased line costs between the United States and Asia. For example, typical costs for these leased lines were around $5,000.00 per month per 128 Kbps of bandwidth, with some route costs as high as $10,000.00 per month per 128 Kbps of bandwidth.

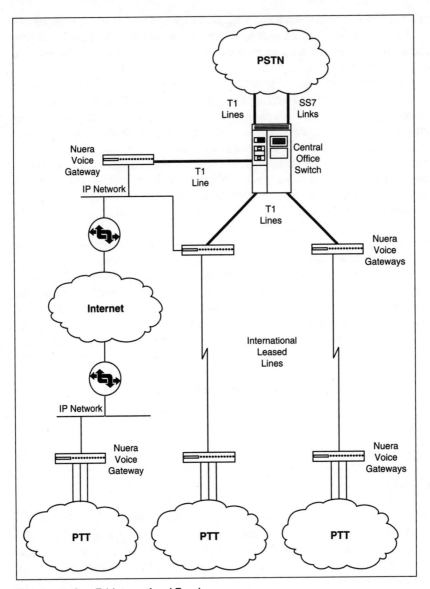

Figure 2-3: OpenTel International Topology

(Courtesy of Nuera Communications, Inc.)

Two options were available: reduce the bandwidth required per call or reduce the cost of that bandwidth. The first option was rejected because the calls were already being compressed to 4.8 Kbps, and it was determined that further compression could reduce the voice quality and potentially lead to customer dissatisfaction.

In attempting to reduce the cost of that bandwidth, OpenTel considered both frame relay and IP transport alternatives to the existing leased lines. Frame relay connections promised to lower the costs by about 25 percent, but had the downside of a potential reduction in voice quality if congestion occurred. In addition, frame relay connections were not always available in Asia, which would mandate long and expensive leased line tail circuits to reach the service provider POPs.

An IP-based transport solution proved to be much more economical and readily available. The service sites for the Internet were more numerous, which cut down the "last mile" tail circuit costs. Furthermore, the circuit cost was not based on the international bandwidth used, but only on the port speed provided, and was typically in the range of $2,000–$3,000 per month for T1 speeds. On the Asian sides the connection was more expensive, but was still lower than the alternative frame relay connections, with an average cost of $2,000 per 128 Kbps of bandwidth. Therefore, OpenTel concluded that an IP solution was both faster and less expensive to provision than the leased lines or the frame relay network alternatives.

OpenTel started slowly by providing Internet access to the major POPs with known good IP performance. They were able to use the same Nuera gateways they had been using for the frame relay connections by simply reconfiguring these gateways to have IP as their primary route between systems. After about a month of testing, the first T1 circuit was cut over to use IP as the primary route. After a month of testing under live traffic conditions, additional routes were converted to the IP-based infrastructure and several leased lines were removed. An additional benefit of this topology is its redundancy – where existing leased lines are still in place, the Internet can be used as an alternate route in the event that those leased lines experience outages.

Further information on OpenTel Communications services is available in Reference [2-3].

2.4 Voice-Enabled Electronic Commerce

Many potential customers come to a vendor's Web site browsing for information. Sometimes they find what they are looking for, and sometimes they don't. But *browsers* are not necessarily *buyers,* as they may encounter several roadblocks along the way. For example, they may not be able to find the information they are seeking, they may have found some information but still have questions, or perhaps they are ready to make a purchase but are reluctant to enter their credit card information for security reasons.

Cisco Systems, Inc.'s, products respond to these electronic commerce challenges by integrating voice or chat and visual communication in several ways. The Web/call center integrates the capabilities of the Internet, the vendor's PBX, and Automatic Call Director (ACD), the vendor's customer call center, into a single system to enhance customer support. The Web-enabled call center provides the customer with a simple one-click button to connect them with a live customer service agent for further assistance. This further assistance can take a form that best meets the needs of that customer: a telephone call from a customer support representative, an e-mail response, a chat room facility, or a voice over IP connection.

In the case simulated here, a customer of Global Bank uses the Bank's "collaboration server" to explore, discover, and communicate with the bank's customer agent. Using the collaboration server, a Global Bank Contact Center agent has a wide range of tools to work with their customer. Examples of the screens that are seen by both the customer and the call center agent are shown in the following figures.

First, the customer logs onto the Global Bank Web site and clicks the "enter" icon (Figure 2-4a). This takes him to the online banking page, where he can select the "Talk To Us Now" option (Figure 2-4b).

Since the customer has requested a live telephone conversation as his option for communication with the bank, he next enters his contact information on the "Talk-To-Me-Live" screen and sends this form to the call center (Figure 2-4c).

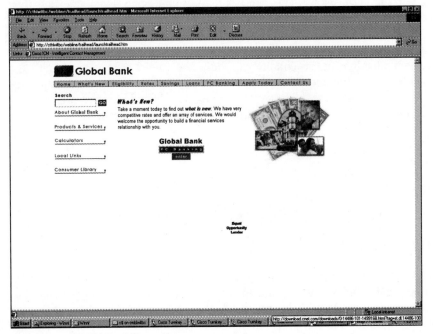

Figure 2–4a: Global Bank Home Page

(Source: Cisco Systems, Inc.)

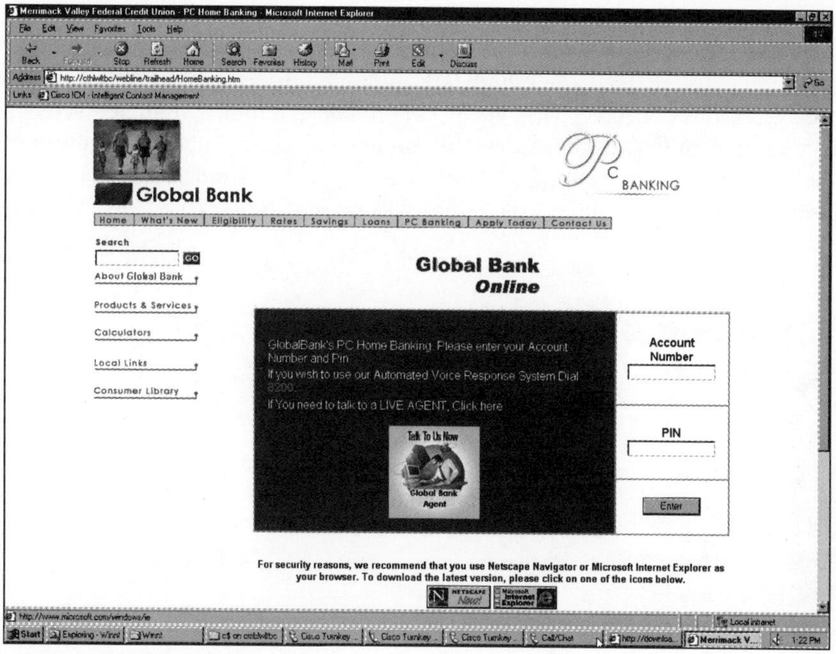

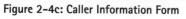

Figure 2-4b: Online Banking Page

(Source: Cisco Systems, Inc.)

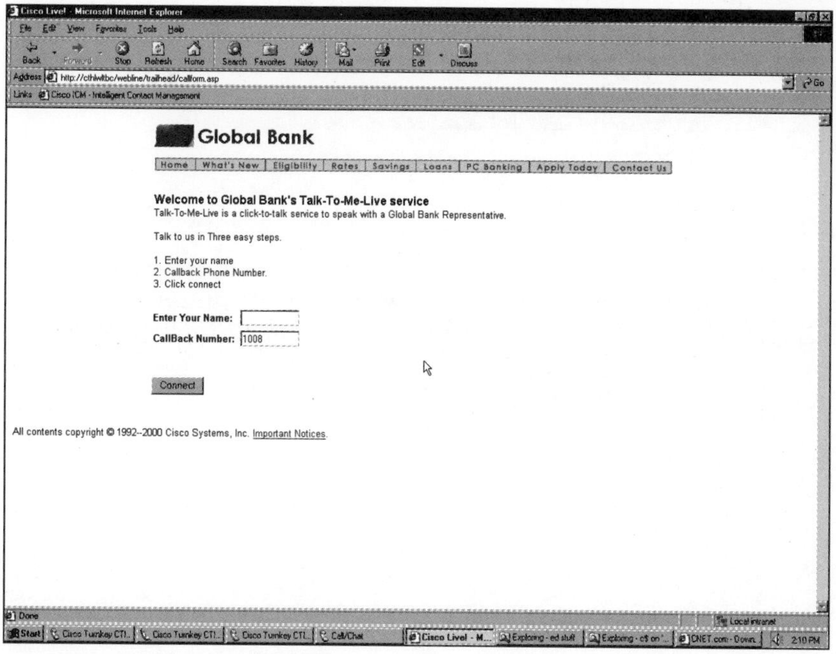

Figure 2-4c: Caller Information Form

(Source: Cisco Systems, Inc.)

At the Global Bank call center, the agents using Cisco's Turnkey Computer Telephony Integration (CTI) product are waiting for the next call. Each agent has a number of options available to communicate with and answer his or her customer's questions. From the CTI screen, the agent can enable a number of shared screens and collaborative functions to address his or her customer's queries. The agent screen splits into two parts: an agent control screen with various content options on the left and the initial content page that will be sent to the caller on the right (Figure 2-4d).

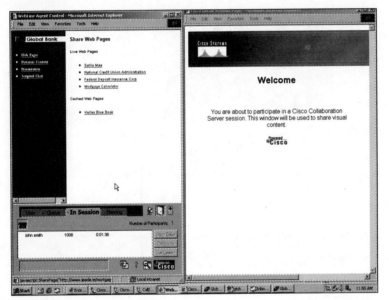

Figure 2–4d: Call Agent Screen

(Source: Cisco Systems, Inc.)

One option is for both the agent and the customer to share Web pages, in this case the home page for a company called United Finance (Figure 2-4e).

In response to a customer question, the agent can request shared dynamic content for the customer (Figure 2-4f). For example, a current stock quotation can be viewed by both agent and customer (Figure 2-4g).

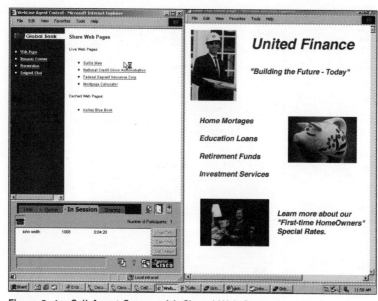

Figure 2-4e: Call Agent Screen with Shared Web Content

(Source: Cisco Systems, Inc.)

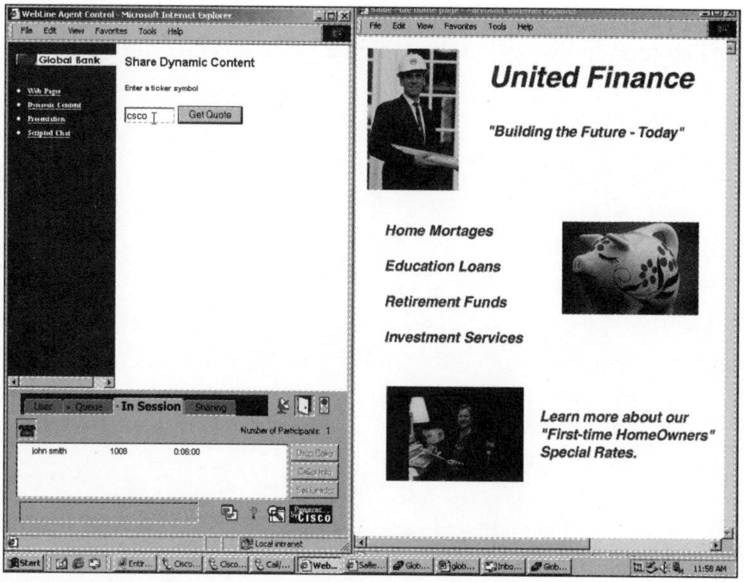

Figure 2-4f: Call Agent Screen Requesting Shared Dynamic Content

(Source: Cisco Systems, Inc.)

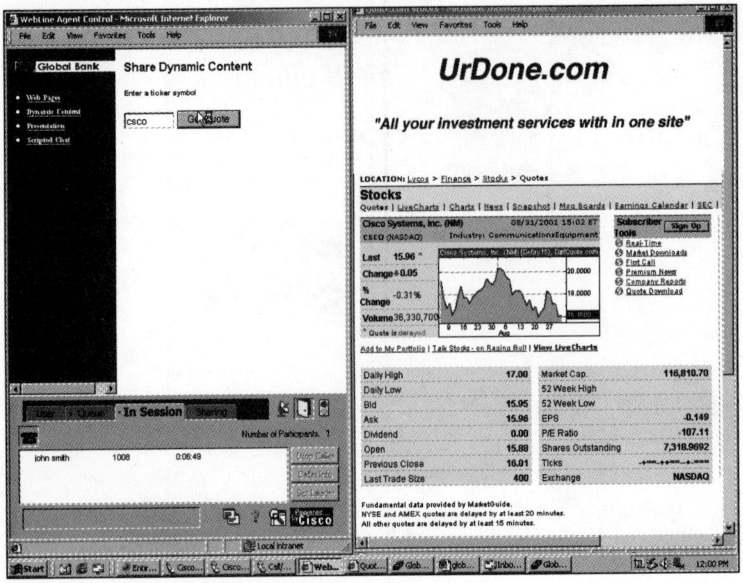

Figure 2-4g: Dynamic Content Sent to Customer

(Source: Cisco Systems, Inc.)

The call agent can also step through a slide presentation with the caller – take note of the left pane in Figure 2-4h – or collaborate using a white board (Figure 2-4i).

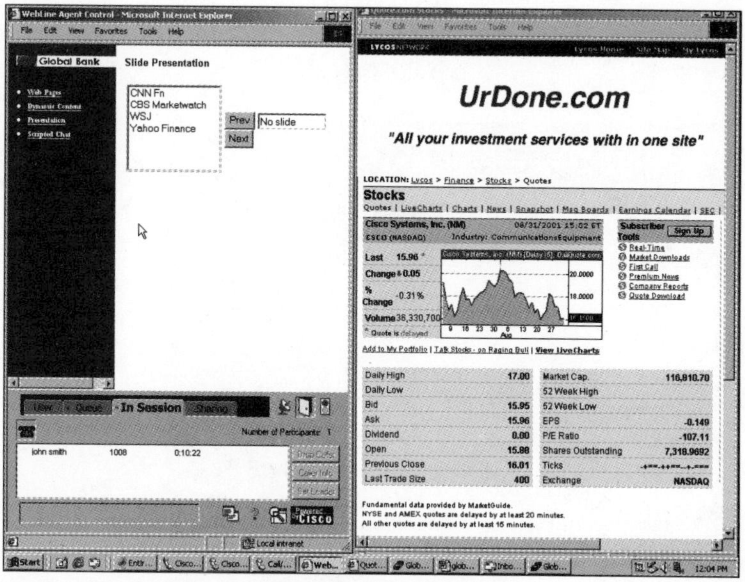

Figure 2-4h: Sharing a Presentation with Customer

(Source: Cisco Systems, Inc.)

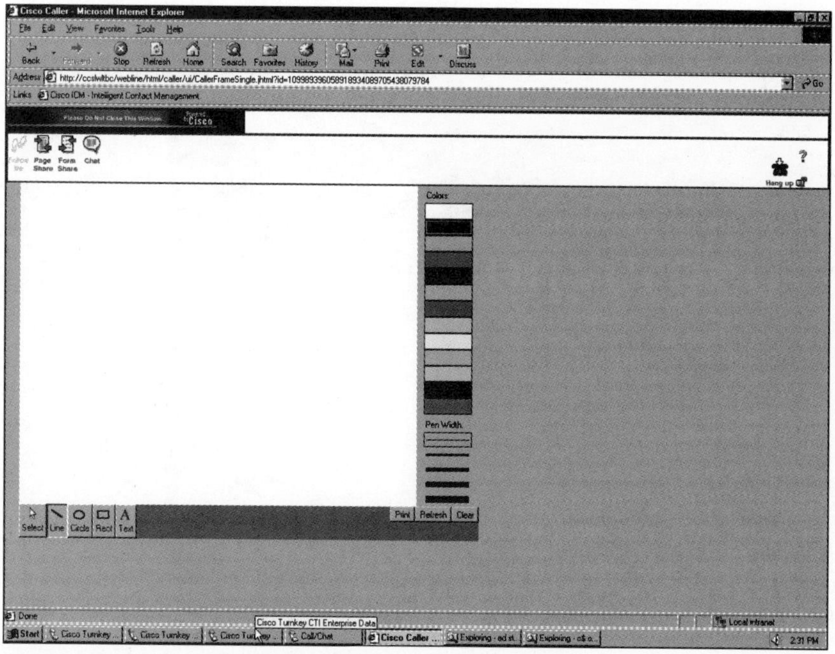

Figure 2-4i: Sharing White Board Information with Customer

(Source: Cisco Systems, Inc.)

An Internet chat session can also be initiated by the customer (Figure 2-4j), to which the agent can respond (Figure 2-4k).

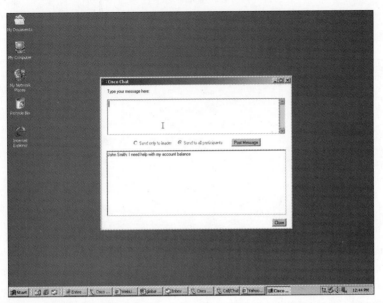

Figure 2–4j: Internet Chat Query

(Source: Cisco Systems, Inc.)

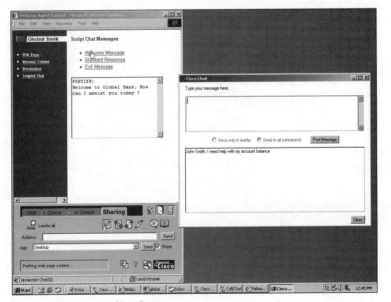

Figure 2–4k: Internet Chat Response

(Source: Cisco Systems, Inc.)

The agent can also initiate an onscreen comparision between two different products (Figure 2-4l), such as the mortgage rates offered by one bank and their competition (Figure 2-4m).

When the caller's questions have all been answered, the call center thanks the customer for their business and enquiry (Figure 2-4n).

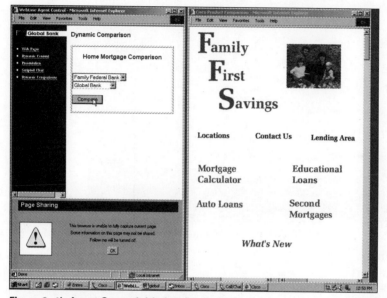

Figure 2-4l: Agent Screen Initiating Comparison

(Source: Cisco Systems, Inc.)

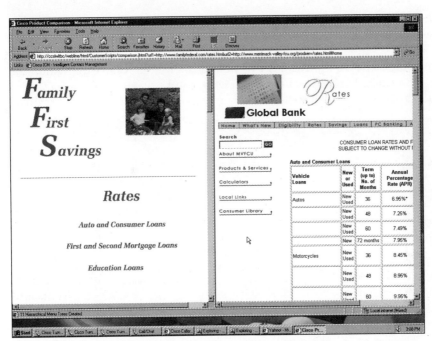

Figure 2–4m: Customer Screen with Comparative Information

(Source: Cisco Systems, Inc.)

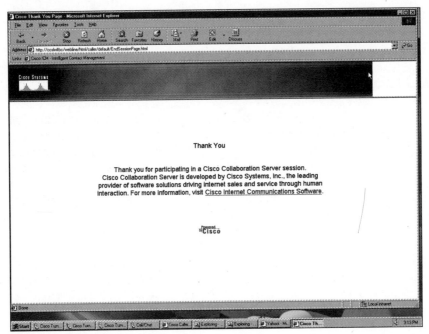

Figure 2–4n: Call Center Thank You Screen

(Source: Cisco Systems, Inc.)

When the call is complete, the call center agent disconnects the call and prepares for the next customer.

In summary, a Web-based call center provides many benefits for both the customer and the vendor. For the customer, questions can be answered immediately, using audio, video, and textual media. For the vendor, individuals that access the Web site and then request live information are more qualified as customers than are those simply approached by a cold call, since they have a genuine interest in the vendor's products or services. When the interactive session is provided, complete information is presented to the prospects, improving the chances of closing a sale.

Further information on Cisco Systems's applications is found in Reference [2-4].

2.5 Voice and Video over IP: The Adirondack Area Network

The concept of a community network throughout the Adirondack region of New York State began to evolve in 1994. Many independent study groups had concluded that the lack of a network infrastructure and customer premises equipment prevented development of any programs to support the varied end-user requirements. The announcement of New York State Advanced Telecommunications Project's (NYSATP) Request for Proposals appeared in this same time period, and the Adirondack Area Network (AAN) was funded by this grant in 1995. The goal of the AAN was to develop a converged network capable of supporting all of the outcomes desired by various groups, since no individual category of end users was large enough to sustain the necessary infrastructure cost-effectively.

The Adirondack region of New York posed a variety of challenges to those creating this network. Technology infrastructure and high bandwidth lines that would be required for the planned applications were lacking in many areas. Of these applications, one of the most desirable was telemedicine, as there was a limited number of health care facilities in the Adirondacks, and therefore limited access to medical specialists. Network applications in support of the medical field included enabling high-resolution data transfers of diagnostic procedures, such as X-ray, magnetic resonance imaging (MRI), and other tests; facilitating access to medical specialists; and expediting patient diagnosis. When consultations were required, physicians at one hospital wanted to easily connect with their colleagues at other network-connected institutions in the area. Another networking challenge was financial, as the ultimate network design and its telecommunications services had to be delivered as cost-effectively as possible.

During the design phase of the network, a number of infrastructure alternatives were considered (see Figure 2-5). The LANs had various technologies, including FDDI, switched segments, and 10BASE-T, which also added to the design challenges. On the WAN side, ATM technology was available in the region but was eliminated because of cost. ISDN was considered, but its low bandwidth and lack of universal service in the region were concerns. Satellite up- and down-links were considered for distance learning, but they were considered too expensive for two-way interactive video conferencing. Fractional T1 lines were also ruled out because of cost and network management issues. Multichannel video was also considered, but was immediately ruled out due to the fiber requirement, the high operational cost, the inability to connect from outside the network, and the general lack of flexibility. As a result, frame relay was identified as the only economical, comprehensive WAN backbone solution. Frame relay did not require fiber build-outs by the carrier, was universally available, was billed at a flat monthly rate, and provided reasonable quality of service.

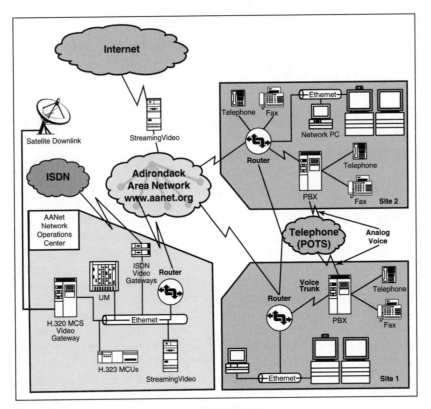

Figure 2-5: The Adirondack Area Network Topology

(Courtesy of Adirondack Area Network)

In order to prove frame relay as an integrated network solution capable of supporting video and data, 5 of the 45 initial sites were chosen as beta video sites. Due to the success of this initial effort, 20 additional video units were connected to the AAN in the first year alone. ISDN capabilities were added for backward compatibility and to enable interactive video connections outside the region. Again, due to the innovative network design, ISDN was added as a shared resource reducing the cost to individual institutions. Moreover, for numerous institutions ISDN is not available at their geographic location. These institutions take advantage of ISDN by using ISDN services offered by the AAN via the frame relay cloud. Internet connectivity was quickly added as well.

When the AAN began, the ITU-T H.323 multimedia networking standard was not yet ratified. Initial interactive video conferencing was supported by encapsulating a related media type, H.320, in IP. (More information on the H.320 family of multimedia standards is found in Chapter 6.) Now that H.323 has been ratified and has become a proven multimedia transport protocol suite, the AAN uses H.323 almost exclusively for video within its network. Video gateways provide connectivity outside the AAN primarily through ISDN using the H.320 standard. Video gateways also enable the AAN to continue to operate its legacy multipoint control units (MCUs) in addition to and in conjunction with native H.323 MCUs. A video gateway to the Internet is also available for low-cost conferences when quality and reliability are not an issue. This is all transparent to the end users who simply "dial" a video number to connect to the desired party or to access a video service. To make a point-to-point video call, a four-digit extension is "dialed." Connecting to a party outside the AAN is accomplished by "dialing" a service number followed by the ISDN number of the party in much the same way as telephone users dial 9 to get an outside line. To connect to a multipoint video call, a service number followed by the conference ID is "dialed." In short, the complexities of integrating video services are hidden from the end users so that they perceive a simple yet reliable system.

New services are constantly being added to the AAN. For example, in 1999, interactive video capabilities, including video streaming and digital archiving for viewing from the Internet, were added as a service to AAN members. The interactive video may be viewed live on the Internet from PCs, but noninteractively, and/or digitally stored and viewed on demand. Alternately, events can be streamed live and/or archived without an interactive video component. The AAN also streams satellite programs from various sources including the State University of New York (SUNY) and the New York State Department of Health.

Voice is also offered as a member service using VoIP, VoFR, or VoATM as appropriate. Institutions can opt for simple voice connectivity between institutions using VoIP or can cascade their PBXs, obtaining all of their PBX features as if their PBXs were cascaded in traditional (and more expensive) methods, by using VoFR or VoATM. For example, one AAN hospital member operates three remote centers. The hospital uses a fully functional PBX complete with voice mail, music on hold, and so on. The remote institutions each have a much smaller PBX with only basic functionality. By cascading the PBX at their main site with the smaller PBXs at their three remote sites over the AAN frame relay network, they can use the enhanced features of their main PBX at each of their remote sites. In addition, each remote institution is a long-distance call from the main site, and they can also avoid the long-distance telephone charges associated with operating these remote institutions. The money they save in long-distance charges more than offsets the cost of their AAN membership. At the same time, AAN membership enables interactive video conferencing, data transfers, and Internet connectivity for all of their sites through the AAN.

Member institutions access AAN through a virtual connection (PVC) into the frame relay network. Frame relay is a flat rate service so there are no long-distance charges within the cloud. Fractional bandwidths are possible and high bandwidth pipes, with transmission rates from 1.5 Mbps (T1) to 45 Mbps (T3), are available. The frame relay network is a shared resource, therefore the cost is substantially less than the cost for traditional dedicated network models such as ISDN or point-to-point connections. By creating logical circuits in the frame relay cloud, each dedicated to video, voice, or data, the AAN guarantees the necessary bandwidth for high-quality video or voice. Instead of costly point-to-point connections, sites need only connect to the nearest access point for the cloud. Sites receive Internet connectivity and high-quality video connections for about the price of Internet connectivity by other means. The audio/video signal is of television/compact disc quality, even at 384 Kbps bandwidth. The video signals can adhere to a number of standards, including ITU-T H.323e, IP encapsulated H.320, or H.323. ISDN is used to connect AAN members to other institutions outside the network. Multipoint video calls are also supported in this environment.

The first network of its kind, AAN has been spotlighted in numerous conferences and publications in the United States and abroad. Due to this notoriety, AAN has been sought after to work with video conferencing users, video conferencing corporations, network providers, and network carriers to implement similar integrated networks. More information about the Adirondack Area Network is available from Reference [2-5].

2.6 The Virginia Community College System Network

The Virginia Community College System (VCCS) network is one of the most extensive educational networks in North America, linking 23 community colleges and their 40 campus locations with the Internet, with universities within the state of Virginia, and with other state agencies for voice, data, and video services. This network serves over 340,000 students, faculty, and staff members.

In the past few years, this organization has been recognized for many technical achievements. These include the first statewide, multivendor ATM broadband network, called NetworkVirginia; the first deployment of classroom video using telephone circuit emulation over ATM; the first statewide network to support Internet 2 technologies; and the first statewide network to deploy voice over IP for long-distance voice communication.

The NetworkVirginia partnership began in 1997, linking the VCCS sites with Virginia Tech and Old Dominion Universities. Each of these educational institutions was equipped with fiber optic DS-3 communication links operating at 45 Mbps and providing TCP/IP transport for data connections, plus voice and video support using circuit emulation over ATM. In the last few years, this network has been enhanced to support converged network applications, including voice over IP, ATM and IP video conferencing, plus streaming desktop video transmission. Excess capacity on this existing statewide ATM network allowed the addition of the voice over IP functions, including in-state long distance, audio conferencing, interactive voice response, and replacements of many customer premises (PBX) and central office-based (Centrex) switching systems. Thus, each location includes a switched Ethernet campus network that supports both data and voice communication, plus a DS-3 link into NetworkVirginia with access into shared facilities and services, such as e-mail, distance education, and streaming video (see Figure 2-6a).

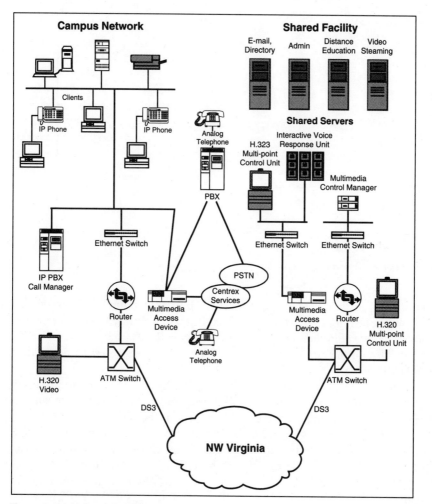

Figure 2–6a: Voice over IP Services

(Courtesy of Virginia Community College System)

The in-state long-distance service is deployed using Cisco routers and IP over any physical media, such as ATM, frame relay, wave division multiplexing, Ethernet, and so on, and provides several key applications. For example, to make an on-net telephone call, the caller enters an access code and a ten-digit number, which is passed to the router. The router matches the ten-digit number to an IP address and routes the call across the network. At the remote location, another router accepts the ten-digit phone number and sends the call to a PBX or Centrex switch (Figure 2-6b).

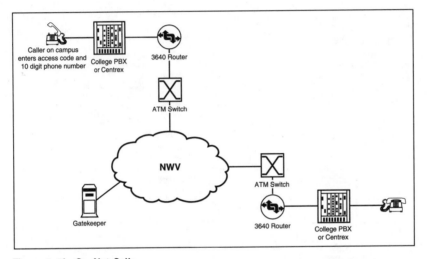

Figure 2–6b: On-Net Calls

(Courtesy of Virginia Community College System)

A caller who is off-campus would enter a ten-digit access number, followed by a ten-digit telephone number via the PSTN. That call would be matched at a router to an IP address and would then be sent across the network to a remote router, which, in turn, would send the call to a PBX or Centrex switch at the desired destination campus (Figure 2-6c).

An interactive voice response (IVR) system, used for course registration and other student information, is a shared application, with central servers that support all the VCCS campuses. To access the IVR application, the caller enters a ten-digit access number, which is passed via the PSTN to a PBX or Centrex on campus. That call would be matched at a router to an IP address, which would then route the call across the network to a remote router, which, in turn, would send the call to the centrally located IVR system (Figure 2-6d). This architecture eliminates the need for IVR servers at each campus, yielding a significant cost savings to the VCCS network.

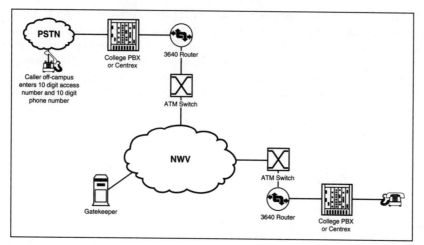

Figure 2-6c: Off-Net to On-Net Calls

(Courtesy of Virginia Community College System)

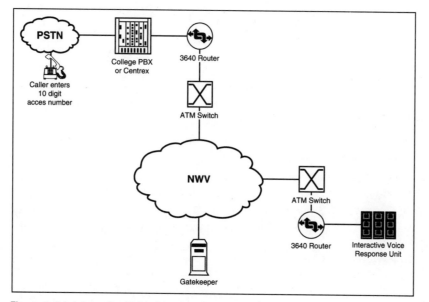

Figure 2-6d: Interactive Voice Response Services

(Courtesy of Virginia Community College System)

The system also supports conference call bridging (Figure 2-6e). An on-campus caller enters a ten-digit telephone number for the conference call plus an access code, and then that call is sent via the PBX or Centrex to a router. The router matches the ten-digit number for the conference call to an IP address and routes the call across the network. The remote router accepts the ten-digit number and routes the call to the Audio Bridge. At the Audio Bridge, the conference access code is validated and the caller is connected.

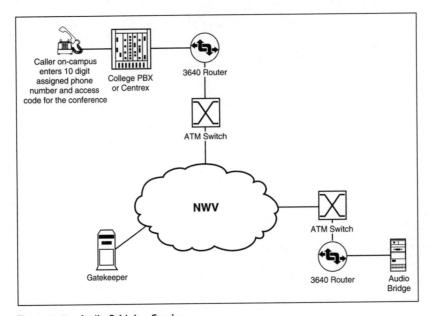

Figure 2–6e: Audio Bridging Services
(Courtesy of Virginia Community College System)

Having proved the viability of the voice over IP network, VCCS next plans to deploy desktop streaming video, providing bidirectional audio and video via IP. Further information on this innovative educational network can be found in Reference [2-6].

2.7 Integrating IP and Wireless Communication within a Manufacturing Environment

Sells Printing Company LLC, located in Milwaukee, Wisconsin, provides integrated communications solutions by offering: complete electronic prepress; sheet-fed and heat-set Web printing; binding, mailing, and distribution services; and CD-ROM and Internet services. Sells Printing serves business-to-business and business-to-consumer segments, and as one of the top 50 fastest-growing printers in the United States, Sells has received numerous industry awards for high-quality printed material. A critical aspect of Sells' continued success hinges on staying technologically current in the marketplace.

As their voice network requirements grew, Sells began to run into more and more obstacles with the continued operation of their existing system. This system caused a number of headaches for telephone relocations — for each phone move it was necessary to remove all the cross connections and punch them down to a new location. The legacy system also led to serious difficulties with equipment availability and servicing, as the age of the system precluded the procurement of new parts and affordable maintenance and programming. Thus, the decision to install a new voice communications system was made.

In looking for a converged solution to replace their legacy system, Sells wanted to maintain operation of their existing voice mail, music on hold, and night ringer, so they needed a vendor who could interoperate with those services. They also wanted to adopt IP and wireless technology early on, rather than wait five years and do a forklift upgrade to remain competitive with a mode of communication they were certain would dominate the market. Support for IP was therefore the first item that Sells listed as a requirement of any new system purchase.

In making the decision to migrate to IP, however, Sells refused to compromise on features and connectivity. The selected vendor had to provide a solution with all the features of a traditional PBX, along with analog signaling. Sells selected the Alcatel OmniPCX 4400 system because it was able to provide this connectivity, along with the reliability and enhanced network ability they were looking for, without compromising on the features they used with the traditional PBX. Alcatel builds next-generation networks, delivering integrated end-to-end voice and data networking solutions to established and new carriers, as well as to enterprises and consumers, worldwide.

Sells' requirements for this new system also included demands for increased mobility and sophisticated voice features such as voice over IP, as well as satisfaction to the network manager requirements for lower operational costs and ease of administration. With hundreds of print jobs every month, customer service representatives needed to communicate not only with customers, but also with fellow employees at Sells, including outside sales representatives, press workers, and purchase order clerks. The firm also needed to select an IP and wireless solution that would be easily serviceable in their 100,000 square-foot printing facility. They decided to equip nearly all of their employees with wireless sets that allow users to take calls anywhere in the main building or the warehouse. These wireless sets, the Alcatel Wireless Reflexes, also share the same advanced PBX features as the desktop IP phones used by coworkers, including dial-by-name, caller ID, voice mail notification and access, and conference calling.

Sells Printing's converged network presently serves approximately 195 employees in two sites, with about 110 wireless sets, 50 IP phones, and 26 wireless base stations to cover their 100,000 square-foot manufacturing facility. They also employ four Alcatel Premium Reflexes sets as attendant consoles for assistants and receptionists. The full-featured receptionist functionality allows the company to steer clear of an automated attendant and retain their commitment to in-person customer service.

A small warehouse with ten IP phones is connected to the main site over a WAN comprised of redundant point-to-point T1s (Figure 2-7). The warehouse benefits from a significant increase in communication functionality with the converged system. Prior to the installation, warehouse employees were not even able to receive voice mail notification on their desk phones; now they are seamlessly integrated into the main site, with no reduction in communication features or services.

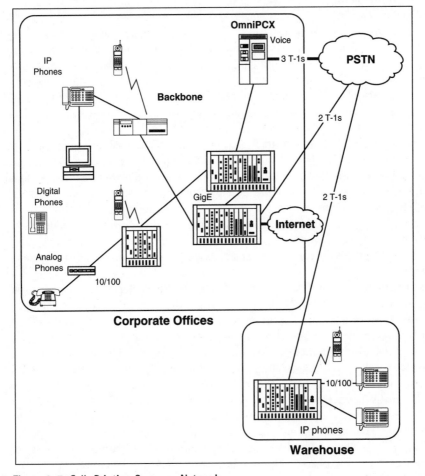

Figure 2-7: Sells Printing Company Network

(Courtesy of Alcatel Internetworking, Inc.)

The use of Alcatel Private Wireless Telecommunication (PWT) phones saves the printing firm money. Prior to their implementation, most employees used cell phones in addition to their desk sets. Sells has been able to eliminate about 30 cell phones, at a savings to the company of $35–40 per month per phone – yielding a total savings of over $1000 per month. The PWTs also increase employee efficiency: if a manager needs to roam the manufacturing floor for an hour, instead of coming back to a dozen voice mails and the ensuing phone tag to return those missed calls, he or she is able to take the calls while mobile.

In addition to the twin set functionality described above, the system allows sophisticated forwarding schemes, enabling mobile employees to forward their desk extension to their cell phone and maintain constant, transparent availability to their customers. Flexibility is also underscored in the procedure for moving desk phones. With the Alcatel system, moves are as simple as logging off the phone, plugging it into a different jack, and then logging back in with the same extension at the new location. In the year prior to the installation of the OmniPCX 4400 system, Sells spent $21,000 on performing moves, adds, and changes alone – a number that has now been reduced to zero.

Sells has plans for future expansion, and one of the things their IT manager evaluated was ease of scalability and connection to new facilities. He concluded that the rollout of an IP-based network would be easier and more cost-effective than the deployment of a nonconverged system. If future expansion brings additional buildings, Sells plans to deploy a remote shelf connected to the Alcatel OmniPCX, further decreasing the total cost of ownership (TCO) of the system. They also plan to implement additional services – such as call center applications – in the next couple of years.

The benefits that Sells has realized with just the *basic* features of their Alcatel OmniPCX system far exceed what they had in their old network. Sells uses IP without forfeiting the availability of other connections, notably analog. They have a true PBX where they can hot-swap line cards, and a reliable UNIX platform that enables the 99.999 percent system uptime they expect from their voice communication system. The ability to conference and to route and forward calls in various configurations has been of particular value, as these features are used on a daily basis throughout the company. The wireless users have gotten a productivity boost from the ability to receive calls anywhere they may be, as if they were at their desks using their fixed phones. Management has been centralized and simplified, and all employees are transparently integrated into the main system, allowing for easy accessibility and continuous availability to customers, suppliers, and colleagues.

Reference [2-7] provides further information on Sells Printing Company and Alcatel Internetworking, Inc., products.

2.8 Looking Ahead

In this chapter, we have considered the wide breadth of applications that can be run over converged networks, supporting voice, fax, data, and video transmission. But the technical viability of these applications is only part of the story – they must be financially viable as well. In the next chapter we will discuss this second part of the story and consider the business case for converged networks.

2.9 References

[2-1] Additional information regarding the itRings! service is available at www.ering.net.

[2-2] Additional information regarding the iBasis network is available at www.ibasis.net.

[2-3] Additional information regarding Nuera Communications, Inc., products is available at www.nuera.com. Additional information regarding OpenTel Communications, Inc.'s, network is available at www.opentel.com.

[2-4] Additional information regarding Cisco Systems products is available at www.cisco.com.

[2-5] Additional information regarding the Adirondack Area Network is available at www.aanet.org.

[2-6] Additional information regarding the Virginia Community College System Network is available at www.vccs.edu.

[2-7] Additional information regarding Sells Printing Company LLC is available at www.sells.com. Additional information regarding Alcatel Internetworking, Inc., products is available at www.alcatel.com.

Chapter 3

The Business Case for Converged Networks

Chapter 1 looked at the principles of converged networks and Chapter 2 considered applications and case studies for those converged networks. At some point along the way, however, someone will likely ask for some cost justification before a converged network design can move beyond the testing phase and into the enterprise-wide implementation phase.

This fundamental cost question may require additional analysis before a clear answer emerges. For example, there may be an assumption that combining voice and data networks into a converged system will lower the overall telecommunication expenses for the enterprise, but one may not know the extent of these savings until the converged network is actually implemented. The amount of network traffic to be rerouted to the converged network is a factor, but so is the mix of domestic and international calls. Since carrier charges may depend on the destination, do you have billing records available that can provide these necessary details? If integrated applications are successfully implemented over that converged system, other benefits are likely – such as more effective use of staff resources, or higher customer satisfaction, both of which could have a positive impact on the organization's financial picture. But again, quantifying these expected benefits prior to implementation may be challenging.

The goal of this chapter is to provide guidelines that will assist in answering financial questions such as these. This chapter considers four examples of financial analysis methods that networking vendors provide their customers, along with a case study taken from one firm's actual experiences, which will be presented at the end of this chapter to summarize some of the key points the chapter covers.

But before we get into this analysis, a couple caveats are in order:

◆ First, internetworks, by their very nature, are enterprise-specific entities. Put another way, your network is unique from any other; the costs associated with your network, and the ways in which you justify those costs are also unique. An expense that I feel is quite appropriate might be considered unreasonable in your circumstances, or for your application. Therefore, some of the assumptions presented in this chapter may require modification in order for them to be applicable to your circumstances.

◆ Second, there are a number of factors in any analysis of this type that are difficult to quantify. What about intangible or "blue sky" factors, such as the value of your customer service reputation? If you significantly change your network infrastructure, are any elements of your current operation at risk? These factors should be considered, as they may impact your financial assumptions.

3.1 Fundamental Financial Assumptions

With the caveats from the introduction to this chapter in mind, the first fundamental assumption for this chapter could be stated as follows:

Assumption 1: Assuming a given level of network performance, operating one network is less expensive than operating two networks.

We will take it as a given that the readers of this book have at least two networks in place: one that serves data networking requirements, and one that serves voice networking requirements (Figure 3-1). If you wanted to extend this discussion further, you could probably subdivide these two categories. For example, the data network might include elements for Internet access, client/server computing, and mainframe database access. The voice network would include dial-up access to the PSTN, but might also include leased line connections supporting a private voice network, such as T1 lines operating at 1.544 Mbps or other tie trunks that connect the PBXs at the various locations.

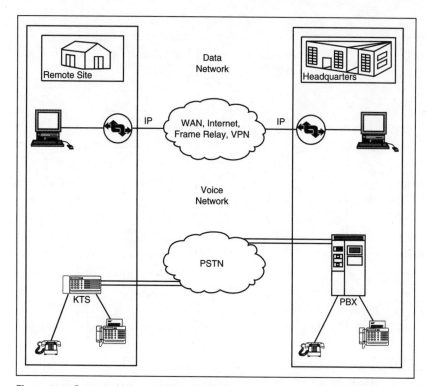

Figure 3-1: Separate Voice and Data Networks

(Courtesy of Nx Networks, Inc.)

Next, we will assume that the topology of an integrated network (Figure 3-2) would include new elements that must be purchased, leased, or otherwise acquired. This would likely involve hardware elements, such as VoIP gateways, but might also include upgrades to existing systems, such as routers and PBXs. Client applications, such as desktop video conferencing equipment, cameras, and so on, might also be involved. Thus, the total cost for the converged network might include several components: acquisition (or first) cost for new equipment, plus the ongoing operating cost for that new equipment, which could include employee training, maintenance contracts, and so on.

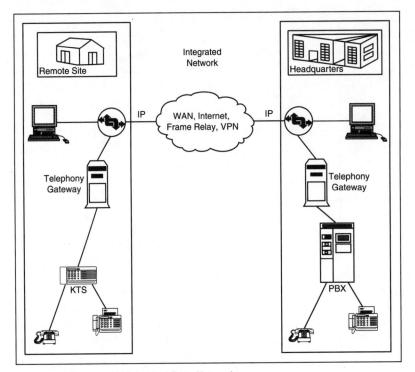

Figure 3–2: Integrated Voice and Data Networks

(Courtesy of Nx Networks, Inc.)

Before we embark on this financial study, a second key assumption needs to be stated:

Assumption 2: Support for new end-user applications will also be a financially motivating factor, but one that is much harder to quantify.

For example, suppose that your proposed application is a Web-enabled call center. You know that your competition recently implemented a similar service and have read industry reports that their sales have substantially increased. (During the same period, you have also noted that your sales have *decreased*, and you have wondered if possibly these two facts are somehow related.) Examples of other decisions that are hard to quantify would include the physical location of your business, the format of your Web page, or the customer benefits of outsourcing your call center.

In any event, you have a second objective when network convergence is considered – protection of your installed base of customers through the implementation of a new customer application. For most people, this is the most difficult part of the analysis – quantifying the "blue sky" elements of that financial decision. Or, stated another way, how do you quantify the impact of *not* implementing the converged network and/or applications? As with most rhetorical questions, formulating an answer is left to the reader.

3.2 Network Traffic Assumptions

Before you develop a business case for a converged network, the technical characteristics of the existing network must be known. An important element of this business case will be the underlying assumptions regarding both current and future network traffic that will impact much of the financial work. For example, if you consider adding voice traffic onto your existing data network, do you know if your data network has the excess capacity to handle that additional traffic? For that matter, do you have baseline or historical information that allows you to predict network growth trends?

Another important factor to consider is whether or not any historical information that you might have available would even be relevant to the new application. In other words, a new application, such as a Web-enabled call center, may be so different in its traffic handling and loading characteristics that any current network statistics do not provide a good indication of how the network might respond to this new application. If that is the case, the network manager will have to make some initial estimates and then refine those estimates as more complete information, perhaps from a lab-based test network, becomes available.

Most vendors of VoIP equipment have software tools available to assist their customers with the design and provisioning of a converged network. However, in order to expedite this process, the network manager should have the following information available before contacting prospective vendors:

- ◆ Network topology information and drawing showing up-to-date network configurations.

- ◆ Network connectivity information showing the types and capacities of the communication lines between various network locations.

- ◆ Network utilization information, including historical data that shows the growth in network traffic on those communication lines over the last 12–24 months.

- ◆ Growth projections, indicating areas in which network traffic is likely to be impacted. For example, the construction of a new manufacturing facility, the acquisition of a smaller, related firm, a joint venture with a business partner, or significant increases or decreases in the number of personnel would all impact network traffic.

- ◆ Impacts on network operation that come from end-user applications or the deployment of new applications. For example, the addition of a new distributed database, a customer support center, a fax-back service, or other communication-intensive application may impact the network traffic and its operation.

◆ Impacts on network operations that are seasonal or cyclical in nature. For example, one would assume that network traffic would increase at the end of the month (payroll processing) and at the end of the quarter (tax return and deposit processing). But if you are in the retail business, you likely have an increase in traffic during December and January as well, as a result of holiday purchases. Have you been able to quantify these cyclical trends?

◆ The sources of traffic on your network, divided by media type such as voice, fax, data, and video. Do you know what percentage of your traffic is a result of fax transmissions? If you do not, then the deployment of a network of fax gateways may be more difficult to justify.

If the preceding list of information prompts any concerns or brings to your attention any unresolved issues, then it would benefit you to do this research before significantly proceeding with any further design or financial commitments. It is difficult to design a network application if you don't know the characteristics of your existing network. Fortunately, a number of tools are available to assist with network monitoring, analysis, and traffic management functions. Further discussion on this subject is beyond the scope of this text; however, a few hours searching industry journals or the World Wide Web for products that would meet your requirements would be a worthwhile investment.

Once these baseline questions can be answered, both the network manager and the prospective vendors are in a better position to proceed. As part of their sales proposal, the vendors are likely to consider additional factors:

◆ The type of access or WAN circuits to be used, such as DSL, frame relay, or ATM

◆ The maximum number of simultaneous calls possible at each location

◆ The traffic matrix, or where most of the calls originate and terminate

◆ The typical length or duration of the calls

◆ The voice compression protocol options available or desirable

◆ Interoperability with existing systems, such as the PBX or voice mail adjunct processor, that may be impacted by this conversion

The sections that follow include examples of various financial scenarios for consideration. As noted previously, these examples are intended to serve as a guide, not necessarily the last word. Any network implementation should pass through the reality check of your own network's objectives and current operation before proceeding.

3.3 Quantifying the Business Case

To summarize the discussion thus far, your interest in moving toward a converged network topology may be rooted in several factors: improving network performance, increasing network redundancy, adding a new application, and/or decreasing communications costs. Putting a value on the first three factors is difficult – how do you quantify the potential payback from a more satisfied customer or determine if the cost of that redundant communication circuit paid off? On the other hand, if you install new equipment and observe that your monthly telecommunications charges decrease, then a value-based analysis is more understandable.

Thus, identifying the financial benefits of networking investments, both in the short and long terms, provides a quantifiable way of determining the viability of the project. Most network managers use a financial measure known as Return on Investment or ROI as a tool to aid with these decisions. A very useful product, known as ROInow!, has been developed by CIOview Corporation (Boxborough, Massachusetts). It comprises a series of powerful yet easy-to-use software packages that enable you to determine the ROI of planned networking expenditures. Reference [3-1] provides further details on the ROInow! software.

The following information, taken from CIOview reference documents [3-2], describes the benefits and outline for such an analysis. Quantitatively defined, ROI is simply the benefits of an investment divided by the costs, expressed in percentage terms, normally over three years. However, when an ROI analysis is completed solely to get an end result number, many of the major benefits of an ROI analysis are not realized. An ROI analysis can dramatically reduce the time and effort associated with the purchase process. By showcasing the business impact of the technology, it becomes easier for senior management to understand *the business implications* of the decision. An ROI analysis also helps to eliminate vendor bias and provides a rational foundation for comparative decision making. It provides a way to standardize on a set of financial assumptions, thus enabling an "apples to apples" comparison between project alternatives. Finally, ROI analysis is a discipline that forces you to look at the costs and benefits of a project. "Costs," "benefits," and "returns" are concepts that senior management is comfortable making decisions by, rather than bits and bytes. By speaking *their* language, technology purchases are related to business goals, improving the chances that the project will be funded.

3.3.1 Financial Terms Used in the Business Case

Before delving further into the concepts of financial analysis, it's important to define a few terms:

◆ **Present Value** is the current value of an investment when the time value of money is taken into account. For example, the value of a $100 bill today is greater than a $100 bill that you promise to give me in one year, since I can take today's $100 bill, put it in a savings account, and earn some interest in the meantime. Another way to look at the same example would be to say that the value of the $100 bill promised for delivery in one year is less than that of the $100 bill that I have in my hand today. The difference between the two values is sometimes referred to the discount factor, which may be expressed in terms of a percentage.

◆ **Return on Investment**, or **ROI**, is perhaps the most common method to evaluate and compare the attractiveness of one business investment to another. The results of an ROI calculation are expressed in percentage terms and are usually qualified by a time period. In other words, an ROI is usually a certain percentage over a certain number of years. Simply speaking, a three-year ROI of 150% means that the benefits you accrue are one and one-half times greater than the cost and resources necessary to implement it.

◆ **Net Present Value**, or **NPV**, is essentially a profit and loss statement for the project. In other words, NPV is the present value of money that takes into account alternative investments that could have been made. It is calculated by summing the present value of the net benefits for each year minus the initial costs of the project. A positive NPV means that the project generates more cash than it took to fund it. A negative NPV means that the project generates a loss.

◆ **Payback Period**, or simply **Payback**, is the time it takes for your project to recoup the funds expended. It designates a time when the project breaks even. It is normally expressed in years or months.

◆ **Internal Rate of Return**, or **IRR**, is the discount factor that you would need to apply to the annual benefit for the net present value of the project to equal zero. In other words, it is the percentage rate by which you have to discount the benefits until the point that they equal all the costs. Many firms set a minimum threshold for IRR as a go/no-go financial decision point for proposed projects.

3.3.2 Calculating Project Benefits

The next sections show how some of these financial measures can be calculated.

3.3.2.1 PRESENT VALUE

Money held now could be invested in a bank account and is therefore more valuable than the same amount of money to be received in 12 months. Present value seeks to account for this. It equals the rate by which you have to discount future benefits for you to be indifferent between a benefit received now and a benefit received at the end of the specified time period. The equation for present value is:

benefit / (1 + discount rate)

Suppose you are an IT manager at a manufacturing company planning a small new software rollout.

If the current discount rate is 10 percent and your benefit at the end of year 1 is $5,000, the present value of that benefit right now is equal to $5,000 / (1+0.10) = $4,545.45. $4,500 received now is the same to you as $5,000 received in 1 year if the discount rate is 10%, because if you invest that $4,500 and take inflation into account, it will be the equivalent of $5,000 in 1 year. Since software often provides a benefit over a number of years and interest is compounded, present value calculations can often be complex. For example, if your annual net benefit is $5,000 for three years, the present value would equal:

$5,000 / (1.1) + $5,000 / (1.1)^2 + $5,000 / (1.1)^3 = $12,434.26

Fortunately, most spreadsheet programs incorporate these financial analysis functions, thus minimizing the mathematical strain on the end user.

Thus, the result would not be $5,000 + $5,000 + $5,000 = $15,000. The basic principle of present value, or the time value of money, is central to several of the different ways of measuring the financial attractiveness of one investment over another.

3.3.2.2 RETURN ON INVESTMENT

Return on Investment (ROI) is arguably the most popular metric used to compare the attractiveness of one business investment to another. Your ROI equals the present value of your accumulated net benefits (gross benefits less ongoing costs) over a certain time period divided by your initial costs. It is expressed as a percentage over a specific amount of time; in IT purchasing, three years is the most common time span, since technology is often effectively obsolete after three years. The equation for a three-year ROI is:

(net benefit year 1 / (1 + discount rate) + net benefit year 2 / (1 + discount rate)^2 + net benefit year 3 / (1 + discount rate)^3) / initial cost

If the initial cost for your manufacturing company's small new software rollout was $10,000, your annual benefits minus annual costs are constant at $5,000 for the next three years, and the discount rate is 10 percent, your three-year ROI would be:

($5,000 / (1 + 0.10) + $5,000 / (1 + 0.10)^2 + $5,000 / (1 + 0.10)^3)/$10,000 = 124%

While ROI tells you what percentage return you will get over a specified period of time, it does not tell you anything about the magnitude of the project. So, while a 124 percent return may seem initially attractive, would you rather have a 124 percent return on a $10,000 project or a 60 percent return on a $300,000 investment? That is why you will often want to know the Net Present Value.

3.3.2.3 NET PRESENT VALUE

The Net Present Value (NPV) gives you the dollar value of your expected return and therefore indicates the magnitude of your project. It is calculated by summing the present value of the net benefits for each year over a specified period of time and then subtracting the initial costs of the project. A positive NPV means that the project generates a profit, while a negative NPV means that the project generates a loss. The equation for a three-year NPV is:

(net benefit year 1 / (1 + discount rate) + net benefit year 2 / (1 + discount rate)^2 + net benefit year 3 / (1 + discount rate)^3) – initial costs

Using the same hypothetical manufacturing company's new software rollout example used in the last section, you find the NPV would equal:

$5,000 / (1 + 0.10) + $5,000 / (1 + 0.10)^2 + $5,000 / (1 + 0.10)^3 – $10,000 = $2,434

The great thing about NPV is that it tells you about the dollar value of your savings; the downside is that it doesn't tell you when savings will occur.

3.3.2.4 PAYBACK PERIOD

Simple payback period is used to find out how long it will take for an investment to show a profit. It is important when time and cash flow are an issue. It is the time it takes for your project to recoup the funds expended and is normally expressed in years or months. The equation for a simple payback period is:

initial cost / annual net benefit.

If you use the same new software rollout example as before, your simple payback period is:

$10,000 / $5,000 = 2 years

Payback is very easy to calculate, but it doesn't tell you about the magnitude of your savings or even how your investment performs after your benefits equal the initial costs.

3.3.2.5 INTERNAL RATE OF RETURN

Internal Rate of Return (IRR) is the most sophisticated of the metrics discussed in these sections and is often used to analyze large, multiyear investments. IRR equals the percentage rate by which you have to discount the net benefits for your time period until the point that they equal the initial costs. IRR is closely related to Net

Present Value. The rate of return calculated by IRR is the discount rate you would need to apply to your benefits to obtain a Net Present Value of zero. The expression for IRR (in this case, a three-year IRR) is:

initial costs = net benefit year 1 / (1 + IRR) + net benefit year 2 / (1+IRR)^2 + net benefit year 3 / (1+IRR)^3

IRR is often calculated through a trial and error process or data table since solving the above equation is very time-consuming; however, spreadsheet functions can be quite useful in solving this equation as well. If you use the same new software roll-out example used in previous sections, the IRR would equal 23 percent. This gives an NPV of ($5000 / 1.23 + $5000 / 1.23^2 + $5000 / 1.23^3) – $10,000 = 0.

IRR may be thought of as a kind of turbo-charged ROI. It still suffers from ROI's main weakness, which is that it does not give any indication of the magnitude of the project involved.

In truth, each of these financial measures has its strengths and weaknesses. Different companies place varying amounts of emphasis on each of the different metrics. To get a clear and complete picture of a prospective investment, you will benefit from having access to all five of these measures. For further information on these terms or the ROInow! software, see Reference [3-1].

The examples in Sections 3.5 through 3.8 consider various network reconfiguration scenarios, provided by four converged network equipment vendors, that could potentially increase the productivity of a network while also reducing the expenses of that network. In addition, each vendor's financial analysis methods are detailed. Note that some vendors use ROI while others use payback period or some other financial measure to quantify the benefits of their implementation. Also note that our focus in these sections is on *analysis methodology,* instead of on the merits of the network design or plausibility of the reconfiguration. In other words, you may disagree on the *technical approach* the vendor has taken, but don't lose sight of the *financial approach* that is being presented. As has been discussed before, synthesize the best elements of all four of these examples to derive a methodology that will work for your network application.

3.4 Example Cost Reduction Scenarios

Converging voice and data networks into a single system may solve a number of networking challenges and provide a number of benefits. The examples given in this section, taken from Reference [3-3], illustrate scenarios where cost savings may occur. As noted above, modification of these scenarios to incorporate network-specific factors would be required in most, if not all, of these examples.

3.4.1 Summarizing Cost Reduction Information

Your business case should be principally based on the hard numbers (such as decreases in monthly telecommunications expenses) rather than the soft numbers (such as customer satisfaction). A simple spreadsheet could be used to summarize this information and determine how quickly the investment in new equipment would pay for itself. For example, suppose that a network with four offices was converted from separate voice and data networks to a converged VoIP network. For each office, estimates could be made regarding the monthly expenses, such as toll charges, personnel, maintenance, and so on, that would be saved by converting to the converged VoIP network, as seen in Column A of Worksheet 1 (Figure 3-3). Similarly, the costs to purchase the new equipment to support the converged network could be determined for each location, as seen in Column B of Worksheet 1. Dividing the Total Cost from Column B by the Monthly Savings from Column A would determine the approximate number of months needed for this new equipment to pay for itself.

Suppose that some of these offices are located outside of the United States, and a traffic analysis indicates that some of the toll charges between locations could be eliminated if a converged network were installed. A comparison between the expected savings and the expected costs of the new equipment would determine the payback period of this investment. To take this example a step further, suppose that an analysis strictly based on these hard cost savings indicates that return on this project is somewhat marginal. A more thorough analysis could then be made, which could take into account the value of the soft factors, such as customer satisfaction, potential increased sales, and so on, that might show the project in a more favorable light.

A similar analysis could be made if the equipment at each location were leased instead of purchased, as seen in Worksheet 2 (Figure 3-4). In this case, the monthly savings in network expenses (Column A) would be compared with the monthly lease payment for the new equipment (Column B), with the net monthly savings determined in Column C. As before, consideration of the easily quantifiable (hard) cost savings should be made before considering any of the more intangible (soft) cost savings.

Column A		Column B	
Office A: monthly savings in network expenses	$	**Office A:** cost for VoIP equipment	$
Office B: monthly savings in network expenses	$	**Office B:** cost for VoIP equipment	$
Office C: monthly savings in network expenses	$	**Office C:** cost for VoIP equipment	$
Office D: monthly savings in network expenses	$	**Office D:** cost for VoIP equipment	$
Subtotal:	$		$
Federal, State, and Local Taxes:	$		$
Total:	$		$

Figure 3-3: Worksheet 1: Payback Period Calculations for Purchased VoIP Equipment

(Courtesy of Nx Networks, Inc.)

Column A		Column B		Column C	
Office A: monthly savings in network expenses	$	**Office A:** monthly lease payment for VoIP equipment	$	**Office A:** net monthly savings	$
Office B: monthly savings in network expenses	$	**Office B:** monthly lease payment for VoIP equipment	$	**Office B:** net monthly savings	$
Office C: monthly savings in network expenses	$	**Office C:** monthly lease payment for VoIP equipment	$	**Office C:** net monthly savings	$
Office D: monthly savings in network expenses	$	**Office D:** monthly lease payment for VoIP equipment	$	**Office D:** net monthly savings	$
Subtotal:	$		$		$
Federal, State, and Local Taxes:	$		$		$
Total:	$		$		$

Figure 3–4: Worksheet 2: Monthly Savings Calculations for Leased VoIP Equipment

(Courtesy of Nx Networks, Inc.)

3.4.2 Reducing Interoffice Toll Charges

Corporate interoffice long distance is one of the greatest telecommunications expenses that managers of large voice and data networks face. Aside from the company's sales staff, the average manager of any firm is on the phone much of the day conferring with coworkers at other offices of the same corporation. This is especially true in high-technology firms where engineers must collaborate with teammates around the world. In many cases, these voice and data networks link the same pairs of locations, or, in other words, are *parallel networks*. If these two parallel networks can be integrated into a single network infrastructure, some economies of scale are likely to be realized.

If the business routes its interoffice long-distance voice traffic over its existing corporate data WAN, virtual private network (VPN), the public Internet, or a public frame relay network, these economies are likely to be realized, and the expense for the interoffice toll charges reduced.

To implement such a converged topology requires additional equipment in the form of a VoIP gateway, adjunct to the existing voice PBX, or other hardware. Worksheet 1 (Figure 3-3) can be used to determine the payback period for this additional hardware. To complete Column A of that worksheet, the network manager must examine the interoffice traffic between that location and all other company locations. An estimate of the savings in monthly toll charges, assuming that the two parallel networks are combined into a single integrated network, is entered in Column A. This estimate should be based on the current network utilization, the amount of excess capacity available on those voice and data links, and the voice compression efficiencies that are anticipated. The cost to purchase the associated VoIP equipment is entered in Column B. By dividing the value in Column A into the value in Column B, a payback period, given in months, can be calculated. For example, suppose that the toll charge savings at Office A are estimated at $800 per month and that the VoIP equipment costs for Office A are $8,000. The resulting payback period (without considering the cost of money) would be $8,000/$800, or 10 months.

In some cases, it will be more desirable to lease the VoIP equipment than to make an outright purchase. Worksheet 2 (Figure 3-4) is used for this situation. In this case, the monthly savings in interoffice toll charges (in Column A) would be used to offset the monthly lease expenses (in Column B). The difference between these two numbers represents the net monthly savings (in Column C).

3.4.3 Reducing Non-Interoffice Toll Charges

Is much of your long-distance traffic destined for the same calling areas, such as area codes 303, 408, 212, 612, and so on? By installing a VoIP gateway in each of these local calling areas and activating the off-net dialing function of the gateway, end users can dial in from their location, get a dial tone in those local calling areas or overseas, and call any number in that local calling area, thereby incurring no long-distance charges (Figure 3-5). A firm can further reduce its costs for its VoIP equipment and WAN connections by leasing ports on its gateway or even by selling connect time minutes to other firms.

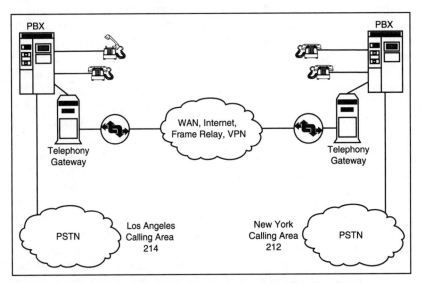

Figure 3-5: Using Off-Net Dialing to Eliminate Non-Interoffice Toll Charges

(Courtesy of Nx Networks, Inc.)

3.4.4 Reducing Inbound Customer Call Charges

Many organizations provide toll-free (800/888) numbers for their customers' convenience. If VoIP gateways are installed on the premises of these regular customers, then calls from those customers are routed via an IP network to that vendor (Figure 3-6). As a result, those calls do not incur the typical charges associated with the use of the toll-free number. The payback period for this scenario can be calculated by comparing the monthly toll-free savings at each location with the cost of purchasing the VoIP equipment to support that location.

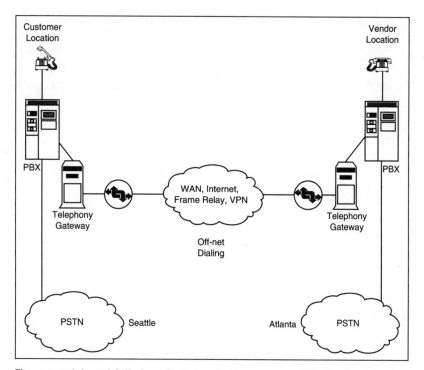

Figure 3–6: Inbound Calls from Customers to Vendors Using VoIP Points of Presence

(Courtesy of Nx Networks, Inc.)

3.4.5 Reducing Inbound Call Center Charges

Now, I'll extend the inbound call center scenario by considering that multiple, separate customers are calling about a vendor's products or services. For example, perhaps your organization has recently focused its advertising efforts in four cities: Los Angeles, Denver, Chicago, and New York. As a result, a high percentage of your inbound customer calls are from area codes 213, 303, 312, and 212. Or perhaps you are in the banking industry, with a number of branch banks scattered around the country. You would like to provide your customers with a local telephone number for customer service yet have those calls go to a centralized processing center.

Both of these challenges share a common solution: installing a VoIP point of presence (POP) in the local calling area and addressing that POP with a local telephone number (Figure 3-7). Using that local number, the customers access a VoIP gateway installed in their local calling area. That gateway connects to an IP-based network connection and communicates with a similar gateway at the distant call center location. From the customer's perspective, the call and the call center are both local operations. In this case, both the customer and the vendor benefit – the customer does not have to make a toll call to access the call center, and the vendor pays for local telephone circuits instead of toll circuits. The payback period for this scenario can be calculated by comparing the savings in communication line charges (the difference between the 800/888 access lines and the local access lines) with the cost of the VoIP equipment to support each location.

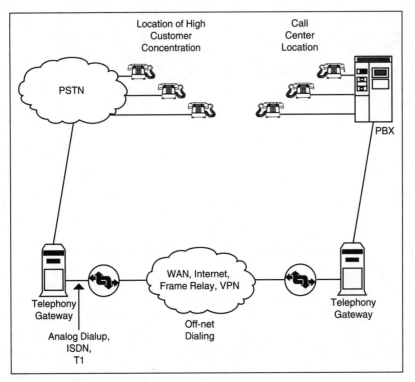

Figure 3–7: Inbound Calls from Areas of High Customer Concentration to a Call Center Using VoIP Points of Presence

(Courtesy of Nx Networks, Inc.)

3.4.6 Consolidating Network Operations within One Calling Area

If all corporate offices are in the same local calling area, and thus no toll charges apply, VoIP technologies can still be deployed for potential cost savings. These savings are derived by reducing the number of trunk lines that are required from the local exchange carrier (LEC). By routing the voice traffic over a firm's WAN or even the public Internet, the firm need not lease so many lines from the local exchange carrier. In effect, the data network replaces the local loop (Figure 3-8). The number of lines that could be replaced would be based on the results of the traffic studies, as is discussed earlier in this chapter in Section 3.2. In addition, good disaster recovery procedures dictate that some voice lines from the LEC remain in place for contingency purposes.

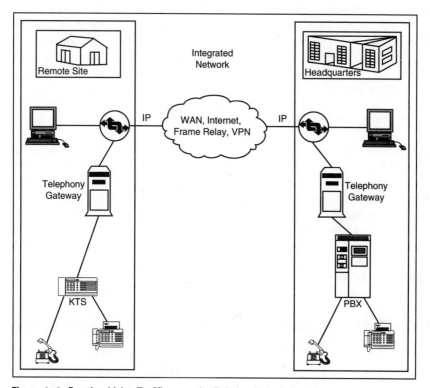

Figure 3–8: Routing Voice Traffic over the Existing Data Network

(Courtesy of Nx Networks, Inc.)

3.5 Financial Model 1: Network Migration Analysis

Mitel Networks (Ottawa, Ontario, Canada) is a well-known manufacturer of PBX and key telephone systems and has migrated their product line in support of converged networks. Mitel's white paper entitled "IP Telephony – The TCO Value Proposition" [3-4] presents an analysis method that considers the Total Cost of Ownership (TCO) of a network and how converged systems can reduce those costs.

Through the presentation of three different business scenarios using real-world data from a VoIP user, this paper provides the return on investment for typical single and multisite organizations migrating to VoIP over a three- to five-year period.

The results of the analysis indicate that there is a significant up-front investment in technology required to start the migration for most organizations (for example, network upgrades to add additional bandwidth and quality of service support). However, over a multiyear migration program, TCO can be reduced, particularly for multisite organizations and those with rapid growth and a dynamic user community.

Mitel acknowledges that toll bypass can result in savings for some organizations, but the real savings from IP Telephony are a result of decreased capital and support costs over the long term. These cost factors include reduced capital infrastructure to support a single network; consolidation of support skills and required personnel; simplification of and reduced cost of moves/adds/changes (MACs) of personnel; and easier integration and support for home office/teleworkers.

3.5.1 Assumptions Made and Inputs Required

Some key assumptions are made regarding the inputs to their business analysis. Citing research from Renaissance Worldwide and the Gartner Group, Mitel assumes that voice network costs are divided into three major categories, each of which contributes a different allocation of cost: capital (24 percent), staff (43 percent), and facilities (42 percent). Similarly, data networks have three major cost components, but with different allocations: capital (35 percent), staff (56 percent), and facilities (9 percent). For both the voice and data network cases, the staff expense is the highest. This yields the conclusion that VoIP network financials can be optimized by paying careful attention to the personnel costs, such as the time that is spent in network configuration activities, collectively known as moves, adds, and changes (MAC).

Mitel also builds other financial assumptions into their analysis (the particular values for your network may vary):

◆ The annual voice budget is approximately $1,500 per user, per year.

◆ The annual data budget is approximately $1,000 per user, per year.

◆ The annual rounded "loaded labor rates" for support personnel are $80,000 per year (for voice networks) and $92,000 per year for data networks.

◆ The average burdened cost per user is $750 for IP Telephony, which is based on Mitel's IP PBX pricing and includes the cost per user for an IP PBX license and a fully featured dual-port IP phone, plus the estimated LAN upgrade costs per user to enable VoIP.

◆ Annual data hardware and software maintenance charges total 8 percent of the capital cost.

◆ Annual PBX hardware and software maintenance charges total 6 percent of the capital cost.

Networking assumptions built into the analysis include the following (as before, the particular values for your network may vary):

◆ Data connections between offices in all multisite networks are over redundant frame relay (FR) circuits (ATM was not considered in this study). The costs associated with supporting voice on the FR network assume an upgrade from an existing 64 Kbps frame relay connection to a 128 Kbps connection. Assuming G.729 compression, this would allow up to 16 simultaneous calls between offices.

◆ A multiprotocol router for data networking to the branch office already exists; therefore, only the cost of QoS upgrades to support VoIP is included in the analysis.

To summarize, the following cost inputs would be required for this type of analysis:

1. Corporate Environment:

   ■ Number of employees

   ■ Expected growth of the organization

   ■ Length of migration period in years

2. Financial Information:

   ■ Data network budget per user

   ■ Voice network budget per user

   ■ Personnel salary for both data and voice network technicians

3. Facilities:

   ■ Number of different sites

   ■ Percent of facility costs devoted to long-distance communications between sites

   ■ Percent of support time devoted to MACs in an existing telecom network

3.5.2 Large Multisite Business Enterprise

This analysis looks at a typical scenario in a large corporation with expansion of new offices (see Figure 3-9 and Table 3-5a). Key inputs that determine this model are:

◆ 2,000 employees in year one, growth of 20 percent per year

◆ Opening small branch office in NA in year two

◆ Opening small European/UK office in year three

◆ Saving of one voice network employee in year four

◆ Analysis over a five-year period

◆ 20 percent of the long-distance calls are for intersite traffic

◆ 14 percent of their support staff labor spent in managing moves

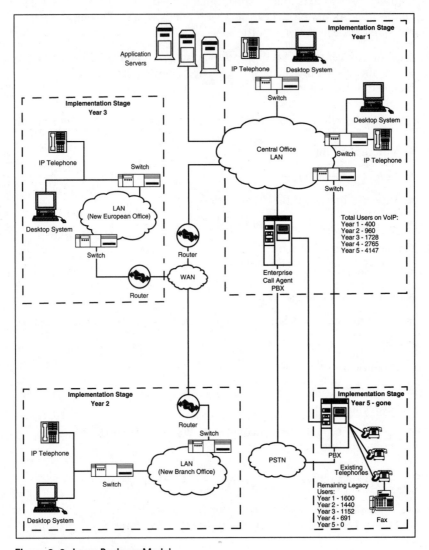

Figure 3-9: Large Business Model

(Courtesy of Mitel Corporation)

TABLE 3-5a LARGE BUSINESS SCENARIO (COURTESY OF MITEL CORPORATION)

	Year 1	Year 2	Year 3	Year 4	Year 5
Implementation Costs					
Capital Costs	$300,800	$363,552	$430,902	$503,337	$581,414
Staff Costs	$8,046	$10,132	$13,324	$17,166	$23,970
Facilities Costs	$19,248	$45,761	$83,057	$113,491	$150,266
Total Costs	$328,094	$419,445	$527,283	$633,994	$755,650
Savings					
Capital Savings	$-	$270,000	$291,600	$314,928	$340,122
Staff Savings	$63,000	$149,778	$253,155	$428,929	$592,105
Facilities Savings	$61,200	$120,960	$179,950	$238,854	$298,377
Total Savings	$124,200	$540,738	$724,705	$982,711	$1,230,605
Return on Investment	(62)%	29%	37%	5%	63%

3.5.3 Small-to-Medium Multisite Enterprise (SME) Business Scenario

This analysis looks at a typical scenario in a small-to-medium-sized corporation with expansion of new small branch offices (see Figure 3-10 and Table 3-5b). Key inputs that determine this model are:

◆ 200 employees in year one, growth of 20 percent per year

◆ Opening small branch office in year two

◆ Saving of one voice network employee in year four

◆ Analysis over a four-year range

◆ 20 percent of the long-distance calls are for intersite traffic

◆ 14 percent of their support staff labor spent in managing moves

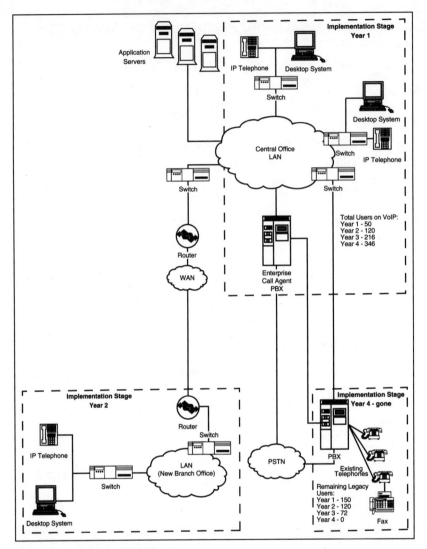

Figure 3-10: Multisite SME Model

(Courtesy of Mitel Corporation)

TABLE 3-5b SMALL-TO-MEDIUM MULTISITE BUSINESS MODEL (COURTESY OF MITEL CORPORATION)

	Year 1	Year 2	Year 3	Year 4
Implementation Costs				
Capital Costs	$37,600	$45,444	$53,863	$62,917
Staff Costs	$3,092	$2,850	$2,838	$2,302
Facilities Costs	$2,406	$8,485	$10,743	$14,624
Total Costs	$43,098	$56,779	$67,444	$79,843
Savings				
Capital Savings	$-	$27,000	$29,160	$31,493
Staff Savings	$7,875	$19,441	$32,372	$94,863
Facility Savings	$7,650	$15,120	$22,494	$29,857
Total Savings	$15,525	$61,561	$84,026	$156,212
Return on Investment	(64)%	8%	25%	96%

3.5.4 Small-to-Medium Standalone Enterprise Scenario

This analysis looks at a typical scenario in a small single-site corporation (see Figure 3-11 and Table 3-5c). Key inputs that determine this model are:

♦ 100 employees in year one, growth of 20 percent per year

♦ Analysis over a three-year range

♦ 14 percent of their support staff labor spent in managing moves

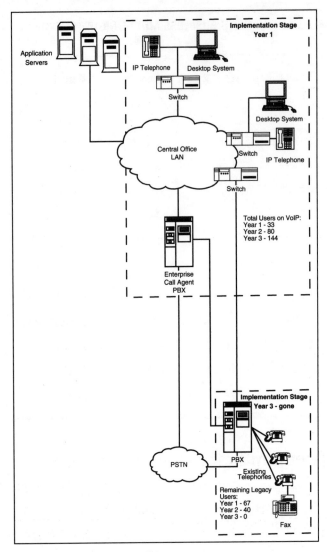

Figure 3-11: Single-Site SME Model

(Courtesy of Mitel Corporation)

TABLE 3-5c SMALL-TO-MEDIUM STANDALONE ENTERPRISE (COURTESY OF MITEL CORPORATION)

	Year 1	Year 2	Year 3
Implementation Costs			
Capital Costs	$25,064	$30,293	$35,905
Staff Costs	$2,856	$2,503	$2,339
Facility Costs	$1,604	$3,550	$5,865
Total Costs	$29,524	$36,345	$44,109
Savings			
Capital Savings	$-	$13,500	$14,580
Staff Savings	$5,249	$13,196	$21,810
Facility Savings	$1,500	$3,240	$5,248
Total Savings	$6,749	$29,936	$41,638
Return on Investment	(77)%	(18)%	(6)%

3.5.5 Scenario Comparisons

Comparison of the results for the different business scenarios is given in Table 3-5d.

TABLE 3-5d COMPARISON OF RETURN ON INVESTMENT (COURTESY OF MITEL CORPORATION)

Site Classification	Year 1	Year 2	Year 3	Year 4	Year 5
Large Multisite	(62)%	29%	37%	55%	63%
SME Multisite	(64)%	8%	25%	96%	
SME Single Site	(77)%	(18)%	(6)%		

As detailed in Table 3-5d, a significant up-front investment is involved in the transition to VoIP. Depending on the characteristics of the organization, the positive return on investment may take two or more years before showing a net positive return, strictly from a costing perspective.

The analysis shows that ROI is significantly affected by:

◆ Cost per user of data and voice networks

◆ The amount of MACs that the company supports in a year

◆ The growth rate of the organization

◆ The amount of intrasite communications currently incurring toll charges

In some cases (that is, in a single-site SME organization), there are no obvious cost savings in moving to VoIP. This is no surprise, because single-site small organizations typically do not have a highly dynamic workforce moving between locations. Also, without interbranch long-distance communications or a need to reduce costs by downsizing support personnel (often support is outsourced), the opportunities to save costs with VoIP are not obvious. In these organizations, the benefits from the migration to VoIP would be likely derived from the applications it enables or the scalability it offers.

In large organizations with multiple offices and a highly dynamic workforce, the opportunity for cost savings is high. When comparing results with those of the "typical" large corporation, it appears that savings for some corporations far exceed the norm for anticipated cost savings. This may be due to a high percentage of intrasite long-distance calls (80 percent) as compared to the typical business offered as an example earlier in the chapter (20 percent), and a three-year migration plan versus the typical five-year model used for large businesses.

A number of key cost factors emerge when reviewing the major cost drivers associated with a transition to VoIP. By removing one of these parameters from the equation, you are able to determine the relative importance of each of these factors. The following list demonstrates the relative ranking (in decreasing order of positive returns) for the key cost factors to be considered when contemplating a transition to VoIP:

◆ Cost per user in the budget for support of the current voice network

◆ Cost of labor used to support the day-to-day MACs to the office environment

◆ The expected growth of the company in terms of new employees (versus new sites)

◆ The amount of interoffice voice/fax traffic that could be sent over the corporation's data network (that is, the avoidance of long-distance toll charges)

Further details regarding Mitel's analysis can be found in Reference [3-4].

3.6 Financial Model 2: Total Cost of Ownership Analysis

Artisoft, Inc. (Cambridge, Massachusetts), develops software-based phone systems, known as the TeleVantage, which can be a valuable asset yielding real cost savings and revenue gains for a small- to medium-sized business. To assist their customers in determining the costs associated with that system, Artisoft provides a TeleVantage Cost Justification Workbook (Reference [3-5]), which is a useful model for evaluating a purchase decision for a phone system. It uses inputs from the business communications infrastructure and the specific configuration of the phone system. The workbook includes a Needs Analysis, Cost Comparison Worksheet, Return on Investment Worksheet, and Productivity Increase Calculation.

3.6.1 Business Communication Needs Analysis

Starting with an analysis of the customer's business needs, Artisoft assists the customer in understanding the critical requirements of the business and then moving to a comparison of alternative solutions. Using the Business Communication Needs Analysis (Table 3-6a), the customer fills in information regarding call statistics, users, phones, network, and functionality. The Needs Analysis is a critical step in the decision to purchase a phone system, since it forces the decision-maker to identify the requirements of the business. By completing this exercise early in the sales cycle, both the prospect and the TeleVantage Solution Provider can be sure that a comprehensive proposal covers key requirements and that surprise requirements do not arise later on.

TABLE 3-6a BUSINESS COMMUNICATIONS NEEDS ANALYSIS (COURTESY OF ARTISOFT, INC.)

BUSINESS INFORMATION AND STATISTICS

Call Statistics

Daily inbound calls

Daily outbound calls

Busy hour

Average call duration

Hours of operation

Number of Users

Internal

Remote

Number of Existing Standalone Phones

Internal

Remote

Briefly outline future growth plans, such as additional locations, users, and functionality.

CURRENT PHONE SYSTEM CONFIGURATION
Draw a diagram of the existing system layout. Include all existing telephony equipment (that is, CSU/DSU, PBX, ACD, IVR, and so on).

TELEVANTAGE CALL FLOW
Draw a diagram of the call flow desired. Include any changes to basic IVR functionality provided by the TeleVantage system, database lookups, ACD queues, and so on.

CURRENT NETWORK INFORMATION

LAN Operating System (check all that apply)

TCP/IP   ❏

Novell   ❏

Other _____ ❏

Messaging Application

None   ❏

Microsoft Exchange   ❏

Lotus Notes   ❏

Novell Groupwise   ❏

Other   ❏

Client Operating Systems Used

Windows 95   ❑

Windows NT   ❑

JAVA   ❑

Other _____   ❑

TELEPHONY INFORMATION

Current Configuration

Existing Switch/PBX Type

Model

Software Release

Proposed TeleVantage System Configuration (choose only one)

TeleVantage server connected directly to public network (serving as PBX)   ❑

The current PBX/ACD will front-end the TeleVantage server   ❑

The TeleVantage server will front-end the current PBX/ACD   ❑

Other (please describe) _____   ❑

Telephony Interfaces Connected to TeleVantage

Line Type	Quantity	Inbound	Outbound	Both
Analog				
T1				
ISDN				
Number of DID lines included in above				

HIGH LEVEL APPLICATION REQUIREMENTS

Check all that will be included in the Proposed Business Communication Solution:

TeleVantage Functionality

PBX	❏
PBX Integration	❏
IVR	❏
ACD	❏
VM/Unified Messaging	❏
Fax	❏
Screen Pop	❏
Web	❏
Other Application Integration	❏
Database Application Integration	❏
Call Center Recording	❏

Please complete the Application Functionality Detail sections below for all those features checked.

APPLICATION FUNCTIONALITY DETAIL

PBX

What criterion determines how inbound calls are routed?

	Yes	No
Is toll restriction required on outbound calls?	❏	❏
Will TeleVantage serve remote employees?	❏	❏
Is paging required?	❏	❏

PBX Integration

With what switch will TeleVantage be required to integrate?

	Yes	No
Will the communication be bidirectional between TeleVantage and the switch?	❏	❏
What is the anticipated call volume/day between TeleVantage and the switch?		

Draw a diagram of a sample call flow between the existing switch and the TeleVantage system.

IVR

	Data Repository (e.g., Accounting)	Database Type (e.g., Oracle)
Access will be required to the following:		
What is the estimated number of menu choices?		
How many languages are required?		

ACD

What is the required number of queues?

	Yes	No
Are queue statistics required?	❏	❏
What general routing schemes are required?		
What is the queue escalation process?		

FAX

	Yes	No
Is fax to the desktop required?	❏	❏
Is automatic creation and distribution of a fax from a database required?	❏	❏
Is outbound fax from desktop required?	❏	❏
Is interactive fax-on-demand required?	❏	❏

Screen Pop

What application must be popped?

What is the underlying database?

	Yes	No
Is the application COM or DDE compliant?	❏	❏

If not, what data protocol is supported?

Web

	Yes	No
Is Web chat required?	❏	❏
Is Web-based IVR/database access required?	❏	❏
If so, what kind of database?		
Will users be accessing documents via the Web?	❏	❏

Call Recording

Please describe what kind of recording will be done (why and by whom).

At what intervals are calls recorded?

What is the average duration of a recorded call?

What is the estimated number of recorded calls per day?

Other Application Integration

What other applications must be integrated with TeleVantage?

What is the operating system and version?

What is the database and version?

Please describe the integration and required data.

Other Database Integration

What type of other database must be integrated?

Oracle	❏
Informix	❏
Sybase	❏
Other _____	❏

OTHER NOTES:

3.6.2 Cost Comparisons

Total Cost of Ownership is a concept that was developed as business managers began to recognize that there is far more to the "cost" of a phone system than its initial purchase price. In fact, the initial purchase price of a phone system usually represents only a small fraction of the total cost of using and supporting the system over time. The Artisoft Workbook includes a Cost Comparison model (Table 3-6b) for calculating the Total Cost of Ownership, with a focus on comparing all initial costs of different types of phone systems, including software, hardware, and applications. Important environmental factors that affect the operational cost of a phone system, such as the business' growth, desired applications, and evolving needs for future voice technology involving the Internet, are considered.

TABLE **3–6b** COST COMPARISON WORKSHEET (COURTESY OF ARTISOFT, INC.)

Cost Components		TeleVantage		Competition
	Unit	MSRP	Extended	
Software				
Server	1	200	200	
Trunks	24	200	4800	
Station	24	100	2400	
Client	12	100	1200	
IP Trunk		250	0	
Call Center Reporter (1)		1000	0	
Hardware				
Analog Kits (2)			0	
Digital T1 Kits (2)	1	5000	5000	
Trunk Cards (2)			0	
IP Trunk Cards (2)			0	
Station/Phone Cards (2)			0	
Server hardware and software	1	3000	3000	
Handsets (3)			0	

Cost Components	TeleVantage			Competition
	Unit	MSRP	Extended	
Features/Applications				
Voice Mail/Port		included	0	
Auto Attendant		included	0	
ACD		included	0	
Initial Investment			**$16,600**	$

Notes:
(1) Reporter module per 20 agents
(2) Dialogic MSRP estimate
(3) No cost if using existing equipment

3.6.3 Return on Investment

Most modern phone systems use software to perform advanced switching functions; however, the functionality within a closed system is dependent on proprietary hardware. Artisoft's TeleVantage is an open standards software system that can accommodate many hardware alternatives. Because of this ability to leverage existing software and hardware investments, the TeleVantage system provides businesses with significant cost savings over time when compared to alternative business solutions, such as proprietary PBXs. In addition, the software-based system can be regularly upgraded, giving end users the opportunity to enjoy the benefits of a "new" phone system at a fraction of the cost.

Artisoft's product can enable businesses to increase the volume of calls, to increase the amount of revenue per call by improving sales productivity, and also to increase the productivity of individual employees. The Artisoft TeleVantage Return on Investment Worksheet (Table 3-6c) can be used to track both the revenue gains and the expense reductions associated with the implementation of the new phone system. This spreadsheet calculates ROI by quantifying the revenue and productivity gains projected from the system over time, compared to the initial investment. In this final worksheet in the model, data from previous stages is required. In addition, revenues derived from productivity increases are also an input to the ROI analysis (see Table 3-6d). Quantifying the ROI for the TeleVantage system demonstrates that the system will pay back its initial cost in a reasonable period of time and enable the business to actualize expense reductions through savings in productivity, based on the hours saved each week for each employee. Further savings are realized through reduced service charges for telecom maintenance and reduced facilities expense due to VoIP routing or other lower-cost telecommunications alternatives. As discussed before, all of these parameters may not directly apply to your network application, but the *process* described by Artisoft's analysis is worthy of consideration.

TABLE 3-6c RETURN ON INVESTMENT WORKSHEET (COURTESY OF ARTISOFT, INC.)

	Input	Monthly	Annual
1. Revenue			
TeleVantage increases revenue by reducing number of abandoned calls.			
Your total number of calls per week	7,974		
Current abandonment rate (%)	8%		
Current abandoned calls per week	638		
Reduction in abandonment rate with TeleVantage (avg. = 10% – 20%)	10%		
Weekly reduction in abandoned calls	64		
Revenue/value per call	$320	$86,757	$1,041,085
Total revenue gain		$86,757	$1,041,085
Operational Cost			
Employee Wages (1)		($58,333)	($699,996)
Operation/Administrative Costs (2)		($10,000)	($120,000)
Total revenue gain		$18,424	$221,089
2. Expense Reduction			
Savings from employee productivity (3)		$1,458	$17,500
Software subscription		$(150)	$(1,800)
Reduced service charges for telecom maintenance	5%	$69	$830
Reduced telecom facilities expense		$2,000	$24,000
Annual operational gain from using TeleVantage		$3,378	$40,530

	Input	Monthly	Annual
3. Total Revenue Gain			
Total revenue generated from TeleVantage		$21,802	$261,619
TeleVantage Initial Investment (from Cost Comparison)			$16,600
Average Annual Return on Investment over 5 years	60		26%

Notes:
(1) Based on 20 employees with a $35,000 annual salary
(2) Includes supporting staff and monthly usage charges
(3) See Table 3-6d Annual Revenue from Increased Productivity

Artisoft recommends that this analysis discussed all throughout Section 3.6 of this chapter, called a Total Cost of Ownership study, be repeated every six to nine months using new data, revisiting the data in the TeleVantage Cost Justification Workbook and reinforcing the benefits of the initial investment. Software subscription updates are generally rolled out within this time frame and should be included in the analysis. Using objective concepts such as TCO and ROI assists the end user in narrowing down the selections appropriate for their business. The phone system purchase decision should be made to maximize the value of this investment over time and to ensure that the asset can continue to meet business demands in the long term, as the company expands and its communications requirements evolve.

For further information on Artisoft, Inc., and its products, see Reference [3-5].

TABLE 3-6d ANNUAL REVENUE FROM INCREASED PRODUCTIVITY (COURTESY OF ARTISOFT, INC.)

Number of Employees	Projected Hours Saved Per Week									
	1	2	3	4	5	6	7	8	9	10
5	$4,375	$8,750	$13,125	$17,500	$21,875	$26,250	$30,625	$35,000	$39,375	$43,750
10	$8,750	$17,500	$26,250	$35,000	$43,750	$52,500	$61,250	$70,000	$78,750	$87,500
15	$3,125	$26,250	$39,375	$52,500	$65,625	$78,750	$91,875	$105,000	$118,125	$131,250
20	$17,500	$35,000	$52,500	$70,000	$87,500	$105,000	$122,500	$140,000	$157,500	$175,000
25	$21,875	$43,750	$65,625	$87,500	$109,375	$131,250	$153,125	$175,000	$196,875	$218,750
30	$26,250	$52,500	$78,750	$105,000	$131,250	$157,500	$183,750	$210,000	$236,250	$262,500
35	$30,625	$61,250	$91,875	$122,500	$153,125	$183,750	$214,375	$245,000	$275,625	$306,250
40	$35,000	$70,000	$105,000	$140,000	$175,000	$210,000	$245,000	$280,000	$315,000	$350,000
45	$39,375	$78,750	$118,125	$157,500	$196,875	$236,250	$275,625	$315,000	$354,375	$393,750
50	$43,750	$87,500	$131,250	$175,000	$218,750	$262,500	$306,250	$350,000	$393,750	$437,500
55	$48,125	$96,250	$144,375	$192,500	$240,625	$288,750	$336,875	$385,000	$433,125	$481,250
60	$52,500	$105,000	$157,500	$210,000	$262,500	$315,000	$367,500	$420,000	$472,500	$525,000
65	$56,875	$113,750	$170,625	$227,500	$284,375	$341,250	$398,125	$455,000	$511,875	$568,750
70	$61,250	$122,500	$183,750	$245,000	$306,250	$367,500	$428,750	$490,000	$551,250	$612,500

75	$65,625	$131,250	$196,875	$262,500	$328,125	$393,750	$459,375	$525,000	$590,625	$656,250
80	$70,000	$140,000	$210,000	$280,000	$350,000	$420,000	$490,000	$560,000	$630,000	$700,000
85	$74,375	$148,750	$223,125	$297,500	$371,875	$446,250	$520,625	$595,000	$669,375	$743,750
90	$78,750	$157,500	$236,250	$315,000	$393,750	$472,500	$551,250	$630,000	$708,750	$787,500

(Based on an annual expense of $35,000 per employee, which includes wages, taxes, and benefits)

3.7 Financial Model 3: Time Savings Analysis

Unified messaging is the unification of two or more applications – including voice mail, fax, and electronic mail – into a single, easy-to-use system, which may incorporate elements of IP-based message delivery. Captaris, Inc. (Kirkland, Washington), has developed a product called CallXpress Unified Messaging, which provides access to all received messages (voice, fax, and e-mail) together, through either the telephone or the computer. When traveling, a telephone might be the easiest way to access messages, although a laptop computer or Web browser could be used as well. When in the office, the e-mail interface is typically used to manage and access voice, fax, and e-mail messages.

Converged networks are implemented for a number of reasons, including improved worker productivity, improved contact with existing/potential customers, and cost savings. Captaris provides financial information and example case studies to support their customer business cases and to justify the purchase of unified messaging systems (Reference [3-6]). Many organizations are combining their voice and data communications departments and have reported that a unified approach saves a great deal of time and effort in supporting their users. Captaris believes that consolidating voice and fax messages in the e-mail client is a logical approach, because many companies already have an e-mail system that is unified messaging–ready, such as the current releases of Microsoft Exchange and Lotus Notes.

3.7.1 Time and Motion Testing

In order to quantify the advantages of unified messaging, Captaris selected three communications challenges that are frequently reported by its client base, for which unified messaging can provide solutions. This study identified and documented the time required to perform these communications functions, first using the typical manual systems found in most offices and then using unified messaging systems and services.

The time and motion studies conducted in the Captaris Usability Lab consisted of gathering typical office users; acquainting them with traditional faxing, voice mail, and e-mail operations; and timing a variety of office activities using these methods. After establishing benchmarks using traditional methods, these same users received training on Captaris' CallXpress unified messaging and were asked to repeat their earlier tasks. Times were again measured and savings calculated. In addition, the required training time was observed. The test participants were office users typically well-acquainted with traditional methods, but almost all were unfamiliar with unified messaging.

The time and motion portion of this study documented time savings for three general areas of communications functions that can also be supported inside a unified messaging system:

1. Time savings for an in-office staff member using a networked computer and a single graphical interface for accessing and reacting to e-mail, voice mail, and faxes versus the same staff member using three separate computer or manual systems for these functions

2. Time savings for a remote staff member or traveling employees using dial-up networking to connect a remote computer that uses a single graphical interface for accessing and reacting to e-mail, voice mail, and faxes versus the remote staff member using three separate computer or manual systems to perform these functions

3. Time savings for in-office staff responsible for sorting and distributing received faxes (incoming) or for administrative staff sending faxes (outbound)

In the first test displaying all message types – voice, fax, and e-mail – in a single interface, significant productivity gains were realized for office professionals. Users were able to quickly identify and act on a particular message type, receive message notification in a consistent manner, and respond to all message types in a consistent fashion. Using unified messaging, the sample voice, fax, and e-mail messages were effectively managed in less than half the time it took with traditional manual methods.

Providing information to remote and traveling employees often requires that a main-office employee locate the remote/traveling employee to ensure that information is delivered. With unified messaging, all three message types are delivered to the remote employee's single mailbox in whatever form is desired – voice, fax, or e-mail. The study observed an average time of almost 17 minutes for a remote or traveling employee to access all three message types using traditional means. With Caparis' CallXpress unified messaging, all three message types were accessed in just over 5 minutes. This yields a savings of 12 minutes each time that all messages are checked.

For the in-office staff that is sending and receiving faxes, the time and motion studies showed a time savings of 80 percent for unified messaging over the total time required to send a fax in the traditional manner. Savings were also observed with the receipt of faxes. With unified messaging, faxes are delivered directly to the intended recipient, eliminating the time required to distribute the fax.

3.7.2 Unified Messaging Example 1

Table 3-7a illustrates a 200-user system with 20 remote/traveling employees. Conservative values were used for average salary cost per hour; many companies will experience much higher costs. Costs were estimated at $250 per seat for a turnkey unified messaging system including hardware, server, and seat licenses (results may differ for individual companies who supply their own hardware).

TABLE 3-7a CAPTARIS 200-SEAT COMPARISON – EXAMPLE 1 (COURTESY OF CAPTARIS, INC.)

	Office-based	Remote/Traveling	Total
Number of employees	180	20	200
Time-savings (in hours/day)	0.25	0.4	
Average hourly salary cost	$12	$25	
Savings per day	$540	$200	$740
System costs	$45,000	$5,000	$50,000
Payback in days			67.56

The system in this example pays for itself in 67.56 business days, exclusive of desktop hardware/software and other incidental expenses.

3.7.3 Unified Messaging Example 2

The second example, shown in Table 3-7b, uses the same 200-user system with 20 remote/traveling employees, but with higher cost estimates and lower cost savings. Costs were estimated at $250 per seat for the turnkey unified messaging system including hardware, software, server, and seat licenses, plus an additional $250 per seat for additional desktop hardware and software, additional e-mail server hardware and software, internal and external technical support costs, and internal and external training.

Again, representative estimated values were used on the average time savings per day, the average hourly salary, and the resulting daily cost savings based on information gathered from Captaris clients. This example assumes that cost savings are lower on the first day but will scale up over time as more applications are activated and more users are placed on the unified messaging system, based on a phased implementation process.

TABLE 3-7b CAPTARIS 200-SEAT COMPARISON – EXAMPLE 2 (COURTESY OF CAPTARIS, INC.)

	Office-based	Remote/Traveling	Total
Number of employees	180	20	200
Time-savings (in hours/day)	0.125	0.20	

	Office-based	Remote/Traveling	Total
Average hourly salary cost	$12	$25	
Savings per day	$270	$100	$370
System costs	$90,000	$10,000	$100,000
Payback in days			270.27

The system in the above example pays for itself in 270.27 business days, including all hard and soft dollar costs. Using approximately 240 business days per year, this system has a payback period of approximately 13 and one-half months.

Thus, the Captaris study examined three functions or communications challenges many organizations typically face that can be addressed using unified messaging systems and services. For each of these functions, time and motion studies substantiate that valuable time savings are possible using the unified messaging system versus a combination of separate electronic and manual systems. The actual value of these time savings must be realized through the effective reallocation of this saved staff time to more productive use in meeting the organization's goals and/or doing more profitable work. Further details regarding this study can be found in Reference [3-6]. An ROI calculator, based on this type of study, can be found in Reference [3-7].

3.8 Case Study: ALARIS Medical Systems

As an example of the business processes that a firm must consider when converging its voice and data networking infrastructures into a single, cohesive system, consider the experiences of ALARIS Medical Systems of San Diego, California (www.alarismed.com). ALARIS Medical's principal line of business is the design, manufacture, and marketing of intravenous infusion therapy products and patient monitoring instruments. In addition to its San Diego world headquarters and manufacturing facility, the company operates manufacturing facilities in Creedmoor, North Carolina; Basingstoke, England; and Tijuana, Mexico. The firm has several strategic business units that operate in North America plus international locations, including Europe, Asia, Australia, and Latin America.

The need for additional bandwidth over their WAN has grown significantly as a result of the recent additions of SAP/R3 applications and a new corporate e-mail system, Microsoft Outlook. The firm quickly found itself lacking the bandwidth needed to support these applications. Rather than invest in additional expensive T1 lines, they enlisted a local consulting group to identify other alternatives.

A conversion to an asynchronous transfer mode (ATM) backbone was considered; however, that would have required an entirely new routing structure as well as a significant capital investment. Voice over IP systems were then researched and appeared to provide a viable solution. However, a VoIP solution needed to be compatible with the existing voice network, which consisted of networked NEC NEAX PBX systems.

The NEC NEAX PBX uses a proprietary signaling protocol called Common Channel Interoffice Signaling, or CCIS. The CCIS protocol is based on the well-known Signaling System 7 (SS7) protocol that provides transparent network voice connectivity between PBXs. For example, CCIS operations facilitate functions such as call forwarding, centralized call accounting, voice mail, and attendant services. This CCIS channel operates within the confines of a T1 circuit in much the same way that an ISDN D-channel operates on an ISDN Primary Rate Interface (PRI) circuit, by providing a specific amount of reserved bandwidth for interswitch communications. This signaling channel must operate at a full 64 Kbps rate, without compression or echo cancellation functions being applied. In summary, a VoIP solution would have to accommodate the existing investment in NEC PBXs and their proprietary CCIS channel in order for the converged network topology to be viable.

After reviewing a number of vendors' VoIP proposals, ALARIS selected the Network Exchange 2210 gateway, manufactured by Nx Networks, Inc., of Herndon, Virginia. This gateway could fully support the CCIS signaling protocol, thus requiring no change to ALARIS' existing voice infrastructure.

The first VoIP connections were between the headquarters facility in San Diego, California, and a remote office in Creedmoor, North Carolina (Figure 3-12). This installation replaced a T1 private line between the facilities, which distributed the voice and data channels using a drop and insert Channel Service Unit/Data Service Unit (CSU/DSU).

Due to the distance between the two locations, signal echoes can occur. ALARIS used the built-in echo cancellation features of the Nx Networks gateway to solve this challenge. Therefore, ALARIS did not have to purchase the echo cancellation capability from their WAN provider, which would have been an additional expense. In addition, they tested various voice compression algorithms that are available for the Nx Networks gateway and found one that provided near toll-quality voice without impairing the data transmission characteristics of the circuit. The Nx Networks gateways also have built-in voice activity detectors that can minimize the bandwidth consumption of voice circuits that are not in use, thus providing additional bandwidth resources for data transmission. (The characteristics of voice transmission, compression algorithms and quality are covered in detail in Chapter 6.) A second installation connected the San Diego headquarters with a remote facility in Hillsboro, Oregon. Like the previous connection, this circuit provided ample bandwidth for both voice and data connectivity.

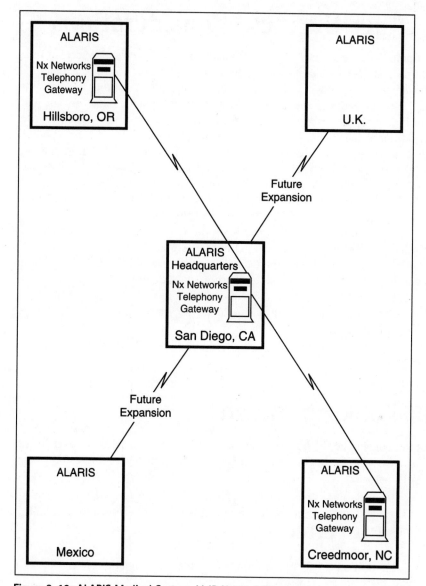

Figure 3-12: ALARIS Medical Systems VoIP Network Topology

(Courtesy of ALARIS Medical Systems)

As a result of the gateway's voice optimization algorithms, ALARIS had more bandwidth between the locations than was actually required and was therefore able to eliminate one T1 line from each location, saving over $10,000 per month in circuit charges. This resulted in a payback period of about three months for the VoIP equipment. As a result of these positive experiences, ALARIS plans to expand their VoIP network and install Nx Networks gateways in Mexico and the United Kingdom.

3.9 Other Business Considerations

VoIP technologies give the promise of reduced telephone charges and access to new applications designed to increase the productivity of a firm's staff, customers, or both. But since every network implementation is unique, a thorough analysis of business goals, objectives, and network traffic is required to make an adequate judgment regarding the viability of these technologies for your specific enterprise.

Two additional factors may enter into the decision process. First, firms with a significant percentage of international voice and data traffic will find that the charges for these connections may bias their results. In most cases, rates for domestic United States telephone service can be negotiated for $0.10 per minute or less. In contrast, rates for international calls are considerably higher – often 10 to 30 times higher, depending on the desired destination and the time of the call. Thus, a significant amount of international toll traffic on the voice network may dramatically improve the business case for VoIP equipment investments.

Second, some firms negotiate long-term contracts with their carriers to obtain more favorable rates. In some cases, termination charges would be applied if a traditional network connection contract were cancelled in favor of an IP-based solution. Any such termination charges should be factored into the business case calculations accordingly.

References [3-8] through [3-13] are additional resources for those readers wishing to dig deeper.

3.10 Looking Ahead

This chapter considered the business case aspects for planning a Voice over IP network. The next chapter begins examining the underlying technologies that comprise a VoIP network.

3.11 References

[3-1] Information on the ROInow! series of software financial analysis tools is available from www.cioview.com.

[3-2] CIOview Corporation provides a number of white papers that describe various aspects of financial analysis for Information Technology (IT) investments. For details, see www.cioview.com/white/.

[3-3] Ohrtman, Frank. "Make All Your Calls Local Calls." Nx Networks, Inc. White Paper, July 1999.

[3-4] Mitel Corporation. "IP Telephony – The TCO Value Proposition." Release 3, May 2001. Available at www.mitel.com/products/3200icp/3200_wp2.pdf.

[3-5] Artisoft, Inc. "Financial Analysis of the Decision to Purchase Artisoft's TeleVantage System – Determining the Total Cost of Ownership and Return on Investment for a Software-Based PBX." See www.artisoft.com for more information.

[3-6] COMGroup and Captaris, Inc. "Unified Messaging Time Savings Study." Available at www.captaris.com/ctg/what_is_unified_messaging/um_market/time_saving_study/timesavingsstudybyavt.pdf, January 2000.

[3-7] An online ROI calculator for fax operations, which complements the Captaris, Inc., study, is available from Snaps, Inc., at www.snapsinc.com/roi.htm.

[3-8] Swenson, Ann. "IP Telephony: Making the Business Case." White paper available at www.crmxchange.com/sessions/column/aug99.html, 1999.

[3-9] The Tolly Group. "Total Cost of Application Ownership (TCA)." White paper number 199503, available at wp.bitpipe.com/resource/org_905740864_63/199503c.pdf, 1999.

[3-10] Lucent Technologies, Inc. "Voice-over-IP Profit Guide for Service Providers." White paper, available at www.lucent.com/livelink/140020_Whitepaper.pdf, October 1999.

[3-11] VanZwol, Jeff. "The Economics of Packet Voice." White paper, available at http://206.103.61.200/pdf/Packet_Voice_WP.pdf, 2000.

[3-12] Sprint Communications Company. "Looking at the Total Cost of Ownership for Sprint ION." White paper available at www.sprintbiz.com/ion/tco.pdf, March 2000.

[3-13] Avaya, Inc. "Business Case Considerations for Deploying IP Telephony in the Enterprise." White paper available at www1.avaya.com/enterprise/whitepapers/icb1050.pdf, March 2001.

Chapter 4

Protocols for Converged Networks

Thus far, we have discussed the principles of network convergence, applications that can operate over converged networks, and some of the business decisions that may be required before implementing these technologies. This chapter considers the infrastructure of an Internet Protocol system, looking at the historical background of the Internet Protocol, the architecture and protocols of IP-based internetworks that support data transport, and, finally, the additional protocols that are required to support VoIP applications.

Some readers are already familiar with the architecture and operation of IP-based internetworks. You may feel comfortable with the details of the IPv4 and IPv6 packet headers; IPv4 and IPv6 addressing formats; routing protocols, such as RIP and OSPF; the purpose of the Domain Name Service; and the functional differences between UDP and TCP. If you fall into this category, skip directly to Section 4.8 and read about the additional protocols that are required to support voice and video transport over IP networks. However, if you feel lacking in any of the above topics, proceed with Section 4.1 so that you will more fully understand the advanced topics that come later in this text. The protocol information in this chapter is revisited and extended in Chapter 6, with a discussion of the various standards that have been designed to support VoIP systems.

4.1 The ARPA Network Architecture

You may recall from the discussion in Chapter 1 that the Internet protocols were developed, in part, by the U.S. Advanced Research Projects Agency (ARPA). The ARPA internetwork architecture (Figure 4-1) consisted of networks connected by gateways [4-1]. The ARPA model assumed that each network used packet switching technology and could connect to a variety of transmission media (LAN, WAN, radio, and so on). Note that the term *gateway* is somewhat historic and has been replaced with the term *router*. Subsequent references in this text will use the term *router*.

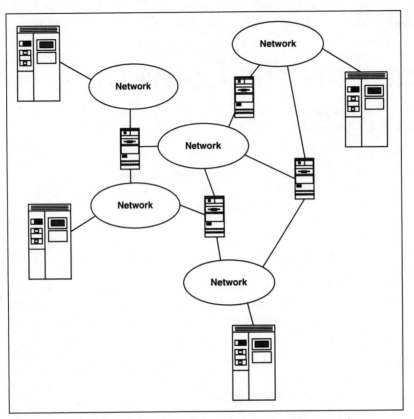

Figure 4-1: Networks Connected with Gateways to Form an Internetwork

The ARPA Internet architecture consisted of four layers (Figure 4-2). The lowest layer was called the Network Interface Layer (it was also referred to as the Local Network or Network Access Layer). It comprised the physical link (for example, LAN) between devices. The Network Interface Layer existed in all devices, including hosts and gateways.

The second layer, the Internet Layer, insulated the hosts from network-specific details, such as addressing. The Internet Protocol (IP) was developed to provide end-to-end datagram service for this layer. (Datagram service is analogous to a telegram in which the information is sent as a package.) The Internet Layer (and, therefore, IP) existed only in hosts and gateways.

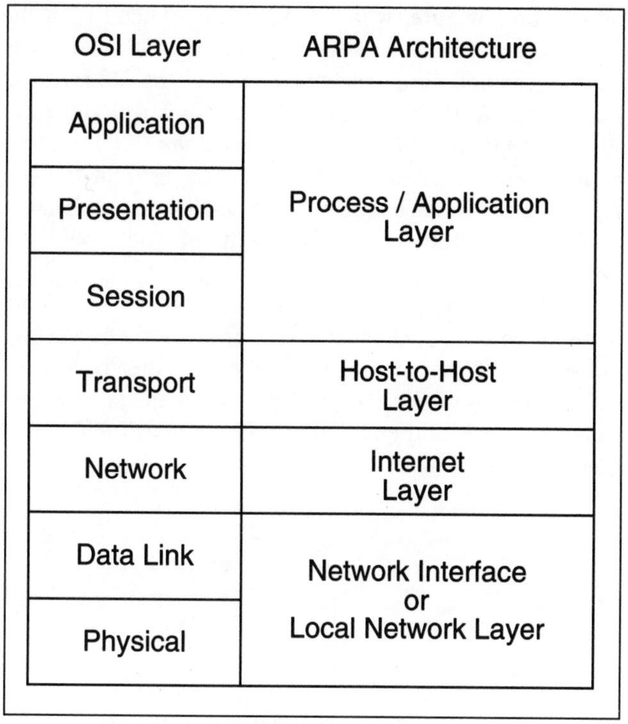

OSI Layer	ARPA Architecture
Application	Process / Application Layer
Presentation	Process / Application Layer
Session	Process / Application Layer
Transport	Host-to-Host Layer
Network	Internet Layer
Data Link	Network Interface or Local Network Layer
Physical	Network Interface or Local Network Layer

Figure 4-2: Comparing OSI and ARPA Models

While the Internet Layer provided end-to-end delivery of datagrams, it did not guarantee their delivery. Therefore, a third layer, known as the Service Layer (now called the Host-to-Host Layer), was provided within the hosts. As its name implies, the Service Layer defined the level of service the host applications required. Two protocols were created for the Service Layer: the Transmission Control Protocol (TCP) for applications needing reliable end-to-end service and the User Datagram Protocol (UDP) for applications with less stringent reliability requirements. A third protocol, the Internet Control Message Protocol (ICMP), allowed hosts and gateways to exchange monitoring and control information. All three of these protocols – TCP, UDP, and ICMP – are employed with VoIP networks. TCP is used to establish the VoIP call, a function that requires high reliability. UDP is used to transport voice samples, a function that requires maximum efficiency with a minimum of over-head. ICMP is used by IP-based VoIP equipment to verify connectivity and resolve communication problems.

The highest ARPA layer, the Process/Application Layer, resided only in hosts and supported user-to-host and host-to-host processing or applications. A variety of standard applications were developed. These included the Telecommunications Network (TELNET) for remote terminal access, the File Transfer Protocol (FTP) for file transfer, and the Simple Mail Transfer Protocol (SMTP) for electronic mail.

Figure 4-2 compares the OSI architecture, which is more theoretical, with the ARPA architecture, which is more practical and better describes how IP-based networks, including VoIP systems, are actually implemented. Note that the OSI Physical and Data Link Layers represent the ARPA Network Interface (or Local Network) Layer; the OSI Network Layer corresponds to the Internet Layer; the OSI Transport Layer is functionally equivalent to the Host-to-Host (Service) Layer; and the OSI Session, Presentation, and Application Layers comprise the ARPA Process/Application Layer. Reference [4-2] further describes the development of the ARPANET Reference Model and protocols.

To connect to LANs, the Network Interface Layer must exist in all hosts and routers, although its implementation may change across the internetwork (see Figure 4-3). Thus Host A must have a consistent attachment to Router B, but the destination Host Z may be of a different type. In other words, you can start with an Ethernet, traverse a frame relay network, and end with a token ring as long as you maintain pair-wise consistencies.

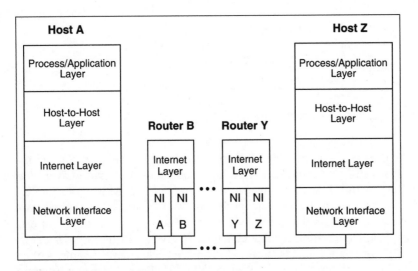

Figure 4-3: Host and Router Connections

The Internet transmission frame that originates at a host, and then subsequently passes through the routers on its way to the destination host, is illustrated in Figure 4-4. This frame would have the format of the local or wide area network in use, such as Ethernet or frame relay. A local network header would begin the frame and would contain addressing information required to deliver that frame to the appropriate location, such as the router, on a local network. The upper layer headers, IP, UDP/TCP, and Application, would follow the local network header. At the end of the frame would be the local network trailer, which would include error control information such as a checksum.

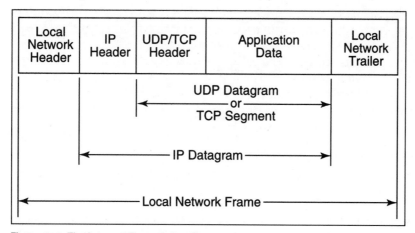

Figure 4–4: The Internet Transmission Frame

Review Figure 4-3 and note that the local network frame formats may change as they pass through various topologies. For example, if the transmission started on an Ethernet LAN, the initial frame format would adhere to the Ethernet specification. If this Ethernet then connected to a frame relay WAN, a conversion in the frame format from Ethernet to frame relay would be made at the first router with a frame relay connection. This frame relay frame would travel to the destination LAN (such as a token ring), where another frame format conversion would be made. Through this process, the packet inside that frame (the IP header, UDP/TCP header, Application Data, and so on) would be largely undisturbed, unless a packet size conversion (known as fragmentation and reassembly) became necessary.

4.2 The ARPA Protocols

The ARPA model is the architecture upon which all of the Internet Protocols were based. To better understand the interworkings of a VoIP system, one must first have a good grasp on the underlying protocols, including the architecture surrounding those protocols.

The ARPA model was designed to connect hosts serving the academic, research, government, and military populations, primarily in the United States. In contrast, the Open Systems Interconnection Reference Model (OSI-RM) was broader in scope. It was designed to address a much broader charter, the interconnection of Open Systems, and was not constrained by the type of system to be connected (for example, academic or military). As a result, the OSI-RM added additional granularity to the definitions of the layer functions and developed a seven-layer model in contrast to ARPA's four-layer model. To summarize, the ARPA world was more specific, the OSI world more general. The result was two architectures that are almost, but not quite, parallel, as shown in Figure 4-5.

ARPA Layer	Protocol Implementation								OSI Layer
Process / Application	Hypertext Transfer	File Transfer	Electronic Mail	Terminal Emulation	Domain Names	File Transfer	Client / Server	Network Management	Application
	Hypertext Transfer Protocol (HTTP)	File Transfer Protocol (FTP)	Simple Mail Transfer Protocol (SMTP)	TELNET Protocol	Domain Name System (DNS)	Trivial File Transfer Protocol (TFTP)	Sun Microsystems Network File System Protocols (NFS) RFCs 1014, 1057, and 1094	Simple Network Management Protocol (SNMP) v1: RFC 1157 v2: RFC 1901-10 v3: RFC 2571-75	Presentation
		MIL-STD-1780 RFC 959	MIL-STD-1781 RFC 2821	MIL-STD-1782 RFC 854					Session
	RFC 2068				RFC 1034, 1035	RFC 783			
Host-to-Host	Transmission Control Protocol (TCP) MIL-STD-1778 RFC 793				User Datagram Protocol (UDP) RFC 768				Transport
Internet	Address Resolution ARP RFC 826 RARP RFC 903		Internet Protocol (IP) MIL-STD-1777 RFC 791			Internet Control Message Protocol (ICMP) RFC 792			Network
Network Interface	Network Interface Cards: Ethernet, Token Ring, ARCNET, MAN and WAN RFC 894, RFC 1042, RFC 1201 and others								Data Link
	Transmission Media: Twisted Pair, Coax, Fiber Optics, Wireless Media, etc.								Physical

Figure 4-5: Comparing ARPA Protocols with OSI and ARPA Architectures

We see some of these parallels when we look at the protocols that are implemented in support of IP-based internetworks. Consider our earlier discussion and recall that the first layer of the ARPA model is the Network Interface Layer, sometimes called the Network Access Layer or Local Network Layer; it connects the local host to the local network hardware. As such, it comprises the functions of the OSI Physical and Data Link Layers; it makes the physical connection to the cable system, it accesses the cable at the appropriate time (for example, using a Carrier Sense Multiple Access with Collision Detection (CSMA/CD) or token passing algorithm), and it places the data into a frame. The frame is a package that envelops the data with information, such as the hardware address of the local host and a check sequence to ensure data integrity. The frame is defined by the hardware in use, such as an Ethernet LAN or a frame relay interface into a WAN. The ARPA model shows particular strength in this area – it includes a standard for virtually all popular connections to LANs, MANs, and WANs. (Internet standards are defined in Request for Comments documents, or RFCs. Further details on these Internet standards are provided in Appendix F.) These include Ethernet (RFC 894); IEEE 802 LANs (RFC 1042); ARCNET (RFC 1201); Fiber Distributed Data Interface – FDDI (RFC1188); serial lines using the Serial Line Internet Protocol or SLIP (RFC 1055); PSPDNs (RFC 1356); frame relay (RFC 2427); Switched Multimegabit Data Service or SMDS (RFC 1209); and the Asynchronous Transfer Mode (ATM), defined in RFC 2684.

The Internet Layer transfers packets from one host (the computing device that runs application programs) to another host. Note that I said *packet* instead of *frame*. The packet differs from the frame in that it contains address information to facilitate its journey from one host to another through the internetwork; the address within the frame header gets the frame from host to host on the same local network. The protocol that operates the Internet Layer is known as the Internet Protocol (the IP in TCP/IP). Several other protocols are also required, however.

The Address Resolution Protocol (ARP) provides a way to translate between IP addresses and local network addresses, such as Ethernet, and is discussed in RFC 826. The Reverse Address Resolution Protocol (RARP), explained in RFC 903, provides the complementary function, translating from the local address (again, such as Ethernet) to IP addresses. (In some architectural drawings, ARP and RARP are shown slightly lower than IP to indicate their close relationship to the Network

Interface Layer. In some respects, ARP/RARP overlap the Network Interface and Internet Layers.)

The Internet Control Message Protocol (ICMP) provides a way for the IP software on a host or gateway to communicate with its peers on other machines about any problems it might have in routing IP datagrams. ICMP, which is explained in RFC 792, is a required part of the IP implementation. One of the most frequently used ICMP messages is the Echo Request, commonly called the PING, which allows one device to test the communication path to another.

As the datagram traverses the Internet, it may pass through multiple routers and their associated local network connections. There's a risk that packets may be lost or that a noisy communication circuit may corrupt data. The Host-to-Host Layer guards against these problems, however remote, and ensures the reliable delivery of a datagram sent from the source host to the destination host.

The Host-to-Host Layer defines two protocols: the User Datagram Protocol (UDP) and the Transmission Control Protocol (TCP). The minimum security UDP, described in RFC 768, provides minimal protocol overhead. UDP restricts its involvement to higher layer port addresses, defining the length and a checksum. TCP, detailed in RFC 793, defines a much more rigorous error control mechanism. TCP (of the TCP/IP nomenclature) provides much of the strength of the Internet Protocol suite. TCP provides reliable data stream transport between two host applications by providing a method of sequentially transferring every octet (8-bit quantity of data) passed between the two applications.

End users interact with the host via the Process/Application Layer. Because of the user interface, a number of protocols have been developed for this layer. As its name implies, the File Transfer Protocol (FTP) transfers files between two host systems. FTP is described in RFC 959. To guarantee its reliability, FTP is implemented over TCP. When economy of transmission is desired, you may use a simpler program, the Trivial File Transfer Protocol (TFTP), described in RFC 783. TFTP runs on top of UDP to economize the Host-to-Host Layer as well.

Electronic mail and terminal emulation are two of the more frequently used Internet applications. The Simple Mail Transfer Protocol (SMTP), given in RFC 2821, sends mail messages from one host to another. When accessing a remote host via the Internet, one must emulate the type of terminal the host wishes to see. For example, a Digital host may prefer a VT-100 terminal while an IBM host would rather see a 3278 or 3279 display station. The Telecommunications Network (TELNET) protocol, defined in RFC 854, provides remote host access and terminal emulation.

As internetworks become more complex, system management requirements increase as well. A large number of vendors, including Hewlett-Packard, IBM, Microsoft, SunSoft, and others, have developed network management systems that supply these needs. Common to all of these platforms is the use of a protocol, the Simple Network Management Protocol (SNMP), that was originally developed to meet the needs of TCP/IP-based internets. As its name implies, SNMP uses minimal overhead to communicate between the Manager (that is, management console) and the Agent (that is, the device, such as a router, being managed). There are presently three different versions of SNMP defined: version 1 (RFCs 1155, 1157, and 1213), version 2 (RFCs 1901–1910), and version 3 (RFCs 2571–2575).

Many other protocols are defined for the Internet suite that provide address resolution, control, and routing functions; these are illustrated in Figure 4-6. Note that the address resolution protocols are functionally lower than the ARPA Internet Layer, and that the control and routing functions are functionally higher than the Internet Layer.

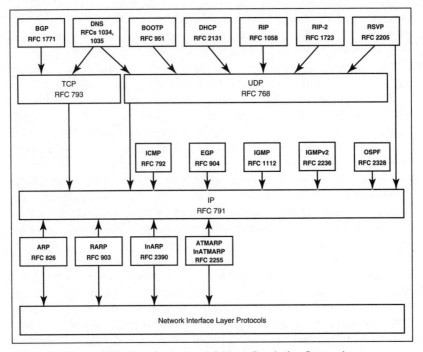

Figure 4–6: Internet Routing, Control, and Address Resolution Protocols

Thus, an IP-based internetwork is composed of a number of distinct protocols, all of which must be used at one time or another to transport information from one point to another. These protocol functions – such as address resolution and routing information updates – are independent of the information content of the data being sent. In other words, ARP, ICMP, TCP, UDP, and the other elements of the ARPA protocol suite must be present independent of whether the information that is being transmitted is a file (using FTP), a network management query (using SNMP), or a short sample of digitized voice (which, as Section 4.8 shows later in the chapter, needs other protocols as well). With that background into the Internet protocols, the next section considers the protocols that facilitate packet transport: IPv4 and IPv6.

4.3 Packet Transport: IPv4, IPv6, and ICMP

This section considers the protocols that forward Internet packets: the two versions of the Internet Protocol, IPv4 and IPv6. In addition, we discuss a complementary protocol that handles communication within the IP-based network infrastructure, the Internet Control Message Protocol (ICMP). We consider these protocols individually in the sections that follow and look at how each relates to Voice over IP.

4.3.1 Internet Protocol version 4

IP, as defined in RFC 791 [4-3], is responsible for the delivery of packets (or *datagrams* as they are known in IPv4 parlance). In other words, the IP destination address facilitates the routing of the datagram to the correct host on the specified network. A port address, found in the UDP or TCP header, then facilitates the routing of the application data within the host to the correct host process.

To deliver datagrams, IP deals with two issues: *addressing* and *fragmentation*. The address ensures that the datagram arrives at the correct destination. Datagram transmission is analogous to mailing a letter. When you mail a letter, you write source and destination addresses on the envelope, place the information to be sent inside, and drop the resulting message into a mailbox. With the postal service, the mailbox is a blue (or red, depending on where you live) box. With the Internet, the mailbox service is the node where you enter the network.

Fragmentation is necessary because the sequence of LANs and WANs that any particular datagram may traverse can have differing frame sizes, and the IP datagram must fit within these varying frames (review Figure 4-4). For example, if the endpoint is attached to an IEEE 802.3 LAN with a maximum data field size of 1500 octets, IP must fragment the large IP datagram into smaller pieces (fragments) that will fit into the constraining frame. The distant node then reassembles the fragments back into a single IP datagram.

As you can see in Figure 4-7, the IP header contains at least 20 octets of control information, divided into a number of distinct fields. Ver (4 bits) defines the current version of IP and should be equal to four. Internet Header Length or IHL (4 bits) measures the length of the IP header in 32-bit words. (The minimum value would be five 32-bit words, or 20 octets.) The IHL also provides a measurement (or offset) for where the higher layer information, such as the TCP header, begins within the datagram. Type of Service (8 bits) tells the network the quality of service requested for this particular datagram. Values include:

Bits	Precedence (or relative importance of this datagram)
Bits 0–2:	111 – Network Control
	110 – Internetwork Control
	101 – CRITIC/ECP
	100 – Flash Override
	011 – Flash
	010 – Immediate
	001 – Priority
	000 – Routine
Bit 3:	Delay, 0 = Normal, 1 = Low
Bit 4:	Throughput, 0 = Normal, 1 = High
Bit 5:	Reliability, 0 = Normal, 1 = High
Bits 6–7:	Reserved for future use (set to 0)

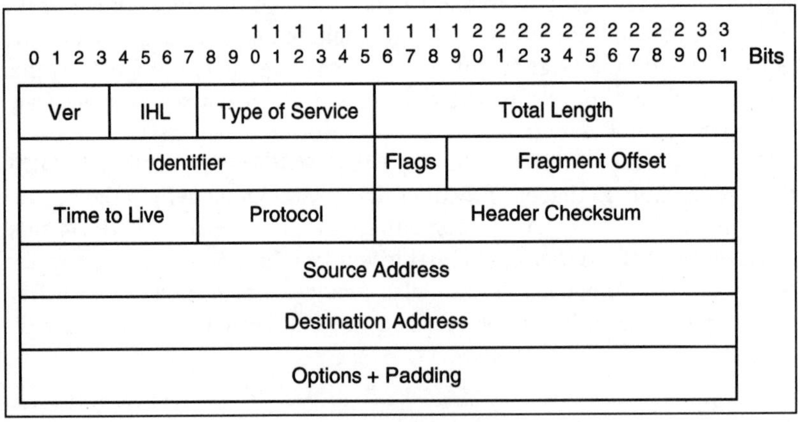

```
                    1 1 1 1 1 1 1 1 1 1 2 2 2 2 2 2 2 2 2 2 3 3
    0 1 2 3 4 5 6 7 8 9 0 1 2 3 4 5 6 7 8 9 0 1 2 3 4 5 6 7 8 9 0 1   Bits
```

Ver	IHL	Type of Service	Total Length		
Identifier			Flags	Fragment Offset	
Time to Live		Protocol	Header Checksum		
Source Address					
Destination Address					
Options + Padding					

Figure 4–7: Internet Protocol (IPv4) Header Format

The Total Length field (16 bits) measures the length, in octets, of the IP datagram (the IP header plus higher layer information). The 16-bit field allows for a datagram of up to 65,535 octets in length, although at minimum all hosts must be able to handle datagrams of 576 octets in length.

The next 32-bit word contains three fields that deal with datagram fragmentation/reassembly. The sender assigns the Identifier field (16 bits) to reassemble the fragments into the datagram. Three Flags indicate how the fragmentation process is to be handled:

Bit 0:   Reserved (set to 0)

Bit 1:   (DF) 0 = May fragment, 1 = Don't fragment

Bit 2:   (MF) 0 = Last fragment, 1 = More fragments

The last field within this word is a 13-bit Fragment Offset, which indicates where in the complete message this fragment belongs. This offset is measured in 64-bit units.

The next word in the IP header contains a Time-to-Live (TTL) measurement, which is the maximum amount of time that the datagram is allowed to live within the Internet. When TTL = 0, the datagram is destroyed. This field is a fail-safe measure that prevents misaddressed datagrams from wandering around the Internet forever. TTL may be measured in either router hops or seconds, with a maximum of 255 of either measurement. If the measurement is in seconds, the maximum of 255 seconds is equivalent to 4.25 minutes (a long time to be "lost" within today's high-speed internetworks).

The Protocol field (8 bits) identifies the higher layer protocol following the IP header. Examples include:

Decimal	Keyword	Description
1	ICMP	Internet Control Message Protocol
6	TCP	Transmission Control Protocol
17	UDP	User Datagram Protocol

RFC 1700, "Assigned Numbers," or the online version [see Reference 4-4], provides a more detailed listing of the protocols defined. A 16-bit Header Checksum completes the third 32-bit word.

The fourth and fifth words of the IP header contain the Source and Destination Addresses, respectively. Addressing may be implemented at several architectural layers. For example, hardware addresses are used at the ARPA Network Interface Layer (or OSI Data Link Layer) and are associated with a specific network interface card, usually burned into an address ROM on the card. The addresses within the IP header are the Internet Layer (or OSI Network Layer) addresses. The Internet address is a logical address that routes the IP datagram through the Internet to the correct host and network (LAN, MAN, or WAN).

4.3.2 Internet Control Message Protocol

If internetworks never experienced errors, datagrams would always be routed to their intended destination without errors. Unfortunately, this is not the case. As discussed previously in this chapter, IP provides a connectionless service to the attached hosts but requires an additional module, known as the Internet Control Message Protocol (ICMP), to report any errors that occur in the processing of datagrams. Examples of errors would be undeliverable datagrams or incorrect routes. The protocol is also used to test the path to a distant host (known as a PING) or to request an address mask for a particular subnet. ICMP is an integral part of IP and must be implemented in IP modules contained in hosts and routers. The standard for ICMP is RFC 792 [4-5].

IP datagrams contain ICMP messages. In other words, ICMP is a user (client) of IP, and the IP header precedes the ICMP message. The datagram would thus be IP header, ICMP header, and finally ICMP data. Protocol = 1 identifies ICMP within the IP header. A Type field within the ICMP header further identifies the purpose and format of the ICMP message. Any data required to complete the ICMP message follows the ICMP header.

Thirteen ICMP message formats have been defined, each with a specific ICMP header format. Two of these formats (Information Request/Reply) are considered obsolete, and several others share a common message structure. The result is six unique message formats, as shown in Figure 4-8.

```
                    1 1 1 1 1 1 1 1 1 1 2 2 2 2 2 2 2 2 2 2 3 3
  0 1 2 3 4 5 6 7 8 9 0 1 2 3 4 5 6 7 8 9 0 1 2 3 4 5 6 7 8 9 0 1  Bits
 ┌──────────────┬──────────────┬────────────────────────────────┐
 │     Type     │     Code     │            Checksum            │
 ├──────────────┴──────────────┼────────────────────────────────┤
 │         Identifier          │        Sequence Number         │
 ├─────────────────────────────┴────────────────────────────────┤
 │                             Data                             │
 └──────────────────────────────────────────────────────────────┘
```

Echo and Echo Reply Messages

```
                    1 1 1 1 1 1 1 1 1 1 2 2 2 2 2 2 2 2 2 2 3 3
  0 1 2 3 4 5 6 7 8 9 0 1 2 3 4 5 6 7 8 9 0 1 2 3 4 5 6 7 8 9 0 1  Bits
 ┌──────────────┬──────────────┬────────────────────────────────┐
 │     Type     │     Code     │            Checksum            │
 ├──────────────┴──────────────┴────────────────────────────────┤
 │                           Unused                            │
 ├──────────────────────────────────────────────────────────────┤
 │        Internet Header + 64 bits of Original Datagram Data   │
 └──────────────────────────────────────────────────────────────┘
```

Destination Unreachable, Source Quench and Time Exceeded Messages

```
                    1 1 1 1 1 1 1 1 1 1 2 2 2 2 2 2 2 2 2 2 3 3
  0 1 2 3 4 5 6 7 8 9 0 1 2 3 4 5 6 7 8 9 0 1 2 3 4 5 6 7 8 9 0 1  Bits
 ┌──────────────┬──────────────┬────────────────────────────────┐
 │     Type     │     Code     │            Checksum            │
 ├──────────────┼──────────────┴────────────────────────────────┤
 │   Pointer    │                   Unused                      │
 ├──────────────┴───────────────────────────────────────────────┤
 │        Internet Header + 64 bits of Original Datagram Data   │
 └──────────────────────────────────────────────────────────────┘
```

Parameter Problem Message

```
                    1 1 1 1 1 1 1 1 1 1 2 2 2 2 2 2 2 2 2 2 3 3
  0 1 2 3 4 5 6 7 8 9 0 1 2 3 4 5 6 7 8 9 0 1 2 3 4 5 6 7 8 9 0 1  Bits
 ┌──────────────┬──────────────┬────────────────────────────────┐
 │     Type     │     Code     │            Checksum            │
 ├──────────────┴──────────────┴────────────────────────────────┤
 │                   Gateway Internet Address                  │
 ├──────────────────────────────────────────────────────────────┤
 │        Internet Header + 64 bits of Original Datagram Data   │
 └──────────────────────────────────────────────────────────────┘
```

Redirect Message

```
                    1 1 1 1 1 1 1 1 1 1 2 2 2 2 2 2 2 2 2 2 3 3
  0 1 2 3 4 5 6 7 8 9 0 1 2 3 4 5 6 7 8 9 0 1 2 3 4 5 6 7 8 9 0 1  Bits
 ┌──────────────┬──────────────┬────────────────────────────────┐
 │     Type     │     Code     │            Checksum            │
 ├──────────────┴──────────────┼────────────────────────────────┤
 │         Identifier          │        Sequence Number         │
 ├─────────────────────────────┴────────────────────────────────┤
 │                      Originate Timestamp                    │
 ├──────────────────────────────────────────────────────────────┤
 │                      Receive Timestamp                      │
 ├──────────────────────────────────────────────────────────────┤
 │                      Transmit Timestamp                     │
 └──────────────────────────────────────────────────────────────┘
```

Timestamp and Timestamp Reply Messages

```
                    1 1 1 1 1 1 1 1 1 1 2 2 2 2 2 2 2 2 2 2 3 3
  0 1 2 3 4 5 6 7 8 9 0 1 2 3 4 5 6 7 8 9 0 1 2 3 4 5 6 7 8 9 0 1  Bits
 ┌──────────────┬──────────────┬────────────────────────────────┐
 │     Type     │     Code     │            Checksum            │
 ├──────────────┴──────────────┼────────────────────────────────┤
 │         Identifier          │        Sequence Number         │
 ├─────────────────────────────┴────────────────────────────────┤
 │                        Address Mask                         │
 └──────────────────────────────────────────────────────────────┘
```

Address Mask Request and Address Mask Reply Messages

Figure 4–8: Internet Control Message Protocol (ICMP) Message Formats

Network managers need to understand each of these ICMP messages because they contain valuable information about network status. All the headers share the first three fields. The Type field (1 octet) identifies one of the 13 unique ICMP messages. These include:

Type Code	ICMP Message
0	Echo Reply
3	Destination Unreachable
4	Source Quench
5	Redirect
8	Echo
11	Time Exceeded
12	Parameter Problem
13	Timestamp
14	Timestamp Reply
15	Information Request (obsolete)
16	Information Reply (obsolete)
17	Address Mask Request
18	Address Mask Reply

The second field is labeled Code (1 octet) and elaborates on specific message types. For example, the Code field for the Destination Unreachable message indicates whether the network, host, protocol, or port was the unreachable entity. The third field is a Checksum (2 octets) on the ICMP message. The ICMP message formats diverge after the third field.

The Echo message (ICMP Type = 8) tests the communication path from a sender to a receiver via the Internet. On many hosts, this function is known as PING. The sender transmits an Echo message, which may contain an Identifier (2 octets) and a Sequence Number (2 octets) as well as data. When the intended destination receives the message, it reverses the source and destination addresses, recomputes the checksum, and returns an Echo Reply (ICMP Type = 0). The contents of the Data field (if any) would also return to the sender.

The Destination Unreachable message (ICMP Type = 3) is used when the router or host is unable to deliver the datagram. This message is returned to the source host of the datagram in question, and its Code field includes the specific reason for the delivery problem:

Code	Meaning
0	Net Unreachable
1	Host Unreachable
2	Protocol Unreachable
3	Port Unreachable
4	Fragmentation Needed and DF Set
5	Source Route Failed

Routers use codes 0, 1, 4, or 5. Hosts use codes 2 or 3. For example, when a datagram arrives at a router, it does a table lookup to determine the outgoing path to use. If the router determines that the destination network is unreachable (that is, a distance of infinite hops away), it returns a Net Unreachable message. Similarly, if a host is unable to process a datagram because the requested protocol or port is inactive, it would return a Protocol Unreachable or Port Unreachable message, respectively. Included in the Destination Unreachable message is the IP header plus the first 64 bits (8 octets) of the datagram in question. This returned data helps the host diagnose the failure in the transmission process.

The advantage of the datagram's connectionless nature is its simplicity. The disadvantage is its inability to regulate the amount of traffic into the network. As an analogy, consider the problem that your local post office faces. To handle the maximum possible number of letters, it needs enough boxes to handle the holiday rush. Building many boxes might be wasteful, however, because many of the boxes may not be used fully during the summer. If a router or host becomes congested with datagrams, it may send a Source Quench message (ICMP Type = 4) asking the source of those datagrams to reduce its output. This mechanism is similar to traffic signals that regulate the flow of cars onto a freeway. The Source Quench message does not use the second 32-bit word of the ICMP header, but fills it with zeros. The rest of the message contains the IP header and the first 8 octets of the datagram that triggered the request.

Hosts do not always choose the correct destination address for a particular datagram and occasionally send one to the wrong router. This scenario can occur when the host is initialized and its routing tables are incomplete. When such a routing mistake occurs, the router receiving the datagram returns a Redirect message to the host specifying a better route. The Code field in the datagram would contain the following information:

Code	Message
0	Redirect datagrams for the network
1	Redirect datagrams for the host
2	Redirect datagrams for the type of service and network
3	Redirect datagrams for the type of service and host

The Redirect message (ICMP Type = 5) contains the router (gateway) address necessary for the datagram to reach the desired destination. In addition, the IP header plus the first 8 octets of the datagram in question return to the source host to aid the diagnostic processes.

Another potential problem of connectionless networks is that datagrams can get lost within the network. Alternatively, congestion could prevent all fragments of a datagram from being reassembled within the host's required time. Either of these situations could trigger an ICMP Time Exceeded message (ICMP Type = 11). This message contains two codes: time-to-live exceeded in transmit (code = 0), and fragment reassembly time exceeded (code = 1). The rest of the message has the same format as the Source Quench message: the second word contains all zeros and the rest of the message contains the IP header and the first 8 octets of the offending datagram.

If a datagram cannot be processed because of errors, higher layer processes recognize the errors and discard the datagram. Parameter problems within an IP datagram header (such as incorrect Type of Service field) would trigger the sending of an ICMP Parameter Problem message (ICMP Type = 12) to the source of that datagram, identifying the location of the problem. The message contains a Pointer that identifies the octet with the error. The rest of the message contains the IP datagram header plus the first 8 octets of data, as before.

The Timestamp message (ICMP Type = 13) and Timestamp Reply message (ICMP Type = 14) either measure the round-trip transit time between two machines or synchronize the clocks of two different machines. The first two words of the Timestamp and Timestamp Reply messages are similar to the Echo and Echo Reply messages. The next five fields contain timestamps, measured in milliseconds since midnight, Universal Time (UT). The Timestamp requester fills in the Originate field when it transmits the request; the recipient fills in the Receive Timestamp upon its receipt. The recipient also fills in the Transmit Timestamp when it transmits the Timestamp Reply message. With this information, the requester can estimate the remote processing and round-trip transit times. (Note that these are only estimates, since network delay is a highly variable measurement.) The remote processing time is the Received Timestamp minus Transmit Timestamp. The round-trip transit time is the Timestamp Reply message arrival time minus the Originate Timestamp. With these two calculations, the two clocks can be synchronized.

The subnetting requirements (RFC 950) added the Address Mask Request (ICMP Type = 17) and Address Mask Reply (ICMP Type = 18) to the ICMP message set. It is assumed that the requesting host knows its own Internet address. (If not, it uses RARP to discover its Internet address.) The host broadcasts the Address Mask Request message to destination address 255.255.255.255 and fills the Address Mask field of the ICMP message with zeros, and the IP router that knows the correct address mask responds. For example, the response for a Class B network (when subnet addresses are not used) would be 255.255.0.0. A Class B network using an 8-bit subnet field would be 255.255.255.0.

4.3.3 Internet Protocol version 6

As the applications for the Internet expanded in the early 1990s, and more organizations began using this worldwide communications resource, some of the shortcomings of the original Internet Protocol became evident. The most noticeable of these shortcomings was the 32-bit IPv4 address space; there were concerns that this address space would soon be exhausted, thus limiting growth of the Internet. As a result, the Internet Engineering Task Force chartered the Internet Protocol Next Generation (IPng) working group. This working group was tasked with defining the requirements and specifications for the protocols that would take the Internet to the next level of growth.

In December 1993, RFC 1550 was distributed, titled "IP: Next Generation (IPng) White Paper Solicitation." This RFC invited any interested party to submit their comments regarding any specific requirements for the IPng or any key factors that should be considered during the IPng selection process. Twenty-one responses were submitted that addressed a variety of topics, including: security (RFC 1675), a large corporate user's view (RFC 1687), a cellular industry view (RFC 1674), and a cable television industry view (RFC 1686).

The IPng Area commissioned RFC 1726, "Technical Criteria for Choosing IP The Next Generation (IPng)," to define a set of criteria that would be used in the IPng evaluation process. Seventeen criteria were noted:

- **Scale:** The IPng Protocol must scale to allow the identification and addressing of at least 10^{12} end systems and 10^9 individual networks.

- **Topological Flexibility:** The routing architecture and protocols of IPng must allow for many different network topologies.

- **Performance:** A state-of-the-art, commercial-grade router must be able to process and forward IPng traffic at speeds capable of fully using common, commercially available, high-speed media at the time.

- **Robust Service:** The network service and its associated routing and control protocols must be robust.

- ◆ **Transition:** The protocol must have a straightforward transition plan from the current IPv4.

- ◆ **Media Independence:** The protocol must work across an internetwork of many different LAN, MAN, and WAN media, with individual link speeds ranging from ones-of-bits per second to hundreds of gigabits per second.

- ◆ **Unreliable Datagram Service:** The protocol must support an unreliable datagram delivery service.

- ◆ **Configuration, Administration, and Operation:** The protocol must permit easy and largely distributed configuration and operation. The automatic configuration of hosts and routers is required.

- ◆ **Secure Operation:** IPng must provide a secure network layer.

- ◆ **Unique Naming:** IPng must assign all IP-Layer objects global, ubiquitous, Internet unique names.

- ◆ **Access and Documentation:** The protocols that define IPng, its associated protocols, and the routing protocols must be published in the standards track RFCs, be freely available, and be without licensing fees for implementation.

- ◆ **Multicast:** The protocol must support both unicast and multicast packet transmission.

- ◆ **Extensibility:** The protocol must be extensible; it must be able to evolve to meet the future service needs of the Internet.

- ◆ **Network Service:** The protocol must allow the network to associate packets with particular service classes and must provide them with the services specified by those classes.

- ◆ **Mobility:** The protocol must support mobile hosts, networks, and internetworks.

- ◆ **Control Protocol:** The protocol must include elementary support for testing and debugging networks.

- ◆ **Private Networks:** IPng must allow users to build private internetworks on top of the basic Internet infrastructure.

Of the criteria noted above, those most relevant to our discussion of VoIP applications are the multicast and network service requirements. Multicasting allows the same packet to be distributed to more than one destination, such as with an audio or video conference call. The network service criteria notes that a particular flow of packets, such as those from that real-time conference call, could be identified for special processing to provide more timely packet delivery. In addition, the overall architecture of IPv6 is designed around 64-bit processors, which run real-time operations more effectively than those processors with a smaller word size (such as 16- or 32-bit machines).

These criteria were used to develop IP version 6, which is currently specified in RFC 2460 [4-6]. The functions necessary to support the design criteria are included within the IPv6 base header and extension headers.

4.3.3.1 THE IPV6 HEADER

The IPv6 header is 40 octets long, with eight fields (Figure 4-9).

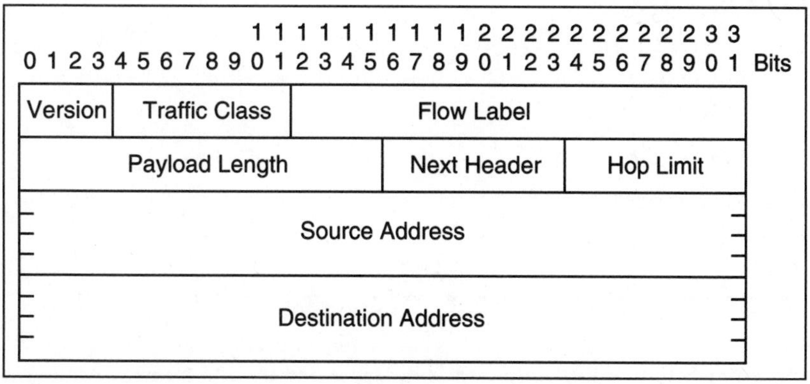

Figure 4–9: Internet Protocol version 6 (IPv6) Header Format

The Version field is 4 bits long and identifies the version of the protocol. For IPv6, Version = 6.

The Traffic Class field is 8 bits long and enables a source to identify the desired delivery criteria for its packets.

The Flow Label field is 20 bits long and may be used by a host to request special handling for certain packets, such as those with a nondefault quality of service.

The Payload Length field is a 16-bit unsigned integer that measures the length, given in octets, of the payload (that is, the balance of the IPv6 packet). Payloads greater than 65,535 octets are allowed and are called jumbo payloads.

The Next Header field is 8 bits long and identifies the header immediately following the IPv6 header. This field uses the same values as the IPv4 Protocol field. Examples are:

Value	Header
0	Hop-by-Hop Options
1	ICMPv4
4	IP in IP (encapsulation)

Continued

Value	Header
6	TCP
17	UDP
43	Routing
44	Fragment
50	Encapsulating Security Payload
51	Authentication
58	ICMPv6
59	None (no next header)
60	Destination Options

The Hop Limit field is 8 bits long and is decremented by one by each node that forwards the packet. When the Hop Limit equals zero, the packet is discarded and an error message is returned.

The Source Address is a 128-bit field that identifies the originator of the packet. (Note that this represents a substantial increase in address field size over what was provided with IPv4.)

The Destination Address field is a 128-bit field that identifies the intended recipient of the packet, although it might not be the ultimate recipient of the packet if a Routing header is present.

4.3.3.2 EXTENSION HEADERS

The IPv6 design simplified the existing IPv4 header by placing many of the existing fields in optional headers. In this way, the processing of ordinary packets is not complicated by undue overhead, while the more complex conditions are still provided for. An IPv6 packet, which consists of an IPv6 packet plus its payload, may consist of zero, one, or more extension headers, as shown in Figure 4-10.

The Hop-by-Hop Options header carries information that must be examined and processed by every node along a packet's delivery path, including the destination node. As a result, the Hop-by-Hop Options header, when present, must immediately follow the IPv6 header. The other extension headers are not examined or processed by any node along a packet's delivery path until the packet reaches its intended destination(s). When processed, the operation is performed in the order in which the headers appear in the packet.

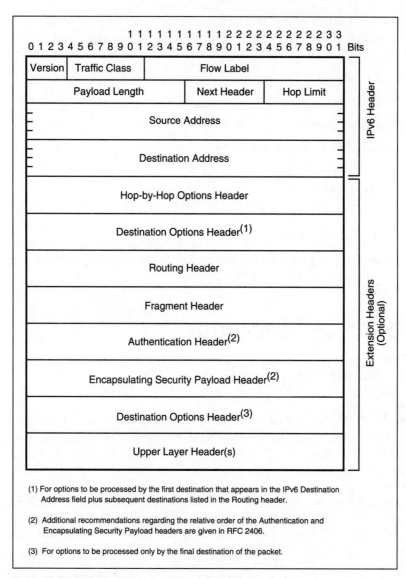

Figure 4–10: Internet Protocol version 6 (IPv6) Packet Format

The IPv6 specification recommends that the extension headers be placed in the IPv6 packet in a particular order:

◆ IPv6 header

◆ Hop-by-Hop Options header

◆ Destination Options header (for options to be processed by the first destination that appears in the IPv6 Destination Address field, plus any subsequent destinations listed in the Routing header)

◆ Routing header

◆ Fragment header

◆ Authentication header

◆ Encapsulating Security Payload header

◆ Destination Options header (for options to be processed by the final destination only)

◆ Upper Layer header (TCP and so on)

Figure 4-10 illustrates the IPv6 and optional headers, with their suggested order. Further details on IPv6 standards and implementations are available from the two key IPv6 Web sites, noted in Reference [4-7].

4.4 Packet Addressing

Following the format of the previous discussion, this section discusses packet addressing for IPv4 and IPv6, respectively.

4.4.1 IPv4 Addressing

Each 32-bit IPv4 address is divided into Host ID and Network ID sections and takes one of five formats ranging from Class A to Class E, as shown in Figure 4-11. The formats differ in the number of bits they allocate to the Host IDs and Network IDs and are identified by the first four bits.

Class A addresses are designed for very large networks with many hosts. They are identified by Bit 0 = 0. Bits 1 through 7 identify the network, and Bits 8 through 31 identify the host. With a 7-bit Network ID, only 128 Class A network addresses are available. Of these, addresses 0 and 127 are reserved.

The majority of organizations that have distributed processing systems including LANs and hosts use Class B addresses. Class B addresses are identified with the first 2 bits having a value of 10 (binary). The next 14 bits identify the network. The remaining 16 bits identify the host. A total of 16,384 Class B network addresses are possible; however, addresses 0 and 16,383 are reserved.

Class C addresses are generally used for smaller networks, such as LANs. They begin with a binary 110. The next 21 bits identify the network. The remaining 8 bits identify the host. A total of 2,097,152 Class C network addresses are possible, with addresses 0 and 2,097,151 reserved.

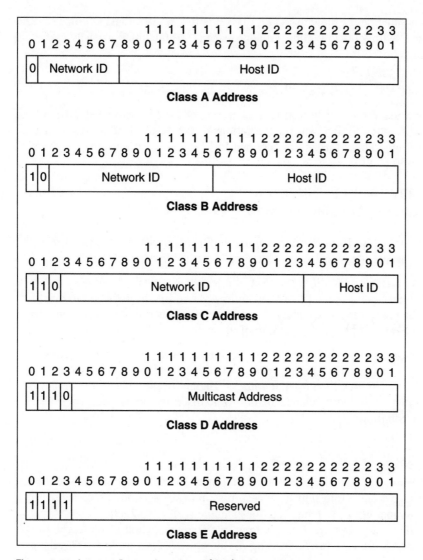

Figure 4–11: Internet Protocol version 4 (IPv4) Address Formats

Class D addresses begin with a binary 1110 and are intended for multicasting. Class E addresses begin with a binary 1111 and are reserved for future use.

All IP addresses are written in dotted decimal notation, in which each octet is assigned a decimal number from 0 to 255. For example, network [10.55.31.84] is represented in binary as 00001010 00110111 00011111 1010100. The first bit (0) indicates a Class A address, the next 7 bits (0001010) represent the Network ID (decimal 10), and the last 24 bits (00110111 00011111 1010100) represent the Host ID.

Class A addresses begin with 1–127, Class B with 128–191, Class C with 192–223, and Class D with 224–239. Thus, an address of [150.100.200.5] is easily identified as a Class B address.

4.4.2 IPv6 Addressing

As was discussed previously in this chapter, one of the incentives behind the IPng effort that resulted in IPv6 was the limitations of the 32-bit IPv4 address structure. The new IPv6 address formats are defined in RFC 2373, "IP Version 6 Addressing Architecture" [4-8].

4.4.2.1 IPV6 ADDRESS TYPES
RFC 2373 defines three different types of IPv6 addresses:

◆ Unicast: An identifier to a single interface. A packet sent to a unicast address is delivered to the interface identified by that address.

◆ Anycast: An identifier for a set of interfaces (typically belonging to different nodes). A packet sent to an anycast address is delivered to one of the interfaces identified by that address (the "nearest" one, according to the routing protocol's measure of distance).

◆ Multicast: An identifier for a set of interfaces (typically belonging to different nodes). A packet sent to a multicast address is delivered to all interfaces identified by that address. The multicast replaces the broadcast function, but with added capabilities to discriminate between packet destinations.

4.4.2.2 IPV6 ADDRESS REPRESENTATION
IPv4 addresses are typically represented in dotted decimal notation. As such, a 32-bit address is divided into four 8-bit sections, and each section is represented by a decimal number between 0 and 255, for example [129.144.52.38].

Since IPv6 addresses are 128 bits long, a different method of representation is required. As specified in the Addressing Architecture document, RFC 2373, the preferred representation is:

```
X:X:X:X:X:X:X:X
```

where each x represents 16 bits, and each of those 16-bit sections is defined in hexadecimal. For example, an IPv6 address could be of the form:

```
FEDC:BA98:7654:3210:FEDC:BA98:7654:3210
```

Note that each of the 16-bit sections is separated by colons, and that four hexadecimal numbers are used to represent each 16-bit section. Should any one of the 16-bit sections contain leading zeros, those zeros are not required. For example:

`1080:0000:0000:0000:0008:0800:200C:417A`

can be simplified to:

`1080:0:0:0:8:800:200C:417A`

If long strings of zeros appear in an address, a double colon "::" may be used to indicate multiple groups of 16-bits of zeros, which further simplifies the example shown above:

`1080::8:800:200C:417A`

The use of the double colon is restricted to appearing only once in an address, although it may be used to compress either the leading or the trailing zeros in an address. For example, a loopback address of:

`0:0:0:0:0:0:0:1`

could be simplified as:

`::1`

For additional details, see RFC 2373.

4.4.2.3 IPV6 ADDRESS ARCHITECTURE

The 128-bit IPv6 address may be divided into a number of subfields to provide maximum flexibility for both current and future address representations. The leading bits, called the *format prefix*, define the specific type of IPv6 address. RFC 2373 defines a number of these prefixes, as shown in Figure 4-12. Note that address space has been allocated for NSAP, IPX, aggregatable global, site local, and other addresses. Also note that multicast addresses begin with the binary value 11111111; any other prefix identifies a unicast address. Anycast addresses are part of the allocation for unicast addresses and are not given a unique identifier.

A number of forms for unicast addresses have been defined for IPv6, some with more complex structures that provide for hierarchical address assignments. The simplest form would be a unicast address with no internal structure – in other words, with no address-defined hierarchy. The next possibility would be to specify a subnet prefix within the 128-bit address, thus dividing the address into a subnet prefix (with n bits) and an interface ID (with 128 – n bits). For applications where more hierarchy is required, a specific type of address, called the Aggregatable Global Unicast Address, is defined. This address type allows multiple levels of hierarchy, starting with network providers of IPv6 service and graduating down to the networks, subnetworks, and finally to the end-user devices. In summary, with a 128-bit address space available, a number of addressing structures are possible. RFC 2373 illustrates many of these.

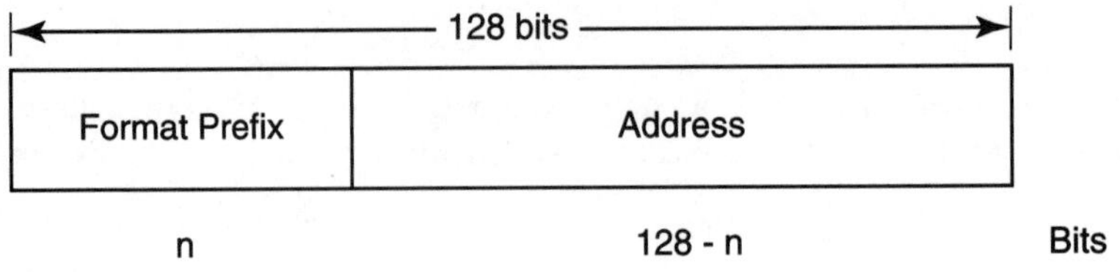

Prefix (binary)	Allocation
0000 0000	Reserved
0000 0001	Unassigned
0000 001	Reserved for NSAP Allocation
0000 010	Reserved for IPX Allocation
0000 011	Unassigned
0000 1	Unassigned
0001	Unassigned
001	Aggregatable Global Unicast Addresses
010	Unassigned
011	Unassigned
100	Unassigned
101	Unassigned
110	Unassigned
1110	Unassigned
1111 0	Unassigned
1111 10	Unassigned
1111 110	Unassigned
1111 1110 0	Unassigned
1111 1110 10	Link Local Unicast Addresses
1111 1110 11	Site Local Unicast Addresses
1111 1111	Multicast Addresses

Figure 4–12: Internet Protocol version 6 (IPv6) Addressing Architecture

Two addresses have special meanings. The address 0:0:0:0:0:0:0:0 (also represented as 0::0) is defined as the *unspecified address* and indicates the absence of an address. This address might be used upon startup when a node has not yet had an address assigned. The unspecified address can never be assigned to any node.

The address 0:0:0:0:0:0:0:1 (also represented as 0::1) is defined as the *loopback address*. This address is used by a node to send a packet to itself.

Two special addresses have been defined for IPv4/IPv6 transition networks. The first such address is called an IPv4-Compatible IPv6 address. It is used when two IPv6 devices (such as hosts or routers) need to communicate via an IPv4 routing infrastructure. The devices at the edge of the IPv4 would use this special unicast address, which carries an IPv4 address in the low order 32 bits. This address has a prefix of 96 bits of zeros. The second type of transition address is called an IPv4-Mapped IPv6 address. This address is used by IPv4-only nodes that do not support IPv6. For example, an IPv6 host would use an IPv4-Mapped IPv6 address to communicate with another host that supported only IPv4. This prefix is 80 bits of zeros, followed by 16 bits of ones.

4.5 Packet Routing: RIP, OSPF, EGP, and BGP

So far, this chapter has covered how hosts transmit datagrams and use a 32-bit address to identify the source and destination of each datagram. The host drops the datagram into the internetwork, and the datagram somehow finds its way to its destination. That "somehow" is the work of routers, which examine the Destination address, compare that address with their internal routing tables, and send the datagram on the correct outgoing communication circuit (Figure 4-13).

Router operation involves several processes. First, the router creates a routing table to gather information from other routers about the optimum path between two endpoints. This table may be *static* (that is, manually built and fixed for all network conditions) or *dynamic* (that is, constructed by the router according to the current topology and conditions). Dynamic routing is considered the better technique because it adapts to changing network conditions. The router uses a *metric*, or measurement, of the shortest distance between the two endpoints to help determine the optimum path. It determines the metric using a number of factors, including the shortest distance, or least cost path, to the destination. The router plugs the metric into one of two algorithms to make a final decision on the correct path. A Distance Vector algorithm makes its choice based on the distance to a remote node. A Link State algorithm also includes information about the status of the various links connecting the nodes and the topology of the network.

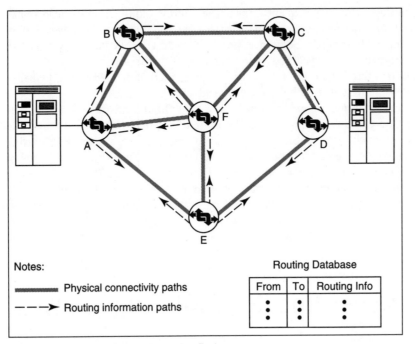

Figure 4-13: Routing Table Information Exchange

The various routers within the network use the Distance Vector or Link State algorithms to inform each other of their current status. Because routers use them for intranetwork communication, the protocols that make use of these algorithms are referred to as Interior Gateway Protocols (IGPs). The Routing Information Protocol (RIP) is an IGP based on a Distance Vector algorithm. The Open Shortest Path First (OSPF) protocol is an IGP based on a Link State algorithm. We'll look at these two algorithms separately in the following sections. If one network wishes to communicate routing information to another network, it uses an exterior gateway protocol. Examples of exterior gateway protocols are the Exterior Gateway Protocol (EGP) and the Border Gateway Protocol (BGP).

In this section, we focus on routing within IPv4-based networks. Updates to the various routing protocols in support of IPv6 are under development and implementation. Current information regarding these updates can be found on the IPv6 Industry Home Page [4-7].

4.5.1 Routing Information Protocol

The Routing Information Protocol, described in RFC 1058 [4-9], is used for inter-router (or intergateway) communications. RIP is based on a Distance Vector algorithm, in which the routers periodically exchange information from their routing tables. The routing decision is based on the best path between two devices, which is often the path with the fewest hops or router transversals.

RFC 1058 acknowledges several limitations to RIP. RIP allows a path length of 15 hops, which may be insufficient for large internetworks. Routing loops are not possible for internetworks containing hundreds of networks because of the time required to transmit updated routing table information. Finally, the metrics used to choose the routing path are fixed and do not allow for dynamic conditions, such as a measured delay or a variable traffic load.

RIP assumes that all devices (hosts and routers) contain a routing table. This table includes several entries: the IP address of the destination; the metric, or cost, to get a datagram from the host to the destination; the address of the next router in the path to the destination; a flag indicating whether the routing information has been recently updated; and timers.

Routing information is exchanged via RIP packets, shown in Figure 4-14, which are transmitted to/from UDP port number 520. The packet begins with a 32-bit header and may contain as many as 25 messages giving details on specific networks. The first field of the header is 1 octet long and specifies a unique command. Values include:

Command	Meaning
1	Request for routing table information
2	Response containing routing table information
3	Traceon (obsolete)
4	Traceoff (obsolete)
5	Reserved for Sun Microsystems
9	Update Request (from RFC 2091)
10	Update Response (from RFC 2091)
11	Update Acknowledge (from RFC 2091)

The second octet contains a RIP Version Number. Octets 3 and 4 are set equal to zero. The next two octets identify the Address Family being transmitted within that RIP packet. For IP, the defined Address Family value is 2.

The balance of the RIP packet contains entries for routing information. Each entry includes the destination IP address and the metric to reach that destination. Metric values must be between 1 and 15, inclusive. A metric of 16 indicates that the desired destination is unreachable. Up to 25 of these entries (from the Address Family Identifier through the Metric) may be contained within the datagram.

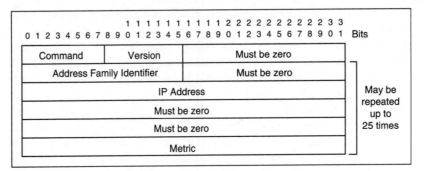

Figure 4-14: Routing Information Protocol (RIP) Packet Format

An extension to the Routing Information Protocol, called RIP version 2, is defined in RFC 2453 [4-10]. This enhancement expands the amount of useful information carried in RIP messages and also adds a measure of security to those messages. The RIP version 2 packet format is very similar to the original format, containing a 4-octet header and up to 25 route entries of 20 octets each in length. Within the header, the Command, Address Family Identifier, IP Address, and Metric fields are identical to their counterparts in the original RIP packet format. The Version field specifies version number 2, and the 2-octet unused field (filled with all zeros) is ignored. The Route Tag field carries an attribute assigned to a route that must be preserved and readvertised with a route, such as information defining the routing information's origin (either intra- or internetwork). Within each route entry, the Subnet Mask field (4 octets) defines the subnet mask associated with a routing entry. The Next Hop field (also 4 octets) provides the immediate next hop IP address for the packets specified by this routing entry. The spaces now occupied by the Subnet Mask and Next Hop fields were previously filled with all zeros.

4.5.2 Open Shortest Path First Protocol

The Open Shortest Path First protocol, defined in RFC 2328 [4-11], is a Link State algorithm that offers several advantages over RIP's Distance Vector algorithm. These advantages include the following abilities: to configure hierarchical (instead of flat) topologies; to quickly adapt to changes within the internet; to allow for large internetworks; to calculate multiple minimum-cost routes that allow traffic load to be balanced over several paths; to authenticate the exchange of routing table information; and to permit the use of variable-length subnet masks. The protocol uses the IP address and Type of Service field for its operation. An optimum path can be calculated for each Type of Service.

4.5.2.1 LINK STATE ALGORITHM OPERATION

OSPF, a Link State algorithm (LSA), improves on RIP, a Distance Vector algorithm (DVA), in several ways. Before considering the improvements, let's review some of the characteristics of Distance Vector algorithms. First, a DVA routes its packets based on the distance, measured in router hops, from the source to the destination.

With RIP the maximum hop count value is 15, which is a possible limitation for large networks. A DVA-based network is a flat network topology, without a defined hierarchy to subdivide the network into smaller, more manageable pieces. In addition, the hop count measurement does not account for other factors in the communication link, such as the speed of that link or its associated cost. Furthermore, RIP broadcasts its complete routing table to every other router every 30 seconds. Recall that the RIP packet may contain information for up to 25 routes. If a router's table contains more entries, say 100 routes, then transmitting all of these routes would require a total of four RIP packets. This requires considerable overhead at each router for packet processing, and it consumes valuable bandwidth on the WAN links in between these routers.

The improvements obtained with a Link State algorithm come in several areas. First, an LSA is based on type of service routing, not hop counts. This allows the network manager to define the least-cost path between two network points based on the actual cost, delay characteristics, reliability factors, and so on. Second, OSPF defines a hierarchical, not a flat network topology. This allows the routing information to be distributed to only a relevant subset of the routers in the internetwork instead of to all of the routers. This hierarchical structure reduces both the router processing time and the bandwidth consumed on the WAN links.

An *autonomous system* (AS), used with an LSA, is defined as a group of routers that exchange routing information via a common routing protocol. The AS is subdivided into *areas*, which are collections of contiguous routers and hosts that are grouped together, much like the telephone network is divided into area codes. The topology of an area is invisible from outside that area, and routers within a particular area do not know the details of the topology outside of that area. When the AS is partitioned into areas, it is no longer likely (as was the case with a DVA) that all routers in the AS are storing identical topological information in their databases. A router would have a separate topological database for each area it is connected to; however, two routers in the same area would have identical topological databases. A backbone is also defined, which connects the various areas and is used to route a packet between two areas.

Different types of routers are used to connect the various areas. *Internal routers* operate within a single area, connect to other routers within that area, and maintain information about that area only. An *area border router* attaches to multiple areas, runs multiple copies of the basic routing algorithm, and condenses the topological information about their attached areas for distribution to the backbone. A *backbone router* is one that has an interface to the backbone, but it does not have to be an area border router. Lastly, an *AS router* is one that exchanges information with routers that belong to other autonomous systems.

4.5.2.2 OSPF OPERATION AND PACKET FORMATS

The basic routing algorithm for OSPF provides several sequential functions, as defined in RFC 2328, Section 4: discovering a router's neighbors and electing a Designated Router for the network using the OSPF Hello protocol; forming adjacencies between pairs of routers and synchronizing the databases of these adjacent routers; performing calculations of routing tables; and flooding the area with link state advertisements.

These protocol operations are performed using one of five OSPF packets. The OSPF packets are carried within IP datagrams and are designated as IP protocol = 89. If the datagram requires fragmentation, the IP process handles that function. The five OSPF packet types have a common 24-octet header, as shown in Figure 4-15. The first 32-bit word includes fields defining a Version Number (1 octet), an OSPF Packet Type (1 octet), and a Packet Length (2 octets), which measures the length of the OSPF packet including the header. The five packet types defined are:

Type	Packet Name	Protocol Function
1	Hello	Discover/maintain neighbors
2	Database Description	Summarize database contents
3	Link State Request	Database download
4	Link State Update	Database update
5	Link State Acknowledgment	Flooding acknowledgment

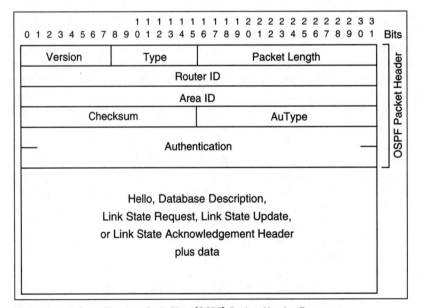

Figure 4-15: Open Shortest Path First (OSPF) Packet Header Format

The next two fields define the Router ID of the source of that packet (4 octets) and the Area ID (4 octets) that the packet came from. The balance of the OSPF packet header contains a Checksum (2 octets), an Authentication Type or AuType (2 octets), and an Authentication field (8 octets), which is used to validate the packet.

4.5.3 Exterior Gateway Protocol

Recall from our earlier discussion that there are two general categories of routing protocols: Interior Gateway Protocols and Exterior Gateway Protocols. In short, the interior protocols are concerned with routing within a network. In contrast, exterior protocols are concerned with routing between autonomous systems, which are generally described as a group of routers that all fall within a single administrative domain. In other words, exterior protocols facilitate your communication with networks outside of your router's domain. In this section, we briefly study the Exterior Gateway Protocol (EGP), defined in RFC 904 [4-12]. In the next section, we go into greater detail about the Border Gateway Protocol (BGP), defined in RFC 1771 [4-13], which is a higher function replacement for EGP.

EGP is used to convey network reachability information between neighboring gateways (or routers) that are in different autonomous systems. EGP runs over IP and is assigned IP protocol number 8. Three key mechanisms are present in the protocol. The Neighbor Acquisition mechanism allows two neighbors to begin exchanging information using the Acquisition Request and Acquisition Confirm messages. The Neighbor Reachability mechanism maintains real-time information regarding the reachability of its neighbors, using the Hello and I Hear You (I-H-U) messages. Finally, Update messages are exchanged that carry routing information.

The specific messages, as defined in RFC 904, are:

Message	Function
Request	Request acquisition of neighbor and/or initialize polling variables
Confirm	Confirm acquisition of neighbor and/or initialize polling variables
Refuse	Refuse acquisition of neighbor
Cease	Request de-acquisition of neighbor
Cease-ack	Confirm de-acquisition of neighbor
Hello	Request neighbor reachability
I-H-U	Confirm neighbor reachability
Poll	Request net-reachability update
Update	Net-reachability update
Error	Error

The general structure of the EGP messages is shown in Figure 4-16. A common message header precedes each message type. The header consists of the EGP Version Number field (1 octet); the Type field (1 octet), which identifies the message type; the Code field (1 octet), which identifies a subtype; the Status field (1 octet), which contains message-specific status information; the Checksum field (2 octets), used for error control; the Autonomous System Number (2 octets), which is an assigned number that identifies the particular autonomous system; and the Sequence Number (2 octets), which maintains state variables.

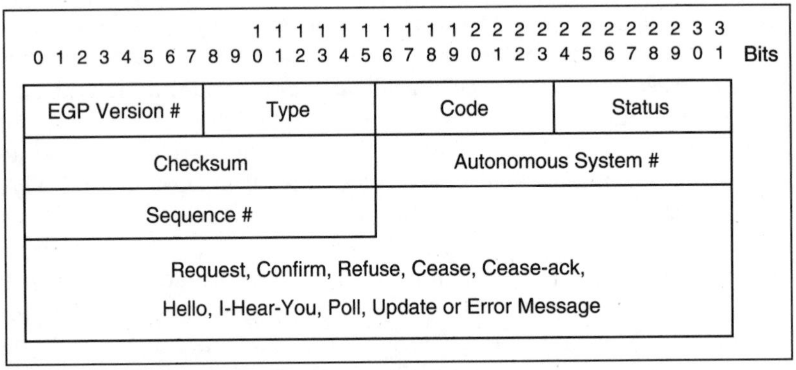

Figure 4-16: Exterior Gateway Protocol (EGP) Message Header Format

Further details on the use and specific formats of the various messages can be found in RFC 904.

4.5.4 Border Gateway Protocol

The Border Gateway Protocol, currently in its fourth version (BGP-4), is defined in RFC 1771 [4-13]. BGP is an inter-autonomous system (AS) protocol, which builds upon and enhances the capabilities of EGP. For example, where EGP runs on IP, BGP runs on TCP, thus ensuring a connection-oriented data flow and greater reliability. BGP is assigned TCP port number 179. BGP also supports Classless Domain Routing (CLDR) and the aggregation of routes.

The system running BGP is called a *BGP speaker*. Connections between BGP speakers in different autonomous systems are called *external links*, while connections between BGP speakers in the same autonomous system are called *internal links*. In a similar fashion, a BGP peer in another AS is referred to as an *external peer*, while a peer within the same AS is called an *internal peer*. After the TCP connection has been established in support of BGP, the two BGP systems exchange their entire routing tables. Updates are then sent as those routing tables change. As a result, the BGP speaker will maintain the current version of the routing tables for all of its peers. That routing information is stored within a Routing Information Base, or RIB.

The BGP message consists of a fixed message header that is 19 octets long, followed by one of four messages: OPEN, UPDATE, NOTIFICATION, or KEEPALIVE. The OPEN, UPDATE, and NOTIFICATION messages add additional information to the BGP message header, while the KEEPALIVE consists of only the annotated message header.

The BGP message header is shown in Figure 4-17 and consists of three fields plus message-specific information. The Marker field (16 octets) contains a value that the receiver can predict. For example, an OPEN message would use a Marker of all ones. Otherwise, the Marker can be incorporated into some authentication mechanism. The Length field (2 octets) indicates the total length of the message, including the header, given in octets. The valid range of the Length field is 19–4,096 octets. The Type field (1 octet) specifies the type of the message as follows:

Type	Message	Function
1	OPEN	The first message sent after transport connection is established
2	UPDATE	Transfers routing information between BGP peers
3	NOTIFICATION	Indicates detection of an error and closure of the connection
4	KEEPALIVE	Periodic confirmation of reachability

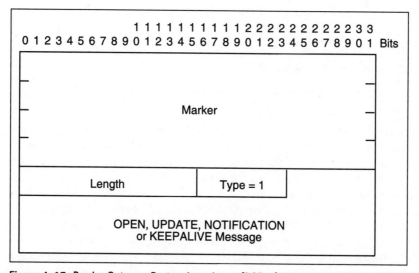

Figure 4–17: Border Gateway Protocol version 4 (BGP-4) Message Header Format

Further details on the operation of BGP-4 can be found in RFC 1771.

4.6 Host Name – Address Translation

The IPv4 and IPv6 addresses and the various classes defined for these addresses provide an extremely efficient way to identify devices on an internetwork. Unfortunately, remembering all of these addresses can be overwhelming. To solve that problem, a system of hierarchical naming known as the Domain Name System (DNS) was developed. DNS for IPv4 is described in RFCs 1034 [4-14] and 1035 [4-15]. Updates to support DNS for IPv6 are described in RFC 1886 [4-16]. In this section, we concentrate on the IPv4 case.

DNS is based on several premises. First, it arranges the names hierarchically, like the numbering plan devised for the telephone network. Just as a telephone number is divided into a country code, an area code, an exchange code, and finally a line number, the DNS root is divided into a number of top-level domains, defined in RFC 920. These are:

Domain	Purpose
MIL	U.S. Military
GOV	Other U.S. Government
EDU	Educational
COM	Commercial
NET	NICs and NOCs
ORG	Nonprofit Organizations
CON	Two-letter country code, e.g., US represents the United States, CA represents Canada, and so on

The top-level domains noted above have been in existence for many years. These, like many other operational parameters, are quickly becoming consumed as a result of the rapid growth of the Internet. To address this problem, the Internet Corporation for Assigned Names and Numbers (ICANN) developed seven new domains: .aero (for the air-transport industry), .biz (for businesses), .coop (for cooperatives), .info (unrestricted use), .museum (for museums), .name (for registration of individual names), and .pro (for professionals, such as accountants, lawyers, and physicians). At the time of this writing, various registration agencies are in the process of implementing these new top-level domains. Up-to-date information regarding these new implementations is posted on the ICANN Web site: www.icann.org.

The second DNS premise is that devices are not expected to remember the IP addresses of remote hosts. Rather, Name Servers throughout the internetwork provide this information. The requesting device thus assumes the role of a client, and the Name Server provides the necessary information, known as a *resource record*, or RR. RRs provide a mapping between domain names and network objects, such as IP addresses. Many different types of RRs are defined in RFCs 1034 and 1035. Examples of RRs include the A record, which is used to map a host address; the MX record, which provides a mail exchange for the domain and is used with the SMTP; the NS record, which defines the name server for a domain; and the PTR record, which is a pointer to another part of the domain name space.

The format for client/server interaction is a DNS message, shown in Figure 4-18. The message header is 12 octets long and describes the type of message. The next four sections provide the details of the query or response.

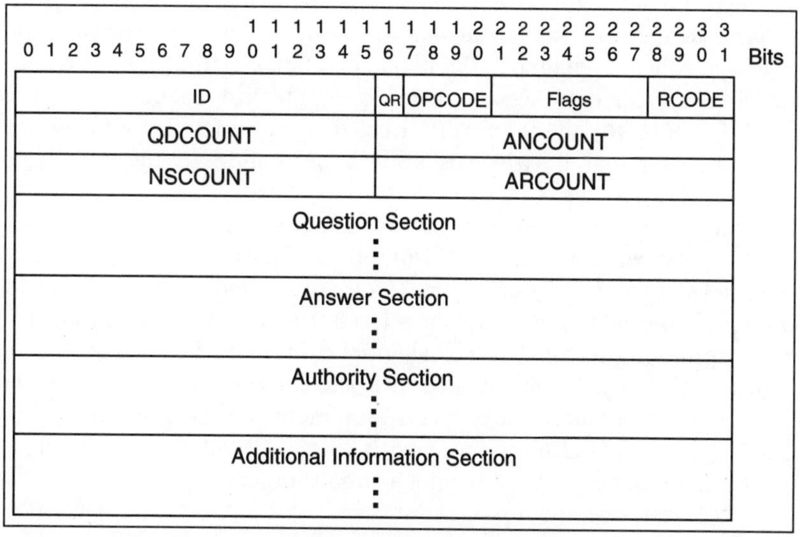

Figure 4–18: Domain Name System (DNS) Message Format

The first field within the header is an Identifier (16 bits) that correlates the queries and responses. The QR bit identifies the message type as a Query (QR = 0) or a Response (QR = 1). An OPCODE field (4 bits) further defines a Query. Four Flags are then transmitted to further describe the message, and a Response Code (RCODE) completes the first word. The balance of the header contains fields that define the lengths of the remaining four sections: Question, Answer, Authority, and Additional Information.

A good resource on DNS is the DNS Resources Directory Web site [4-17].

4.7 End-to-End Reliability: UDP and TCP

Routing the datagram from the source to the destination is only part of the story — the reliability of that transmitted information must be ensured. Since IP provides a connectionless (or unreliable) network service, protocols at a layer above IP are required to ensure reliable delivery of the information between hosts. That reliability is the job of two protocols that are considered in this section: the User Datagram Protocol (UDP) and the Transmission Control Protocol (TCP).

4.7.1 User Datagram Protocol

UDP provides a connectionless host-to-host communication path for the host's message. A connectionless path is one in which the communication channel is not established prior to the transmission of data. Instead, the network transmits the data in a package called a datagram. The datagram contains all of the addressing information necessary for that message to reach its intended destination. UDP is described in RFC 768 [4-18] and is an ARPA Host-to-Host (or OSI Transport) Layer protocol. UDP assumes that IP, which is also connectionless, is the underlying ARPA Internet (or OSI Network) Layer protocol.

The UDP service requires minimal overhead and therefore uses the relatively small UDP header shown in Figure 4-19. Note in the figure that each horizontal group of bits, called a word, is 32 bits wide. The first two fields in the UDP header are the Source and Destination Port numbers (each 2 octets long), which identify the higher layer protocol process that the datagram carries. The Source Port field is optional, and when not used contains all zeros. The Length field (2 octets) is the length of the UDP datagram, which has a minimum value of 8 octets. The Checksum field (2 octets) is also optional and is filled with all zeros if the upper layer protocol (ULP) process does not require a checksum.

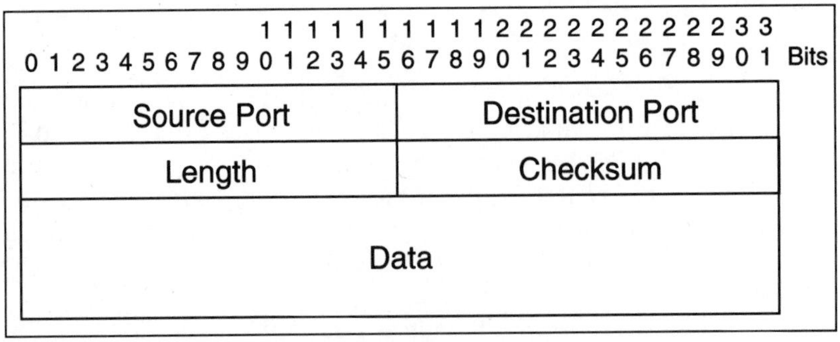

Figure 4-19: User Datagram Protocol (UDP) Header Format

Other host processes that use UDP as the Host-to-Host protocol include the Time protocol, port number 37; the Domain Name Server (DNS), port number 53; the Bootstrap Protocol (BOOTP) server and client, port numbers 67 and 68, respectively; the Trivial File Transfer Protocol (TFTP), port number 69; and the Sun Microsystems Remote Procedure Call (SunRPC), port number 111. All of these applications are designed with the assumption that if the Host-to-Host connection fails, some higher layer process would provide error notification or error recovery procedures. For example, if a network management message transmission were to fail, a Trap message (defined by the Simple Network Management Protocol, or SNMP) might be sent as a notification of that failure.

However, some applications require more reliable end-to-end data transmissions and therefore use the more rigorous Transmission Control Protocol (TCP) instead of UDP. As we see in the next section, TCP provides a number of error control procedures that UDP lacks.

4.7.2 Transmission Control Protocol

TCP, defined in RFC 793 [4-19], is a connection-oriented protocol that is responsible for reliable communication between two end processes. The unit of data transferred is called a *stream*, which is simply a sequence of octets. The stream originates at the upper layer protocol process and is subsequently divided into TCP segments, IP datagrams, and Local Network frames.

TCP handles six functions: basic data transfer, reliability, flow control, multiplexing, connections, and precedence/security. These functions are performed by the various fields within the TCP header, which has a minimum length of 20 octets (Figure 4-20). This header contains a number of fields – relating to connection management, data flow control, and reliability – that UDP did not require. The TCP header starts with two Port addresses (2 octets each) to identify the logical host processes at each end of the connection.

The Sequence Number field (four octets) is the sequence number given to the first octet of data. When the SYN flag bit is set, the sequence number indicates the Initial Sequence Number (ISN) selected. The first data octet sent would then use the next sequence number [ISN+1]. (For example, if ISN = 100, then the data would begin with SEQ = 101. If the sequence number was not advanced by one, the process would end up in an endless loop of transmissions and acknowledgments.) The sequence number ensures the sequentiality of the data stream, which is a fundamental component of reliability.

The Acknowledgment Number field (4 octets) verifies the receipt of data. This protocol process is called Positive Acknowledgment or Retransmission (PAR). The process requires that each unit of data (the octet in the case of TCP) be explicitly acknowledged. If it is not, the sender will time-out and retransmit. The value in the acknowledgment is the next octet (that is, the next sequence number) expected from the other end of the connection. When the Acknowledgment field is in use (that is, during a connection), the ACK flag bit is set.

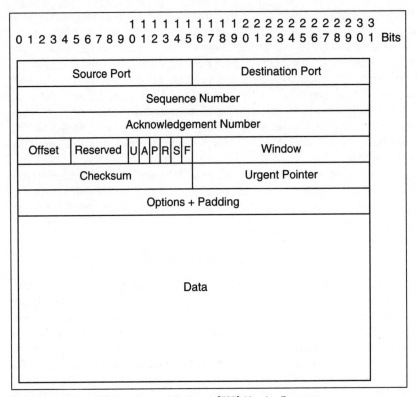

Figure 4–20: Transmission Control Protocol (TCP) Header Format

The next 32-bit word (octets 13–16 in the header) contains a number of fields used for control purposes. The Data Offset field (4 bits) measures the number of 32-bit words in the TCP header. Its value indicates where the TCP header ends and the upper layer protocol (ULP) data begins. The Offset field is necessary because the TCP header has a variable, not fixed, length; therefore, the position of the first octet of ULP data may vary. Since the minimum length of the TCP header is 20 octets, the minimum value of the Data Offset field would be five 32-bit words. The next 6 bits are reserved for future use and are set equal to zero.

Six flags that control the connection and data transfer are transmitted next. Each flag has its own 1-bit field. These flags include:

- ♦ **URG:** Urgent Pointer field significant

- ♦ **ACK:** Acknowledgment field significant

- ♦ **PSH:** Push function

◆ RST: Reset the connection

◆ SYN: Synchronize Sequence numbers

◆ FIN: No more data from sender

The Window field (2 octets) provides end-to-end flow control. The number in the Window field indicates the quantity of octets, beginning with the one in the Acknowledgment field, that the sender of the segment can accept. Note that, like the Acknowledgment field, the Window field is bidirectional. Since TCP provides a full-duplex communication path, both ends send control information to their peer process at the other end of the connection. In other words, my host provides both an acknowledgment and a window advertisement to your host, and your host does the same for mine. In this manner, both ends provide control information to their remote partner.

The Checksum field (2 octets) is used for error control.

The Urgent Pointer field (2 octets) allows the position of urgent data within the TCP segment to be identified. This field is used in conjunction with the Urgent (URG) control flag and points to the sequence number of the octet that follows the urgent data. In other words, the Urgent Pointer indicates the beginning of the routine (nonurgent) data.

Options and Padding fields (both variable in length) complete the TCP header. The Options field is an even multiple of octets in length and specifies options required by the TCP process within the host. The Padding field contains a variable number of zeros that ensure that the TCP header ends on a 32-bit boundary.

4.8 Protocols Supporting VoIP: Multicast IP, RTP, RTCP, RSVP, RTSP, SDP, SAP, SIP, and ENUM

Thus far in Chapter 4, we have looked at the underlying infrastructure and protocols that are used to route and reliably deliver IP datagrams through an internetwork. These protocols, such as IP, RIP, OSPF, UDP, TCP, and the others we studied, were developed with data applications in mind: e-mail, file transfers, remote terminal access, and so on. In this section, we briefly consider some of the additional protocols, primarily at the higher layers, that are required to support real-time and multimedia applications such as VoIP. These protocols are revisited in the case studies presented in Chapter 9. A summary of these protocols, plus their dependencies, is shown in Figure 4-21.

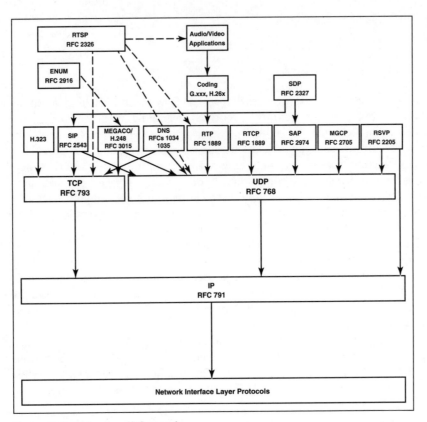

Figure 4–21: Voice over IP Protocols

4.8.1 Multicast IP

The term *multi* is derived from a Latin term that means *much* or *many*. In the case of IP datagrams, the objective is to send one packet and have it be received at many destinations. This *one* to *many* packet transport mechanism can be used in a number of applications, including audio and video conferencing, news broadcasts, stock quotation distribution, and distance learning.

When datagrams are multicast, instead of individual copies of the message being sent to each recipient, the bandwidth of the communications infrastructure is conserved. A single stream of information from one source is delivered to the destination end stations, instead of multiple streams from that one source being delivered to those end stations (Figure 4-22).

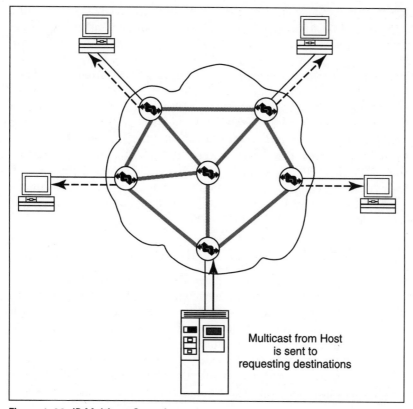

Figure 4-22: IP Multicast Operation

The concepts of multicast transmission over IP-based internetworks were first described in RFC 1112, "Host Extensions for IP Multicasting," published in 1989 [4-20]. To support multicast applications, the end stations must be able to support the Internet Group Management Protocol (IGMP, also described in RFC 1112 and further defined in RFC 2236 [4-21]), which enables multicast routers to determine which end stations on their attached subnets are members of multicast groups. These groups are identified by special multicast addresses. IPv4 Class D addresses are reserved to support multicast applications and range in value from 224.0.0.0 through 239.255.255.255.

From these values, the Internet Assigned Numbers Authority (IANA) has assigned specific values for particular multicast functions. For example, the range of addresses between 224.0.0.0 and 224.0.0.255, inclusive, is used for routing protocols and other topology and maintenance functions. Within this range, address 224.0.0.1 identifies "all systems on this subnet" and 224.0.0.2 identifies "all routers on this subnet." Other values have been specified RIP2 routers (224.0.0.9), DHCP Server/Relay Agents (224.0.0.12), audio and video transport, and others. Addresses in the range from 239.0.0.0 through 239.255.255.255 are reserved for local applications. A complete listing of the assigned multicast addresses is available in the "Assigned Numbers" document (currently RFC 1700, or available online), and also in Reference [4-22].

In order to propagate these datagrams to multiple destinations, the routers within the network infrastructure operate with modified routing protocols. Two examples of these multicast routing protocols are the Distance Vector Multicast Routing Protocol (DVMRP), described in RFC 1075 [4-23], and the Multicast Extensions to OSPF (MOSPF), described in RFC 1584 [4-24]. These multicast routing protocols construct logical spanning trees, which describe how the multicast traffic flows to the end stations. A good source of information on multicasting in general is the IP Multicast Initiative (IPMI) [4-25].

4.8.2 Real-Time Transport Protocol

Recall from our earlier discussions that IP networks provide connectionless (CON) data transport services. One of the main characteristics of CON networks is their absence of delay characteristics. In other words, you drop a packet into the network, and if all works as planned, it reaches the intended destination. However, you cannot make any statements regarding the timeframe that will be required for that packet to travel from the source to the destination. Perhaps it will travel slowly, or perhaps it will travel quickly (or perhaps it will get clobbered and not get there at all, but we optimists will dismiss that alternative for the moment and assume successful packet delivery).

So the next question becomes, how do you take data from an application, such as voice or video, which is real-time, and send it through a network that cannot (by definition and design) guarantee reliable delivery? The answer is found in the use of the Real-time Transport Protocol (RTP), which is defined in RFC 1889 [4-26]. A companion protocol, the RTP Control Protocol (RTCP), monitors the quality of service and conveys information about the participants in the communication session. RTCP is discussed in Section 4.8.3 later in this chapter.

RTP provides end-to-end delivery services for data that requires real-time support, such as interactive audio and video. According to RFC 1889, the services provided by RTP include payload type identification, sequence numbering, timestamping, and delivery monitoring. Applications typically run RTP on top of UDP to make use of UDP's multiplexing and checksum services, and as such both RTP and UDP contribute parts of the transport protocol functionality. Provisions are defined, however, to use RTP with other underlying network or transport protocols.

It is also important to note the functions that RTP does not provide. For example, RTP itself does not provide any mechanism to ensure timely delivery or provide other quality-of-service guarantees, but relies on the lower layer services for these functions. It does not guarantee packet delivery or prevent out-of-order packet delivery, nor does it assume that the underlying network is reliable and delivers packets in sequence. The sequence numbers included in RTP allow the receiver to reconstruct the sender's packet sequence, but sequence numbers might also be used to determine the proper location of a packet, for example in video decoding, without necessarily decoding packets in sequence.

There are two parts of RTP defined in RFC 1889: the Real-time Transport Protocol (RTP), which carries data that has real-time properties, and the RTP Control Protocol (RTCP), which monitors the quality of service and conveys information about the participants in an ongoing session. In addition to the protocol specification given in RFC 1889, a companion document, RFC 1890 [4-27], provides a profile specification that defines a set of payload type codes and their mapping to payload formats, such as various media encodings. For example, RFC 1890 defines a profile specification with minimal session control. In other words, this profile is designed for sessions where no negotiation or membership control is used. Examples of the use of RTP and its profiles are given in both RFC 1889 and RFC 1890.

Before discussing the RTP packet format, a few definitions, taken from RFC 1889, are in order:

◆ **RTP payload:** The data transported by RTP in a packet, for example audio samples or compressed video data.

◆ **RTP packet:** A data packet consisting of the fixed RTP header, a possibly empty list of contributing sources (as defined below), and the payload data.

◆ **RTCP packet:** A control packet consisting of a fixed header part similar to that of RTP data packets, followed by structured elements that vary depending on the RTCP packet type. The formats are defined in RFC 1889, Section 6.

◆ **Port:** The addressing mechanism that uniquely identifies different applications within a host. For example, the File Transfer Protocol (FTP) and the Simple Network Management Protocol (SNMP) have different port numbers. RTP depends on the lower layer protocol to provide some mechanism such as ports to multiplex the RTP and RTCP packets of a session.

◆ **Transport address:** The combination of a network address and port that identifies a transport-level endpoint, for example an IP address and a UDP port. Packets are transmitted from a source transport address to a destination transport address.

◆ **RTP session:** The association among a set of participants communicating with RTP. For each participant, the session is defined by a particular pair of destination transport addresses (one network address plus a port pair for RTP and RTCP). The destination transport address pair may be common for all participants, as in the case of IP multicast, or it may be different for each, as in the case of individual unicast network addresses plus a common port pair. In a multimedia session, each medium is carried in a separate

RTP session with its own RTCP packets. The multiple RTP sessions are distinguished by different port number pairs and/or different multicast addresses.

◆ **Synchronization source (SSRC):** The source of a stream of RTP packets, identified by a 32-bit numeric SSRC identifier carried in the RTP header so as not to be dependent upon the network address. All packets from a synchronization source form part of the same timing and sequence number space, so a receiver groups packets by synchronization source for playback. Examples of synchronization sources include the sender of a stream of packets derived from a signal source such as a microphone or a camera, or an RTP mixer (as defined below). A synchronization source may change its data format, for example, its audio encoding mechanism, over time.

◆ **Contributing source (CSRC):** A source of a stream of RTP packets that has contributed to the combined stream produced by an RTP mixer (as defined below). The mixer inserts a list of the SSRC identifiers of the sources that contributed to the generation of a particular packet into the RTP header of that packet. This list is called the CSRC list. An example application is audio conferencing, where a mixer indicates all the talkers whose speech was combined to produce the outgoing packet, allowing the receiver to indicate the current talker even though all the audio packets contain the same SSRC identifier (that of the mixer).

◆ **End system:** An application that generates the content to be sent in RTP packets and/or consumes the content of received RTP packets. An end system can act as one or more synchronization sources in a particular RTP session, but typically acts only as one.

◆ **Mixer:** An intermediate system that receives RTP packets from one or more sources, possibly changes the data format, combines the packets in some manner, and then forwards a new RTP packet. Since the timing among multiple input sources will not generally be synchronized, the mixer will make timing adjustments among the streams and generate its own timing for the combined stream. Thus, all data packets originating from a mixer will be identified as having the mixer as their synchronization source.

◆ **Translator:** An intermediate system that forwards RTP packets with their synchronization source identifier intact. Examples of translators include devices that convert encodings without mixing, replicators from multicast to unicast, and application-level filters in firewalls.

◆ **Monitor:** An application that receives RTCP packets sent by participants in an RTP session, in particular the reception reports, and estimates the current quality of service for distribution monitoring, fault diagnosis, and long-term statistics.

◆ **Non-RTP:** Protocols and mechanisms that may be needed in addition to RTP to provide a usable service. In particular, for multimedia conferences, a conference control application may distribute multicast addresses and keys for encryption, negotiate the encryption algorithm to be used, and define dynamic mappings between RTP payload type values and the payload formats they represent for formats that do not have a predefined payload type value.

Given the above functional definitions, consider the RTP message header format that is shown in Figure 4-23. The first 12 octets are present in every RTP packet, while the list of CSRC identifiers is present only when inserted by a mixer.

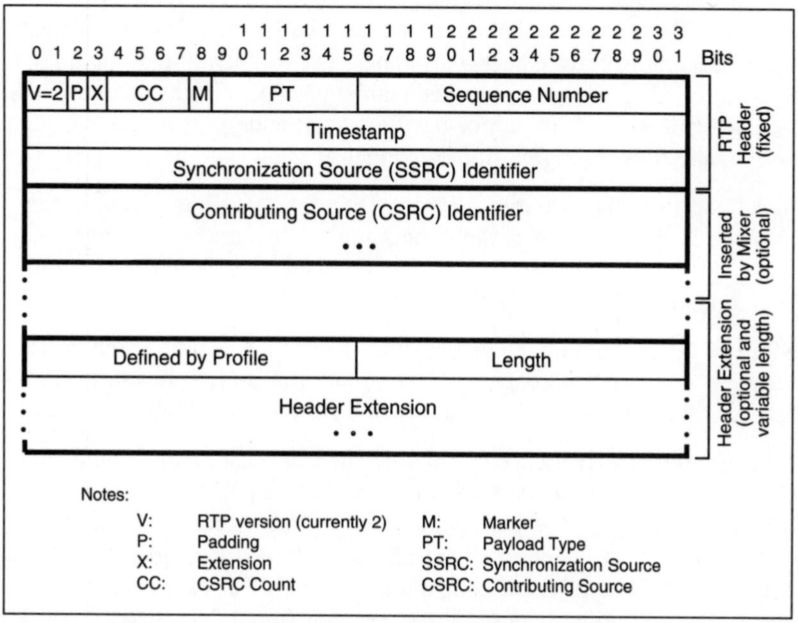

Figure 4–23: Real-Time Transport Protocol (RTP) Message Header

The fields of the RTP header are:

◆ **Version (V, 2 bits):** Identifies the version of RTP, currently 2.

◆ **Padding (P, 1 bit):** If the padding bit is set, the packet contains one or more additional padding octets at the end that are not part of the payload. The last octet of the padding contains a count of how many padding octets should be ignored. Padding may be needed by some encryption algorithms with fixed block sizes or for carrying several RTP packets in a lower layer protocol data unit.

◆ **Extension (X, 1 bit):** If the extension bit is set, the fixed header is followed by exactly one header extension, with a format defined in RFC 1889, Section 5.3.1.

◆ **CSRC count (CC, 4 bits):** The CSRC count contains the number of CSRC identifiers that follow the fixed header.

◆ **Marker (M, 1 bit):** The interpretation of the marker is defined by a profile. It is intended to allow significant events such as frame boundaries to be marked in the packet stream.

◆ **Payload type (PT, 7 bits):** Identifies the format of the RTP payload and determines its interpretation by the application.

◆ **Sequence number (16 bits):** The sequence number increments by one for each RTP data packet sent, and may be used by the receiver to detect packet loss and to restore packet sequence. The initial value of the sequence number is random (unpredictable) to make attacks on encryption more difficult, even if the source itself does not encrypt (because the packets may flow through a translator that does).

◆ **Timestamp (32 bits):** The timestamp reflects the sampling instant of the first octet in the RTP data packet. The sampling instant must be derived from a clock that increments monotonically and linearly in time to allow synchronization and jitter calculations.

◆ **SSRC (32 bits):** The SSRC field identifies the synchronization source. This identifier is chosen randomly, with the intent that no two synchronization sources within the same RTP session will have the same SSRC identifier.

◆ **CSRC list (0 to 15 items, 32 bits each):** The CSRC list identifies the contributing sources for the payload contained in this packet. The number of identifiers is given by the CC field. If there are more than 15 contributing sources, only 15 can be identified. CSRC identifiers are inserted by mixers, using the SSRC identifiers of contributing sources. For example, for audio packets the SSRC identifiers of all sources that were mixed together to create a packet are listed, allowing correct talker indication at the receiver.

◆ **RTP Header Extension (variable length):** An optional extension mechanism is provided with RTP to allow individual implementations to experiment with new functions that require additional information in the RTP header.

Specific details regarding the use of these header fields is given in RFC 1889.

4.8.3 Real-Time Control Protocol

The RTP control protocol (RTCP) is defined in RFC 1889 and is based on the periodic transmission of control packets to all participants in the session, using the same distribution mechanism as the data packets. The underlying protocol must provide multiplexing of the data and control packets, such as using separate port numbers with UDP. The following RTCP functions are identified in RFC 1889:

1. Providing feedback on the quality of the data distribution. This is an integral part of RTP's role as a transport protocol and is related to the flow and congestion control functions of other transport protocols. The feedback may be directly useful for control of adaptive encodings, but experiments with IP multicasting have shown that it is also critical to get feedback from the receivers to diagnose faults in the distribution. Sending reception feedback reports to all participants allows one who is observing problems to evaluate whether those problems are local or global. With a distribution mechanism like IP multicast, it is also possible for an entity such as a network service provider that is not otherwise involved in the session to receive the feedback information and act as a third-party monitor to diagnose network problems. This feedback function is performed by the RTCP sender and receiver reports, described in RFC 1889, Section 6.3.

2. Carrying a persistent transport-level identifier for an RTP source called the canonical name or CNAME. Since the SSRC identifier may change if a conflict is discovered or a program is restarted, receivers require the CNAME to keep track of each participant. Receivers also require the CNAME to associate multiple data streams from a given participant in a set of related RTP sessions, for example to synchronize audio and video.

3. The first two functions require that all participants send RTCP packets; therefore, the rate must be controlled in order for RTP to scale up to a large number of participants. By having each participant send its control packets to all the others, each can independently observe the number of participants.

4. An optional function of conveying minimal session control information, for example, participant identification to be displayed in the user interface. This is most likely to be useful in "loosely controlled" sessions where participants enter and leave without membership control or parameter negotiation. RTCP serves as a convenient channel to reach all the participants, but it is not necessarily expected to support all the control communication requirements of an application.

RFC 1889 defines five different RTCP packet formats:

◆ **SR or Sender Report:** For transmission and reception statistics from participants that are active senders

◆ **RR or Receiver Report:** For reception statistics from participants that are not active senders

◆ **SDES or Source Description Items:** Includes CNAME

◆ BYE: Indicates the end of participation

◆ APP: Application-specific functions

Each RTCP packet begins with a fixed part similar to that of RTP data packets, followed by structured elements that may be of variable length according to the packet type, but always end on a 32-bit boundary. The alignment requirement and a length field in the fixed part are included to make RTCP packets "stackable." Multiple RTCP packets may be linked together without any intervening separators to form a compound RTCP packet that is sent in a single packet of the lower layer protocol, for example UDP. There is no explicit count of individual RTCP packets in the compound packet since the lower layer protocols are expected to provide an overall length to determine the end of the compound packet.

The formats of these RTCP packets vary by function and are rather complex. Interested readers are referred to RFC 1889, Section 6, for these details.

Details on the operation of RTP can be found in RFC 1889 [4-26] and RFC 1890 [4-27]. Reference [4-28] is an excellent resource for RTP information.

4.8.4 Resource Reservation Protocol

As more time-sensitive applications have been developed for the Internet, defining a Quality of Service (QoS) and the mechanisms to provide that QoS have become requirements. The Resource Reservation Protocol (RSVP), defined in RFC 2205 [4-29] and updated in RFC 2750 [4-30], is designed to address those requirements. When a host has an application such as real-time video or multimedia, it may use RSVP to request an appropriate level of service from the network in support of that application. But for RSVP to be effective, every router in that path must support that protocol – something that some router vendors and ISPs are not yet equipped to do. In addition, RSVP is a control protocol, and therefore works in collaboration with – not instead of – traditional routing protocols. In other words, the routing protocol, such as RIP or OSPF, determines which datagrams are forwarded, while RSVP is concerned with the QoS of those datagrams.

RSVP requests that network resources be reserved to support data flowing on a simplex path, and that reservation is initiated and maintained by the receiver of the information. Using this model, RSVP can support both unicast and multicast applications. Review Figure 4-6; RSVP messages may be sent directly inside IP datagrams (using IP Protocol = 46) or encapsulated inside UDP datagrams, using Ports 1698 and 1699.

RSVP defines two basic message types: Reservation Request (or Resv) messages and Path messages (Figure 4-24). A receiver transmits Resv messages upstream toward the senders. These Resv messages create and maintain reservation state information in each node along the path or paths. A sender transmits Path messages downstream toward the receivers, following the paths prescribed by the routing protocols that follow the paths of the data. These Path messages store path state information in each node along the way.

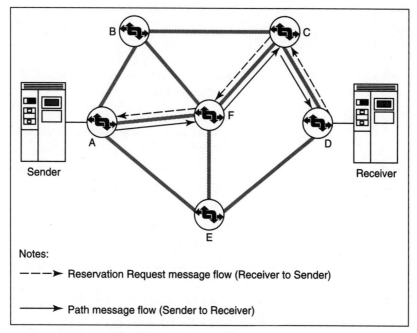

Notes:

– – –► Reservation Request message flow (Receiver to Sender)

——► Path message flow (Sender to Receiver)

Figure 4–24: Resource Reservation Protocol (RSVP) Operation

The RSVP message consists of three sections: a Common Header (8 octets), an Object Header (4 octets), and Object Contents (variable length), as shown in Figure 4-25. The Version field (four bits) contains the protocol version (currently 1). The Flags field (four bits) is reserved for future definition. The Message Type field (1 octet) specifies one of seven currently defined RSVP messages:

Message Type	Message Name	Function
1	Path	Path message, from sender to receiver, along the same path used for the data packets.
2	Resv	Reservation message with reservation requests, carried hop-by-hop from receiver to senders.
3	PathErr	Path error message; reports errors in processing Path messages, and travels upstream toward senders.

Continued

Message Type	Message Name	Function
4	ResvErr	Reservation error message; reports errors in processing Resv messages, and is sent downstream toward receivers.
5	PathTear	Path teardown message, initiated by senders or by a timeout, and sent downstream to all receivers.
6	ResvTear	Reservation teardown message, initiated by receivers or by a timeout, and sent upstream to all matching senders.
7	ResvConf	Reservation confirmation message, acknowledges reservation requests.

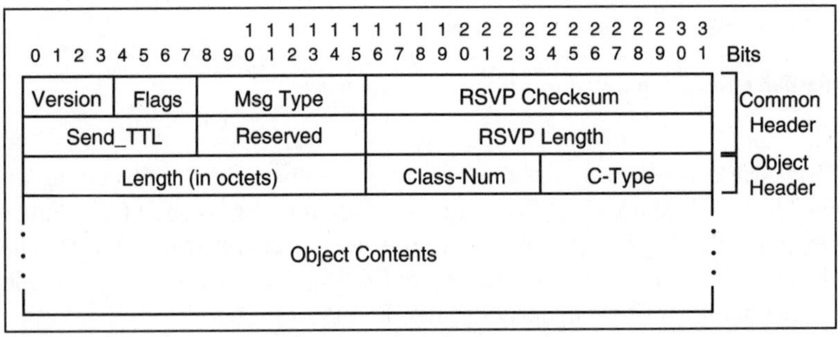

Figure 4–25: Resource Reservation Protocol (RSVP) Message Header

The RSVP Checksum field (2 octets) provides error control. The Send_TTL field (1 octet) is the IP Time to Live field value with which the message was sent. The RSVP Length field (2 octets) is the total length of the RSVP message, given in octets.

Every object consists of one or more 32-bit words with a 1-octet Object Header. This second header includes a Length field (2 octets), which is the total length of the object (with a minimum of 4 octets, and also a multiple of 4 octets); a Class Number (1 octet), which defines the object class; and a C-Type field (1 octet), which is an object type that is unique with the Class Number. The Object Contents complete the message.

Details on the operation of RSVP can be found in RFC 2205 [4-29] and RFC 2750 [4-30]. Reference [4-31] is a good resource for RSVP information.

4.8.5 Real-Time Streaming Protocol

The Real-Time Streaming Protocol, defined in RFC 2326 [4-32], is an Application Layer protocol that controls the delivery of data that has real-time properties, such as audio and video. RTSP does not typically deliver the continuous streams itself, although interleaving of the continuous media stream with the control stream (such as RTCP) is possible. In effect, RTSP acts as a "network remote control" for multimedia servers.

There is no notion of an RTSP connection; instead, a server maintains a session labeled by an identifier. An RTSP session is in no way tied to a transport-level connection such as a TCP connection. During an RTSP session, an RTSP client may open and close many reliable transport connections to the server to issue RTSP requests. Alternatively, it may use a connectionless transport protocol such as UDP.

The streams of information controlled by RTSP may use RTP; however, RTSP's operation is independent of the underlying transport mechanism. RTSP is intentionally similar in syntax and operation to the Hypertext Transfer Protocol (HTTP), version 1.1, defined in RFC 2616 [4-33] and updated by RFC 2817 [4-34], so that extension mechanisms to HTTP can in most cases also be added to RTSP. However, RTSP differs in a number of important aspects from HTTP, including its client/server operation, protocol identifier, and typical out-of-band data transport.

RFC 2326 defines the following operations that RTSP supports:

- ◆ **Retrieval of media from media server:** The client can request a presentation description via HTTP or some other method. If the presentation is being multicast, the presentation description contains the multicast addresses and ports to be used for the continuous media. If the presentation is to be sent only to the client via unicast, the client provides the destination for security reasons.

- ◆ **Invitation of a media server to a conference:** A media server can be "invited" to join an existing conference, either to play back media into the presentation or to record all or a subset of the media in a presentation. This mode is useful for distributed teaching applications. Several parties in the conference may take turns "pushing the remote control buttons."

- ◆ **Addition of media to an existing presentation:** Particularly useful for live presentations, the server can tell the client about additional media becoming available.

Details of RTSP operation can be found in RFC 2326.

4.8.6 Session Description and Session Announcement Protocols

The Session Description Protocol (SDP), defined in RFC 2327 [4-35], is used to describe a multimedia session for the purposes of session announcement, session invitation, and other forms of session-related initiation. SDP conveys information about media streams in multimedia sessions to allow the recipients of a session description to participate in that session. SDP provides a means to communicate the existence of the session, and it also conveys sufficient information to enable another station to join and participate in that session.

A conference session is announced by periodically multicasting an announcement packet to a well-known address and port using the Session Announcement Protocol (SAP), defined in RFC 2974 [4-36], which is transmitted using UDP. The payload of the SAP packet may contain an SDP packet that describes the session of interest. That description includes:

◆ Session name and purpose

◆ Time(s) the session is active

◆ The media comprising the session

◆ Information to receive those media, such as addresses, ports, formats, and so on

◆ Information about the bandwidth to be used by the conference

◆ Contact information for the person responsible for the session

As noted in RFC 2327, the purpose of SDP is to define a format for describing session information while allowing for different transports to convey that information. As such, SDP information may be transported using SAP (as described above and shown in Figure 4-21), or using the Session Initiation Protocol (SIP), the Real-time Streaming Protocol (RTSP), electronic mail with Multimedia Internet Mail Extensions (MIME) format, or the Hypertext Transfer Protocol (HTTP).

4.8.7 Session Initiation Protocol

Thus far, we have considered Multicast IP, RTP, RTCP, RSVP, RTSP, SDP, and SAP as adjuncts to our familiar TCP/IP and/or UDP/IP protocol infrastructures. These protocols enhance the functions of IP to allow real-time information to be effectively communicated. (Recall that IP was developed in the 1970s to support data communication, which is non-real-time information, in contrast to the current requirements to support voice and video, which are real-time.) But before that information can be transmitted, a communication session between the two endpoints must be established. This is the purpose of the Session Initiation Protocol (SIP), defined in

RFC 2543 [4-37]. SIP is a control or signaling protocol used for creating, modifying, and terminating sessions between participants. These sessions may include multimedia conferences, telephone calls, distance learning, or other types of multimedia distribution. The parties to that session may or may not be human end users — robots, such as media storage devices, could also be participants in that session.

Thus, SIP is a part of the Internet multimedia protocol architecture, which includes the other protocols like RTP, SAP, and SDP that have already been discussed. Review Figure 4-21 and note that SIP can carry SDP data, and that the SIP information can use either TCP or UDP for transport. SIP's call control functionality is somewhat similar to control protocols defined by the ITU-T, including H.323 and others, such as H.225.0 and H.245. Because of these functional parallels, we will postpone a more detailed discussion of SIP functions until Chapter 6. At that time we will consider call control in the larger context of VoIP architectures and look at gateways and gatekeepers, plus the protocols such as the Media Gateway Control Protocol (MGCP) used for those communication functions.

4.8.8 Electronic Numbers

Thus far, we have considered a large number of protocols that are required for the proper operation of a voice, fax, or video over IP network. But one more challenge remains. Telephone, fax, or videoconferencing systems are identified by telephone numbers, such as +1.303.555.1212. In contrast, IP-connected devices are identified by an IP address, such as [10.222.18.66]. So which number do you enter to make a Voice over IP call?

That challenge is addressed by a process known as ENUM, which is an abbreviation for *electronic number*. The ENUM work is based on DNS and is documented in RFC 2916 [4-38]. ENUM bridges the gap between telephone numbers, defined by ITU-T E.164, and IP addresses. These services support all forms of IP-based communication, including voice, fax, voice mail retrieval, messaging, and others. When an IP-based call is made from an end user, the connected system will query the ENUM system to determine if an IP address has been registered for the destination party. If such an IP address exists, the call is completed using IP on an end-to-end basis. If the IP address is not registered, the call is then redirected to the PSTN for completion. Thus, the telephone number supports both PSTN and IP-based network communication. The ENUM process uses the DNS for much of its communication activities, thus retaining compatibility with IP network systems in current use. Reference [4-39] details further resources for readers who wish to dig deeper.

4.9 Looking Ahead

In this chapter, we have looked at the ARPA protocol suite in general and the protocols that support VoIP services in particular. A summary of what we have learned is shown in Figure 4-26, a composite Voice over IP packet that includes the IPv4 header, the UDP header, the RTP header, and a 20 millisecond sample of packetized voice information. We will return to this composite figure in the following chapters to better understand how this information is originated at the sender, transmitted through an IP network, and eventually sent to the ultimate destination.

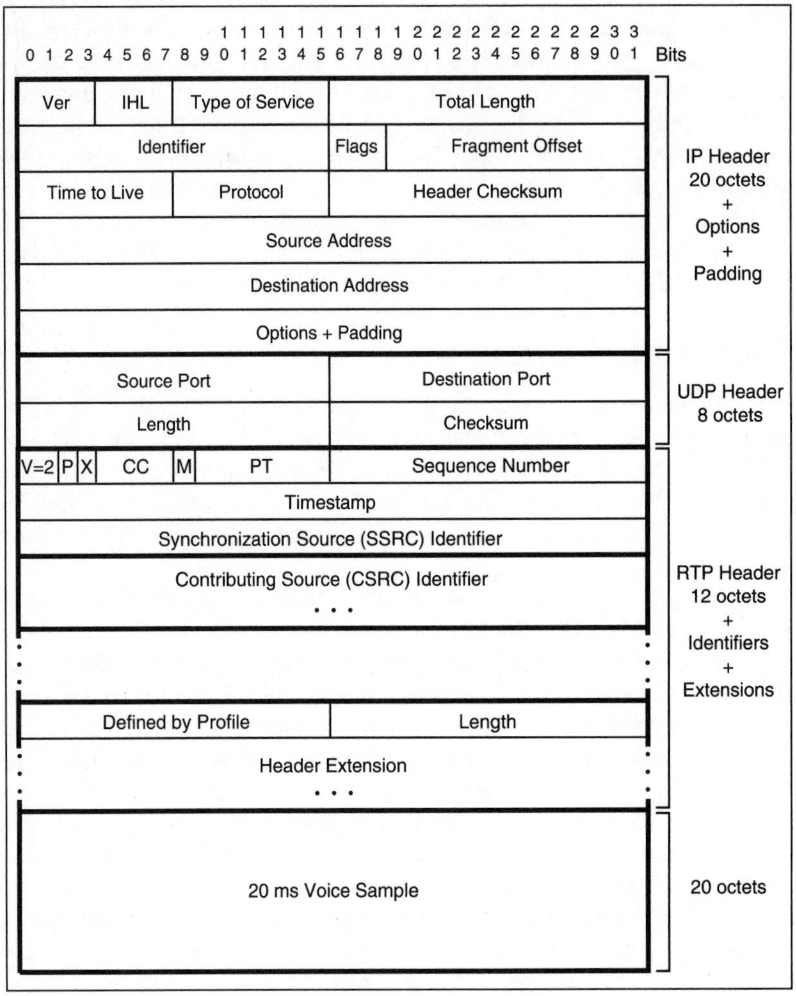

Figure 4–26: Voice over IP Packet Format

In the Chapter 5, we will bring the wide area transport into the equation and consider a number of WAN systems that support the transmission of the Internet Protocol.

4.10 References

[4-1]   Leiner, B. M., et al. "The ARPA Internet Protocol Suite." RS-85-153, included in the *DDN Protocol Handbook*, Volume 2: 2-27–2-49.

[4-2]   Padlipsky, M. A. "A Perspective on the ARPANET Reference Model." RFC 871, The Mitre Corp., September 1982.

[4-3]   Postel, J. "Internet Protocol." RFC 791, September 1981.

[4-4]   Reynolds, J., and J. Postel. "Assigned Numbers." RFC 1700, October 1994. Protocol information assigned by the Internet Assigned Numbers Authority (IANA) is also available online at www.iana.org/numbers.htm.

[4-5]   Postel, J. "Internet Control Message Protocol." RFC 792, September 1981.

[4-6]   Deering, S., and R. Hinden. "Internet Protocol, Version 6 (IPv6) Specification." RFC 2460, December 1998.

[4-7]   Further information on IPv6 standards and implementations is available at www.ipv6forum.com.

[4-8]   Hinden, R., and S. Deering. "IP Version 6 Addressing Architecture." RFC 2373, July 1998.

[4-9]   Hedrick, C. "Routing Information Protocol." RFC 1058, June 1988.

[4-10] Malkin, G. "RIP Version 2." RFC 2453, November 1998.

[4-11] Moy, John. "OSPF Version 2." RFC 2328, April 1998.

[4-12] Mills, D. L. "Exterior Gateway Protocol Frame Specification." RFC 904, April 1984.

[4-13] Rekhter, Y., and T. Li. "A Border Gateway Protocol 4 (BGP-4)." RFC 1771, March 1995.

[4-14] Mockapetris, P. "Domain Names: Concepts and Facilities." RFC 1034, November 1987.

[4-15] Mockapetris, P. "Domain Names: Implementation and Specification." RFC 1035, November 1987.

[4-16] Thomas, S., and C. Huitema. "DNS Extensions to Support IP version 6." RFC 1886, December 1995.

[4-17] A good resource for directory information is www.dns.net/dnsrd.

[4-18] Postel, J. "User Datagram Protocol." RFC 768, August 1980.

[4-19] Postel, J. "Transmission Control Protocol." RFC 793, August 1980.

[4-20] Deering, S. "Host Extensions for IP Multicasting." RFC 1112, August 1989.

[4-21] Fenner, W. "Internet Group Management Protocol, version 2." RFC 2236, November 1997.

[4-22] A complete listing of IP multicast addresses can be found at: `http://www.iana.org/assignments/multicast-addresses`.

[4-23] Waitzman, D., et al. "Distance Vector Multicast Routing Protocol." RFC 1075, November 1988.

[4-24] Moy, J. "Multicast Extensions to OSPF." RFC 1584, March 1994.

[4-25] A good resource for IP Multicast information is the IP Multicast Initiative's Web site: `www.ipmulticast.com`.

[4-26] Schulzrinne, H., et al. "A Transport Protocol for Real-Time Applications." RFC 1889, January 1996.

[4-27] Schulzrinne, H. "RTP Profile for Audio and Video Conferences with Minimal Control." RFC 1890, January 1996.

[4-28] A good resource for RTP information is `www.cs.columbia.edu/~hgs/rtp/.html`.

[4-29] Braden, R., editor. "Resource Reservation Protocol (RSVP) Version 1 Functional Specification." RFC 2205, September 1997.

[4-30] Herzog, S. "RSVP Extensions for Policy Control." RFC 2750, January 2000.

[4-31] A good resource for RSVP information is the RSVP Project at `www.isi.edu/div7/rsvp/rsvp-home.html`.

[4-32] Schulzrinne, H., et al. "Real Time Streaming Protocol (RTSP)." RFC 2326, April 1998.

[4-33] Fielding, R., et al. "Hypertext Transfer Protocol – HTTP/1.1." RFC 2616, January 1999.

[4-34] Khare, R., and S. Lawrence. "Upgrading to Transport Layer Security (TLS) within HTTP/1.1." RFC 2817, May 2000.

[4-35] Handley, M., and V. Jacobson. "SDP: Session Description Protocol." RFC 2327, April 1998.

[4-36] Handley, M., et al. "Session Announcement Protocol." RFC 2974, October 2000.

[4-37] Handley, M., et al. "SIP: Session Initiation Protocol." RFC 2543, March 1999.

[4-38] Falstrom, P. "E.164 number and DNS." RFC 2916, September 2000.

[4-39] Good sources of information regarding ENUM are available from the ENUM World Reference page, at `www.ngi.org/enum`; the teleDNS Project information page, `www.enumworld.com`; and the NetNumber.com, Inc., information page at `www.netnumber.com`.

Chapter 5

WAN Transport for Converged Networks

Previous chapters have discussed the principles of converged networks from several perspectives: the end user's objectives, the applications, the business and financial considerations, and the protocols that comprise an IP-centric network architecture.

This chapter extends our discussion to the operation and protocols of the wide area network (WAN) transport, which connects end-user systems and provides a transmission mechanism between the end users and the applications that those end users are running. In the previous chapters, this issue was cleverly avoided by using what are called *cloud diagrams* (Figure 5-1). The WAN transport is shown as a big cloud, with the end users on the outside and the carriers on the inside. The end users are depicted as being on the outside looking in – they are users of the WAN's service but do not know the intimate details of how that service operates. This cloud diagram also implies that the carriers are on the inside looking out – they are the providers of the WAN service but do not necessarily know the details of the systems their customers are using to connect to the network. Thus, the cloud diagram obscures both the details of the users' network and the internal operation of the WAN.

This chapter aims to lift the fog surrounding the internal workings of the WAN cloud. We briefly consider a number of WAN transport alternatives, including digital leased lines such as T1 or T3 lines, Integrated Services Digital Network (ISDN) connections, frame relay, asynchronous transfer mode (ATM), and Digital Subscriber Line (DSL) options.

The information in this chapter is primarily aimed at readers who have come from the local area networking side of the data communications industry and who may not be familiar with all of the WAN transport alternatives that are available. However, readers who are experienced with the many wide area alternatives may also find this information useful. Specifically, an existing WAN transport – be that ISDN, frame relay, ATM, or some other technology – was probably installed to support a single application, such as voice *or* data, and may now be under consideration to support both voice *and* data. A reasonable question is whether that existing infrastructure is capable of doing both, or whether a higher-capacity alternative should be deployed. To better answer this question, consideration of all of the available alternatives, as overviewed in this chapter, would be appropriate.

Chapter 7 considers the other side of the cloud and examines end-user equipment for VoIP networks.

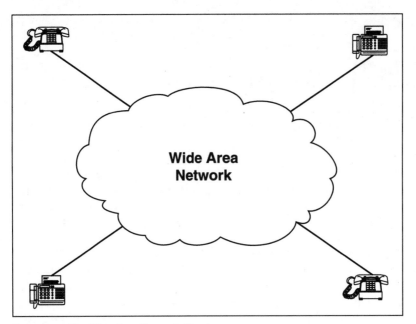

Figure 5-1: The Wide Area Network Cloud

5.1 WAN Transport Alternatives

Perhaps the greatest challenge in navigating through the WAN cloud is sorting through all of the transmission alternatives presented by carriers. As you might expect, some of these alternatives are used for very specialized applications and are not good fits for converged network applications.

Consider Figure 5-2, which shows the various WAN alternatives organized into a hierarchy. The first distinction defines the transmission format, either analog or digital. Generally, analog lines have a lower bandwidth and are more susceptible to noise and other error-causing disturbances than digital lines. Analog lines come in two types: switched (or dialup) and dedicated (or leased). Switched telephone lines are used to access the Public Switched Telephone Network (PSTN) and provide service for pay telephones, fax machines, low-speed modems, and the like. Since the local telephone loops vary in their quality (some are decades old), PSTN transmission characteristics can be somewhat random. In other words, sometimes you get a good connection, and sometimes you don't. When you don't, your best alternative is to hang up and redial, and hope for better luck next time.

Dedicated analog lines are archaic by today's standards, but met specific requirements in the early days of data communications (circa 1970). Since the dedicated line provided a fixed path between two points, that line could be conditioned through the use of filters, amplifiers, and other electronic devices to optimize its transmission characteristics. Nevertheless, most analog leased line configurations were designed to support modems in the 2.4 to 9.6 Kbps range, which by today's standards is inadequate. For VoIP applications you would only want to use analog circuits for connections from a single end user into the network via the PSTN, but not for the transport of any multiuser or higher-speed data.

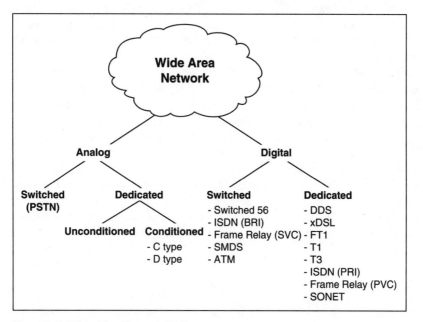

Figure 5–2: Wide Area Network Options

In contrast to their problematic analog cousins, digital lines are designed for high-speed data applications and serve as the primary transport mechanisms for voice, fax, data, and video over IP applications. Like analog lines, digital lines can be divided into switched or dedicated connections. The fundamental building block for these digital circuits is a DS0 channel, which provides a bandwidth of either 56 or 64 Kbps. Multiple DS0 channels can be multiplexed together to satisfy the requirements for greater amounts of bandwidth. We discuss these multiplexing processes later in this chapter.

A number of switched digital lines have been developed, although not all of these may be available from each Local Exchange Carrier (LEC) or Inter-exchange Carrier (IXC). Switched 56 service provides a 56 Kbps link between two locations and provides one DS0 of bandwidth. The next step up is Integrated Services Digital Network (ISDN) service, with a Basic Rate Interface (BRI). The ISDN-BRI provides two DS0 channels that operate at 64 Kbps, plus an additional D channel that supplies a lower rate (typically 16 Kbps, although 9.6 Kbps is provisioned in some areas). Frame relay service may operate in two modes: Switched Virtual Connections (SVCs), where calls are established and terminated using call setup procedures, and Permanent Virtual Connections (PVCs), where connections are established on an end-to-end basis and appear to the end user like a leased line.

Frame relay service is provided at a number of transmission rates, ranging from 64 Kbps to 45 Mbps. Switched Multimegabit Data Service (SMDS) is a high-speed data transmission that was developed by Bell Communications Research, Inc. (Bellcore, now Telcordia Technologies, Inc.). SMDS operates at 1.5 Mbps or 45 Mbps but is available only in limited areas. Asynchronous Transfer Mode (ATM) is a cell-based switched network architecture that was designed to carry a wide range of traffic types: packet-switched data, circuit-switched data, voice, video, and so on. ATM can operate at a wide variety of data rates, beginning at 1.5 Mbps.

A number of dedicated digital lines have also been developed. The lowest speeds are typically called DDS (Digital Data Service) lines. DDS lines operate at 2.4, 4.8, 9.6, 19.2, 56, and 64 Kbps, and are typically used for terminal-to-host applications such as point-of-sale terminals. The Digital Subscriber Line (xDSL) services are available in some areas and have access rates in the hundreds of kilobits per second rate, with even higher rates planned in some areas. Various carriers support different versions (and therefore various transmission rates) of DSL services, hence the "x" in the xDSL acronym. T1 lines operate at a rate of 1.544 Mbps, which is known as the Digital Signal Level 1, or DS1 rate. The T1 line has a capacity of 24 DS0 channels. In many areas, customers are given the option of subscribing to only a portion of a T1, known as a Fractional T1 or FT1 service. Thus, if you only need the equivalent of six DS0 channels (384 Kbps data rate), you do not have to pay for a complete T1 connection. T3 lines operate at a rate of 44.736 Mbps, which is known as the Digital Signal Level 3, or DS3, rate. A T3 line is equivalent to 28 T1 lines, or 672 DS0 channels. Primary Rate Interface ISDN service (ISDN-PRI) operates at the same transmission rate (1.544 Mbps) as a T1 line but divides its information-carrying channels into 23 B-channels for information transfer and one D-channel for call setup and control purposes. The individual ISDN-PRI B- and D-channels are equivalent to a DS0 channel. Synchronous Optical Network (SONET) services are available in larger metropolitan areas and provide fiber-optical-based transmission at the DS1 and DS3, and in some cases higher, rates.

The next few sections look at the specific WAN infrastructures that are most likely to be used to carry IP traffic on converged networks and are consequently the types of interfaces likely to be found on converged network components such as VoIP gateways. The WAN technologies that we discuss in the next sections are T1 and T3 lines, ISDN, frame relay, ATM, and DSL.

5.2 T1/T3 Digital Lines

The T-carrier system was developed to multiplex voice signals onto a digital transmission line. It was designed in response to the "one pair – one conversation" problem, which limited telephone conversations to the number of physical copper pairs between two points. As the usage of the telephone network grew, and as services such as dial-up modem applications became more widespread, the telephone network started running out of available copper pairs to provide those circuits. And since those copper pairs were in cables (which, in turn, were likely buried in conduits under city streets), a practical limit on how many physical pairs could be installed between two locations was reached. The solution, which was called a *pair-gain system*, was to deploy digital instead of analog transmission, and to use two pairs for the transmission system – one pair for transmit and one pair for receive. For T1 lines, two pairs carry 24 voice or data channels, which results in a pair-gain of 12.

Thus, the T1 circuit is a digital, full-duplex transmission facility operating at 1.544 Mbps and is part of a hierarchy of multiplexed digital signals. The fundamental building block of this hierarchy is called the Digital Signal Level 0 (DS0) channel, which carries 64 Kbps of bandwidth. (As an aside, the 64 Kbps is derived from the analog to digital conversion process that is used to create the digital telephone signal. The analog signal is sampled, or measured, 8,000 times per second. Each sample is then converted into an 8-bit code. The resulting digital signal – 8 bits times 8,000 times per second – yields a data rate of 64 Kbps.)

Note the distinction between the T1 *circuit* and the DS1 *signal*. The T1 designation refers to the technology (such as a digital telephone system over copper pairs). The DS1 designation refers to the format of the data that is sent over that circuit. This digital multiplexing hierarchy includes the following:

Signal Level	Carrier System	Equivalent DS0 Channels	Equivalent DS1 Channels	Data Rate (Kbps)
DS0	N/A	1	N/A	64
DS1	T1	24	1	1,544
DS1C	T1C	48	2	3,152
DS2	T2	96	4	6,312
DS3	T3	672	28	44,736
DS4	T4	4,032	168	274,760

The multiplexing hierarchy is illustrated in Figure 5-3. Of the various signal rates noted, the DS0, DS1, and DS3 signals are the ones most likely to be used for customer-provided network equipment, such as VoIP gateways and IP routers. The DS1C, DS2, and DS4 signals are typically reserved for internal carrier circuits only. Also note that there are rather large steps in bandwidth capacity between the DS0, DS1, and DS3 signals that end users employ. In other words, if a T1 line (operating at 1.544 Mbps) is insufficient, your next step is a T3 line (operating at 44.736 Mbps), which is a 28-fold increase in capacity – a rather large jump!

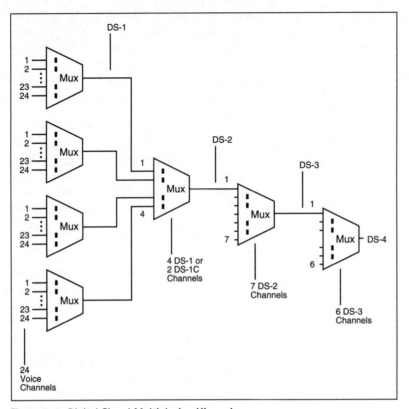

Figure 5-3: Digital Signal Multiplexing Hierarchy

After the format of the data is specified, a method of distinguishing between the individual channels (which may be distinct telephone conversations or data circuits) must be established. For DS1 signals, this framing is accomplished by adding one additional bit, dubbed the 193rd bit, to each frame, as illustrated in Figure 5-4. This extra bit adds 8,000 bps to the DS1 signal bandwidth. Thus, the DS1 data rate of 1.544 Mbps is derived from 24 DS0 channels at 64 Kbps, or 1,536 Kbps, plus 8 Kbps (the framing bit), yielding 1,544 Kbps or 1.544 Mbps.

DS1 frames are typically delivered to the end-user equipment in a larger format that allows more efficient use of the framing bits. This larger delivery package is called a *superframe*. There are two superframe formats defined: the D4 superframe and the extended superframe, or ESF.

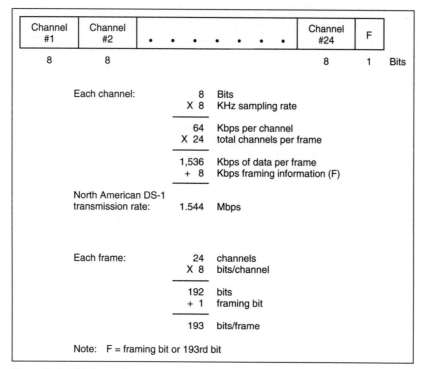

Figure 5–4: DS1 Frame Format

D4 framing uses the 193rd bit strictly for framing purposes (Figure 5-5). A total of 12 individual frames are combined into the D4 superframe. A pattern of the sampled 193rd bits (bit numbers 193, 386, 579, and so on) is used to identify individual DS0 channels within each DS1 frame. This framing pattern (100011011100) is repeated every 12 frames (or superframe). Signaling information (used for central office–to–central office messages) appears in bit 8 of frames 6 and 12. When this signaling information is present, the effective throughput of that channel is reduced to 56 Kbps. (This is because only 7 bits are available to carry end-user information. With each bit having a capacity of 8 Kbps, the resulting channel capacity is 56 Kbps. And since you don't know if the carrier has inserted these signaling bits in the data stream after that data has left your premises, it is wise to count on only 56 Kbps of capacity per channel, instead of the 64 Kbps that would normally be available.)

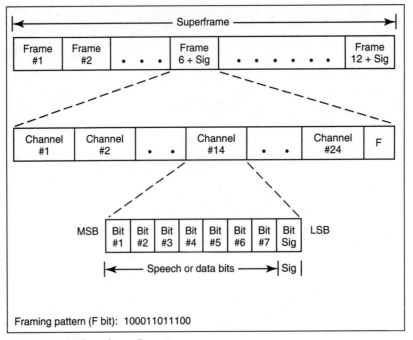

Figure 5-5: D4 Superframe Format

(Source: ANSI T1.107)

The extended superframe format (ESF) is illustrated in Figure 5-6. ESF extended the superframe from 12 to 24 DS1 frames, which resulted in a total of 24 of the framing (or 193rd) bits. With 24 bits instead of 12 to work with, two additional capabilities became available (see Figure 5-7). The signaling capabilities were expanded to four options (T, 2, 4, 16) and are shown in the traffic and signaling columns in Figure 5-7. Signaling information (if used) is present in frames 6, 12, 18, and 24.

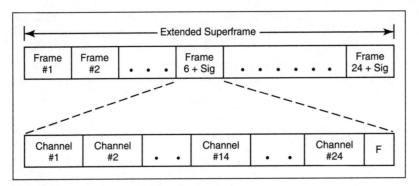

Figure 5-6: Extended Superframe Format

(Source: ANSI T1.107)

There are three uses for the framing function (shown as F in Figure 5-6): Framing itself (Fe); Data Link (DL); and Block Check (BC). The Data Link function provides a 4 Kbps communications link between circuit end points. Transmissions on this data link would typically consist of maintenance and performance messages. The Block Check framing function (BC) provides a six-bit Cyclic Redundancy Check (CRC-6), which is used to verify the accuracy of the entire superframe. Any individual line errors would cause a violation of the CRC-6, thus alerting the intermediate transmission equipment of the problem. The advantage of the ESF framing format over that of the D4 is its ability to monitor the network and then notify a network management console of any difficulties.

Frame Number	Information Coding Bits	Signaling Bit	ESF Signaling Options			
			T	2 State	4 State	16 State
1	1-8					
2	1-8					
3	1-8					
4	1-8					
5	1-8					
6	1-7	8	–	A	A	A
7	1-8					
8	1-8					
9	1-8					
10	1-8					
11	1-8					
12	1-7	8	–	A	B	B
13	1-8					
14	1-8					
15	1-8					
16	1-8					
17	1-8					
18	1-7	8	–	A	A	C
19	1-8					
20	1-8					
21	1-8					
22	1-8					
23	1-8					
24	1-7	8	–	A	B	D

Notes:
Option T: Transparent (bit 8 used for information coding).
Option 2 State: Two state Option provides one 1,333 bps signaling channel (A).
Option 4 State: Four state option provides two 667 bps signaling channels (A and B).
Option 16 State: Sixteen state option provides four 333 bps signaling channels (A, B, C, and D).

Figure 5–7: Extended Superframe Format Coding

(Source: ANSI T1.107)

It is important to ask the carrier if D4 or ESF formats are used on the DS1 circuits being provided. If these superframe formats are used, and network signaling is required, then there is a good possibility that the effective data rate of each DS0 channel (or at least the capacity that can be assured) is 56 Kbps instead of 64 Kbps. This is a useful bit of information to know when planning the capacities of access lines between your network and the carrier.

As a final note, a different multiplexing hierarchy is used in Europe. This hierarchy is sometimes referred to as the CEPT hierarchy, which stands for the Conference of European Postal and Telecommunications Administrations. The CEPT hierarchy defines different rates from the North American (DS) hierarchy. These include E1 (2.048 Mbps), E2 (four multiplexed E1 channels with a transmission rate of 8.448 Mbps), and E3 (16 multiplexed E1 channels with a transmission rate of 34.368 Mbps). The E1 channel is based on 32 DS0 channels, where 30 of these channels carry end-user information, one carries framing information, and one carries signaling information.

Further technical details on the digital signal hierarchy can be found in ITU-T G.704 [5-1] and ANSI T1.107 [5-2]. Reference [5-3] identifies an excellent resource for technical details on these WAN circuits.

5.3 ISDN Connections

Integrated Services Digital Network, or ISDN, service is available in many areas. There are two standard interfaces for ISDN service: the Basic Rate Interface, or BRI, and the Primary Rate Interface, or PRI. ISDN service has been standardized by both the International Telecommunications Union – Telecommunications Standards Sector (ITU-T) for international connections and the American National Standards Institute (ANSI) for use within the United States. Both the BRI and the PRI provide serial, synchronous, full duplex connections (Figure 5-8).

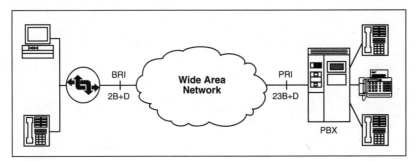

Figure 5-8: ISDN Interfaces

The BRI is defined in ITU-T I.430 [5-4] and transmits with a line rate of 192 Kbps. Some of that information is devoted to timing, framing, and other control overhead; as a result, 144 Kbps of bandwidth is delivered to the end user. This bandwidth is divided into two B-channels at 64 Kbps each (equivalent to a DS0), plus a D-channel at 16 Kbps. The B- (or Bearer) channels transport end-user information. The D-channel carries signaling information or packet-switched data. The BRI can be configured for either point-to-point or multipoint connections and is typically used for residential and small business applications. ISDN BRI service is provided by the Local Exchange Carrier (LEC) and is typically delivered to the end user on a 4-pin modular (RJ-11) or 8-pin modular (RJ-45) connector. For applications with converged networks and VoIP service, the ISDN BRI is most likely to be used in small office–home office (SOHO) applications for access to a headquarter's location.

The PRI is defined in ITU-T I.431 [5-5] and transmits at one of two rates: 1.544 Mbps, which is used in North America, Japan, and some of the Pacific Rim countries; and 2.048 Mbps (the E1 channel), which is used in Europe. The PRI definition is based on the T1/E1 standards that are discussed in Section 5.2 earlier in the chapter. The PRI is configured for point-to-point connections only and is typically used for high-capacity trunks between PBXs or between the carrier's access point and a PBX. As such, this interface would be optionally available on most routers and VoIP gateways that connect the customer's premises to the WAN and is also found on digital PBXs that integrate the premises' voice and data communication functions.

5.4 Transmitting IP Datagrams over Serial Lines

Two protocols have been developed to support TCP/IP-based data transmission over switched and dedicated serial lines: the Serial Line IP (SLIP) and the Point-to-Point Protocol (PPP).

Serial Line IP (SLIP), described in RFC 1055 [5-6], frames IP datagrams on a serial line. SLIP is not an Internet Standard protocol; therefore, specific implementations may vary. SLIP defines two characters: END (C0H or octal 300 or decimal 192) and ESC (DBH or octal 333 or decimal 219), as shown in Figure 5-9. To transmit, the SLIP host begins sending the IP datagram (see Figure 5-9). It replaces any data octet equivalent to the END character with the two-octet sequence of ESC plus octal 334 (DB DCH). It replaces any octet equal to the ESC character with the two-octet sequence of ESC plus octal 335 (DB DDH). After completing the datagram transmission, it sends an END character. (Note that the ESC character used with SLIP is not the ASCII escape character.) SLIP does not have a defined maximum packet size; however, many systems adhere to the maximum packet size used by the Berkeley UNIX SLIP of 1,006 octets (excluding the SLIP framing characters). An enhancement to SLIP, known as Compressed SLIP or CSLIP, compresses the TCP/IP header for transmission over low-speed serial lines. CSLIP is defined in RFC 1144 and is often referred to as Van Jacobson header compression. This technique minimizes the protocol overhead being sent, partially compensating for the lower speed of the transmission system.

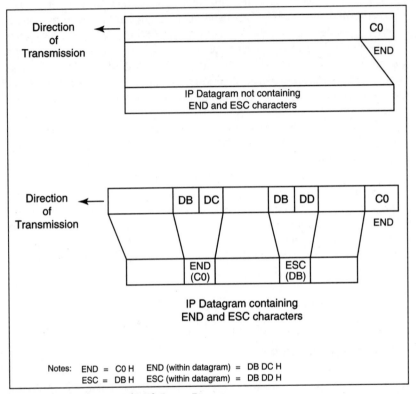

Figure 5-9: Serial Line IP (SLIP) Frame Format

The Point-to-Point Protocol (PPP), described in RFC 1661 [5-7], is the second protocol used for serial line connections. Unlike SLIP, PPP is an Internet Standard protocol for use over asynchronous or synchronous serial lines. RFC 1661 describes three main components of PPP: a method of encapsulating multiprotocol datagrams, a Link Control Protocol (LCP), and a family of Network Control Protocols (NCPs). LCP packets initialize the Data Link Layer of the communicating devices. NCP packets negotiate the Network Layer connection between the two endpoints. Once the LCP and NCP configuration is complete, datagrams can be transmitted over the link. RFC 2153 details vendor extensions that can provide supplementary information.

The PPP frame is based on the ISO High Level Data Link Control (HDLC) protocol (known as ISO 3309), which has been implemented by itself and has also been incorporated into many other protocol suites, including X.25, frame relay, and ISDN. (The 1979 HDLC standard addresses synchronous environments; the 1984 modification extends the usage to asynchronous environments. When asynchronous transmission is used, all octets are transmitted with 1 start bit, 8 data bits, and 1 stop bit.)

The PPP frame (see Figure 5-10) includes fields for beginning and ending Flags (set to 07H); an Address (set to FFH, the all-stations address); Control (set to 03H, for Unnumbered Information); Protocol (a 1- or 2-octet field identifying the higher layer protocol in use); Information (the higher layer information, with a default maximum length of 1,500 octets); and a Frame Check Sequence (2 octets). RFC 1662 describes the details of the HDLC-like framing.

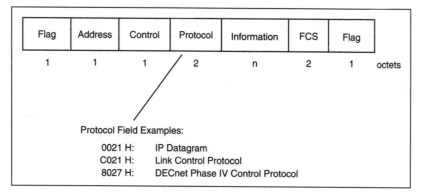

Figure 5-10: Point-to-Point Protocol Frame

The Protocol field is used to distinguish multiprotocol datagrams, with the value contained in that field identifying the datagram encapsulated in the Information field of the packet. RFC 1661 specifies values for the Protocol field that are reserved; the "Assigned Numbers" document (currently RFC 1700) contains specific Protocol field assignments.

The Protocol field is two octets (or four hex characters) long, with possible values from 0000–FFFFH. Values in the 0.xxx–3.xxx range identify the Network Layer protocol of specific packets, and values in the 8.xxx–B.xxx range identify packets belonging to the associated Network Control Protocols (NCPs), if any. Protocol field values in the 4.xxx–7.xxx range are used for protocols with low-volume traffic that have no associated NCP. Protocol field values in the C.xxx–F.xxx range identify packets as link layer Control Protocols (such as LCP). For example, the value of 0021H identifies an IPv4 datagram.

PPP's second component is the Link Control Protocol (LCP), which deals with Data Link Layer issues. LCP defines five steps for link control. The process begins with the Link Dead phase, which indicates that the Physical Layer is not ready. When the Physical Layer is ready to be used, the process proceeds with the Link Establishment phase. In the Link Establishment phase, the Link Control Protocol (LCP) is used to establish the connection through the exchange of Configure packets between the two ends of the link. The Authentication Phase, which is optional, allows the peer at the other end of the link to authenticate itself prior to exchanging Network Layer protocol packets. In the Network Layer Protocol Phase, each Network Layer in operation, such as IP, Novell's IPX, or AppleTalk, is configured by the Network Control Protocol (NCP). The final step, the Link Termination Phase, uses LCP to close the link.

PPP's third objective is to develop a family of NCPs to transmit Network Layer information. A number of NCPs have been defined, each addressing a particular Network Layer protocol. These include DECnet Phase IV, defined in RFC 1762; Banyan VINES, defined in RFC 1763; and Xerox Network Systems (XNS) Internet Datagram Protocol (IDP), defined in RFC 1764. Each of these protocols is defined by a distinct value of the Protocol field.

The IETF Assigned Numbers document, which is available online, contains all the current assignments for the PPP fields [5-8].

5.5 IP over Frame Relay Networks

Frame relay (FR) was developed by the American National Standards Institute (ANSI) and the International Telecommunications Union – Telecommunications Standards Sector (ITU-T) and was derived from earlier work on Integrated Services Digital Networks (ISDNs). As such, the FR protocol is similar to the ISDN protocols and, for that matter, is also similar to the 1970s era X.25 packet switching technologies that preceded ISDN. Frame relay improves on both X.25 and ISDN by streamlining the protocol processing. For example, both X.25 and ISDN are implemented at the three lower layers of the OSI model, that is, the Physical, Data Link, and Network Layers. A significant part of the Data Link and Network Layer functions deals with error control – what to do when the transmission is corrupted. In today's environments, with very reliable networks that are often fiber-optic-based (and therefore less susceptible to transmission errors caused by electromagnetic interference), much of this error control is no longer necessary. The architects of frame relay recognized this change and reduced the complexity of the frame relay protocols accordingly.

Thus, frame relay is implemented at only the Physical and Data Link Layers. Frame relay eliminates the Network Layer (that is, packet) processing and performs only a few Data Link Layer functions. For example, FR checks the frame for errors, but it does not automatically request a retransmission if it discovers one. Should an error occur, the processes within the sender and receiver take responsibility for that function.

Frame relay provides a logical connection, either a switched virtual circuit (SVC) or a permanent virtual circuit (PVC), between end-user systems (Figure 5-11). A virtual circuit is a logical communication channel between the end-user equipment, or Terminal Equipment (DTE), and the frame relay network, or Data Circuit-Terminating Equipment (DCE). In most cases, the DTE is called a Frame Relay Access Device (FRAD), and the DCE is called a Frame Relay Node (FRN) or a Frame Relay Network Device (FRND). The frame relay network interface, called the User-Network Interface, or UNI, is defined as the physical communication line between the FRAD and the FRN or FRND. For frame relay implementations in the United States, the ANSI T1.606 [5-9] standard provides the technical details. Other implementation guidelines are provided in documents produced by a trade organization, the Frame Relay Forum [5-10].

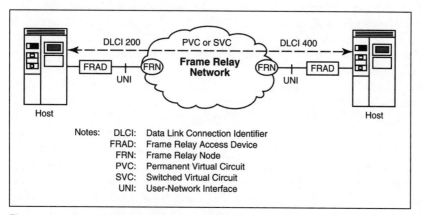

Figure 5-11: Frame Relay Logical Connections

The data to be transmitted across those connections is contained within a frame relay frame, as shown in Figure 5-12. The first two octets of the frame relay frame comprise the frame relay header and are followed by the higher layer information, such as an IP datagram.

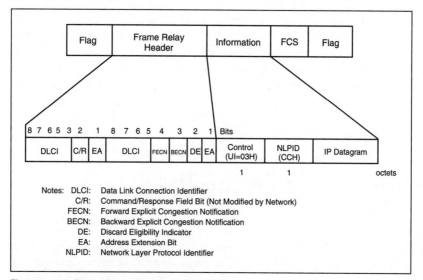

Figure 5-12: Frame Relay Frame with IP Datagram

(Source: ANSI T1.618)

The FR header contains a number of subfields. The longest of these is the Data Link Connection Identifier (DLCI), which identifies the virtual circuit used for any particular communication path. Multiple virtual circuits may exist at this interface. For example, if a router is the FRAD, it may serve 50 workstations on a LAN, which could each conceivably have a virtual circuit (identified with the DLCI field) into the frame relay network. The DLCI field (10 bits long when the default two-octet frame relay header is used) allows up to 1,024 virtual circuits, although some are reserved for network diagnostic purposes. These circuits are further defined as Permanent Virtual Circuits (PVCs) and are established when the FRAD is attached to the frame relay network.

When a frame enters the frame relay network, the FRND examines the Frame Check Sequence (FCS) at the end of the frame for errors. If an error is present, the frame is discarded. If the FCS passes, the FRND examines the DLCI field and a table lookup determines the correct outgoing link. If a table entry does not exist for a particular frame, the frame is discarded. The frame relay header contains three bits to indicate congestion on the frame relay network. The first two bits are known as Explicit Congestion Notification (ECN) bits. Any node within the frame relay network can send an ECN bit in two directions: downstream using the Forward ECN (or FECN) bit and upstream using the Backward ECN (or BECN) bit. The third bit used for congestion control is the Discard Eligibility (DE) bit. The DE bit indicates which frames should be discarded to relieve congestion. ANSI T1.617a [5-11] discusses these congestion management principles. The Command/Response (C/R) and Extended Address (EA) complete the frame relay header. The C/R bit was defined for LAPD but is not used with frame relay networks. The EA bits allow the frame relay header to extend to three or four octets long to accommodate more DLCI addresses.

The Internet standard for frame relay support is RFC 2427 [5-12], which provides specifics for implementing multiprotocol traffic over frame relay networks. Several variations are presented in that document; however, consistent among all the variants are the Control field and the Network Level Protocol ID (NLPID). The Control field may either specify Unnumbered Information (UI) with a field value of 03H or Exchange Identification (XID) with a field value of AF or BFH. ISO and ITU-T administer the NLPID and identify the type of protocol used within the Information field. RFC 2427 defines the value of NLPID = CCH to designate IPv4 datagrams. Other formats for routed and bridged frames have been defined as well; consult RFC 2427 for specific details.

5.6 Voice over Frame Relay Networks

The transmission of voice and fax traffic over frame relay networks is addressed in a Frame Relay Implementation Agreement, FRF.11.1, published by the Frame Relay Forum [5-13]. The technical characteristics of that document address several key functions, including the transport of compressed voice payloads within frame relay frames, multiplexing of up to 255 sub-channels on a single frame relay DLCI, and support for a number of voice compression algorithms.

To support these services, a Voice Frame Relay Access Device (VFRAD) is defined, which would likely be positioned between a voice concentrator (such as a PBX or key system) and the frame relay network if it were a standalone device, or possibly integrated into some other system that supported both voice traffic and a frame relay interface. The VFRAD accesses the frame relay service across the UNI but provides additional functions to the end users, as noted in the previous paragraph. For example, the VFRAD may provide voice/data sub-channel multiplexing, as shown in Figure 5-13. Multiple voice and data connections can be supported over a single PVC. This multiplexing function becomes specific to a single PVC, as illustrated by DLCI 16 in Figure 5-14. Note that other PVCs, such as DLCI 17, could use other frame relay supported services (such as data transport) across the same frame relay physical interface.

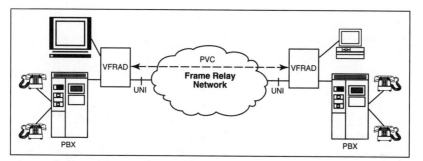

Figure 5-13: Frame Relay Service Multiplexing

(Source: Frame Relay Forum FRF.11.1)

The multiplexing of these various payloads requires an additional level of protocol encapsulation, as illustrated in Figure 5-15. Each voice or data payload is packaged as a distinct sub-frame, and multiple sub-frames are carried within the Information field of the frame relay frame. The sub-frames may be combined within a single frame to increase the efficiencies of the protocol processing and transport functions of the end-user equipment. For example, Figure 5-15 shows three voice channels and one data channel that are all supported over a single DLCI.

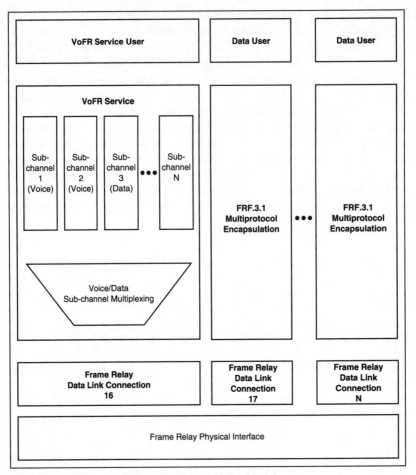

Figure 5-14: Voice over Frame Relay Multiplexing Model

(Source: Frame Relay Forum FRF.11.1)

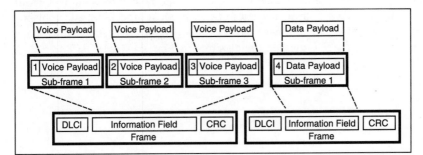

Figure 5-15: Relationship between Frames and Sub-frames

(Source: Frame Relay Forum FRF.11.1)

Each sub-frame consists of a variable length header plus a payload. The sub-frame header carries the multiplexing functions that identify the specific voice/data channels (Figure 5-16a). The sub-frame header consists of six fields. The Extension Indication (EI) and Length Indication (LI) determine the length of the sub-frame header and its functions, which are further defined in Figure 5-16b. The Sub-channel Identification (CID) specifies the particular sub-channel (one of up to 256) in use. The Payload Type field indicates the payload contained in that sub-frame, such as dialed digits, fax information, and so on. The Payload Length field specifies the number of payload octets that follow the header. Finally, the payload itself, as defined by the Payload Type, completes the sub-frame.

8	7	6	5	4	3	2	1	Octets
EI	LI	Sub-channel Identification (CID) (Least significant 6 bits)						1
CID (msb)		0 Spare	0 Spare	Payload Type				1a (Note 1)
Payload Length								1b (Note 2)
Payload								P

Notes: 1. When the EI bit is set, the structure of Octet 1a given in Figure 5-16b applies.

2. When the LI bit is set, the structure of Octet 1b given in Figure 5-16b applies.

3. When both the EI bit and the LI bit are set to 1 both Octet 1a and 1b are used.

Figure 5-16a: Sub-frame Format

(Source: Frame Relay Forum FRF.11.1)

Further details regarding the transport of Voice over Frame Relay networks, plus the various coding options for the VFRAD implementations, are given in FRF.11.1 [5-13].

Extension indication (octet 1)

The extension indication (EI) bit is set to indicate the presence of octet 1a. This bit must be set when a sub-channel identification value is > 63 or when a payload type is indicated. Each transfer syntax has an implicit payload type of zero when the EI bit is cleared.

Length indication (octet 1)

The length indication (LI) bit is set to indicate the presence of octet 1b. The LI bit of the last sub-frame contained within a frame is always cleared and the payload length field is not present. The LI bits are set for each of the sub-frames preceding the last sub-frame.

Sub-channel identification (octets 1 and 1a)

The six least significant bits of the sub-channel identification are encoded in octet 1. The two most significant bits of the sub-channel identification are encoded in octet 1a. A zero value in the two most significant bits is implied when octet 1a is not included in the VoFR header (EI bit cleared). Sub-channel identifiers 0000 0000 through 0000 0011 are reserved in both the short and long format.

Payload type (octet 1a)

This field indicates the type of payload contained in the sub-frame.

Bits				
4	3	2	1	
0	0	0	0	Primary payload transfer syntax
0	0	0	1	Dialed digit transfer syntax
0	0	1	0	Signalling bit transfer syntax
0	0	1	1	Fax relay transfer syntax
0	1	0	0	Silence Information Descriptor

A zero value for the payload type is implied when octet 1a is not included in the header (EI bit cleared).

Payload length (octet 1b)

Payload length contains the number of payload octets following the header. A payload length indicates the presence of two or more sub-frames packed in the information field of the frame.

Payload (octet p)

The payload contains octets as defined by the applicable transfer syntax assigned to the sub-channel or as indicated by the payload type octet 1a.

Figure 5–16b: Sub–frame Format Details

(Source: Frame Relay Forum FRF.11.1)

5.7 IP over ATM Networks

Asynchronous Transfer Mode, or ATM, is a transmission technology that was originally conceived to meet the transport requirements for local, metropolitan, and wide area network applications. As such, ATM technologies operate over a wide range of transmission rates, currently defined from 1.5 Mbps (DS1) to 9.953 Gbps (Optical Carrier Level 192, or OC192), with even higher rates under development. From a practical perspective, however, ATM technologies have been primarily deployed in MAN and WAN environments for backbone transmission. Many other high-speed alternatives exist for LANs, such as Fast Ethernet and Gigabit Ethernet, that are often more cost-effective than an ATM implementation. As a result, the desktop-to-desktop ATM service that was originally conceived is not frequently implemented.

The ATM architecture is connection-oriented and is based on high-speed switches that direct the 53-octet cells of information from their source to the ultimate destination. ATM has a four-layer architecture. This includes the Physical Layer, which handles bit timing and transmission-related issues; the ATM Layer, which is responsible for the transfer of the 53-octet cells; the ATM Adaptation Layer (AAL), which supports the transport of higher layer information by dividing that information into 53-octet cells and incorporating appropriate error control mechanisms; and the higher layers, which contain user information.

The 53-octet ATM cell is composed of a 5-octet header and a 48-octet payload. The format of the cell is standard across all AALs; however, the format of the 48-octet payloads, the various protocol processes, such as segmentation and reassembly, and so on, vary with the AAL type in use. At the present time, five AALs have been defined:

- ◆ AAL0 is the null AAL, where the entire 48-octet payload carries end-user information.

- ◆ AAL1 is typically used for circuit emulation service, which would include both voice and video applications that operate with a constant bit rate. With AAL1, the 48-octet payload is divided into a 1-octet field that contains sequence and error control information, and a 47-octet payload that carries end-user information.

- ◆ AAL2 is intended for delay-sensitive applications with a variable bit rate, such as voice and video. AAL2 is frequently used in conjunction with Digital Subscriber Line (DSL) service to transport voice and data within local exchange environments.

- ◆ AAL3/4 is used for connectionless applications and other applications that need extensive error control capabilities, such as Switched Multimegabit Data Service (SMDS). With AAL3/4, the 48-octet payload carries four octets of sequencing and error control information, plus 44 octets of end-user information.

- ◆ AAL5 provides a straightforward mechanism to send connection-oriented traffic, such as frame relay or X.25. With AAL5, a short header is appended to the original end-user message, and then that message is divided into 48-octet payloads for transmission via ATM cells.

A thorough study of ATM is beyond the scope of this text. However, readers interested in an in-depth study of ATM and its protocols should check out Agilent Technologies papers [5-14], or a companion text, *Analyzing Broadband Networks* [5-15].

Despite the differences between the original ATM architecture and the realities of the marketplace, the transport of IP traffic over ATM infrastructures has been the topic of much research. Much of this research has been under the guidance of the ATM Forum, a consortium of users, vendors, and carriers who have joined together to further develop the technology and publish many documents that detail its implementation [5-16]. The Internet Engineering Task Force (IETF) has also played a key role in the publication of RFC documents that detail how IP-based and ATM-based internetworks can coexist. Four related alternatives for TCP/IP internetworking with ATM have been developed: Multiprotocol Encapsulation over AAL5 (defined in RFC 2684), Classical IP and ARP over ATM (defined in RFC 2225), LAN Emulation – LANE (defined by the ATM Forum), and Multiprotocol over ATM – MPOA (defined by the ATM Forum).

Multiprotocol Encapsulation over ATM Adaptation Layer 5 is documented in RFC 2684 [5-17]. This document describes two methods, each with several options, for carrying network interconnect traffic over ATM AAL5: Logical Link Control (LLC) encapsulation and Virtual Circuit (VC) -based multiplexing. The LLC encapsulation method allows multiplexing of multiple protocols over a single ATM virtual circuit and is typically used when it is not feasible to have a separate VC for each protocol. With the VC-based multiplexing technique, each protocol is carried on a separate VC. This method is used when it is feasible and economical to dynamically create large numbers of virtual circuits.

The LLC encapsulation method, used to carry IP traffic, is shown in Figure 5-17. Information contained within an IEEE 802.2 LLC header and an IEEE 802.1a SNAP header identifies the protocol carried within that PDU. Of particular interest within the SNAP header is the Protocol Identifier (PID) field, which has the value 08 00H for IP traffic. The Protocol Data Unit (PDU) that follows these headers contains up to 65,527 octets of higher layer information, such as the IP datagram. Other packet formats, used to carry other types of routed and bridged traffic, are described in RFC 2684.

RFC 2225, "Classical IP and ARP over ATM" [5-18], considers the application of ATM as a direct replacement for the physical transmission technologies (such as cables and routers) that have heretofore been employed. In this case, the network is assumed to be configured as a Logical IP Subnetwork (LIS), where members of that LIS have the same IP network/subnet number and address mask, are directly connected to the ATM network, and meet other protocol requirements. Hosts connected to ATM communicate directly to other hosts within the same LIS. To communicate with a host outside of the local LIS requires an IP router. Figure 5-18 illustrates such a LIS, where all members have a consistent IP network and subnet address [N.S.x] and use a router for communication outside of the LIS.

For two LIS members to communicate, they must know each other's IP and ATM addresses. IP over ATM uses an enhanced version of the Address Resolution Protocol (ARP) called ATMARP to provide translation between ATM and IP addresses. ATMARP runs on a server that exists at an ATM address that all LIS members are aware of. The IP datagram is encapsulated within an ATM Adaptation Layer 5 (AAL5) message and is then further subdivided into cells for transmission over the ATM network.

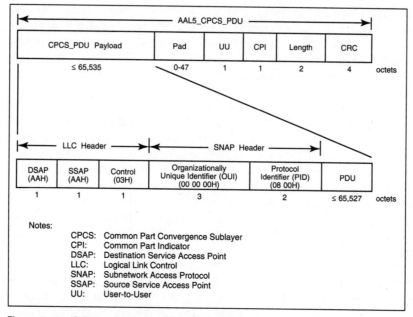

Figure 5-17: IP Datagram Encapsulation over AAL 5

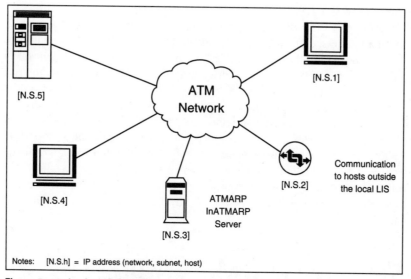

Figure 5-18: Logical IP Subnetwork

LAN Emulation, or LANE as it is commonly known, is a service that allows exist-ing end-user applications to access an ATM network. More importantly, this access appears to the application as if it were using more traditional protocols, such as TCP/IP or Novell's Internetwork Packet Exchange (IPX), and as if it were running over more traditional LANs such as Ethernet or token ring. One of the design constraints is to account for the differences in protocol design – ATM is connection-oriented, whereas IP and IPX are connectionless. A number of functions, including setting up the ATM connection and translating LAN to ATM addresses, must be hidden from the upper layers, thus making the application think it is operating over a traditional network.

The ATM Forum's LAN Emulation version 2.0 specification [5-19] defines two scenarios that are applicable. In the first, an ATM network may be used to interconnect Ethernets to Ethernets, an Ethernet to an ATM device, or an ATM device to another ATM device. The second scenario replaces Ethernet LANs with token ring LANs under similar conditions. The ATM-to-LAN converter sits at the edge of the network, running dual protocol stacks: one that communicates with the LAN (on one side) and another that communicates with the ATM switch (on the other side). Note that this ATM-to-LAN converter is functioning as a bridge, operating independently of the Network and higher layer protocols. The ATM switch (or switches) do not participate in LAN Emulation other than to switch the ATM connections, as would be the case with any other ATM-based network scenario.

An evolution of the ATM Forum's LAN Emulation work is a process known as Multiprotocol over ATM (MPOA) [5-20]. While LANE operates at the MAC Layer (OSI Data Link Layer), MPOA operates at the OSI Network Layer. MPOA is designed to integrate with LAN Emulation and to support the traditional routing functions of protocol filtering with enhanced security through firewalls, while handling both Data Link and Network Layer operations.

MPOA is designed with a client/server architecture, with the MPOA Client (MPC) residing in an edge device or MPOA host, and the MPOA Server (MPS) residing in an MPOA router. Both the MPC and the MPS contain a LAN Emulation Client (LEC) function. The MPC includes a Layer 3 forwarding function, but it does not run internetwork routing protocols. The primary function of the MPC is to act as the initiation and termination points (source and sink, respectively) of internetwork shortcuts. When the MPC recognizes a data flow that could benefit from a shorter path, or shortcut, it requests the establishment of a shortcut to the destination. When the shortcut path is used, performance gains should result, especially for the transmission of stream-oriented traffic such as voice and video.

With this introduction into the transmission of IP over ATM networks, you can next consider some of the research regarding the transmission of voice traffic over ATM networks.

5.8 Voice over ATM Networks

Recall that one of the original design objectives of ATM technology was to incorporate voice, data, video, and other types of media into a cohesive stream of 53-octet cells. The ATM Forum has developed a number of documents that describe the various technologies and the protocols involved in these technologies, which go by the acronym VTOA, *Voice and Telephony over ATM*. These documents, which are all available from the ATM Forum's Web site [5-16], include:

♦ **Circuit Emulation Service 2.0 (af-vtoa-0078.000, January 1997):**
Addresses the need to carry constant bit rate (CBR) or circuit-oriented traffic over ATM networks. One of the goals of the Circuit Emulation Service (CES) is that the performance realized over ATM should be comparable to that experienced with currently available digital technologies, such as DS1 and DS3 lines.

♦ **Voice and Telephony over ATM to the Desktop (af-vtoa-0083.001, February 1999):** Specifies the particular features required to provide voice and telephony service in Broadband ISDN networks, such as ATM. Issues discussed include interworking between Narrowband ISDN (ISDN-BRI or ISDN-PRI) and Broadband ISDN (ATM) environments, along with signaling systems that are required to complete those calls.

♦ **Dynamic Bandwidth Utilization in 64 Kbps Time Slot Trunking over ATM – Using CES (af-vtoa-0085.000, July 1997):** Provides methods for detecting which time slots of a given trunk are active and which are inactive, which optimizes the bandwidth utilization of the ATM network.

♦ **ATM Trunking Using AAL1 for Narrowband Services v. 1.0 (af-vtoa-0089.000, July 1997):** Describes interworking functions between Narrowband services, such as 64 Kbps channels, and ATM trunks for PBX-like applications.

♦ **ATM Trunking Using AAL2 for Narrowband Services (af-vtoa-0113.000, February 1999):** Describes trunking arrangements for transport of voice, voice-band data, circuit mode data, frame mode data, and fax traffic. The document specifies the use of ATM virtual circuits with AAL2 to transport bearer information and ATM virtual circuits with AAL2 or AAL5 to transport signaling information.

♦ **Low Speed Circuit Emulation Service (af-vtoa-0119.000, May 1999):** Discusses the transport of constant bit rate (CBR) traffic over ATM networks, with specific emphasis on the support of low-speed applications (less than 64 kilobits). This document supports interfaces of both Data Terminal Equipment (DTE) and Data Circuit Terminating Equipment (DCE) for applications using EIA-449, EIA-530, and V.35 interfaces.

♦ **ICS for ATM Trunking Using AAL2 for Narrowband Services (af-vtoa-0120.000, May 1999):** This document provides an Implementation Conformance Statement (ICS) for the ATM Trunking using AAL2 for Narrowband Services. The ICS is a statement of which capabilities and options have been implemented; its purpose is to evaluate conformance of a particular implementation.

◆ Low Speed Circuit Emulation Service (LSCES) Implementation
  Conformance Statement Proforma (af-vtoa-0132.000, October 1999):
  This document adds an appendix to the Low Speed Circuit Emulation
  Service (LECES) document (af-vtoa-0119.000) described previously. This
  appendix contains the Implementation Conformance Statement (ICS)
  Proforma, which is used by an implementor to describe compliance with
  the baseline LECES document.

◆ Loop Emulation Service using AAL2 (af-vmoa-0145.000, July 2000):
  This document describes a Loop Emulation Service using AAL2 for
  Narrowband Services, which provides an efficient way of transporting
  voice, voice-band data, fax traffic, plus ISBN B- and D-channels over a
  broadband subscriber line connection such as xDSL, wireless, or other
  technologies.

Of particular interest for voice traffic applications is the ATM AAL2 specification,
defined by the ITU-T in Recommendations I.363.2 [5-21], I.366.1 [5-22], and I.366.2
[5-23], and described by the ATM Forum in the af-vmoa-0145.000 document noted
in the previous bullet list. AAL2 addresses the need to support real-time applications, such as voice and video, within a packet-switched network while, at the same
time, providing the guaranteed Quality of Service that these applications require.
AAL2 provides bandwidth-conserving features such as voice compression, silence
suppression, and the deletion of any voice channels that remain idle.

Figure 5-19, taken from Reference [5-23], and the ATM Forum's paper "Voice
and ATM" [5-24] discuss the various implementation options for carrying voice
over ATM networks. The first, known as Circuit Emulation Service (CES), is defined
in the ATM Forum's *af-vtoa-0078.000* document, noted in the previous bulleted list.
With CES, the ATM network provides a transport mechanism for voice links with
processes that are similar to techniques used within Time Division Multiplexing
(TDM) networks today. An enhancement to this method, known as Dynamic
Bandwidth Circuit Emulation Service (DBCES), is defined in the ATM Forum's *af-
vtoa-0085.000* document. This method detects which of the voice trunks are active
and which are idle and reuses the idle bandwidth for other services. Voice trunking
techniques, which tunnel voice traffic across a network between two endpoints, can
use either AAL1 or AAL2 services for this transport. The AAL2 case is defined in the
ATM Forum's *af-vtoa-0113.000* document, which includes the bandwidth conserva-
tion services just described. The final technique is to encode the voice traffic inside
another protocol, such as IP or frame relay, and then use ATM's high bandwidth
facilities for transport across the network. This final technique is necessarily complex, as additional protocols are involved in support of the encapsulation processes.

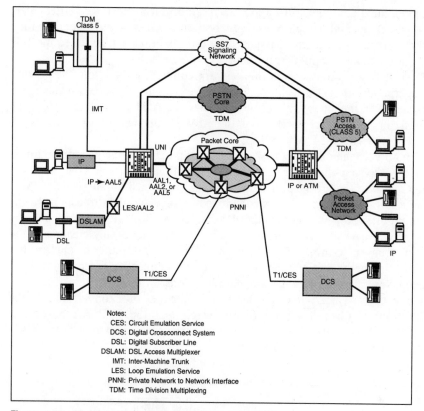

Figure 5-19: Multiple Ways of Carrying Voice over ATM

(Courtesy of Telica, Inc.)

References [5-25] through [5-27] discuss voice over ATM implementation issues in greater detail.

5.9 Voice over DSL

Digital Subscriber Line, or DSL as it is commonly known, provides an integrated voice/data transport service that was derived from ISDN-based technologies. DSL is currently available from many local exchange carriers, although (like ISDN) it may be offered only in areas of high population density [5-28]. There are many different versions of DSL, such as Asymmetric DSL (ADSL), High-bit-rate DSL (HDSL), Symmetric DSL (SDSL), and Single Pair HDSL (SHDSL), all with technical differences in transmission rate, network architecture and equipment, and so on. In most cases, the term xDSL, or simply DSL, is used to discuss the technology, independent of the specific implementation. Because DSL lines provide higher-speed data access than conventional dial-up circuits and modems, most local exchange carriers marketing this service extol its ability for higher-speed Internet access as part of their sales pitch. The industry is also supported by a trade organization called the DSL Forum, which provides many useful resources on their Web site [5-29].

Of interest to our discussion is the network connectivity side of DSL service, which incorporates the ATM technologies that were discussed in the previous section. In particular, the interworking functions between ATM and DSL environments have been the focus of research from the ATM Forum and many vendors, as described in References [5-30] and [5-31].

Since both voice and data signals traverse a DSL network, the generic architecture for these systems includes elements from both the voice (PSTN) and data (Internet) networks (Figure 5-20). The network itself will incorporate either an ATM or frame relay architecture that can support both voice and data transport. In the telco central office, a device known as a DSL Access Multiplexer (DSLAM) delivers the DSL service over copper pairs to the subscriber. For data-only customers, the connection from the central office is terminated with a DSL router or modem. For customers using both voice and data capabilities, the connection is terminated with a device that can access both voice and data functions. At the other side of the network connection, a Voice Gateway is used to deliver the voice conversation to the destination via a Class 5 central office switch and the PSTN. A Subscriber Management System is used to deliver the data packets to the Internet or the destination enterprise network, as appropriate.

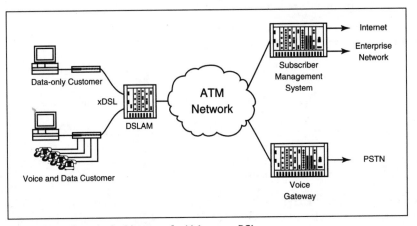

Figure 5-20: Generic Architecture for Voice over DSL

(Courtesy of CopperCom, Inc.)

From the service provider's perspective, there are two architectures that can be deployed: centralized and decentralized, depending on the location and ownership of the Class 5 switch. The centralized architecture is typically used when a Competitive Local Exchange Carrier (CLEC) installs their DSLAMs within the

Incumbent Local Exchange Carrier's (ILEC's) central office (Figure 5-21). The packet network (such as ATM) would concentrate the voice traffic from these DSLAMs into a single Voice Gateway, which would then pass that traffic to the PSTN via a Class 5 switch. By centralizing this concentration function at a regional Point of Presence (POP), the CLEC's initial investment is focused on the DSLAMs, rather than on more expensive switching systems.

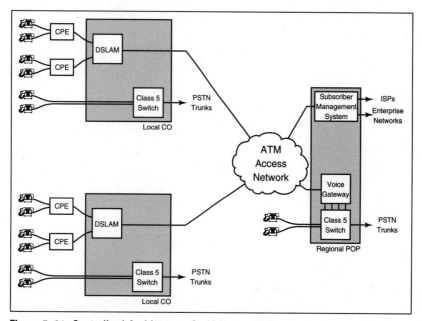

Figure 5-21: Centralized Architecture for Voice over DSL

(Courtesy of CopperCom, Inc.)

In contrast, the distributed architecture can be deployed when a service provider owns both the DSLAMs and the Class 5 switches in the same central office, such as when the ILEC is marketing its own DSL service offering (Figure 5-22). With this architecture, the voice traffic is routed to a Voice Gateway and Class 5 switch within each central office, while the data traffic is passed through the packet network to a central location for further processing. There are two alternatives for this data connection. The first provides an enhanced Voice Gateway that examines the information coming from the DSLAM and sends the voice call to the Class 5 switch, and the data to the packet network. This process is called *data pass through* (the upper portion of Figure 5-22). The second alternative uses a DSLAM with switching capabilities, which directs the voice information to the Class 5 switch, while the data packets are sent to the packet network. Note that the local central offices handle all of the voice connections, while the Regional POP only deals with the data connections.

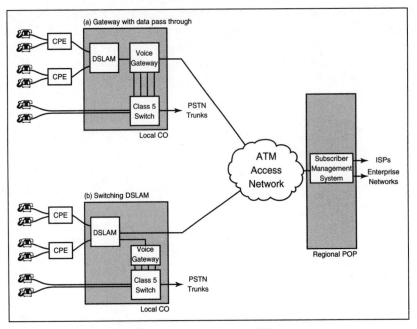

Figure 5-22: Distributed Architecture for Voice over DSL

(Courtesy of CopperCom, Inc.)

The protocols used within the DSL network may vary depending on the type of transport – frame relay (FR) or ATM – that is deployed. When ATM transport is used, the voice information is encoded using ATM's AAL2, as discussed in the previous section, and is then transported from the customer's premises to the DSLAM via DSL. At the DSLAM, those ATM cells are placed on a higher-speed transport, such as a DS3 circuit, to be sent to the Voice Gateway (Figure 5-23).

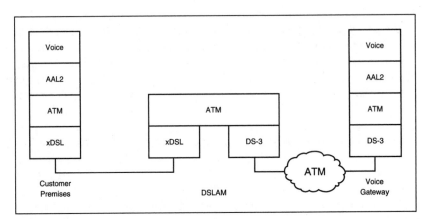

Figure 5-23: Protocol Stacks for Voice over DSL

(Courtesy of CopperCom, Inc.)

If a frame relay connection exists between the customer's premises and the DSLAM, the DSLAM provides a Frame-to-Cell conversion, as defined by the Frame Relay Forum's FRF.8.1 document [5-32], yielding ATM cells using AAL5 to be sent to the Voice Gateway (Figure 5-24). Note that this process involves a Voice over IP over frame relay protocol stack on the customer premises side of the network, and a Voice over IP over ATM AAL5 on the Voice Gateway side of the network.

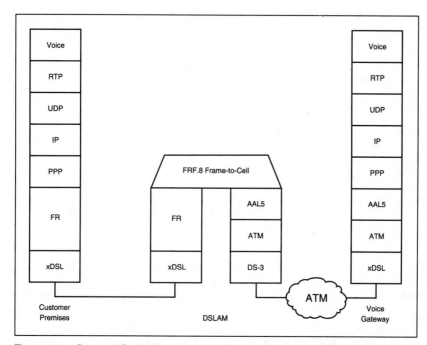

Figure 5-24: Protocol Stacks for Voice over IP with Frame-based DSLAM

(Courtesy of CopperCom, Inc.)

Another architectural alternative is to deploy AAL2, defined by the ATM Forum in support of voice traffic, over the frame relay connection (Figure 5-25). A similar Frame-to-Cell conversion is provided within the DSLAM; however, the Voice Gateway uses both AAL5 (for the connection to the ATM network) and AAL2 for support of the voice traffic.

Details regarding these alternatives can be found in an excellent white paper from networking vendor CopperCom, Inc., entitled "Mastering Voice over DSL: Network Architecture" [5-33].

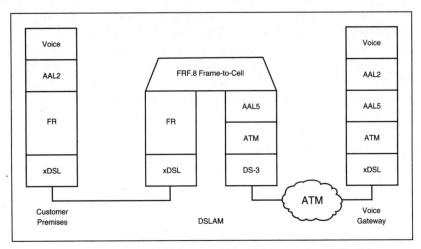

Figure 5-25: Protocol Stacks for Voice over AAL2 with Frame-based DSLAM

(Courtesy of CopperCom, Inc.)

5.10 Carriers Providing IP Transport Services

Now that you have examined various transport alternatives — T1 lines, frame relay circuits, ATM switched connections, DSL, and so on — Table 5-1 lists some of the carriers that provide these IP-based transport alternatives. A few words of caution, however: the carrier marketplace has become extremely competitive in the past few years, with many acquisitions, mergers, and bankruptcies. Therefore, spend adequate time in due diligence research before committing to a long-term carrier contract.

TABLE 5-1 CARRIERS PROVIDING IP TRANSPORT SERVICES

Carrier	Contact	Notes
Access Power, Inc.	www.accesspower.com	Worldwide service
CoolCall.com, Inc.	www.coolcall.com	North America, Internationally
deltathree, Inc.	www.deltathree.com	Worldwide phone-to-phone and PC-to-phone service
DialCom, Inc.	www.dialcomusa.com	Worldwide service

Carrier	Contact	Notes
EasyLink Services, Corporation	www.easylink.com	Serves Africa, Asia Pacific, Europe, Americas, and Middle East
Ecocom	www.ecocomusa.com	Worldwide service
Fnet Corp.	www.fnet.net	Worldwide phone/fax service
Genuity, Inc.	www.genuity.com	Worldwide service
GlobalNet Telecom, Inc.	www.globalnettelecom.com	Worldwide fax, voice service
Glocalnet AB	www.glocalnet.com	Serves Sweden
GRIC Communications, Inc.	www.gric.com	Serves Europe, U.S., and other countries
IBasis, Inc.	www.ibasis.net	Worldwide service
IPVoice Communications, Inc.	www.ipvoice.com	Worldwide service
Iscom, Inc.	www.iscom.net	Worldwide service
ITXC Corporation	www.itxc.com	Worldwide service
Level(3) Communications, Inc.	www.level3.com	Serves North America, Asia, and Europe
Net2Phone, Inc.	www.net2phone.com	Serves 50 countries worldwide
NetVoice Technologies Corp.	www.netvoice.net	Serves Texas and Southern U.S.
Networks Telephony Corp.	www.networkstelephony.com	Serves North America, Asia, and Europe
1World Telecommunications, Inc.	www.1worldconnect.com	Worldwide
OzEmail Interline Pty Ltd.	www.ozemail.com.au	Serves Australia, New Zealand, U.K., and U.S.

Continued

TABLE 5-1 CARRIERS PROVIDING IP TRANSPORT SERVICES *(Continued)*

Carrier	Contact	Notes
Poptel GmbH	www.poptel.com	Serves Germany, France, Switzerland, and U.S.
Qwest Communications International, Inc.	www.qwest.net	U.S. phone/fax service
Rapid Link, Inc.	www.rapidlink.com	Worldwide
Sonera Info Communications Ltd.	www.sonera.fi	Serves North America, Europe, and Asia
Startec Global Communications Corporation	www.startec.com	Worldwide service
TalkingNets, Inc.	www.talkingnets.com	Worldwide
Teleconomico, Inc.	www.hottelephone.com	Serves U.S. and 25 countries worldwide
Teleglobe, Inc.	www.teleglobe.com.	Worldwide
VocalTec Communications Ltd.	www.vocaltec.com	Worldwide
WorldCom, Inc.	www.worldcom.com	Serves 65 countries worldwide
World Interactive Network	www.win-inc.com	Worldwide fax and voice service
XO Communications	www.xo.com	Serves U.S. and Europe

5.11 Looking Ahead

This chapter considered the WAN infrastructures that are used to transport IP-based traffic, whether it is voice, fax, data, or video traffic. The next chapter deals with the signaling standards that are used to establish the connection on an end-to-end basis.

5.12 References

[5-1] International Telecommunication Union – Telecommunications Standardization Sector. *General Aspects of Digital Transmission Systems – Terminal Equipments – Synchronous Frame Structures Used at 1544, 6312, 2048, 8448, and 44 736 kbit/s Hierarchical Levels.* Recommendation G.704, October 1998.

[5-2] American National Standards Institute. *Telecommunications – Integrated Services Digital Network (ISDN) – Digital Hierarchy – Formats Specifications.* ANSI T1.107, 1995.

[5-3] Network test equipment vendor Acterna, LLC. (formerly Wavetek, Wandel & Goltermann) provides a number of resources describing the architectures and analysis procedures for digital leased lines, including T1, T3, ISDN, frame relay, ATM, and others. These papers are available at www.acterna.com/technical_resources/.

[5-4] International Telecommunication Union – Telecommunications Standardization Sector. *Integrated Services Digital Network (ISDN) – ISDN User-Network Interfaces – Basic User-Network Interface – Layer 1 Specification.* Recommendation I.430, November 1995.

[5-5] International Telecommunication Union – Telecommunications Standardization Sector. *Integrated Services Digital Network (ISDN) – ISDN User-Network Interfaces – Primary User-Network Interface – Layer 1 Specification.* Recommendation I.431, March 1993.

[5-6] J. Romkey. "A Nonstandard for Transmission of IP Datagrams Over Serial Lines: SLIP." RFC 1055, June 1988.

[5-7] W. Simpson. "The Point-to-Point Protocol (PPP)." RFC 1661, July 1994.

[5-8] The IETF Assigned Numbers document is available online at www.iana.org/numbers.html.

[5-9] American National Standards Institute. *Integrated Services Digital Network (ISDN) – Architectural Framework and Service Description for Frame-Relaying Bearer Service.* ANSI T1.606, 1990 (R1996).

[5-10] The Frame Relay Forum can be contacted at Frame Relay Forum North American Office, 39355 California Street, Suite 307, Fremont, CA 94538; Tel: (510) 608-5920, Fax: (510) 608-5917, E-mail: frf@frforum.com, Web address: www.frforum.com.

[5-11] American National Standards Institute. *Integrated Services Digital Network (ISDN) – Signaling Specification for Frame Relay Bearer Service for Digital Subscriber Signaling System Number 1 (DSS1) (Protocol Encapsulation and PICS).* ANSI T1.617a, 1994 (R1999).

[5-12] Brown, C., and A. Malis. "Multiprotocol Interconnect over Frame Relay." RFC 2427, September 1998.

[5-13] Frame Relay Forum. Voice over Frame Relay Implementation Agreement. FRF.11.1. December, 1998, with Annex J added in March 1999. Available from www.frforum.com.

[5-14] Network test equipment vendor Agilent Technologies (formerly part of the Hewlett-Packard Company) provides a number of resources to assist with the analysis of frame relay networks. These papers are available at onenetworks.comms.agilent.com/WhitePapers.asp.

[5-15] Miller, Mark A. *Analyzing Broadband Networks*, Third Edition. McGraw-Hill (New York, NY), 2001.

[5-16] The ATM Forum can be contacted at ATM Forum Worldwide Headquarters, 404 Balboa Street, San Francisco, CA, 94118; Tel: (415) 561-6275, Fax: (415) 561-6120, E-mail: info@atmforum.com, Web address: www.atmforum.com.

[5-17] Grossman, D., and J. Heinanen. "Multiprotocol Encapsulation over ATM Adaptation Layer 5." RFC 2684, September 1999.

[5-18] Laubach, M., and J. Halpern. "Classical IP and ARP over ATM." RFC 2225, April 1998.

[5-19] The ATM Forum. *LAN Emulation Over ATM Version 2 – LUNI Specification*, Document AF-LANE-00084.000, July 1997.

[5-20] The ATM Forum. *Multiprotocol over ATM (MPOA) Specification 1.1*, Document AF-MPOA-0114.000, May 1999.

[5-21] International Telecommunication Union – Telecommunications Standardization Sector. *Integrated Services Digital Network– Overall Network Aspects and Functions – Protocol Layer Requirements – B-IDSN ATM Adaptation Layer Specification; Type 2 AAL*. Recommendation I.363.2, September 1997.

[5-22] International Telecommunication Union – Telecommunications Standardization Sector. *Integrated Services Digital Network – Overall Network Aspects and Functions – Protocol Layer Requirements – Segmentation and Reassembly Service Specific Convergence Sublayer for the AAL type 2*. Recommendation I.366.1, June 1998.

[5-23] International Telecommunication Union – Telecommunications Standardization Sector. *Integrated Services Digital Network – Overall Network Aspects and Functions – Protocol Layer Requirements – AAL type 2 Service Specific Convergence Sublayer for Trunking*. Recommendation I.366.2, February 1999.

[5-24] Kafel, Ali. "Voice and ATM." January 2001. Available at www.telica.com/news/voice&atm.pdf.

[5-25] The ATM Forum. "Speaking Clearly with ATM — A Practical Guide to Carrying Voice over ATM," 2001. Available from www.atmforum.com/pages/library/whitepapers/2.html.

[5-26] Newbridge Networks Corp. "Integrating Voice Services onto ATM: Engineering Considerations," October 1998. Available at www.newbridge.com/doctypes/techwhitepaper/pdf/voatm_wp.pdf.

[5-27] Nortel Networks. "Packet Voice Convergence Using ATM Adaptation Layer-2 (AAL-2) Protocol." Document number 55043.25/07-99 Issue I, July 1999. Available from www.nortelnetworks.com/products/library/collateral/55043.25-07-99.pdf.

[5-28] Dobrowski, George, and Ajay Sharma. "Standards Update: AAL2 — Making It Happen for VoDSL." *Broadband World* (Fall 2000): 12–13. Also available electronically at www.globespan.net/resources/resources2.html.

[5-29] The DSL Forum. "DSL Anywhere," 2001. Available at www.dslforum.org.

[5-30] The ATM Forum. "ATM Interworks with DSL," 2001. Available at www.atmforum.com/pages/interworksw/dsl.html.

[5-31] Alcatel Internetworking, Inc. "Voice over DSL — The Key to Next Generation Voice/Data Services," February 2001. Available at www.cid.alcatel.com/doctypes/techpaper/pdf/10625_VoDSL_tp.pdf.

[5-32] Frame Relay Forum. Frame Relay/ATM PVC Service Interworking Implementation Agreement, Document FRF8.1, February 2000. Available from www.frforum.com.

[5-33] Taylor, Martin. "Mastering Voice over DSL: Network Architecture," 1999. Available at www.coppercom.com/pdf/wp-mastering.pdf.

Chapter 6

Signaling Standards for Converged Networks

Converged networks are composed of a number of elements (Figure 6-1). Suppose you wish to communicate with a colleague over an IP-based infrastructure. On your end, the communications path includes a Voice over IP client application; a local network that supports IP; and a wide area network that supports IP, such as an ISDN or a T1 line. Your colleague requires a similar connection on their end. These three elements are studied in Chapters 2, 4, and 5, respectively.

But there is one fundamental question that must be answered: How does the communication path get established? The answer to that question is found in a process known as *signaling*. Signaling is defined as the procedure or procedures undertaken to establish (or set up), manage (or supervise), and terminate (or disconnect) a communication session between two endpoints. There are several assumptions built into these procedures. First, it must be assumed that the two endpoints have a need to communicate, and that that need is being driven by some higher layer protocol or process (such as an application like an e-mail client that needs to communicate with the e-mail server, or a human who needs to call home). Second, it must be assumed that these two endpoints have the ability to reach each other, share a common addressing scheme, and have some way of determining each other's address. For example, it would do me no good to try to contact you on my amateur radio station if you don't own a compatible transmitter and receiver, or if you are not presently on the air, or if I don't know your identifying address or call sign. Third, the signaling procedures may have to traverse several networks, possibly using different protocols, in order to reach the destination. For example, if the call is initiated on an IP-based network but terminated on an analog telephone attached to the PSTN, both IP-based and PSTN-based signaling will be involved (Figure 6-2).

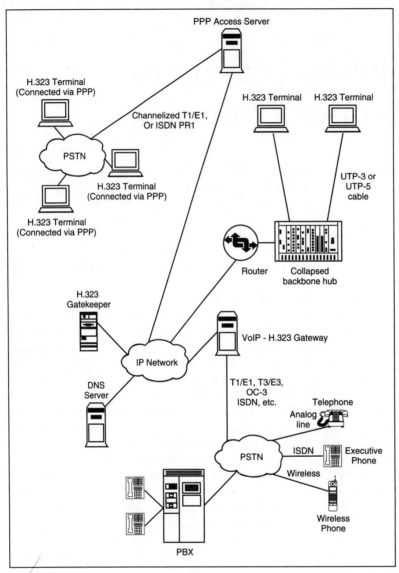

Figure 6-1: Voice over IP Network Elements

(Courtesy of the Voice over IP Forum)

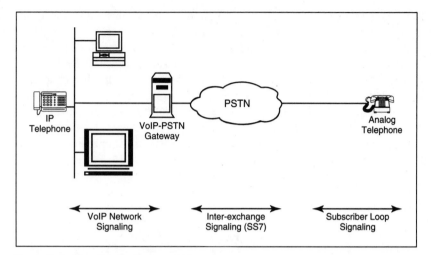

Figure 6–2: Signaling Systems and Messages

Thus, the signaling functions can be divided into two broad categories: signaling that occurs within the telephone network, and signaling that occurs within the packet network. Signaling within the PSTN is defined by a protocol known as Signaling System 7 (SS7), defined by the ITU-T for international calls (Reference [6-1]) and by ANSI for calls within the United States (Reference [6-2]). PSTN signaling is divided into two elements. The first part occurs between the telephone set and the local central office switch and is known as subscriber loop signaling. Loop signaling conveys indications of on/off hook status, ringing signals, and so on to the subscriber's terminal. The second part, known as inter-exchange signaling, conveys call information between central office switches. SS7 is a complex protocol beyond our discussion of enterprise-based VoIP networks. Reference [6-3] is an excellent resource for readers needing an overview of SS7.

Signaling within the packet network can be accomplished using some combination of four protocols: the H.323, developed by the ITU-T; the Session Initiation Protocol (SIP), developed by the IETF; the Media Gateway Control Protocol (MGCP), developed by the IETF; and the MEGACO/H.248 protocol, jointly developed by the IETF and the ITU-T. Depending on the network architecture and the components involved, one or more of these protocols may be deployed, although, as you will see, some provide very similar functions and would not necessarily be used simultaneously.

The next three sections summarize the functions of these four signaling protocols, beginning with H.323. A few words of caution are in order, however. All of these protocols are quite complex, and the documentation very extensive (for example, the baseline H.323 specification is 225 pages long, and RFC 2543, which defines SIP, is 149 pages long). Therefore, what is presented in this chapter is intended as a summary of the key functions of these protocols, not a complete summary of all of the possible operational conditions. Also, standards are always subject to change, so make sure you have the most current document available for your research. Readers wishing to learn more about network signaling and its use within VoIP networks should consult References [6-4] through [6-7]. Readers wishing to dig deeper into a specific protocol should consult the references noted in the following sections.

6.1 The H.323 Multimedia Standard

The first of the VoIP signaling standards this chapter looks at, H.323, was developed by the ITU-T and is currently in its fourth revision. The original title of the ITU-T H.323 standard, approved in 1996, was lengthy but described its purpose: *Visual Telephone Systems and Equipment for Local Area Networks Which Provide a Non-guaranteed Quality of Service* (the new title, displayed in Reference [6-8], is more succinct!). If we dissect the title, we see two key elements: visual telephone systems (in contrast to just audio telephone systems) and their use over LANs that do not provide a guaranteed quality of service, or QoS. To better understand the scope of this standard, it helps to put it in context with other ITU-T Series H Recommendations that deal with audiovisual and multimedia systems. These other standards include:

- ◆ **H.320:** Narrowband visual telephone systems and terminal equipment (used with narrowband ISDN services).

- ◆ **H.321:** Adaptation of H.320 terminals to broadband ISDN (ATM) environments.

- ◆ **H.322:** Visual telephone systems and equipment for local area networks that provide a guaranteed quality of service.

- ◆ **H.323:** Packet-based multimedia communications systems.

- ◆ **H.324:** Terminal for low bit rate multimedia communications (used for PSTN and wireless applications).

H.323 assumes that the transmission medium is a LAN that does not provide guaranteed packet delivery. A typical Ethernet would be a good example – if two Ethernet workstations transmit at the same time, a collision occurs. Since the probability of such a collision is difficult to predict, defining a specific quality of service is also difficult. Other standards in this family address other network types, such as H.320 (ISDN), H.321 (ATM), and H.324 (low bit rate connections), or, in the case of H.322, networks that provide QoS guarantees. Thus, the H.323 standard is designed to work with the local and wide area network types that are most commonly found – those that do not provide guarantees on the QoS provided.

6.1.1 Standards Associated with H.323

In addition to the network implementation standards noted above, there are other standards that fall within the umbrella of the H.323 recommendation. These include:

◆ **H.225.0:** Terminal to Gatekeeper signaling functions, as defined in Reference [6-9].

◆ **H.245:** Terminal control functions that are used to negotiate channel usage, capabilities, and other functions, as defined in Reference [6-10].

◆ **Q.931:** Call signaling functions to establish and terminate the call, as defined in Reference [6-11].

◆ **T.120:** Data conferencing, which might include shared whiteboarding and still image transfer applications, as defined in Reference [6-12].

6.1.2 H.323 Terms and Definitions

Before delving into the H.323 standard in greater detail, a few terms, as defined in that standard, should be mentioned:

◆ **Call:** A point-to-point multimedia communication between two H.323 endpoints, which begins with the call setup procedure and ends with the call termination procedure.

◆ **Endpoint:** An H.323 terminal, Gateway (GW), Gatekeeper (GK), or Multipoint Control Unit (MCU). The endpoint can call and be called, and generates and/or terminates streams of information.

◆ **Gatekeeper (GK):** An entity on the LAN that provides address translation and controls access to the LAN for other devices, such as terminals, Gateways, and MCUs.

◆ **Gateway (GW):** An endpoint on the LAN that provides real-time, two-way communications between H.323 terminals on the LAN and other ITU terminals on a WAN, or to another H.323 Gateway.

◆ **H.323 Entity:** Any H.323 component, which includes terminals, Gateways, Gatekeepers, Multipoint Controllers (MCs), Multipoint Processors (MPs), and Multipoint Control Units (MCUs).

◆ **Multipoint Control Unit (MCU):** An endpoint on the LAN that provides the capability for three or more terminals and Gateways to participate in a multipoint conference. The MCU includes a mandatory MC and optional MPs.

◆ **Multipoint Controller (MC):** An entity on the LAN that provides for the control of three or more terminals participating in a multipoint conference.

◆ **Multipoint Processor (MP):** An H.323 entity on the LAN that provides for the centralized processing of audio, video, and/or data streams in a multipoint conference.

◆ **Terminal (Tx):** An endpoint on the LAN that provides for real-time, two-way communications with another H.323 terminal, Gateway, or Multipoint Control Unit.

◆ **Zone:** A collection of all terminals, Gateways, and Multipoint Control Units managed by a single Gatekeeper.

6.1.3 H.323 Components

The various building blocks that comprise a typical H.323 network are illustrated in Figure 6-3. Note that the building blocks imply that each of these functions is in a distinct box. However, one physical box often contains more than one functional element. For example, both MCU and Gatekeeper functions could be located in the same physical device. A typical H.323 environment might include Gateways to other networks, such as the PSTN or ISDN, as shown in Figure 6-4. Chapter 7 delves into the architectures of terminals, Gateways, Gatekeepers, and other components in greater detail. For the moment, I will restrict the discussion of these components to the larger scale, functional perspective, as defined in Section 6.1.2.

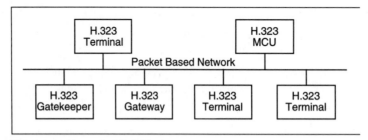

Figure 6–3: H.323 Building Blocks

(Source: ITU-T Recommendation H.323)

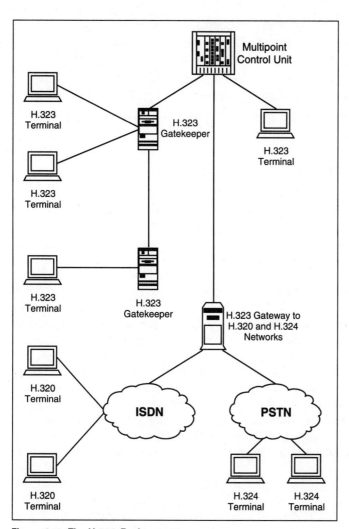

Figure 6–4: The H.323 Environment

Multimedia networks must support a number of different end-user applications; therefore, H.323 must support different streams of information. These are:

◆ **Audio:** Digitized and coded speech signals. The audio signal is accompanied by an audio control signal.

◆ **Video:** Digitized and coded motion video. The video signal is accompanied by a video control signal.

◆ **Data:** Still pictures, facsimile, computer files, and so on.

◆ **Communications Control:** Information that passes control data between like functional elements (such as terminal-to-terminal control) to exchange capabilities between these devices, to open and close logical channels, to control transmission modes, and to perform other functions.

◆ **Call Control:** Information that includes call establishment and call disconnect functions.

6.1.4 H.323 Signaling

Call signaling is defined in H.323 environments to establish a call, to request changes in the bandwidth of that call, to determine the status of endpoints associated with the call, and to terminate or disconnect the call. The call signaling messages are specified in H.225.0, noted earlier in the chapter. H.323 entities are identified using two levels of addressing structures, a Network address and a TSAP identifier. The Network address is a unique identifier for that entity on the network and is specific to that network environment in which the entity resides. For the case of IP-based networks, the Network address would be the IP address assigned to the device. The TSAP identifier is used to multiplex several Transport Layer connections into an entity that has a single Network address. (The term TSAP comes from the Transport Service Access Point — an addressing scheme used at the OSI Transport Layer and defined as part of the Open Systems Interconnection Reference Model.) For IP applications, the TSAP could be the UDP or TCP port number. H.225.0, Appendix IV, defines the transmission of H.225.0 messages over various transport protocol stacks, including UDP/IP and TCP/IP, and gives examples of addresses to be used. For example, [224.0.1.41] is the UDP Address and 1718 is the UDP port for multicast communication with Gatekeepers. We will discuss other specific addresses as they arise in examples and case studies.

Recall from the definitions in Section 6.1.2 that the Gatekeeper is the device that controls access to the network. When endpoints are initialized on networks that contain a Gatekeeper, they register their presence with that Gatekeeper. The logical channel that is used to carry that type of communication between endpoints and Gatekeepers is called the Registration, Admissions, and Status channel, or simply RAS for short. The RAS channel is known as an unreliable channel, meaning that for IP-based networks it would use IP/UDP (the more efficient connectionless transport) instead of the more rigorous TCP/IP transport (called a reliable channel).

Since it is possible for multiple Gatekeepers to exist on a network, each endpoint uses a process known as Gatekeeper Discovery, which may operate either manually or automatically, to determine which of the Gatekeepers to register with. The manual process provides a static association, such as from a configuration file. The automatic process is called Auto Discovery and is illustrated in Figure 6-5. (The type of illustration displayed in Figure 6-5, and several subsequent figures, is called a *ladder diagram*, which shows the protocol interactions between two (or more) devices. The time sequence goes down the page, with earlier events at the top of the ladder and later events at the bottom of the ladder. The protocol interactions between devices are shown as the rungs of the ladder.)

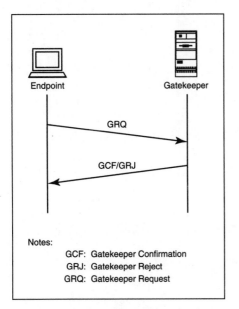

Figure 6–5: H.323 Auto Discovery Process

(Source: ITU-T Recommendation H.323)

In the case of Auto Discovery, the endpoint (such as an H.323 terminal) multicasts a Gatekeeper Request (GRQ) message asking, "Who is my Gatekeeper?" Gatekeepers willing to provide that function respond with a Gatekeeper Confirmation (GCF) message, which contains the transport address of the Gatekeeper's RAS channel. Gatekeepers unwilling to serve in that capacity return a Gatekeeper Reject (GRJ) message. When more than one Gatekeeper indicates a willingness to serve, the endpoint chooses one of the Gatekeepers that has provided a positive response.

Endpoints must register with the Gatekeeper prior to attempting any calls and at other significant times, such as a cold start, to provide that Gatekeeper with the address(es) being used by the endpoint. This process, known as Endpoint Registration, is shown in Figure 6-6. The endpoint sends a Registration Request (RRQ) message to the Gatekeeper's RAS Channel Transport Address. The Gatekeeper responds with either a Registration Confirmation (RCF) or a Registration Reject (RRJ) message. Endpoint registrations are cancelled by sending an Unregister Request (URQ) to the other entity, with either an Unregister Confirmation (UCF) or an Unregister Reject (URJ) returned as appropriate (see Figure 6-6).

Several other messages can be exchanged between the endpoint and the Gatekeeper. The Location Request (LRQ) can be initiated by either device to determine the contact information, including the Call Signaling Channel and RAS Channel addresses (Figure 6-7).

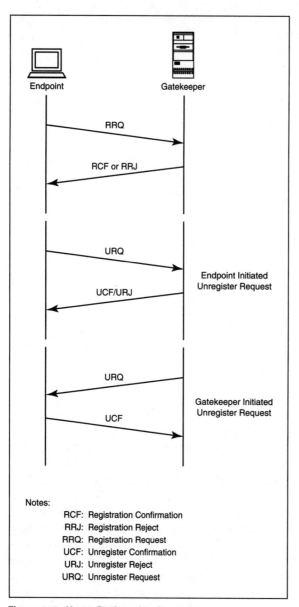

Figure 6–6: H.323 Registration Processes

(Source: ITU-T Recommendation H.323)

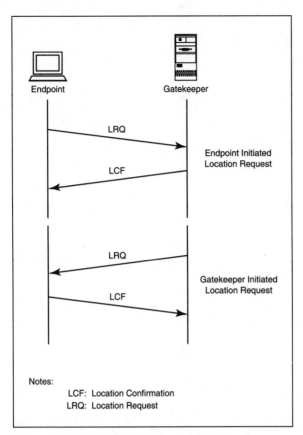

Figure 6-7: H.323 Location Information Processes

The RAS channel can also be used to transmit Admissions, Bandwidth Change, Status, and Disengage messages. The Admissions Request (ARQ) specifies the bandwidth the endpoint is requesting for the call, which may be reduced by the Gatekeeper in the Admissions Confirm (ACF) message. If the Gatekeeper denies admission, an Admissions Reject (ARJ) is returned. Either entity may attempt to modify the call bandwidth during the call using the Bandwidth Change Request (BRQ) message, with a corresponding Bandwidth Change Confirm (BCF) or Bandwidth Change Reject (BRJ) returned as appropriate (Figure 6-8).

Once the endpoint has been admitted to the network, a call can be initiated using the call signaling messages. For networks that do not contain a Gatekeeper, such as an IP phone–to–IP phone connection, the signaling messages are passed between the two endpoints directly (Figure 6-9).

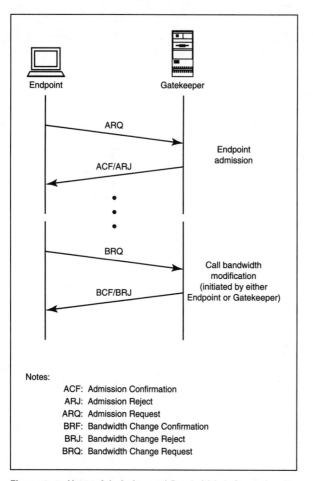

Figure 6–8: H.323 Admission and Bandwidth Information Processes

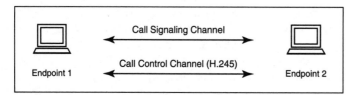

Figure 6–9: H.323 Call Signaling without Gatekeeper

For networks that contain a Gatekeeper, the endpoint first requests admission to the network. In the Admission Confirm message, the Gatekeeper indicates whether to route that call information via the Gatekeeper or to send the call signaling directly to the distant endpoint. If the Gatekeeper is involved in the call signaling, the process is known as Gatekeeper Routed Call Signaling, as shown in Figure 6-10. Note that for this case, both the RAS and the call signaling messages flow between the endpoints and the Gatekeeper. For the case of the Gatekeeper Routed Call Signaling, the H.245 control messages that flow between the two endpoints may be routed via the Gatekeeper or sent directly between the endpoints. For simplicity, these H.245 messages are not shown in Figure 6-10.

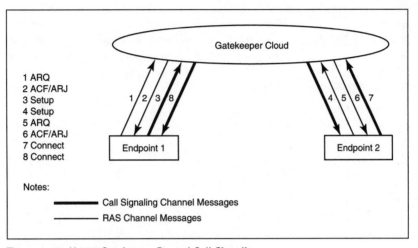

Figure 6-10: H.323 Gatekeeper Routed Call Signaling

(Source: ITU-T Recommendation H.323)

In the second case, known as Direct Endpoint Call Signaling (Figure 6-11), the RAS messages flow between the endpoints and the Gatekeeper, while the signaling messages flow between the endpoints directly. The Gatekeeper determines which method, Routed or Direct, will be employed.

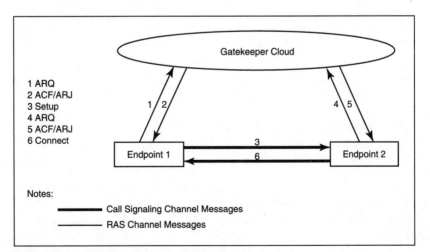

Figure 6-11: H.323 Direct Endpoint Call Signaling

(Source: ITU-T Recommendation H.323)

Now that we have laid the groundwork for the endpoints to be admitted to the network using RAS (if, of course, a Gatekeeper is in use) and have described additional requirements for the call signaling messages that are subsequently sent, it's time to take a look at the complete operation.

The simplest procedure is where no Gatekeepers are in use and the two endpoints send signaling information directly to each other (Figure 6-12). The calling endpoint (Endpoint 1 in this case) sends a Setup message to the well-known Call Signaling Channel TSAP address of the called endpoint (Endpoint 2 in this case). The Connect message from Endpoint 2 would include with the response a Call Proceeding message that would contain the H.245 Control Channel Transport address for use with H.245 control messages.

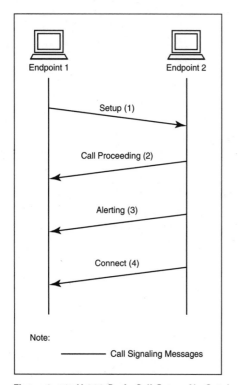

Figure 6-12: H.323 Basic Call Setup, No Gatekeepers

(Source: ITU-T Recommendation H.323)

When both of the endpoints are registered with the same Gatekeeper, and that Gatekeeper has chosen the Direct Call Signaling method (review Figure 6-11), the process begins with the calling endpoint (Endpoint 1 in this case) requesting admission from the Gatekeeper (Figure 6-13). After admission, Endpoint 1 then sends a Setup message to Endpoint 2. If Endpoint 2 wishes to accept the call, it returns a Call Proceeding message and requests admission from the Gatekeeper. If an

Admission Reject (ARJ) message is returned from the Gatekeeper, Endpoint 2 would return a Release Complete message to Endpoint 1 (not shown in Figure 6-13). If a positive response (ACF) is received from the Gatekeeper, Endpoint 2 sends Alerting and Connect messages to Endpoint 1, with the H.245 Control Channel Transport address contained within the Connect message.

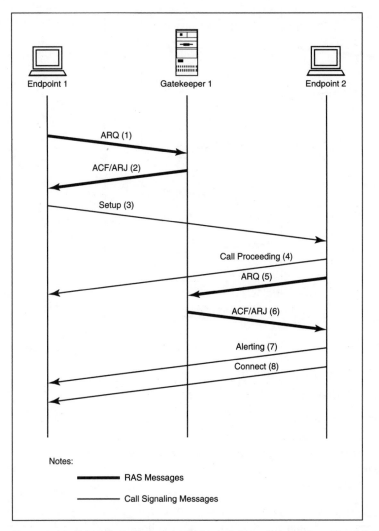

Endpoint 1   Gatekeeper 1   Endpoint 2

ARQ (1)

ACF/ARJ (2)

Setup (3)

Call Proceeding (4)

ARQ (5)

ACF/ARJ (6)

Alerting (7)

Connect (8)

Notes:

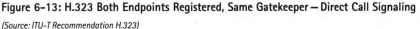 RAS Messages

——— Call Signaling Messages

Figure 6-13: H.323 Both Endpoints Registered, Same Gatekeeper — Direct Call Signaling

(Source: ITU-T Recommendation H.323)

When Gatekeeper Routed Call Signaling is deployed (review Figure 6-10), the process is very similar except that the signaling messages (Setup, Call Proceeding, and so on) are passed through the Gatekeeper in a two-step process (Figure 6-14).

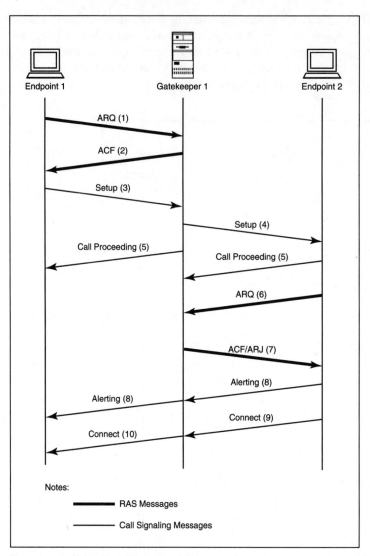

Figure 6–14: H.323 Both Endpoints Registered, Same Gatekeeper — Gatekeeper Routed Call Signaling

(Source: ITU-T Recommendation H.323)

As a final example, consider the case where both endpoints are registered with different Gatekeepers, and both of these Gatekeepers deploy Direct Call Signaling (Figure 6-15). In this case, Endpoint 1 initiates the call by requesting admission to the network from Gatekeeper 1, and, upon admission, transmits a Setup message to Endpoint 2. This Setup message is sent to the well-known Call Signaling Transport address of Endpoint 2, or the Call Signaling Transport address (specific to Endpoint 2) if that specific address was returned by Gatekeeper 1 in the ACF response. If Endpoint 2 wishes to accept the call, it requests admission to the network from Gatekeeper 2 and subsequently sends a Connect message that contains an H.245 Control Channel Transport address to be used with the H.245 signaling functions.

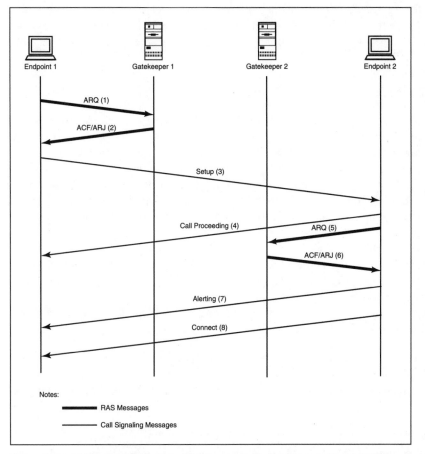

Figure 6-15: H.323 Both Endpoints Registered — Both Gatekeepers Direct Call Signaling

(Source: ITU-T Recommendation H.323)

For those readers wanting further study, many other network topology permutations and associated call scenarios are described in H.323. In addition, References [6-13] through [6-15] provide tutorial information on H.323 architecture and protocol procedures. The H.323 Forum Web site is another good resource (Reference [6-16]). The next section considers an IETF-developed alternative to H.323, known as the Session Initiation Protocol, or SIP.

6.2 Session Initiation Protocol

The second VoIP signaling protocol this chapter studies is the Session Initiation Protocol, or SIP, which has been developed by the IETF and documented in RFC 2543 (Reference [6-17]). SIP is an Application Layer control protocol used to create, modify, and terminate sessions between participants. These sessions could take on many forms, including multimedia conferences, Internet telephony, media distribution, and others. SIP has been developed using many of the constructs that are found in other IETF-developed protocols, including the Simple Mail Transfer Procotol (SMTP) for electronic messaging and the Hypertext Transfer Protocol (HTTP) for Web pages.

Much of this similarity is found in the architecture of SIP, which is based on a straightforward client-server model, much like what is found in other systems and protocols, like Web browsers (or clients) and Web servers. In addition, SIP is part of the IETF's multimedia architecture, which includes many of the protocols that were discussed in Chapter 4, including RTP, RTSP, SAP, and SDP. In contrast to H.323 — which is, as discussed in the previous section, really an umbrella for a number of standards (H.225.0, H.245, and so on) — SIP is based on IP and IP-derived technologies, such as IP addressing schemes, URLs, and so on. As a result, many feel that SIP is much simpler to implement and is therefore advantageous for certain applications. An excellent comparison between these two signaling protocols is found in Reference [6-18]. Other good resources are the industry group known as the SIP Forum and the vendor-sponsored SIP Center (Reference [6-19]), which chronicle various industry conferences, interoperability testing events, and other functions in support of SIP development and deployment.

The discussion of SIP begins by considering some of the key terms and definitions found in RFC 2543.

6.2.1 SIP Terms and Definitions

RFC 2543 defines a number of terms related to the functions of SIP. Following are some of the most important:

- ◆ **Call:** A call consists of all participants in a conference invited by a common source. The SIP call is identified by a globally unique call ID.

- ◆ **Conference:** A multimedia session that is identified by a common session description. A conference may take on many different forms, including a multicast conference, a full-mesh conference, or a two-party telephone call or connection.

◆ **Initiator, calling party, or caller:** The party initiating a conference invitation, which may or may not be the same as the one creating the conference.

◆ **Invitation:** A request sent to a user (or service) requesting participation in a session. A successful SIP invitation consists of two transactions: an INVITE request followed by an ACK request.

◆ **Invitee, invited user, called party, or callee:** The person or service that the calling party is trying to invite to a conference.

◆ **Location server:** A service used by a SIP Redirect or Proxy server to obtain information regarding a callee's possible location(s). Location servers may be co-located with a SIP server.

◆ **Proxy or proxy server:** An intermediary program that acts as both a server and a client for the purpose of making requests on behalf of other clients.

◆ **Redirect server:** A server that accepts a SIP request, maps the address into zero or more new addresses, and returns these addresses to the client.

◆ **Registrar:** A server that accepts REGISTER requests.

◆ **Server:** An application program that accepts requests in order to service those requests and sends back responses to those requests. Servers are proxy, redirect, user agent, or registrar servers.

◆ **Session:** A multimedia session is a set of multimedia senders and receivers and the data streams flowing from senders to receivers.

◆ **Transaction:** A SIP transaction occurs between a client and a server and comprises all messages from the first request sent from the client to the server up to a final response sent from the server to the client.

◆ **User agent client (UAC) or calling user agent:** A client application that initiates the SIP request.

◆ **User agent server (UAS) or called user agent:** A server application that contacts the user when a SIP request is received and returns a response on behalf of the user.

◆ **User agent (UA):** An application that contains both a user agent client and a user agent server.

The next section looks at how these various terms and definitions are realized within a SIP architecture.

6.2.2 SIP Components and Messages

There are two key components in a SIP-based network, User Agents and Servers, which yield a straightforward, simplistic operation. The SIP User Agents contain a User Agent Client (UAC) and a User Agent Server (UAS), as shown in Figure 6-16a. The UAC function initiates the SIP requests, while the UAS function contacts the user when a request is received and returns a response on behalf of that user. The response may be an acceptance, a rejection, or a redirection of the request.

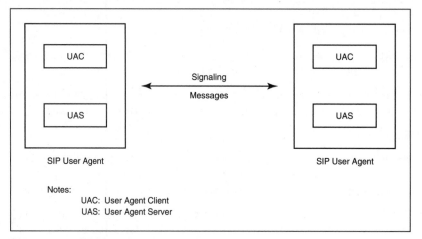

Figure 6–16a: SIP Agent Communication

A SIP server may also be deployed to perform specific functions within the network (Figure 6-16b). A Proxy server makes requests on behalf of other clients and possibly translates a message, as necessary, before forwarding. A Redirect server accepts a SIP request, maps the address into another address, and then returns the new address to the Client. The Registrar server accepts REGISTER requests and may be co-located with the Proxy or Redirect servers. Finally, the Location server provides a service to the Proxy or Redirect servers by obtaining information regarding the callee's possible location. Location servers may also be co-located with another SIP server. Another architectural view of a SIP environment, which shows call agents and many of the servers, is shown in Figure 6-17. (We will return to the numbered sequence shown in Figure 6-17 later in this section.)

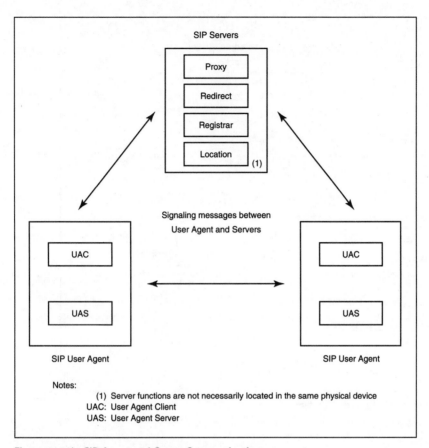

Figure 6-16b: SIP Agent and Server Communication

SIP components are identified with a SIP Uniform Resource Locator, or URL, which takes a form similar to that used with e-mail systems, such as *user@host*. The *user* part could consist of a user name or telephone number, while the *host* part could consist of a domain name or a numeric network address. Thus, brutus@ diginet.com, 3035551212@diginet.com, brutus@10.3.12.91, and 3035551212@ 10.10.31.1 are all possible examples of SIP addresses.

A SIP message can either be a *request* from a client to a server, or a *response* from a server to a client. The request message defines the operation requested by the client, while the response message provides information from the server to the client indicating the status of that request.

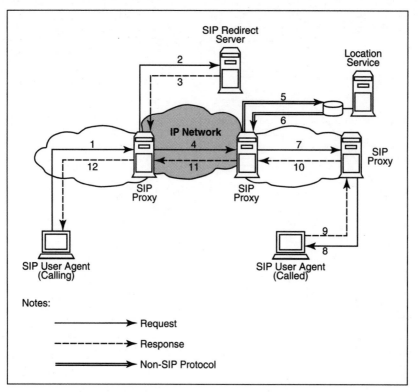

Figure 6-17: SIP Network Architecture

(Courtesy of RADVISION, Inc.)

There are six types of request messages, distinguished by what is called a *method*:

- ◆ **INVITE:** Indicates that the user or service is being invited to participate in a session. The body of this message would include a description of the session to which the callee is being invited.

- ◆ **ACK:** Confirms that the client has received a final response to an INVITE request, and is only used with INVITE requests.

- ◆ **OPTIONS:** Is used to query a server about its capabilities.

- ◆ **BYE:** Is sent by a User Agent Client to indicate to the server that it wishes to release the call.

- ◆ **CANCEL:** Is used to cancel a pending request.

- ◆ **REGISTER:** Is used by a client to register an address with a SIP server.

The response messages contain Status Codes and Reason Phrases that indicate the current condition of a request. The Status Code values are divided into six general categories:

- ◆ **1xx: Informational** – The request has been received and processing is continuing.

- ◆ **2xx: Success** – An ACK, which indicates that the action was successfully received, understood, and accepted.

- ◆ **3xx: Redirection** – Further action is required to process this request.

- ◆ **4xx: Client Error** – The request contains bad syntax and cannot be fulfilled at this server.

- ◆ **5xx: Server Error** – The server failed (for internal reasons) to fulfill an apparently valid request.

- ◆ **6xx: Global Failure** – The request cannot be fulfilled at any server.

Specific details on the SIP message formats, Status Codes, and other parameters are specified in RFC 2543.

6.2.3 SIP Signaling

As the previous sections have indicated, SIP is not as complex as H.323 (for example, SIP does not use Gatekeepers). As a result, the signaling processes are also less complex. A simple case of a SIP session between two user agents is illustrated in Figure 6-18. This process begins with the calling user agent sending an INVITE message to the called user agent. Included with that INVITE are parameters that indicate the calling party address, a description of the session, typically using the Session Description Protocol (SDP), and a call identifier. The called user agent responds with an OK message (Response Code = 200), which is followed by an ACK from the calling user agent as the final step in the call setup process. The two agents then exchange the audio and/or video information, and, when finished, one of the agents sends the BYE message to indicate that it wishes to release the call. An OK message response is returned, and then the call termination is complete.

RFC 2543 details a SIP connection when a Proxy server is required to complete the connection (Figure 6-19). The Proxy server accepts the INVITE request and queries the Location server for more complete addressing information. When this addressing information is returned, the Proxy server issues an INVITE to the address(es) returned from the Location server, which triggers the called user agent to indicate an incoming call (ringing). The called user agent accepts the call with a SIP Response Code of 200 (OK message), which is passed via the Proxy server to the calling user agent. The calling user agent returns an ACK message which, in turn, is passed via the Proxy server to the called user agent, thus completing the call setup.

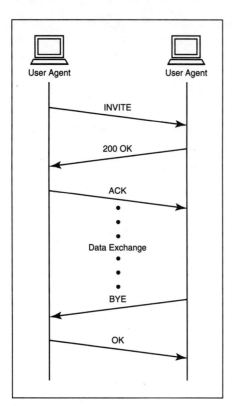

Figure 6-18: SIP Call Signaling

The Proxy server was able to identify the called user agent because it had registered its location with the Registrar server (Figure 6-20). Recall from the earlier definitions that the Registrar server accepts REGISTER requests, is typically co-located with a Proxy or Redirect server, and may also offer Location server functions.

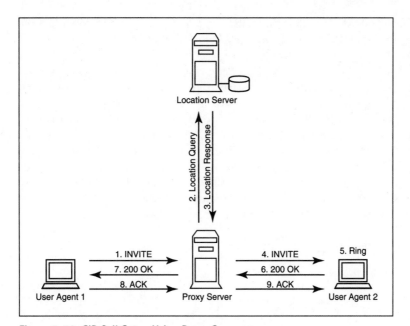

Figure 6-19: SIP Call Setup Using Proxy Server

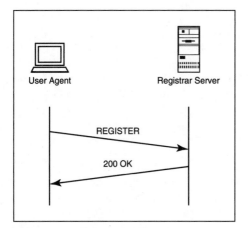

Figure 6-20: SIP Registration

RFC 2543 also details the procedures used when the end user must be located and a Redirect server employed (Figure 6-21). In this case, the called user agent sends the INVITE message to the Redirect server, which consults with the Location server for complete address information, as before. However, in this case, the called user agent has moved, which is indicated with the SIP Response Code of 302 (Moved temporarily). This information is ACK'd to the Redirect server, and then a second INVITE message, this time to the appropriate address of the called user agent, is issued. The INVITE causes the called user agent to ring and then return a SIP Response Code of 200 (OK message), which is then ACK'd by the calling user agent.

Now that you've read about all of the SIP server functions, review Figure 6-17 and consider a scenario in which multiple servers are involved in a call. Note that the calling user agent call request is passed from one Proxy server to a Redirect server (Steps 1–3), through the network (Step 4) to another Proxy server, which accesses the Location service using a non-SIP protocol (Steps 5–6). A second Proxy server is accessed, which reaches the called user agent (Steps 7–8). The called user agent returns the call acceptance message in the opposite direction (Steps 9–12).

As was the case with H.323, more scenarios could be drawn, including support for mobile user agents. The interested reader should refer to RFC 2543 for details, or to References [6-20] through [6-25] for additional discussion. The next section of the chapter considers protocols that are used for signaling between gateways.

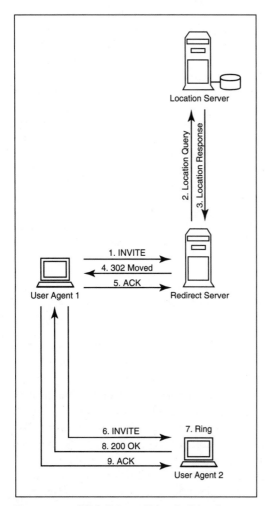

Figure 6–21: SIP Call Setup Using Redirect Server

6.3 Gateway Control Protocols: MGCP and MEGACO/H.248

Thus far, this chapter has considered signaling protocols, H.323 and SIP, that are primarily deployed to control end stations, such as multimedia terminals or video-conferencing systems. These protocols may be resident within the applications or operating systems of these end stations, enabling the end stations to initiate, control, and terminate a call. However, when dissimilar networks are involved in the communication path, such as a workstation attached to an IP network calling an analog telephone connected to the PSTN, gateways between those networks must get involved. A second category of signaling protocols is thus required between the telephony gateways to control their operation and establish paths between those dissimilar networking environments.

A model for communication between gateways has been developed by the European Telecommunications Standards Institute (ETSI), with a research initiative known as the TIPHON project, which stands for Telecommunications and Internet Protocol Harmonization Over Networks [6-26]. The objective of the project is to support worldwide voice communication and to ensure that users connected to IP networks will be able to communicate with those on switched circuit networks (SCNs), such as the PSTN or ISDN environments. ETSI is a European-based organization; however, it cooperates with the ITU-T, the IETF, and various trade organizations in an effort to produce standards that are applicable on a global basis. The TIPHON project is quite broad and covers a number of telecommunications activities, including network architectures, call control procedures and protocols, addressing, service interoperability, and quality of service.

The gateway model developed by ETSI divides the functions of a gateway into three key elements: a Signaling Gateway (SG), a Media Gateway (MG), and a Media Gateway Controller (MGC), as shown in Figure 6-22 and documented in Reference [6-27]. (As an aside, the ITU-T has developed a similar gateway model that is documented in H.323, Section 6.3.1.) Note that, to the outside world, these three elements appear as a single gateway. When implemented, however, they may be distinct, and may also be provided and/or administered by different organizations, such as carriers and enterprise network equipment vendors, thus realizing a distributed gateway architecture. The SG mediates the signaling functions between the IP network and the SCN. For example, it may provide correlation between the H.323 signaling on the packet network side and the SS7 signaling on the PSTN side. The MG mediates the media signals between the IP network and the SCN. For example, it may convert information transported on the IP network using RTP/UDP/IP packet formats to PCM encoded voice on the PSTN side. Finally, the MGC communicates with both the SG and the MG, providing the call processing functions required. The MGC uses either the MGCP or the MEGACO/H.248 protocols for these intergateway communication functions.

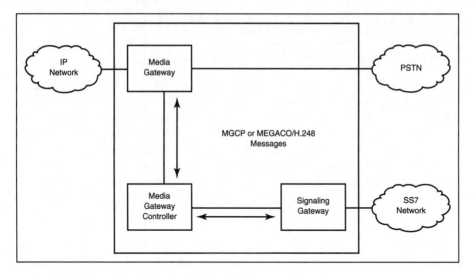

Figure 6-22: Decomposed Gateway Architecture

We start our discussion with MGCP, which was developed first.

6.3.1 MGCP

The Media Gateway Control Protocol (MGCP) was developed by the IETF and is documented in RFC 2705 [6-28]. The MGCP specification details the commands and parameters that are passed between the MGC (also referred to as the Call Agent) and the telephony gateway to be controlled. Examples of gateways that are noted in RFC 2705 that could be controlled using MGCP include:

◆ **Trunking gateways** that interface between a telephone network and a VoIP network, and that typically manage a large number of digital circuits.

◆ **Voice over ATM gateways** that interface to ATM networks.

◆ **Residential gateways** that provide a traditional analog (RJ11) connection to the network, such as cable modems and xDSL devices.

◆ **Access gateways** that provide a traditional analog (RJ11) or digital PBX interface to a VoIP network.

◆ **Business gateways** that provide a traditional digital PBX or software-based PBX interface to a VoIP network.

◆ **Network access servers** that provide data access to the Internet.

◆ **Circuit or packet switches** that offer a control interface to an external call control element.

The call control element (or MGC in TIPHON terms) is referred to as a Call Agent in MGCP. Thus, the purpose of MGCP is to send commands from the Call Agent to one of the above types of gateways in a master/slave fashion. MGCP does not define any communication mechanism for synchronization between Call Agents. MGCP further assumes a connection model and defines both endpoints and connections.

Endpoints are sources or sinks of data and can be either physical (such as an interface terminating a digital trunk or analog line) or virtual (such as a designated audio source). Endpoint identifiers have two components: the domain name of the gateway that is managing the endpoint, and a local name within that gateway.

Connections can be either point-to-point or multipoint in nature. Further, connections are grouped into calls, where one or more connections can belong to one call. The connections and calls are established by the actions of one or more Call Agents.

The information communicated between Call Agents and endpoints is either *events* or *signals*. An example of an event would be a telephone going off hook, while a signal may be the application of dial tone to an endpoint. These events and signals are grouped into what are called *packages*, which are supported by a particular type of endpoint. As illustrated in RFC 2705, one package may support events and signals for analog lines, while another package may support a group of events and signals for video lines. Further, RFC 2705 defines ten of these packages: generic media, DTMF, MF, Trunk, Line, Handset, RTP, Network Access Server, Announcement Server, and Script. Each of these has specific functions and parameters.

Communication between Call Agents and gateways uses MGCP commands, which are transmitted using UDP. There are nine defined MGCP commands, which are constructed using a command verb followed by a set of parameter lines. The commands are the following:

- ◆ **EndpointConfiguration (EPCF):** Instructs the gateway about the coding characteristics expected by the line-side of the endpoint (sent from Call Agent to gateway).

- ◆ **NotificationRequest (RQNT):** Instructs the gateway to watch for specific events such as hook actions or DTMF tones on a specified endpoint (sent from Call Agent to gateway).

- ◆ **Notify (NTFY):** The gateway informs the Call Agent when the requested events occur (sent from gateway to Call Agent).

- ◆ **CreateConnection (CRCX):** Creates a connection that terminates in an endpoint inside the gateway (sent from Call Agent to gateway).

- ◆ **ModifyConnection (MDCX):** Changes the parameters associated with a previously established connection (sent from Call Agent to gateway).

- ◆ **DeleteConnection (DLCX):** Deletes an existing connection or indicates that a connection can no longer be sustained (sent from Call Agent to gateway).

- ◆ **AuditEndpoint (AUEP):** Queries the status of a particular endpoint (sent from Call Agent to gateway).

- ◆ **AuditConnection (AUCX):** Queries the status of a particular connection (sent from Call Agent to gateway).

- ◆ **RestartInProgress (RSIP):** The gateway notifies the Call Agent that the gateway is being taken out of service or is being placed back into service (sent from gateway to Call Agent).

Many parameters may be associated with each of these commands and are detailed in RFC 2705. Further information regarding MGCP operation can be found in References [6-29] and [6-30]. MGCP is currently maintained by the PacketCable initiative [6-31] and Softswitch Consortium [6-32], although no international standards bodies have indicated plans for enhancement or adoption.

6.3.2 MEGACO/H.248

The MEGACO/H.248 protocol was jointly developed by the IETF and the ITU-T, and therefore has a double name: MEGACO, the IETF designation, is documented in RFC 3015 (Reference [6-33]), and Recommendation H.248, the ITU-T designation, is documented in Reference [6-34]. The text for these two documents is identical; therefore, this discussion will use the simplified name of MEGACO going forward. It should be noted that developments of MGCP and MEGACO crossed paths, but the two resulting protocols are not compatible. MEGACO is based on the same type of distributed gateway architecture (defined by TIPHON) as MGCP; however, there are key differences in the protocol. The first difference is in the abstractions used in the connection model. In MGCP, the commands apply to the connections. In MEGACO, the commands apply to *Terminations* that are related to a *Context*, as shown in Figure 6-23, taken from RFC 3015. A Termination sources and/or sinks one or more streams of information; for multimedia conferences, the Termination could also be multimedia and source and/or sink multiple media streams. A Context is an association between a number of Terminations. The Context describes the topology and the media mixing for the cases where more than two Terminations are involved with this association. Contexts are modified using the Add, Subtract, and Modify commands, described next, with a connection created when two or more Terminations are placed in a common Context.

The packages defined with MEGACO specify the characteristics of the Termination. With MEGACO, *properties* and *statistics* are descriptors that are added to the *events* and *signals* that were found in MGCP. In addition, Annex E of RFC 3015 defines different packages from those found with MGCP: Generic, Base Root, Tone Generator, Tone Detection, Basic DTMF Generator, DTMF Detection, Call Progress Tones Generator, Call Progress Tones Detection, Analog Line Supervision, Basic Continuity, Network, RTP, and TDM Circuit.

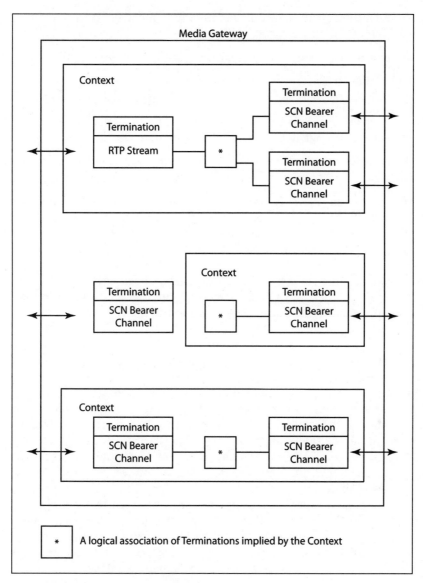

Figure 6-23: MEGACO Connection Model

There are eight MEGACO commands:

◆ **Add:** Adds a Termination to a Context. The Add command on the first Termination in a Context is used to create a Context.

◆ **Modify:** Modifies the properties, events, and signals of a Termination.

◆ **Subtract:** Disconnects a Termination from its Context and returns statistics on the Termination's participation in the Context.

◆ **Move:** Atomically moves a Termination to another Context.

◆ **AuditValue:** Returns the current state of properties, events, signals, and statistics of Terminations.

◆ **AuditCapabilities:** Returns all the possible values for Termination properties, events, and signals allowed by the Media Gateway.

◆ **Notify:** Allows the Media Gateway to inform the Media Gateway Controller of the occurrence of events in the Media Gateway.

◆ **ServiceChange:** Allows the Media Gateway to notify the Media Gateway Controller that a Termination or group of Terminations is about to be taken out of service, or has just been returned to service. A number of ServiceChangeReasons have been defined, which provide further details.

In addition to the differences in the above commands, the transport mechanisms for the two protocols differ. MGCP is defined for UDP/IP transport, and MEGACO is independent of the underlying transport, supporting UDP/IP, TCP/IP, or ATM.

Given its position as a member of the ITU-T standards family, MEGACO/H.248 is referenced in other ITU-T standards, including the H.323 standard, Section 6.3.2. The relationship between H.323 and H.248 is illustrated in Figure 6-24. Note that the Media Gateway Controller is shown at the top of the figure, with connections running H.248 to the access and trunking gateways. The various gateways connect to an RTP/IP-based network on one side and other types of networks on the other side. The connections to the other networks may use different protocols and signaling methods, including channel associated signaling (CAS), ISDN user part (ISUP), and Inter-machine trunks (IMTs). In addition, the H.248 Media Gateway Controller and an H.323 Gatekeeper are illustrated as being co-located, with an interface defined by H.246 Annex C in between.

At the time of this writing, no industry consensus has been reached regarding which standard, MGCP or MEGACO, will receive the most widespread support. MGCP appears to have the greatest industry backing; however, MEGACO has the support of an international standards body, the ITU-T. References [6-35] and [6-36] provide additional information on MEGACO, including functional comparisons between MEGACO and MGCP.

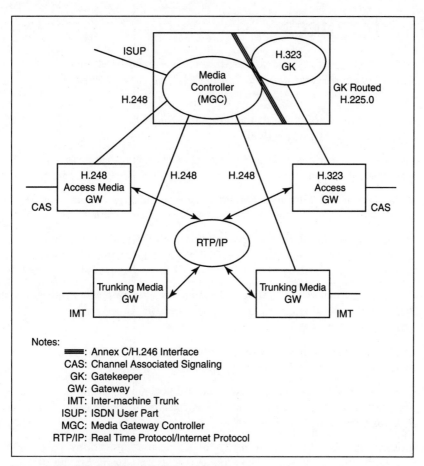

Figure 6–24: Relationship of H.323 and H.248

(Source: ITU-T Recommendation H.323)

6.4 Looking Ahead

This chapter considered the signaling standards that are used to establish the communication channels between converged network endpoints. The next chapter considers these endpoints in greater detail and examines client terminals, gateways, gatekeepers, and the other components that make up the converged network infrastructure.

6.5 References

[6-1] International Telecommunications Union – Telecommunications Standardization Sector. *Introduction to CCITT Signaling System 7.* Recommendation Q.700, March 1993.

[6-2] American National Standards Institute. *Signaling System 7, General Information.* ANSI T1.110, 1999.

[6-3] NMS Communications. *SS7 and Intelligent Networking Applications,* May 2001. White paper available at `www.nmscommunications.com`.

[6-4] Munch, Bjarne. *IP Telephony Signaling,* August 1999. White paper available at `www.ericsson.com/datacom/emedia/ip_telephony.pdf`.

[6-5] Elachi, Joanna. *Standards Snapshot: The State of the Big 3 in VoIP Signaling Protocols,* November 27, 2000. White paper available at `www.commweb.com/article/printableArticle?doc_id=COM20001127S0008`

[6-6] Percy, Alan. *Brooktrout TR Series IP Telephony Inter-Gateway Protocols.* White paper available at `www.brooktrout.com/whitepapers/html_pages/iptel_protocol.html`.

[6-7] Galitizine, Greg. "Pulling Together – Interoperability Through Open Standards." *Internet Telephony* (October 2000): 62–66.

[6-8] International Telecommunications Union – Telecommunications Standardization Sector. *Packet-based Multimedia Communications Systems.* Recommendation H.323, 2000.

[6-9] International Telecommunications Union – Telecommunications Standardization Sector. *Call Signaling Protocols and Media Stream Packetization for Packet-based Multimedia Communication Systems.* Recommendation H.225.0, 2000.

[6-10] International Telecommunications Union – Telecommunications Standardization Sector. *Control Protocol for Multimedia Communication.* Recommendation H.245, 2000.

[6-11] International Telecommunications Union – Telecommunications Standardization Sector. *Digital Subscriber Signaling System No. 1 (DSS 1) – ISDN User-Network Interface Layer 3 Specification for Basic Call Control.* Recommendation Q.931, 1993.

[6-12] International Telecommunications Union – Telecommunications Standardization Sector. *Data Protocols for Multimedia Conferencing.* Recommendation T.120, 1996.

[6-13] Thom, Gary A. "H.323: The Multimedia Communications Standard for Local Area Networks." *IEEE Communications* (December 1996): 52–56.

[6-14] RADVISION, Inc. "What is H.323." White paper available at www.radvision.com/papers/.

[6-15] International Engineering Consortium. "H.323 Web ProForum Tutorial." Available at www.iec.org/online/tutorials/h323.pdf.

[6-16] An excellent source for H.323 information is the H.323 Forum Web site: www.h323forum.org.

[6-17] Handley, M., H. Schulzrinne, et al. *SIP: Session Initiation Protocol.* RFC 2543, March 1999.

[6-18] Nortel Networks, Inc. "A Comparison of H.323v4 and SIP." White paper available at www.cs.columbia.edu/~hgs/sip/drafts/sip_h323v4.doc, January 2000.

[6-19] Excellent sources for SIP information are the SIP Forum Web site: www.sipforum.org, and the vendor-sponsored SIP Center Web site: www.sipcenter.com.

[6-20] Schulzrinne, Henning G., and Jonathan D. Rosenberg. "The Session Initiation Protocol: Providing Advanced Telephony Services Across the Internet." *Bell Labs Technical Journal* (October–December 1998): 144–160. White paper available at www.lucent.com/minds/techjournal/oct-dec1998/pdf/paper09.pdf.

[6-21] Doumas, Thomas. "Next Generation Telephony: A Look at Session Initiation Protocol." White paper available at literature.agilent.com/litweb/pdf/5968-6297.pdf, March 2000.

[6-22] Greenfield, David. "Calling All Carriers." *Network Magazine* (February 2001): 106–110.

[6-23] Zimmerer, Eric. "VoIP Report: SIP Wins the Race." *The ATM & IP Report* (March 2001): 1–3.

[6-24] Michael, Bill. "SIP Ascendant." *Communications Convergence* (June 2001): 28–56.

[6-25] RADVISION, Inc. *What is SIP?* White paper available at www.radvision.com/papers/.

[6-26] Information regarding the European Telecommunications Standards Institute (ETSI) and the TIPHON project can be found at www.etsi.org.

[6-27] European Telecommunications Standards Institute. Telecommunications and Internet Protocol Harmonization over Networks (TIPHON); Network architecture and reference configurations; TIPHON Release 2. Technical Specification ETSI TS 101 314 v1.1.1, September 2000.

[6-28] Arango, M., et al. "Media Gateway Control Protocol (MGCP) Version 1.0." RFC 2705, October 1999.

[6-29] RADVISION, Inc. *Media Gateway Control Protocol (MGCP)*. White paper available at `www.radvision.com/papers/`.

[6-30] Anatel Communications. "MGCP White Paper." White paper available at `www.anatel.net/whitepapers/mgcpwhitepaper2.pdf`.

[6-31] Information on the PacketCable may be obtained at `www.packetcable.com`.

[6-32] The Softswitch Consortium may be reached at `www.softswitch.org`.

[6-33] Cuervo, F., et al. *Megaco Protocol Version 1.0*. RFC 3015, November 2000.

[6-34] International Telecommunications Union – Telecommunications Standardization Sector. *Audiovisual and Multimedia Systems, Infrastructure of Audiovisual Services – Communication Procedures, Gateway Control Protocol*. Recommendation H.248, 2000.

[6-35] RADVISION, Inc. *What is MEGACO/H.248?* White paper available at `www.radvision.com/papers/`.

[6-36] Hughes Software Systems. "Use of MEGACO vis-à-vis MGCP to build a Gateway Solution." White paper available at `www.hssworld.com/whitepapers/whitepaper_pdf/vop2.pdf`.

Chapter 7

Component Systems for Converged Networks

Converged networks are composed of a number of elements and require the implementation of a number of LAN and WAN protocols for operation. Suppose you wish to communicate with a colleague over an IP-based infrastructure. On your end, the communications path includes a Voice over IP client application, a local network that supports IP, and a wide area network that supports IP, such as an ISDN or a T1 line. Likewise, your colleague requires a similar connection on their end. These three elements are discussed in Chapters 2, 4, 5, and 6.

But there is one more element of this network topology that needs to be considered — some additional equipment on the customer's premises that coordinates between the applications, the LAN, and the WAN. Suppose you decide to use your network for an audio/video teleconference. Does sufficient bandwidth exist on the LAN to support this application? What about your existing voice communication systems, such as the Private Branch Exchange (PBX) or your voice mail system? How will the new converged network incorporate these existing systems and allow for legacy investment? What effects will additional traffic have on the WAN circuits?

These issues are addressed by the component systems, typically located at the customer premises, which include gateways, gatekeepers, and interfaces to legacy equipment such as digital PBXs. This chapter studies these converged network-specific devices and considers the next generation of switching systems, both customer premises (PBX) and central office (softswitch) -based. Chapter 8 then considers issues like quality of service, network latency, and interoperability, which are concerns that arise once these component systems are in place.

This discussion begins by examining various converged network environments and their component parts.

7.1 Converged Network Environments

As has been discussed in previous chapters, environments for converged networks contain a number of elements that encompass both local and wide area network infrastructures. The Voice over IP Forum, which is part of the International Multimedia Teleconferencing Consortium (IMTC), has developed an Implementation Agreement (IA) that describes three possible connectivity configurations for converged networks [7-1]. All three of these configurations use some combination of an IP-based network and the PSTN to provide the communication infrastructure required.

In the first configuration, two multimedia-equipped PCs (with microphone and speakers) communicate over an IP network (Figure 7-1). Communication to this IP network could use a number of dial-up or dedicated connections, or a higher-speed connection over a LAN. Two other required elements that are discussed later in this chapter are the H.323 Gatekeeper, which provides network management functions, and a Domain Name Service (DNS) Server, which provides address translation functions.

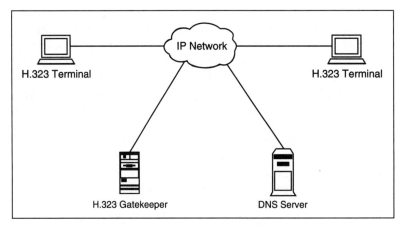

Figure 7-1: Network Elements Used for the PC-to-PC Connection

(Courtesy of the Voice over IP Forum)

The second alternative brings in the PSTN connection (Figure 7-2). In this example, one user accesses the network via a telephone and the PSTN, while another user receives access from an H.323 terminal. This configuration introduces another element into the mix – an H.323 Gateway between the PSTN and the IP network. The operation of this gateway will be discussed in the next section of the chapter. As before, the H.323 Gatekeeper and the DNS Server are also required. Note that since the telephone is assumed to be an audio (not audio/video) device, this configuration would be limited to telephone-like conversations, not multimedia streams as was the case in the previous example.

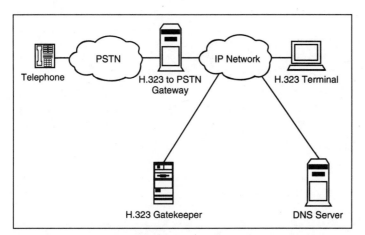

Figure 7-2: Network Elements Used for the PC-to-Phone Connection

(Courtesy of the Voice over IP Forum)

The final scenario deploys two connections to the PSTN and also two gateways (Figure 7-3). In this configuration, two end users can communicate over their standard telephones, with an IP network carrying the traffic between the two PSTN connections. Two analogies can be drawn from this topology. First, this appears to be very similar to the current telephone network in the United States, where the end users connect to Local Exchange Carriers (LECs), and those carriers are interconnected via an Interexchange Carrier (IXC). For example, my offices are located in Colorado. If I want to call a colleague in New Jersey, the local access on my end is through Qwest Communications, and the local access on his end is provided by Verizon. We can select from a number of Interexchange Carriers (AT&T, Worldcom, Sprint, and so on) for the long-distance connection. Second, this PSTN–IP Network–PSTN topology is very similar to the service provided by many Internet Telephony Service Providers (ITSPs), such as iBasis, which is discussed in Chapter 2, Section 2.2. By using an international ITSP, like iBasis' service, the end user circumvents expensive international toll charges. Recognizing this threat to their revenue base, the IXCs in the United States and other countries are beginning to offer IP-based services along with their more standard offerings such as T1 lines and frame relay connections.

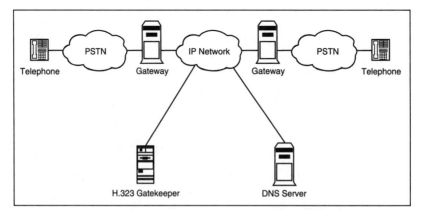

Figure 7–3: Network Elements Used for the Phone-to-Phone Connection

(Courtesy of the Voice over IP Forum)

All the network elements in these varied topologies – the end-user terminals, the gateways, the miscellaneous network devices – share one major feature. They all adhere to a common multimedia networking architecture, such as the ITU-T H.323 [7-2] or the IETF SIP [7-3] standards, which are discussed in Chapter 6.This architecture provides for a consistent flow of both call control and user information between user stations, as illustrated in Figure 7-4. Note that signaling information flows between the end stations, gateways, and gatekeepers. A TCP connection would be established along the path between the end stations via gateways and gatekeepers to support the signaling required for the end-user communication (Steps 1, 2, and 3 in Figure 7-4). The end-user information (such as a telephone conversation) would flow from an end station to a gateway, or between gateways, using UDP (Step 4 in Figure 7-4).

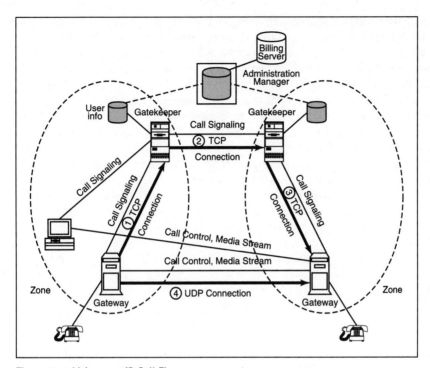

Figure 7-4: Voice over IP Call Flow

(Courtesy of Lucent Technologies)

7.2 Terminals

The end users interact with a terminal, which provides real-time, two-way communication with another compatible device. On that terminal, support for voice communications is required, and support for video and data communications is optional. This results in two important implementation factors. First, by requiring support for voice communication, H.323 or SIP terminals can be used as packet-based replacements for plain old telephone service (POTS) over the PSTN.

Second, by making support for video and data communication optional, the standard opens the door to interoperability problems. On a practical level this means two manufacturers can have products that adhere to a standard, such as H.323, yet are very different in their capabilities. For example, one H.323 terminal product may be a voice client software package, available without charge. Another H.323 terminal may be a very sophisticated video conferencing system that supports voice, video, and data communication and costs tens of thousands of dollars. Both products are compliant with the H.323 standard but may not be interoperable with each other because of the vast difference in their capabilities. But H.323 is a multimedia standard and is designed to address a variety of end-user requirements, so a difference in terminal capabilities exists both by design and necessity. To be fair, these issues could potentially exist between two vendors' SIP-based products, or any other set of products that were designed by independent engineering teams. The standards leave some room for product-specific implementation decisions, and unfortunately, products from different manufacturers do not always work together.

An example of an H.323 terminal and its capabilities is illustrated in Figure 7-5. Note that the video, audio, and data information streams are shown on the left-hand side of the figure, and that the interface to the LAN is shown on the right-hand side. The center of the figure illustrates the scope of H.323. There are five elements that comprise the H.323 implementation. The first two of these employ Coding/Decoding (codec) algorithms that convert the analog signal into a digital format and further optimize that signal for transmission. The video codec encodes the information for transmission from the video source, such as a camera, and decodes the received video information for display. The audio codec encodes the information for transmission from the audio source, such as a microphone, and decodes the received audio for output to a loudspeaker. Video codec standards, such as H.261, and audio codec standards, such as G.711, as well as the issue of delays in codec processing, are discussed in the next section of the chapter.

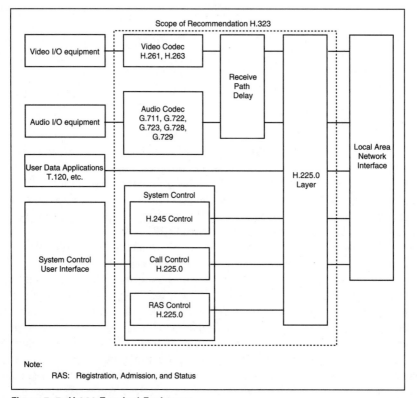

Figure 7-5: H.323 Terminal Equipment

(Source: ITU-T Recommendation H.323)

The data channel supports standardized data conferencing applications, such as file exchange, database access, still image transmission, and electronic whiteboards, as defined in the ITU-T T.120 series of recommendations.

The System Control unit provides signaling functions that are required for the proper operation of the terminal, such as call control, the exchange of terminal capabilities, and so on. The H.245 Control functions allow the terminals to negotiate channel usage and other capabilities. These functions are defined in ITU-T Recommendation H.245 [7-4]. Part of this control is a channel known as the RAS channel, which stands for Registration, Admission, and Status. The Call Control functions are used for call establishment and call termination functions. These functions are derived from a well-known signaling protocol, Q.931 [7-5], that has influenced work in ISDN, frame relay, and ATM network signaling. The RAS channel is used for communication between terminals and gatekeepers. Finally, the H.225.0 Layer formats transmit and receive information [7-6]. For example, this layer sends the information to be transmitted to the network interface and retrieves the received information from that network interface. In conjunction with transmit and receive operations, the H.225 Layer provides sequence numbering, error detection, and other functions.

7.3 Audio and Video Codecs

Review Figure 7-5 and note that the input for the audio and video signals is a codec, which stands for *coder/decoder*. The next sections of this chapter look at voice and video codecs separately.

7.3.1 Voice Codecs

The origins of voice encoding devices can be traced back several decades to the development of digital telephony. Chapter 5 mentions that WAN connections can be divided into two general categories: analog lines and digital lines. Digital lines were developed for several reasons, but one of the key reasons was to pack more information content into the cable pairs that were available. Bell System researchers discovered that they could send 24 voice conversations over two pairs of wire, thus yielding a pair gain of 12 from the older, analog technology.

In order to transport the analog voice signal using a digital transmission line, the voice signal first needs to be processed, which takes several steps. First, a bandwidth is established for the analog signal. For most encoding systems, this bandwidth is 4 KHz, which indicates that telephone-quality signals, having a nominal frequency range between 300 and 3,300 Hz, will be passed (the upper frequency limit is often rounded up from 3,300 to 4,000 Hz to account for imperfect filter response). With some codecs, this analog bandwidth is increased for higher voice quality. For example, the G.722 codec specifies a bandwidth of 50–7,000 Hz and is therefore called a wideband codec. Next, the analog signal is *sampled* (or measured) at a periodic rate. The sampling rate that is most frequently used is 8,000 samples per second. Next these samples (or measurements) are converted from an analog value into an equivalent digital value, which is called *quantizing*. In most cases, an 8-bit scale is used, which yields 256 (2^8) distinct quantization levels. Thus, the basic bit rate becomes the following:

8,000 samples/second × 8 bits/sample = 64,000 bits/second

This basic rate is known as the DS0 rate, which, as is discussed in Chapter 5, Section 5.2, has become the fundamental building block for all digital telephony worldwide (Figure 7-6).

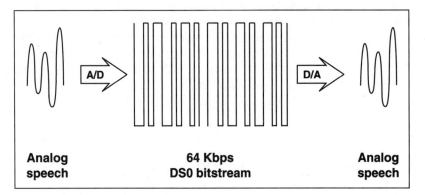

Figure 7–6: Channelized Telephony

(Courtesy of Nx Networks)

However, by current technology standards, voice channels do not need to consume 64,000 bits/second of bandwidth because additional signal processing can be applied after the analog-to-digital conversion (Figure 7-7). This additional process is known as *coding*; it may involve a number of mathematical functions, including data compression, voice activity detection, silence suppression, and so on. A reverse process, aptly called *decoding*, occurs at the receiver. When the coding/decoding is added to the signal processing, much less than 64,000 bits/second is required for each voice channel (Figure 7-7). As a result, more channels can be included in each WAN link, and the overall network costs should decrease.

There are two general categories of voice codecs: those that have been approved by a standards body, such as the ITU-T, and those that are proprietary to a particular vendor. Some vendors choose standardized codecs in their terminals, gateways, and other devices, thus making their products more interoperable with other vendors' designs. Other vendors may have developed a coding algorithm that they feel has superior performance to those that are standardized, and for a number of reasons (market share certainly being one) choose to keep that algorithm proprietary. As a result, the likelihood that one vendor's products will interoperate with another vendor's devices is low (close to zero in some cases). As one might expect, there are differing opinions regarding the use of proprietary versus standardized codecs, and readers can determine which of these two options is best suited to their individual networking environment.

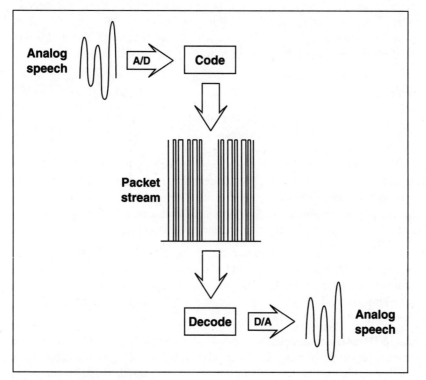

Figure 7–7: Packet Telephony

(Courtesy of Nx Networks)

In any event, most coding algorithms are actually implemented on a Digital Signal Processor, or DSP integrated circuit. As References [7-7] through [7-10] detail, DSP technology has made extensive advances in the last few years that have enabled both the processing complexity and the processing density to increase dramatically. Thus, with more signals being processed per chip, and with more complex algorithms employed, the resulting bandwidth consumption of a typical voice conversation has been dramatically decreased from the benchmark 64,000 bits/second. This decrease means more conversations per circuit, which lowers the telecommunications costs of organizations and allows them to purchase more terminals and gateways. In summary, DSPs have become one of the most significant technologies to fuel the growth of converged networks.

The following bullet list represents a brief summary of the capabilities of the coding algorithms that have been standardized:

◆ **G.711 (1972):** This algorithm operates at 64 Kbps. It uses Pulse Code Modulation (PCM) and produces a frame that contains 125 microseconds of speech. This is the original encoding standard. It produces a high quality of speech against which all other algorithms are compared, but it also has the highest bandwidth consumption, as no compression is involved.

◆ **G.722 (1988):** This algorithm operates at 48, 56, or 64 Kbps and is often referred to as the wideband coder, with an analog bandwidth of 7,000 Hz.

◆ **G.723.1 (1995):** This algorithm operates at 5.3 and 6.4 Kbps. It uses Algebraic Code Excited Linear Prediction (ACELP) for the low-rate coder, and Multipulse Maximum Likelihood Quantization (MP-MLQ) for the high-rate coder. The algorithm produces a frame with 30 milliseconds of speech and a total delay of 37.5 milliseconds. It has been adopted by the International Multimedia Teleconferencing Consortium's Voice over IP Forum in their Implementation Agreement and, as a result, is used in a number of converged network equipment applications.

◆ **G.726 (1990):** This algorithm operates at 16, 24, 32, and 40 Kbps. It uses Adaptive Differential Pulse Code Modulation (ADPCM). The algorithm produces a frame with 0.125 milliseconds of speech and a total delay of 0.125 milliseconds. It was originally designed to optimize bandwidth consumption over T1 networks.

◆ **G.728 (1994):** This algorithm operates at 16 Kbps. It uses Low Delay Code Excited Linear Prediction (LD-CELP). The algorithm produces a frame with 0.625 milliseconds of speech and a total delay of 0.625 milliseconds.

◆ **G.729 (1995):** This algorithm operates at 8 Kbps. It uses Conjugate Structure Algebraic Code Excited Linear Prediction (CS-ACELP). The algorithm produces a frame with 10 milliseconds of speech and a total delay of 15 milliseconds. It was originally designed for wireless environments.

◆ **G.729A (1996):** This algorithm operates at 8 Kbps. It uses a less complex version of the CS-ACELP algorithm implemented in G.729. The algorithm produces a frame with 10 milliseconds of speech and a total delay of 15 milliseconds. It was adapted for integrated voice and data applications and has been adopted by the International Multimedia Teleconferencing Consortium's Interoperability NOW! Activity Group.

The selection of coding algorithms and their associated delay characteristics is revisited during the discussion of converged network implementations in Chapter 8.

7.3.2 Video Codecs

Two codecs have been defined by the ITU-T for use with H.323 systems:

- ◆ **H.261:** This algorithm operates at a multiple of $p \times 64$ Kbps, where p can range in value from 1 to 30. The resulting video bit rate ranges from approximately 40 Kbps to 2 Mbps. H.261 is a required element of H.323.

- ◆ **H.263:** This algorithm is based on H.261, with additional compression. It contains negotiable options and can operate with a number of different video information formats. H.263 is an optional element of H.323.

In most cases, equipment designers, not network managers, select the encoding scheme that will be used in a particular product. Therefore, some knowledge about codec characteristics is valuable; however, the intricate details of the algorithms should be left to the designers. References [7-11] through [7-16] provide further information on voice and video codecs for those readers wishing to dig deeper.

7.4 Client Software

A number of firms have developed client software that supports voice and video over IP applications. Some of this software is available for free download over the Internet, and some of it comes with a cost. As might be expected, the capabilities, ease of use, and other features of these products vary. A sample client package is on the CD-ROM that accompanies this text. As with all software, thorough testing in a lab environment, prior to more widespread enterprise deployment, is advised. Table 7-1 lists some Voice and Video over IP applications you might want to check out.

TABLE 7-1 **VOICE AND VIDEO OVER IP APPLICATIONS**

Company	Product	Platforms
01 Communique, www.01com.com	Communicate! Pro	Windows 95/98, 2000, NT
Buddyphone, www.buddyphone.com	buddyPhone	Windows 95/98, 2000, NT
Callserve, www.callserve.com	React	Windows 95/98, 2000, NT
CineCom Corporation, NTwww.cinecom.com	CineVideo/Direct	Windows 95, NT

Continued

TABLE 7-1 VOICE AND VIDEO OVER IP APPLICATIONS *(Continued)*

Company	Product	Platforms
Cybration, Inc., www.icuii.com	ICUII Video Chat	Windows 95/98, NT 4.0, XP, Macintosh
Dialpad Communications, Inc., www.dialpad.com	Dialpad	Windows 95/98, 2000, Me, NT4, Mac, OSX
Dwyco, www.dwyco.com	CDC31 Dwyco Video Conferencing	Windows 95/98, 2000, Me, NT 4.0
eDial, www.edial.com	eDial	Windows 95/98, 2000, NT
eRing Solutions, Inc., www.eRing.net	itRings!	Windows 95/98, 2000, NT
E-Tech Canada Ltd., www.voxphone.com	Video VoxPhone	Windows 95/98, 2000, NT
Eyematic Interfaces, Inc., www.ivisit.com	iVisit	Windows 95/98, 2000, NT, Mac
Ezonics Corporation, www.ezonics.com	EZPhone Cam	Windows 98, 2000, Me
First Virtual Communications, Inc., www.cuseeme.com	CUseeMe Conference Server	Windows 95/98, 2000, NT, Sun Solaris, Red Hat Linux
iConnectHere.com, www.iconnecthere.com	iConnectHere	Windows 95/98, 2000, NT
INRIA, www-sop.inria.fr/rodeo/ fphone/obtain.html	Free Phone	Windows 95/98, DirectX 6.0, Solaris 2.6, Linux 2.0, SunOS 4.1.3, SGI IRIR 5.3
Intel Corporation, www.intel.com	Internet Video Phone	Windows 95/98, 2000, XP
Internet Communication Technologies, Inc., www.clearphone.com	ClearPhone	Windows 98, 2000, Me, MacOS 9+
IRIS Systems, http://irisphone.com	IRIS Phone	Windows 3.*x*, 95, NT 3.5, 4.0
Livehelper.com LLC, www.livehelper.com	Livehelper	Windows 95/98, NT

Company	Product	Platforms
MediaRing.com, Inc., www.mediaring.com	MediaRing Talk	Windows 95B, 98, 2000, Me
Mediatrix, www.mediatrix.com	APA Softphone	Windows 9x/2000, NT 4.0
Microsoft Corporation, www.microsoft.com/ windows/netmeeting	NetMeeting	Windows 95/98, 9x, 2000, Me, NT 4.0
Nautilus, www.lila.com/nautilus	Nautilus	Windows 95/98, NT, Solaris, Linux, DOS
Netscape Communications Corp., home.netscape.com/ navigator/v3.0/ cooltalk.html	CoolTalk	Windows 3.1, 95, NT, MacOS, Solaris, HP-UX, Digital UNIX, SunOS, IRIX
Net2Phone, Inc., commcenter.net2phone.com	Net2Phone	Windows 3.x, 95/98, 2000, Me, NT, Mac
Open Source Software, www.speakfreely.org	Speak Freely	Windows 95/98, 2000, Me, NT, UNIX
PC-Telephone.com, http://pc-telephone.com	PC-Telephone	Windows 95/98, 2000, NT
PhoneFree.com, www.phonefree.com	PhoneFree	Windows 95/98, 2000, NT
Pixion, Inc., www.picturetalk.com	PictureTalk	Windows 95, 98, 2000, NT, MacOS 8.x, SunOS, SunSolaris 2.x
SecuriPhone, www.securiphone.com	SecuriPhone	Windows 95/98, 2000, XP, Me, NT
Smith Micro Software, Inc., www.smithmicro.com	VideoLinkPro	Windows 95/98, 2000, Me, NT 4.0
VocalTec Communications, www.vocaltec.com	Surf&Call	Windows 95/98, NT 4.0

7.5 Gateways

The gateway provides a communication and connection path between an endpoint on the LAN and the switched circuit network (SCN). If two H.323 endpoints are on the same network, they can communicate directly without gateway intervention. Similarly, two endpoints on the SCN (that are not on the network) can also communicate without gateway intervention. When communication between these two networks is required, however, the gateway translates between the transmission formats and the communication procedures that are used on each side. Gateways can be provided as standalone devices or integrated into other systems, such as a PBX.

Four different types of gateways are defined in H.323; they provide for two different network types (H.323 Terminal and H.323 MCU) and two different SCN types (SCN Terminal and SCN MCU), as shown in Figure 7-8. The SCN side of the gateway communicates with the appropriate network type, such as H.320 (ISDN) or H.324 (PSTN). The Conversion Function provides the necessary conversions of the transmission format, control, audio, video, and data signal streams between the two different networks. In addition, the gateway may also provide for conversion of any signaling messages between the Network side (which uses H.225.0) and the SCN side (which might use Q.921, Q.2931, or some other signaling scheme).

As illustrated in Figure 7-9, the gateway performs a very critical function that allows H.323 systems to coexist with other (legacy) systems, such as ISDN and PSTN video conferencing equipment.

The architecture of a gateway includes three key elements: an interface for the voice side of the network, an interface for the packet side of the network, and the necessary signal processing between these two sides [7-17], as shown in Figure 7-10. The signal processing is most likely performed on a Digital Signal Processor (DSP) integrated circuit, which has been optimized for the processing speed required to support real-time voice and video connections. Signal processing functions include canceling any echoes that exist on the telephone line (thus optimizing the intelligibility of the conversation); encoding/decoding of the analog signal, typically using one of the algorithms discussed above, such as G.711 or G.723.1; adapting the digitally encoded information into a series of IP datagrams (review Figure 4-26); and transmitting those datagrams via a network, such as an Ethernet, to the ultimate destination.

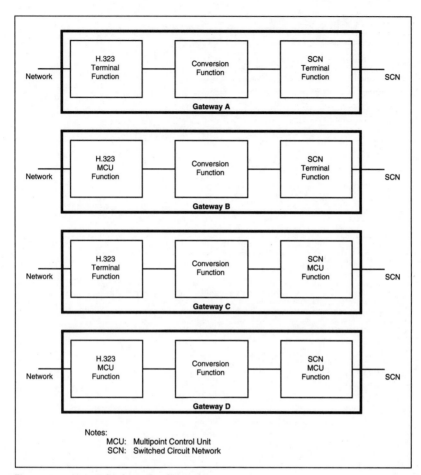

Figure 7-8: H.323 Gateway Configurations

(Source: ITU-T Recommendation H.323)

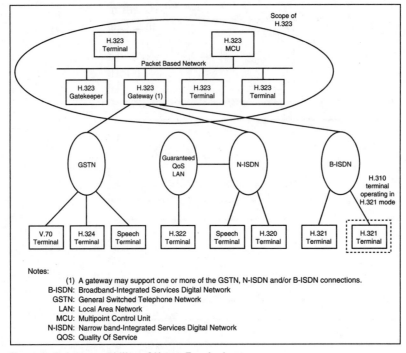

Figure 7-9: Interoperability of H.323 Terminals

(Source: ITU-T Recommendation H.323)

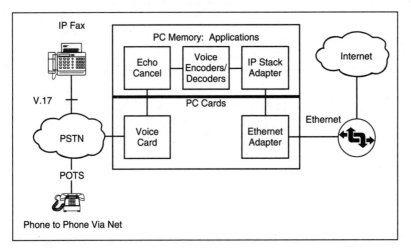

Figure 7-10: IP Telephony Gateway Architecture

(Courtesy of NMS Communications)

As most of these gateway functions are software-related, many manufacturers opt to purchase specialized communication software that can be embedded into their products rather than developing their own code. One of the developers of this type of software is Telogy Networks, Inc., of Germantown, Maryland. Telogy's software module is designed for general Voice over Packet applications, which include transport using ATM, frame relay, and IP-based networking environments [7-18]. The Telogy software is representative of H.323 Gateway design and operation and is further described in References [7-19] and [7-20].

The Telogy software functions can be divided into four general areas: a Voice Packet Module, a Telephony Signaling Module, a Network Protocol Module, and a Network Management Module (Figure 7-11). The Voice Packet Module interacts with the voice signal. It typically runs on a DSP and prepares the voice samples for transmission over the packet network. The Telephony Signaling Module interacts with the telephone network equipment and translates signaling indications (such as on- and off-hook signals) into state changes that can be interpreted by the Network Protocol Module. The Network Protocol Module processes that signaling information and converts it into a format that is compatible with the packet network. Finally, the Network Management Module supports the Simple Network Management Protocol (SNMP) and provides management of the operations.

The Voice Packet Module contains a number of functions (Figure 7-12). The Pulse Code Modulation (PCM) Interface interacts with the voice samples and includes a tone generator to generate the Dual Tone Multifrequency (DTMF) tones as necessary. The Echo Canceler is compliant with the ITU-T G.165/G.168 echo cancellation standards, which improve the clarity of the received signal. The Voice Activity Detector monitors the received signal for voice activity. If no activity is detected, the silence is suppressed, yielding additional savings in transport bandwidth. The Tone Detector receives the DTMF tones and reports them to the host system. The Voice Codec software includes algorithms for many of the codecs (discussed earlier in the chapter in Section 7.3), which compress the voice signal. A Fax Interface Unit is also included; it allows facsimile information to be transmitted and received. The Adaptive Playout Unit provides timing information in both transmit and receive directions, thus controlling packet jitter and packet loss. The Packet Protocol function encapsulates the compressed voice or fax information into a packet for transmission over the network. Finally, the Message Processing Unit controls the exchange of monitoring and control information between this software module and the host equipment that it resides in.

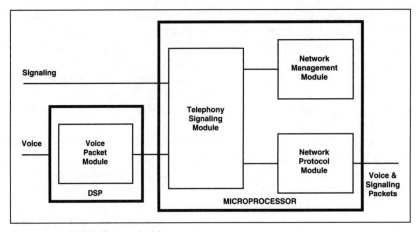

Figure 7–11: VoP Software Architecture

(Courtesy of Telogy Networks, Inc.)

The Telephony Signaling Module detects the presence of a new call and collects the destination address information (via the dialed digits) that will route that call to the intended destination (Figure 7-13). This module's functions include interfaces for various types of channel-associated signaling (CAS) circuits such as Foreign Exchange Station (FXS), Foreign Exchange Office (FXO), Loop Start, Ground Start, Pulse Dialing, and Ear and Mouth (E&M). In addition, various types of common channel signaling (CCS) are supported, including ISDN Primary Rate Interface (PRI) and Basic Rate Interface (BRI) connections, plus other signaling schemes based on the ITU-T Q-series of recommendations (QSG). The Address Translation function maps the telephone or fax number to a number that can be used by the packet network, such as an IP Address, a frame relay Data Link Connection Identifier (DLCI), or an ATM Virtual Path Identifier/Virtual Channel Identifier (VPI/VCI). Also included in this module are control functions for the DSP.

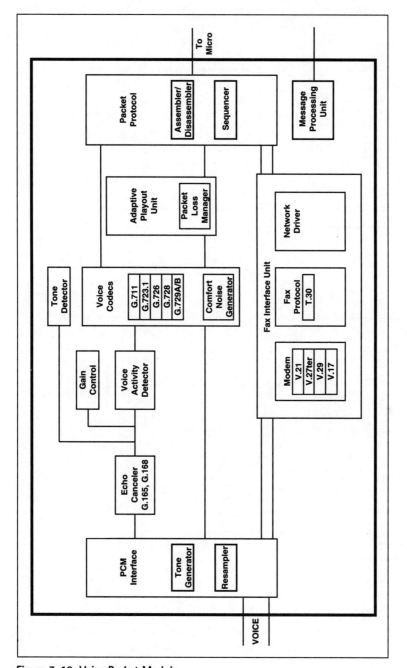

Figure 7-12: Voice Packet Module

(Courtesy of Telogy Networks, Inc.)

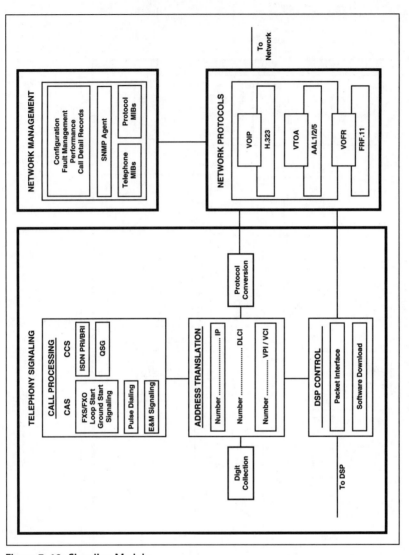

Figure 7-13: Signaling Module

(Courtesy of Telogy Networks, Inc.)

The Network Management Module includes processes that allow the software implementation to be managed effectively. This includes an SNMP Agent, plus Management Information Bases (MIBs) supporting both telephone and network protocol functions.

The Network Protocol Module implements three network options: H.323 for VoIP networks; ATM Adaptation Layers 1, 2, or 5 for Voice Telephony over ATM (VTOA);

and the Frame Relay Forum's Voice over Frame Relay (VoFR) Implementation Agreement, specified in the Frame Relay Forum's FRF.11.1 Implementation Agreement (review Reference [5-13]).

References [7-21] through [7-23] describe and compare various vendors' gateway implementations.

7.6 Terminal–to–Gateway Communication

As has been discussed, terminals support end-user applications, and gateways provide access to other networks, such as an ISDN or the PSTN. Procedures are defined in H.225.0 that specify the communication between the terminal and the gateway. These protocols are illustrated in Figure 7-14, with the terminal functions on the left and the gateway functions on the right. Note that the H.225.0 architecture includes a number of protocols that provide specific communication functions between the terminal and the gateway.

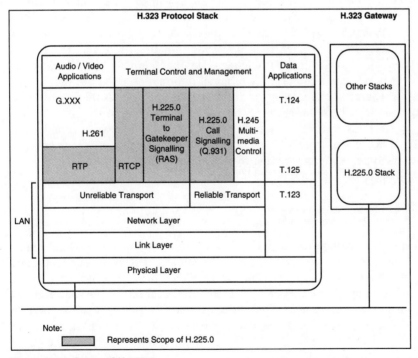

Figure 7-14: Scope of H.225.0

(Source: ITU-T Recommendation H.225.0)

Three types of information streams are shown at the top of the terminal side of the figure: audio and video applications, terminal control and management functions, and data applications. The scope of the H.225.0 is shown in the shaded boxes in the center of the figure. The lower layers (Transport through Physical) illustrate the local network connection and reliability functions.

The Real Time Transport Protocol (RTP) and the Real Time Control Protocol (RTCP), which are covered in Chapter 4, Section 4.8, are used to convey and control the audio/video application information. Note that there are two transport options: an unreliable transport and a reliable transport. As is covered in more detail in Chapter 4, Section 4.7, the User Datagram Protocol (UDP) provides unreliable (or datagram) service, while the Transmission Control Protocol (TCP) provides reliable (or stream-oriented) service. UDP and TCP are two examples of protocols that could be used within the H.225.0 architecture for the unreliable and reliable services, respectively. However, H.225.0 leaves open the option of using other transport protocols and specifically states that the use of the RTP/RTCP is not tied to the use of IP, UDP, or TCP.

Four control protocols are defined within the H.225.0 architecture for terminal control and management functions. The Real Time Control Protocol (RTCP) provides feedback regarding the quality of the data distribution, identification of the RTP data source, and control of the rate of RTP packet transmission; it conveys minimal session control information. A terminal-to-gatekeeper signaling protocol, known as the Registration, Admission, and Status (RAS) protocol, is also defined. Note that RTP, RTCP, and RAS run over unreliable transport. The H.225.0 Call Signaling, which was developed from the Q.931 signaling protocol, provides call establishment and call termination functions. The H.245 protocol (which is outside the scope of H.225.0) is a protocol for terminal information messages that control terminal procedures at the start of or during communication. Note that both the signaling and the call control protocols run over reliable transport.

Data applications include support for the ITU-T T.123 (network-specific data protocol stacks for multimedia conferencing), T.124 (generic conference control), and T.125 (multipoint communication service protocol) standards.

7.7 Gatekeepers

A gatekeeper (GK) manages all activities in a *zone*. A zone, as illustrated in Figure 7-15, is a collection of at least one (or more) terminal(s), gateways, and multipoint control units that are managed by a single gatekeeper. From a logical standpoint, the GK is separate from other H.323 entities. From a physical standpoint, however, the GK may coexist with a terminal, GW, MCU, or other device. Thus, the gatekeeper should be thought of as a *logical function*, instead of as a distinct, physical box.

According to ITU-T H.323, the gatekeeper is an optional entity in the H.323 environment. From a practical implementation perspective, however, the GK is an essential network element [7-24]. When present in a system, the functions of the GK can be divided into two categories: those services that the GK must perform, and those services that the GK may optionally perform.

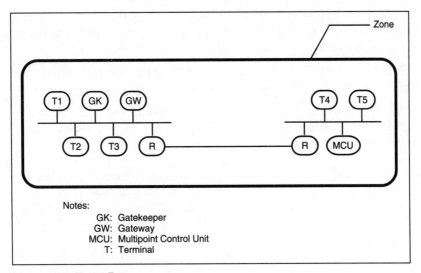

Figure 7-15: H.323 Zone

(Source: ITU-T Recommendation H.323)

When the GK is present in a system, it must perform the following functions:

♦ **Address Translation:** Provides a translation between an alias (such as a name or e-mail address for a terminal or a gateway) and a transport address.

♦ **Admissions Control:** Authorizes access to the network based on call authorization, bandwidth availability, or some other manufacturer-specified criteria. Messages specified in ITU-T H.225.0 are used for this purpose.

♦ **Bandwidth Control:** Monitors and controls the network bandwidth so that the available network bandwidth limits are not exceeded. Messages specified in ITU-T H.225.0 are used for this purpose.

♦ **Zone Management:** Provides the three services noted above for terminals, gateways, and Multipoint Control Units that are registered with that gatekeeper.

Optional functions that the GK may perform include:

♦ **Call Control Signaling:** The GK processes the call control signaling with the endpoints.

♦ **Call Authorization:** The GK rejects a terminal's call because of an authorization failure, such as access restrictions to a particular terminal or gateway or access restrictions during a certain time period.

◆ **Bandwidth Management:** The GK controls the number of H.323 terminals that are permitted to access the network simultaneously and rejects access if sufficient bandwidth does not exist.

◆ **Call Management:** The GK maintains a list of ongoing H.323 calls and is able to indicate if a particular called terminal is busy.

◆ **Other Functions:** A GK management information data structure, bandwidth reservation for terminals, and directory services are functions that have been proposed for further study.

These key services provided by gatekeepers allow functions such as billing for bandwidth-specified services, interoperability between PBX dialing plans and IP-based terminals, and automatic call routing and call distribution features for multimedia call centers. Further details on the services and functions that gatekeepers provide are given in References [7-25] and [7-26].

7.8 Multipoint Control Units

The Multipoint Control Unit (MCU) manages conferences between three or more H.323 terminals and/or gateways. The MCU can also connect two terminals in a point-to-point configuration initially, and then in a multipoint conference developed subsequently. The MCU consists of two parts: a Multipoint Controller (MC), which is mandatory, and Multipoint Processors (MPs), which are optional. For example, a typical MCU might contain one MC and three MPs, each of which would support audio, video, and data traffic.

The MC provides the function of capability negotiation, using the ITU-T H.245 protocol, to ensure that all of the terminals have a common level of communication. The MC may also control resources of the conference, such as the particular terminal that is currently multicasting video. An MC can be located within a terminal, gateway, gatekeeper, or the MCU.

The MP provides for the centralized processing of audio, video, and/or data streams of information in a multipoint conference. These processing functions include mixing and switching of that information under the control of the MC. Depending on the type of conference supported, the MP may process single or multiple streams of media.

Four types of multipoint conferences are defined in H.323: centralized multipoint, decentralized multipoint, hybrid multipoint with centralized audio, and hybrid multipoint with centralized video. In the centralized multipoint case, the endpoints communicate with the MC in a point-to-point manner on the H.245 control channel, and with the MP on the audio, video, and data channels. The MC performs the multipoint control functions using H.245, and the MP transmits the resulting information streams back to the communicating endpoints. With the decentralized multipoint capability, the endpoints communicate with the MC in a point-to-point mode and optionally communicate with the MP on the data channels. The endpoints have the capabilities to multicast their information to all other endpoints in the conference. Figure 7-16 illustrates both the centralized and the decentralized cases, which can both be managed by the MCU.

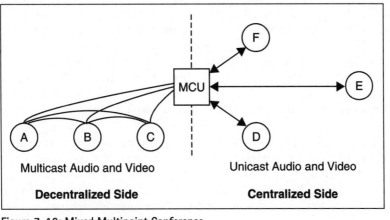

Figure 7-16: Mixed Multipoint Conference

(Source: ITU-T Recommendation H.323)

Hybrid multipoint conferences combine the features of the centralized and the decentralized cases. With the hybrid multipoint–centralized audio case, the endpoints multicast their video channels to other endpoints on the conference under the control of the MC. The endpoints transmit their audio channels to the MP, which performs audio mixing functions and outputs the resulting audio streams to the various endpoints. In the hybrid multipoint–centralized video case, the endpoints multicast their audio channels to other endpoints on the conference under the control of the MC. The endpoints transmit their video channels to the MP, which performs the video switching, mixing, or format conversion functions, and outputs the resulting video streams to the various endpoints.

Details regarding MCU operation are provided in H.323 and H.245.

7.9 Premises Communication Systems

Converged networks, by definition, seek to combine both voice and data networking capabilities within one cohesive system. From the voice networking side of the equation, this concept has been around for about two decades. Customer premises switching systems, frequently called Private Branch Exchanges (PBXs), enhanced their circuit-switched voice capabilities to include data transport many years ago. However, the data applications were typically limited to terminal-to-host communication (at 56/64 Kbps – the DS0 rate) or PBX-to-host communication (at 1.544 Mbps – the DS1 rate).

With the advent of IP-based networking, PBX vendors have been migrating their products from a circuit switching-based architecture to a packet switching-based architecture, thus easing the transition for converged networking applications. The industry has therefore coined the term "IPBX" to indicate the IP-based nature of the new generation of PBX systems. One example of such an architecture is Avaya Inc.'s Enterprise Class IP Solutions (ECLIPS) product line, which integrates voice and data services over an Ethernet/IP-based infrastructure (Figure 7-17). The nerve center of Avaya's architecture is known as the Avaya Communication Server, which supports both gatekeeper and gateway functions. The gatekeeper function is implemented on an interface called the Control LAN (or CLAN) board. This interface implements the H.225.0, H.323, H.245, and Q.931 signaling protocols to facilitate the establishment and termination of connections between IP telephones or other H.323-compatible terminals. The gateway function is implemented on an IP Media Processor board, which handles audio traffic between a time division multiplexing (TDM) bus and the IP network. Included on the IP Media Processor board are DSPs for audio encoding/decoding functions, plus an RTP/UDP/IP protocol stack to handle the packet transport. Reference [7-27] describes the Avaya architecture in greater detail, while References [7-28] through [7-30] provide further resources on IP-based PBX systems.

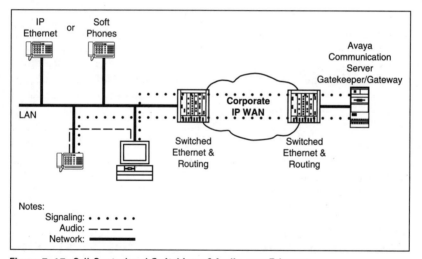

Figure 7-17: Call Control and Switching of Audio over Ethernet

(Reprinted with permission from Avaya Inc.)

7.10 Softswitches

This text has focused the majority of its discussion on enterprise-centric, not carrier-centric, VoIP applications; however, it is nevertheless important to discuss the architecture of a softswitch, which is an IP-based replacement for central office switching systems. As is discussed in Chapter 6, Section 6.3, gateways can be decomposed into three key elements: a Media Gateway (MG), a Signaling Gateway (SG), and a Media Gateway Controller (MGC). In addition, an Application Server (AS) supports end-user functionality. The MGC communicates with the SG and the MG using the MGCP or MEGACO/H.248 protocols, and communicates with legacy networks, such as the ISDN or PSTN, using other protocols, such as Signaling System 7 (SS7), for the purpose of establishing and terminating calls between locations (Figure 7-18, taken from Reference [7-31]).

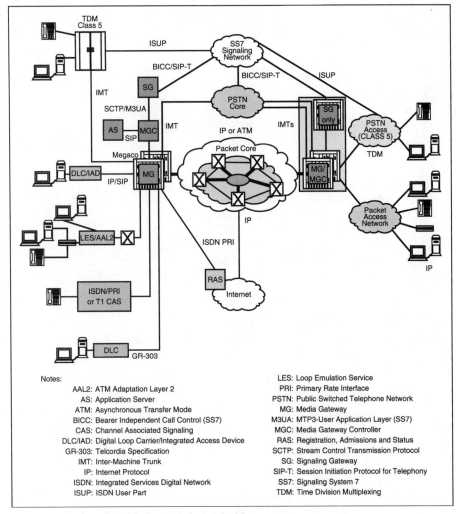

Figure 7-18: Elements of Softswitch-based Architecture

(Courtesy of Telica, Inc.)

The term *softswitch* is used to describe the software running in the MGC, and possibly also in the SG and the AS, that provides for these call connection functions. (The MG is not included in this description, as it provides physical interfaces into ATM, IP, PSTN, or other networks, not a switching function per se.) The softswitch provides for a distributed, open switching architecture between its elements, with a layered architecture that allows an intermix of multivendor systems (Figure 7-19). In addition, applications can be developed by third parties that can be run on top of the call control layer rather than being embedded within proprietary central office switches currently in use. Thus, the softswitch achieves many of the architectural objectives desired for open systems: media independence, interoperability between multiple vendors' products, support for multiple protocols, scalability for larger networks, and open application interfaces. References [7-32] through [7-34] provide further information on softswitch design and functionality.

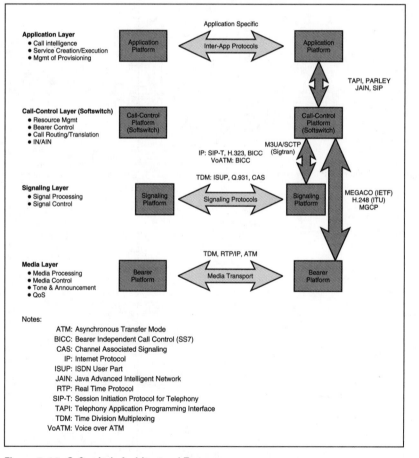

Figure 7-19: Softswitch Architectural Taxonomy

(Courtesy of Telica, Inc.)

7.11 Looking Ahead

This chapter considered the customer premises equipment that comprises a converged network, such as client terminals, gateways, gatekeepers, and various switching systems. For implementers, however, key questions remain: How will all of these new elements integrate into the existing network, and are there any design constraints that should be considered? These questions will be discussed in Chapter 8.

7.12 References

[7-1] Voice over IP Forum. "IMTC Voice over IP Forum Service Interoperability Implementation Agreement 1," December 1997. Available from ftp. imtc-files.org/imtc-site/incoming/VOIP/Voip_I%7E1.doc.

[7-2] International Telecommunications Union – Telecommunications Standardization Sector. *Packet-based Multimedia Communication Systems.* ITU-T H.323, 2000.

[7-3] Handley, M., et al. *Session Initiation Protocol.* RFC 2543, March 1999.

[7-4] International Telecommunications Union – Telecommunications Standardization Sector. *Control Protocol for Multimedia Communication.* ITU-T H.245, 2001.

[7-5] International Telecommunications Union – Telecommunications Standardization Sector. *Digital Subscriber Signaling System No. 1 (DSS 1) – ISDN User-Network Interface Layer 3 Specification for Basic Call Control.* ITU-T Q.931, 1998.

[7-6] International Telecommunications Union – Telecommunications Standardization Sector. *Call Signaling Protocols and Media Stream Packetization for Packet-based Multimedia Communication Systems.* ITU-T H.225.0, 2000.

[7-7] Krapf, Eric. "DSPs – Powering the Packet-Voice Revolution." *Business Communication Review* (October 1998): 2–9.

[7-8] Eyre, Jennifer, and Jeff Bier. "DSPs Court the Consumer." *IEEE Spectrum* (March 1999): 47–53.

[7-9] RadiSys. "C6X Solutions for a Voice over IP Gateway." White paper available at www.radisys.com/files/voip.pdf.

[7-10] Ammon, Steve, and Neal Bradford. "Implementing Embedded DSP-based VoP Systems." *Electronic Products* (September 2001): 16–17.

[7-11] Cox, Richard V. "Three New Speech Coders from the ITU Cover a Range of Applications." *IEEE Communications* (September 1997): 40–47.

[7-12] Rijkse, Karel. "H.263: Video Coding for Low-Bit-Rate Communication." *IEEE Communications* (December 1996): 42–45.

[7-13] Spiro Lab Telecom. "Why Choose G.729?," June 15, 2000.

[7-14] Spiro Lab Telecom. "Why Get a G.729 License?," June 2000.

[7-15] Array Microsystems, Inc. "Video Compression – An Introduction." White paper available at www.array.com/compres.pdf.

[7-16] Cinecom Corporation. "Videoconferencing – A Technical Discussion on Using It over the Internet." White paper available at www.cinecom.com/wpvidc.htm.

[7-17] NMS Communications. "IP Telephony: Powered by Fusion," 1997.

[7-18] Telogy Networks, Inc. "Voice over Packet," 1997. White paper available from www.telogy.com.

[7-19] Carr, Brian. "Building Block Architecture in VoIP Gateways." *Internet Telephony* (October 2000): 82–89.

[7-20] The International Engineering Consortium. "Voice and Fax over Internet Protocol (V/FoIP) Tutorial." Available at www.iec.org/online/tutorials/vfoip.

[7-21] Roberts, Scott. "Elements of an Internet Telephony Gateway." *Internet Telephony* (October 2000): 33–34.

[7-22] Woods, Darrin. "Buyer's Guide: Voice Gateways." *Network Computing* (December 4, 2000): 109–111.

[7-23] Mier, Edwin E., et al. "VoIP Gateways: Bigger and Better." *Business Communications Review* (September 2001): 56–63.

[7-24] Rizzetto, Daniele, and Claudio Catania. "A Voice over IP Service Architecture for Integrated Communications." *IEEE Network* (May/June 1999): 34–40.

[7-25] RADVISION, Inc. "H.323 Gatekeepers." White paper available at www.radvision.com/papers/C1_H.323_Gatekeeper.pdf.

[7-26] The International Engineering Consortium. "Gatekeeper Tutorial." Available at www.iec.org/online/tutorials/gatekeep.

[7-27] Avaya Inc. "Avaya IP Call Processing White Paper." Available at www1.avaya.com/enterprise/whitepapers/IP_Call_Process.pdf.

[7-28] Sulkin, Allan. "The Evolving ICS Platform." *Business Communications Review* (September 2001): 52–55.

[7-29] Woods, Darrin. "PBXes: CO Switches Extended to the Enterprise." *Network Computing* (October 1, 2001): 79–83.

[7-30] Morrissey, Peter. "VoIP Invasion: Are You Ready for It?" *Network Computing* (November 13, 2000): 70–94.

[7-31] Kafel, Ali. "Softswitches and Softswitch-based Architectures." Presentation available from `www.telica.com/news/ip_forum_softswitch.pdf`.

[7-32] Kafel, Ali. "Softswitches enable voice/IP services." *Network World* (May 5, 2001). Available at `www.nwfusion.com/archive/2001/120073_05-07-2001.html`

[7-33] Taylor, Martin. "Convergence in Local Telephone Networks." White paper available at `www.coppercom.com/pdf/wp_convergence.pdf`.

[7-34] Knight, Stefan. "Packet Translation: The Key to True End-to-End Packet Telephony in Next Generation Networks." *The ATM & IP Report* (January/February 2001): 1–4.

Chapter 8

Implementing Converged Networks

This chapter turns your attention to the steps required to begin the implementation phase of a converged network. But before that point, there are additional technical issues to be considered that transcend the topics of applications, local and wide area networks, protocols, and systems that have been addressed in previous chapters. These topics include the design of the converged network, interoperability between converged networks and other systems, and Quality of Service (QoS) factors that affect the satisfaction of the end users of these networks. This chapter begins by looking at one of the biggest challenges facing network managers, the design of the integrated voice/data network, and then moves on to examine a number of other implementation-related topics.

8.1 Designing the Converged Network

This discussion of network implementation begins with the fundamental issue to be considered, the design of that network. Perhaps the importance of that design phase is best illustrated anecdotally. Suppose you are responsible for your organization's data network. This network has evolved over the years and is now a distributed system with subnetworks in several cities that are connected with WAN links. Your upper management goes on a cost-cutting binge and clamps down on corporate business travel, with the intention of replacing business trips with videoconferences. You are now charged with the responsibility of implementing an IP-based voice and video conferencing network across your existing WAN. But does the existing network infrastructure have the capacity to support this type of application? Fortunately, there are a number of both vendor- and third-party-developed tools to assist the network manager with these questions.

Westbay Engineers Ltd. of Crawley, UK, offers a range of network design software tools that includes support for Voice over IP modeling [8-1]. Westbay Engineers Ltd. has a varied customer base ranging from operators of local enterprise networks to the largest telecommunications carriers in the world. Westbay Engineers' flagship product is called Westplan. It analyzes existing networks and optimizes networks to suggest the most appropriate network facilities that should be deployed between networked locations. A demonstration version of Westplan is included with the CD-ROM accompanying this book. The software is time limited and has some features disabled, such as the ability to export reports, but it should offer a good evaluation of Westplan's features.

Westplan's data is organized into projects, each of which shares a common collection of definable network nodes. Each project can also hold an unlimited number of user-defined networks. These define different ways of interconnecting the network nodes. By defining new networks, users are able to investigate various network topologies and to select the most appropriate configuration.

Figure 8-1a shows Westplan in its Outlook Mode. In this mode, it is similar in appearance to Microsoft Outlook with each project being represented by a horizontal shortcut bar on the left side of the main window. Clicking on a project's bar reveals icons representing each of that project's networks. A network can be selected and brought into view by clicking on its icon.

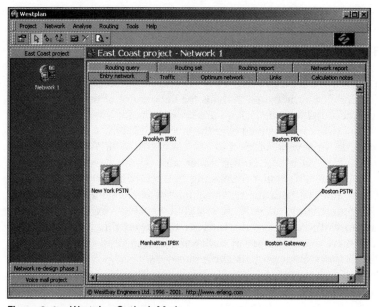

Figure 8-1a: Westplan Outlook Mode

(Courtesy of the Westbay Engineers, Ltd.)

The network drawing is the main application area and is visible when Westplan starts. It contains icons representing each of the current project's nodes and lines representing each link defined in that project's currently selected network.

The example in Figure 8-1a shows a network with three sites on the East Coast of the United States: Manhattan, Brooklyn, and Boston. Manhattan and Brooklyn both have IPBXs that directly support IP connections. These IPBXs are interconnected using a link carrying IP and are both connected to the local PSTN using T1 digital trunks. The PBX at Boston does not directly support IP and connects to the Manhattan IPBX through a locally installed VoIP gateway. Both the gateway and the PBX are connected to the local PSTN using T1 trunks.

New nodes can easily be added to the network drawing by right-clicking the mouse at the new node location and selecting Add Node from the pop-up menu.

The dialog box that appears prompts the user to enter a name for the new node and to provide an estimate of the traffic levels generated by the node (Figure 8-1b). There will be an opportunity to change the default traffic figures (which are essential parameters for the results to be accurately calculated by Westplan) later.

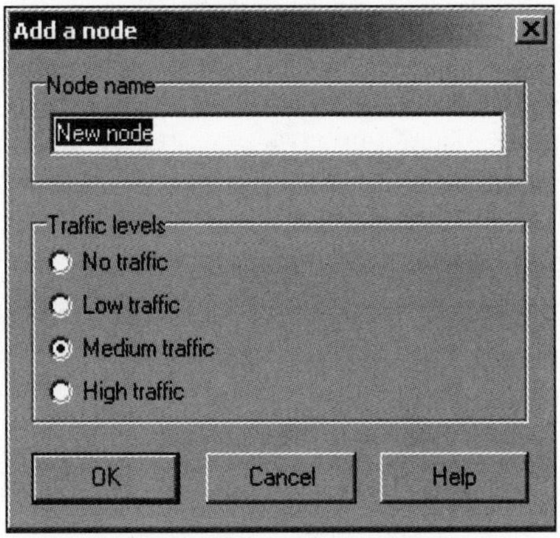

Figure 8-1b: Adding a Node to Westplan

(Courtesy of the Westbay Engineers, Ltd.)

A node can represent a network location, a voice switch, or a routing device. A node should be defined for any network element that can make a routing decision or that converts the transmission medium from one type to another (for example, analog trunks to Voice over IP).

Inserting new links also uses "point and click." Right-click on the network drawing and select Add Link. Move the cursor over one of the two nodes to be connected. When the icon representing that node appears "pressed down," press the left mouse button and hold it down while "dragging" the source node to the destination node. Details concerning the link need to be entered in the resulting dialog box, shown in Figure 8-1c.

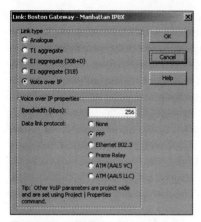

Figure 8–1c: Adding a Link to Westplan

(Courtesy of the Westbay Engineers, Ltd.)

The transmission medium used for the link should be selected using the radio buttons at the top of Figure 8-1c. The choices are *Analogue, T1,* two *E1* formats, and *Voice over IP.* The bottom half of the dialog box changes depending on the first selection, but the example shown relates to VoIP and shows a link of 256 Kbps being defined with a Datalink (Layer 2) protocol of PPP. The 256 Kbps entry is required only if an existing network connection needs to be analyzed. If this were a new network, then this value could be left at its default, because Westplan would dimension the link during its optimization process.

The Add Link dialog box shows only VoIP parameters relating to Layer 2. The remaining parameters are changed on a project-wide basis by selecting Project | Properties from the main menu, bringing up the dialog box shown in Figure 8-1d.

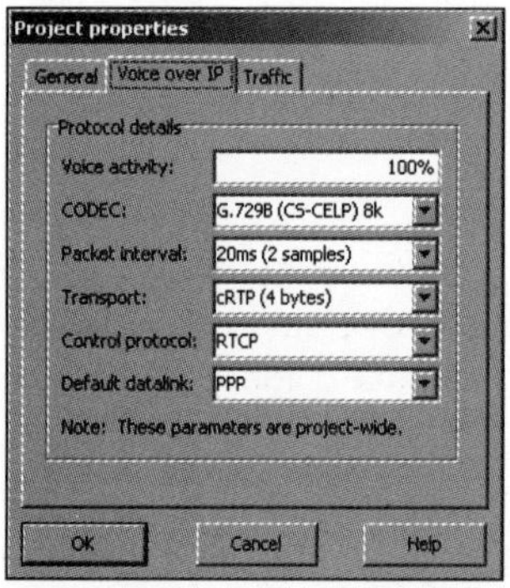

Figure 8–1d: Adding Project Properties in Westplan

(Courtesy of the Westbay Engineers, Ltd.)

Using the Project properties dialog box, the silence suppression characteristics, voice encoding algorithm, packet interval, transport protocol, and control protocol may be entered.

At this point, it should be noted that the design process does not simply involve selecting the VoIP parameters that result in the lowest bandwidth per link. Delay characteristics vary for each voice compression scheme and a designer should always keep in mind that a network must meet quality of service targets such as delay and jitter. However, if these initial design considerations have already been made (for example, codecs, maximum hops, and protocols), then Westplan can model their effects on the network resources that need to be deployed.

Clicking on the Links tab above the network drawing shows a summary of all the links defined in the current network (Figure 8-1e).

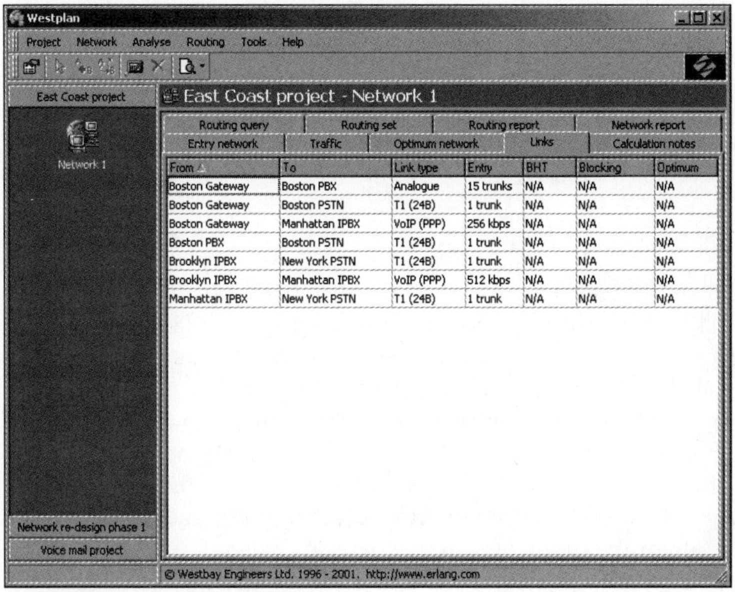

Figure 8-1e: Westplan Link Summary

(Courtesy of the Westbay Engineers, Ltd.)

The Entry Network facilities are shown, but the information is not complete, because at this stage Westplan has not yet analyzed the network.

Before initiating the analysis process, it is important to enter accurate traffic figures. Traffic figures are entered on a spreadsheet that is brought into view by clicking the Traffic tab (Figure 8-1f).

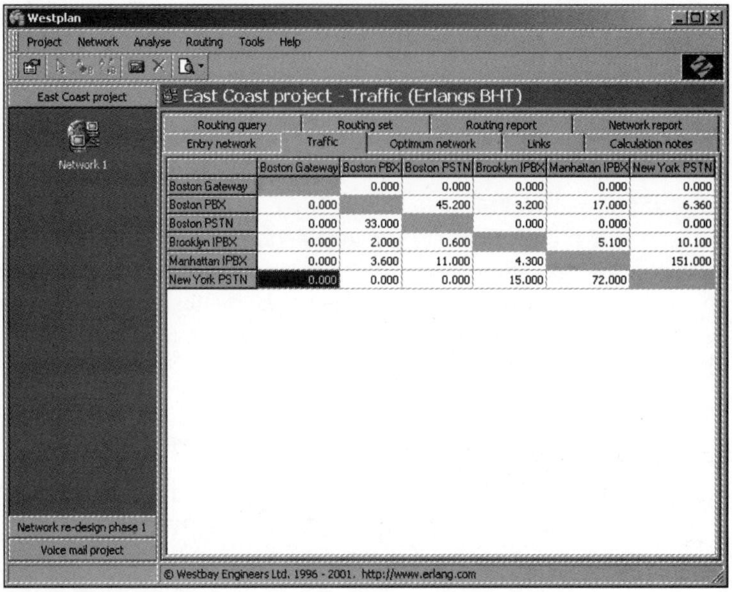

Figure 8-1f: Westplan Traffic Parameters

(Courtesy of the Westbay Engineers, Ltd.)

Traffic figures can be entered in either Erlangs of traffic during the busiest hour or minutes of traffic per day (the unit used can be set as an application-wide option). It is important to enter accurate figures. These can be obtained from call loggers, switch statistics, call detail recorders, telephone company reports, or careful estimates. It is best to try and establish the offered traffic levels at their point of source rather than using traffic levels carried by existing trunk groups. Traffic carried on existing trunks may have suffered a degree of blocking if those trunks have not been correctly sized. This means that a trunk group's traffic figures may not be an accurate reflection of the traffic offered to a network.

In the example shown in Figure 8-1f, traffic is passed among the three PBXs. Traffic is also recorded between each site and that site's local PSTN network. In addition, there are small amounts of traffic from the New York PBXs to the Boston PSTN and from the Boston PBX to the New York PSTN. This represents tail end hop off (TEHO) traffic in which a private network is used to carry telephone calls between two cities, with the "tail end" PBX terminating those calls to its local PSTN. The purpose of TEHO is to save on long-distance call charges.

By default, Westplan assumes that calls will be routed through a network using the shortest number of hops. By clicking on the Routing Query tab, the assumed routing between any two nodes can be displayed as an animated highlighting of the calculated routing (Figure 8-1g).

If this routing is not appropriate, then new routes can be defined for carrying traffic between two nodes. These nonstandard routes are defined using the Routing Set tab and can be displayed in a report using the Routing Report tab (Figure 8-1h).

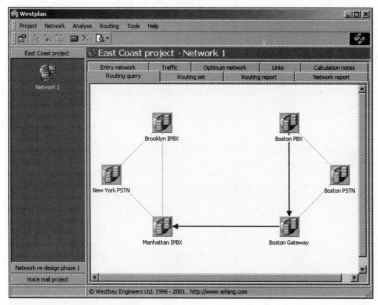

Figure 8-1g: Westplan Routing Query

(Courtesy of the Westbay Engineers, Ltd.)

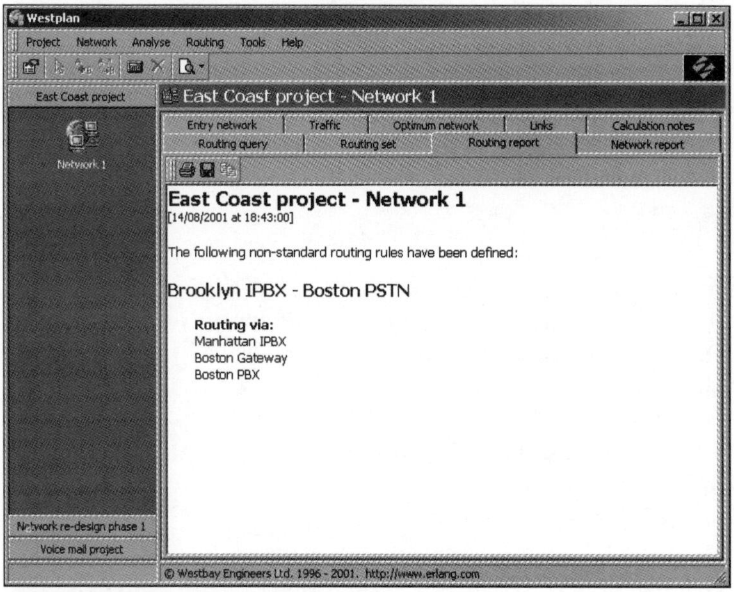

Figure 8-1h: Westplan Routing Rules

(Courtesy of the Westbay Engineers, Ltd.)

In this example, calls from the Manhattan PBX to the Boston PSTN have been set to pass through the Boston PBX rather than being sent to the Boston PSTN directly by the gateway in Boston.

Once you have defined the nodes of a project, the links interconnecting those nodes in a network, and the traffic levels, Westplan is ready to analyze and optimize the current network. Clicking on the Optimum Network tab starts this optimization process (Figure 8-1i).

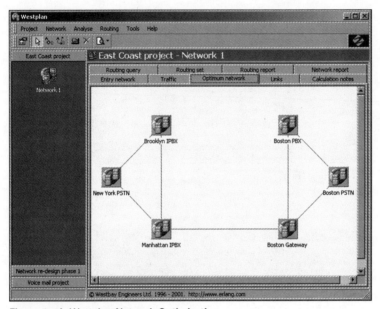

Figure 8-1i: Westplan Network Optimization

(Courtesy of the Westbay Engineers, Ltd.)

During the optimization process, Westplan calculates the traffic offered to each link. The network drawing displayed is the same as the Entry Network drawing, except that the links are color-coded to indicate whether the call blocking experienced is within the limits set for the project. (Call blocking occurs if insufficient lines have been provided on a trunk group and manifests itself as callers hearing a busy tone even if the person they are calling is available.) By clicking on the Links tab, a more detailed set of results can be viewed (Figure 8-1j).

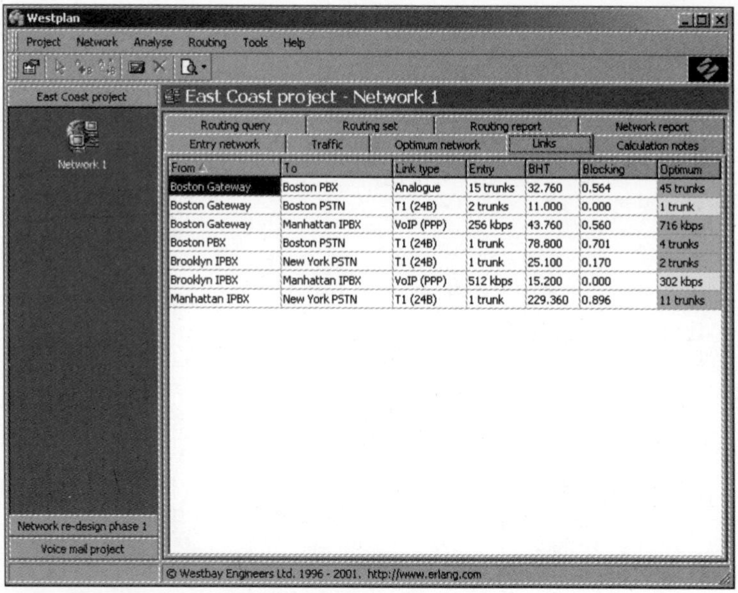

Figure 8-1j: Westplan Optimization Results

(Courtesy of the Westbay Engineers, Ltd.)

For each link, the Links Table now shows the traffic offered in Erlangs and an estimate of the blocking encountered on the link as it was configured when it was defined in the Entry Network. The last column shows an estimate of the optimum facilities that should be engineered for the link in order to keep the blocking within the project's specified call blocking targets. For analog and aggregate links, the number of ideal trunks is shown; for Voice over IP, the optimal bandwidth is shown. Westplan is suggesting that the links be engineered according to the final column. A lower bandwidth or number of trunks would result in call blocking, whereas installing links with higher values of network resource may be overkill. Of course, the final interpretation is always the responsibility of the designer. It might be prudent to slightly overengineer a link in order to protect oneself against unexpectedly higher levels of traffic or against network failures.

Westplan offers full notes to justify its calculations, and this report can be viewed and saved using the Calculation Notes tab (Figure 8-1k).

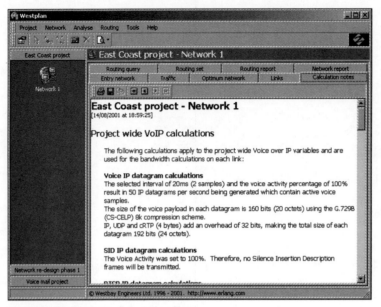

Figure 8-1k: Westplan Calculation Notes

(Courtesy of the Westbay Engineers, Ltd.)

One of the strengths of Westplan is its ability to answer "what if" questions and to test the effects of network reconfigurations or failures. For example, the failure of the PSTN link from the Boston gateway would result in all tail end hop off (TEHO) traffic from the New York IPBXs to the Boston PSTN being routed through the Boston PBX. The traffic from the Manhattan IPBX already routes through the Boston PBX, so the additional traffic load through the Boston PBX would result from TEHO calls from the Brooklyn IPBX (11 Erlangs Busy traffic). This additional traffic would be offered to the link from the Boston gateway to the Boston PBX and the remaining PSTN link to the Boston PBX.

To simulate this failure, return to the Optimum Network tab and select Network | Duplicate from the main menu. The original network will be copied to a new network and will become the currently selected network. Click on the link between the Boston gateway and the Boston PSTN using the mouse and press the delete key. The result is a network with one less link than the previous network (Figure 8-1l).

When the new network is optimized by clicking on the Optimum Network tab, the two links turn from green to red as expected. Again, a more detailed analysis can be seen by clicking on the Links tab (Figure 8-1m).

Westplan
Project Network Analyse Routing Tools Help
East Coast project
Network 1
Boston Gateway PSTN failure
East Coast project - Boston Gateway PSTN failure
Routing query
Routing set
Routing report
Network report
Entry network
Traffic
Optimum network
Links
Calculation notes
Brooklyn IPBX
Boston PBX
New York PSTN
Boston PSTN
Manhattan IPBX
Boston Gateway
Network re-design phase 1
Voice mail project
© Westbay Engineers Ltd. 1996 - 2001. http://www.erlang.com

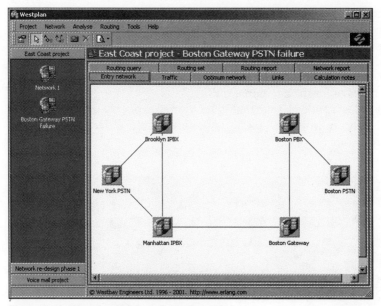

Figure 8-1l: Westplan Network Reconfiguration

(Courtesy of the Westbay Engineers, Ltd.)

Westplan
Project Network Analyse Routing Tools Help
East Coast project
Network 1
Boston Gateway PSTN failure
East Coast project - Boston Gateway PSTN failure
Routing query
Routing set
Routing report
Network report
Entry network
Traffic
Optimum network
Links
Calculation notes
From To Link type Entry BHT Blocking Optimum
Boston Gateway Boston PBX Analogue 45 trunks 43.760 0.095 57 trunks
Boston Gateway Manhattan IPBX VoIP (PPP) 716 kbps 43.760 0.009 716 kbps
Boston PBX Boston PSTN T1 (24B) 4 trunks 89.800 0.043 5 trunks
Brooklyn IPBX Manhattan IPBX VoIP (PPP) 302 kbps 15.200 0.009 302 kbps
Brooklyn IPBX New York PSTN T1 (24B) 2 trunks 25.100 0.000 2 trunks
Manhattan IPBX New York PSTN T1 (24B) 11 trunks 229.360 0.002 11 trunks
Network re-design phase 1
Voice mail project
© Westbay Engineers Ltd. 1996 - 2001. http://www.erlang.com

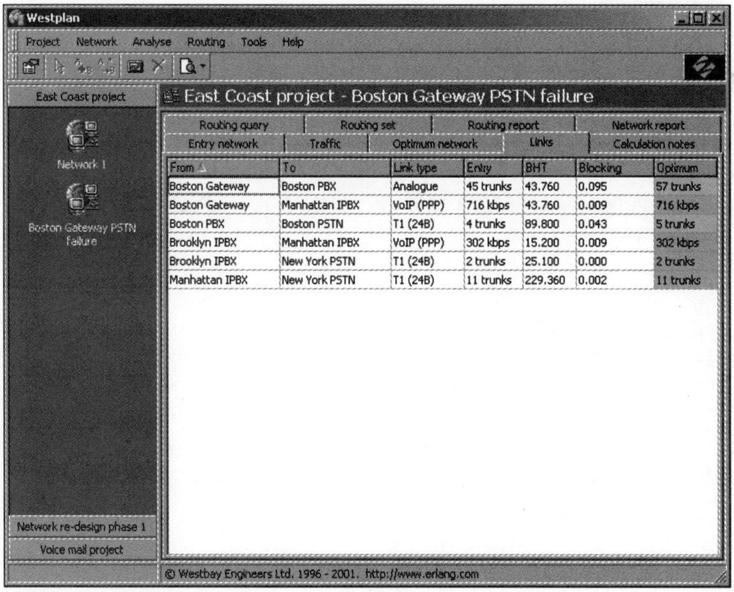

Figure 8-1m: Westplan Network Reconfiguration Analysis

(Courtesy of the Westbay Engineers, Ltd.)

This shows that the blocking on the Boston gateway to Boston PBX circuit becomes 0.095 (9.5 percent), and that in order to restore this link to its optimum call blocking value, the link would need to be increased from 45 to 57 analog trunks. Similarly, unacceptable blocking would be experienced on the PSTN connection to the Boston PBX, and this link would need to be increased from four T1 trunks to five T1 trunks to allow for the additional traffic.

Westplan includes a Guided Tour that gives a brief explanation of the various features of the software while walking the user through the different areas of the program (Figure 8-1n).

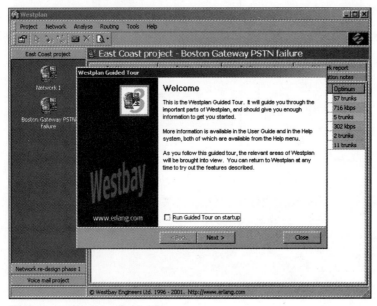

Figure 8-1n: Westplan Guided Tour

(Courtesy of the Westbay Engineers, Ltd.)

Westbay Engineers Ltd. has been providing network design software tools since 1996 and is a trusted supplier of software to organizations around the world. Westbay has also published a number of white papers on network design and traffic analysis that are listed in References [8-2] through [8-4]. Reference [8-5] documents online analysis tools that Westbay makes available on their Web site.

8.2 Interoperability Testing

Interoperability is one of those terms with a fairly simple meaning but widespread implications. If we look at the root terms, we see *inter* (between) and *operate* (to perform a function). So, in other words, *interoperability* defines whether or not two systems work with each other.

With communication networks, interoperability can take on several dimensions: connectivity or configuration, functionality, and performance. For example, will a gateway from Vendor A work with a gateway from Vendor B? Perhaps more importantly, what about the interoperability between legacy network equipment and the new converged network equipment? Or, put another way, will a gateway from Vendor A work with your PBX from Vendor B?

Fortunately, the consortia concerned with network convergence are addressing these challenges head on. The International Multimedia Teleconferencing Consortium (IMTC) [8-6] has sponsored much research into the issue of interoperability. The results of this research, several interoperability frameworks, are the focus of the following sections.

8.2.1 The Voice over IP Forum's Service Interoperability Implementation Agreement

The Voice over IP Forum, affiliated with the IMTC, developed their Service Interoperability Implementation Agreement so that it "combines, clarifies and complements existing standards to provide a complete Internet telephony interoperability protocol." The Implementation Agreement (IA) is based on H.323 and related standards, but it is not intended to replace H.323. Instead, it makes the jobs of the hardware and software developers charged with implementation easier, as it removes some of the inherent ambiguities in all data networking standards.

Thus, when a consensus is reached regarding the interpretation of various elements defined in H.323 prior to product development, the likelihood of vendor-specific interpretations, which could lead to implementations that will not interoperate, is (hopefully) reduced. One could draw an analogy from an old riddle: If you put ten engineers in a room and ask them to read and interpret the same document, how many unique interpretations will you get? The IA is designed to simplify the answer to this question – only one interpretation.

One of the most significant parts of the Interoperability Profile is a recommended protocol stack to be included in each product implementation. As other chapters of this book discuss, multimedia networks encompass many protocol layers ranging from Physical Layer infrastructures to specific applications. For many of these layers, several protocols can be chosen. For example, there are a number of voice encoding algorithms, including ITU-T G.711, G.723.1, G.728, G.729, and others. If one vendor chooses one algorithm (such as G.723.1) and a second vendor chooses another (such as G.728), these two devices will not communicate. They may be able to exchange bits, but there will be no meaningful communication. With choices like this at every level of the protocol stack, the chances that a given vendor's product will operate with any other vendor's product rapidly diminish.

The VoIP Protocol Stack, shown in Figure 8-2, presents specific guidelines organized by functional layer that, if followed, will increase interoperability. Starting at the top of the stack, the Call Establishment and Control function determines the connection setup and disconnect procedures and controls the H.323 session after it has been established. The Presentation function interprets the audio signal and any other audible control information, such as the comfort noise (the background white noise that assures us that the telephone connection is still active) and the Dual Tone Multifrequency (DTMF) signals, or touchtones, that are used for end-user signaling functions. For example, you may use DTMF signals to enter a password to retrieve your voice mail, to navigate your way through an interactive voice response (IVR) system, such as a bank's automated teller system, and so on. The IA specifies two different audio codecs to be used with the Presentation Layer and DTMF: the G.711 codec (64 Kbps) and the G.723.1 codec (5.3 or 6.4 Kbps).

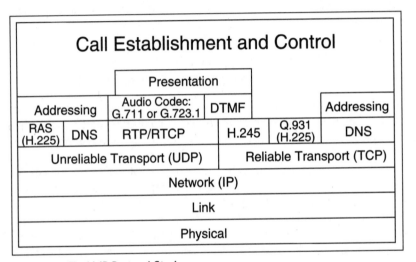

Figure 8–2: The VoIP Protocol Stack

(Courtesy of the IMTC)

The addressing function deals with two issues. First, H.323 terminals may need to locate other terminals by using an H.323 gatekeeper and the Registration, Admission, and Status (RAS) protocol. Second, an H.323 endpoint may need to initially locate an H.323 gatekeeper using the Domain Name System, or DNS. DNS provides a method of associating domain names with IP addresses. Since DNS can operate over both unreliable and reliable transports, it is shown twice in the VoIP Protocol Stack. The Real Time Transport Protocol (RTP) and the Real Time Control Protocol (RTCP) provide control over the digitally encoded analog signals. Recall that both RTP and RTCP are IETF standards, but they are also adopted in the ITU-T H.225.0 recommendation. The H.245 protocol defines control procedures for multimedia communication, such as terminal-to-terminal parameter negotiation messages. Signaling messages, defined in ITU-T Q.931, are also an element of H.225.0. The Q.931 signaling protocol is used with many connection-oriented networks, including ISDN and frame relay. A version of Q.931, known as Q.2931, defines ATM signaling procedures.

Two different transport protocols are specified in the IA. For unreliable transport (connectionless) functions, including RAS, DNS, and audio information transfer, the User Datagram Protocol (UDP) is specified. For reliable (connection-oriented) functions, including terminal parameter negotiation, call signaling, and DNS, the Transmission Control Protocol (TCP) is specified. For both of these cases, the Internet Protocol (IP) is employed at the Network Layer, with the Data Link and Physical Layers left as implementation-independent options.

For those readers wanting to dig deeper, protocol-specific details are described in the IA [8-7].

8.2.2 The iNOW! Standards-Based IP Telephony Interoperability Profile

The Interoperability NOW! (iNOW!) efforts, which are also affiliated with the IMTC, are an extension of the VoIP Forum's Service Interoperability IA research. The IMTC iNOW! Activity Group was formed to serve the needs of both equipment vendors and service providers interested in developing interoperable solutions. ITXC, an Internet Service Provider, spearheaded the formation of the group in 1998 to ensure the interoperability of two of its gateway suppliers, Lucent and VocalTec. After some initial research and development, the partnership demonstrated its interoperability solutions at trade shows, generating interest among other equipment vendors.

A significant result of this effort is the iNOW! Standards-based IP Telephony Interoperability Profile, version 2.1 [8-8]. Five key interoperability issues are addressed in this document:

- ◆ Gateway-to-gateway interoperability (Manufacturer A to/from Manufacturer B)

- ◆ Gatekeeper-to-gatekeeper interoperability (Manufacturer A to/from Manufacturer B)

- ◆ Gatekeeper-to-exchange carrier interoperability (Manufacturer A and Manufacturer B to/from exchange carrier)

- ◆ Phone-to-phone service

- ◆ Fax-to-fax service

The Interoperability Profile extends the work of the VoIP Forum's Implementation Agreement with a specific set of interoperability requirements. These include support for the G.729A (preferred) and G.723.1 (secondary) codecs, as well as support for the T.38 fax protocol. Support for other standards, such as the IETF TCP/IP and UDP/IP protocols, plus the ITU-T V.21, V.27ter, V.29, and V.17 standards, is also required. Reference [8-8] describes the iNOW! objectives and conclusions in greater detail.

8.2.3 H.323 Interoperability Testing

Recent work of the IMTC has focused on interoperability testing between vendors that have developed products compliant with the ITU-T H.323 protocol. This work is part of the Conferencing over IP (CoIP) Activity Group and is documented in Reference [8-9]. The H.323 Interoperability Test Plan includes various scenarios that have been developed to test the systems on an end-to-end basis, evaluating the higher level functions rather than the operation of specific protocol layers. Each of these scenarios is described by defining the H.323 entities involved, such as endpoints, gateways, gatekeepers, and so on; the sequence of tests to be performed; and procedures for scoring the test. In addition, a scoresheet, available as a spreadsheet file, is used to record the testing results. Even though these tests were developed with the vendor community in mind, valuable information can be gleaned for network managers who subject their vendor's products to similar scrutiny. The next several paragraphs describe the various testing scenarios and objectives.

Testing Scenario 0 defines a point-to-point audio/video/data (A/V/D) connection without gatekeeper involvement (Figure 8-3a). In this test, the endpoints take turns calling each other to verify the exchange of call setup messages. The quality of the media channel is then evaluated, and the end stations then terminate the call. This scenario tests the IP addressing, Q.931 signaling messages, H.245 connection establishment, RTP/RTCP payload transmission, and audio codec operation.

Figure 8-3a: Scenario 0: Point-to-Point A/V/D with No Gatekeeper
(Courtesy of the IMTC)

Testing Scenario 1 defines a point-to-point audio/video/data (A/V/D) call within a single zone (Figure 8-3b). In this test, the endpoints interact with the gatekeeper for admission to the network, check the quality of the media path, and then terminate the call to again verify the interaction with the gatekeeper. This test evaluates the end station-to-gatekeeper RAS message handling, such as the ARQ/ACF, DRQ/DCF, and ARQ/ARJ messages, for both the end station and gatekeeper sides of this connection.

Testing Scenario 2 defines a point-to-point audio/video/data (A/V/D) call between multiple zones, which employs two gatekeepers (Figure 8-3c). In this test, an endpoint in one zone calls an endpoint in another zone, the two gatekeepers interact to facilitate the call, the quality of the media transmission is evaluated, and then the call is terminated. This test evaluates the end station-to-gatekeeper and gatekeeper-to-gatekeeper message handling, such as the H.225.0 LRQ, LRJ, DRQ, and DCF messages.

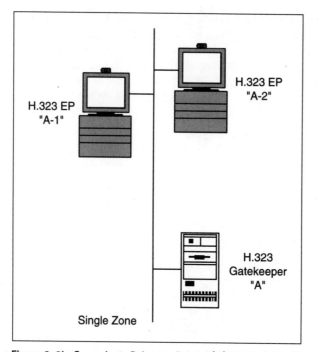

Figure 8–3b: Scenario 1: Point-to-Point A/V/D Call within Single Zone
(Courtesy of the IMTC)

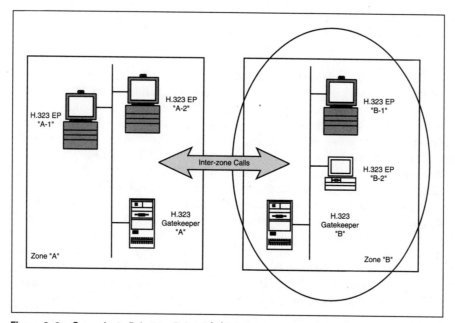

Figure 8–3c: Scenario 2: Point-to-Point A/V/D Call between Multiple Zones
(Courtesy of the IMTC)

Testing Scenario 3 defines a multipoint audio/video/data (A/V/D) call between multiple zones (Figure 8-3d). In this test, two endpoints in one zone interact with the Multipoint Control Unit (MCU) to establish a conference, and then another endpoint is added. The quality of the audio mixing and video switching is evaluated, and then the MCU terminates the conference. This test evaluates the endpoint-to-gatekeeper message handling, plus the interaction between the endpoints and the MCU for conferencing functions.

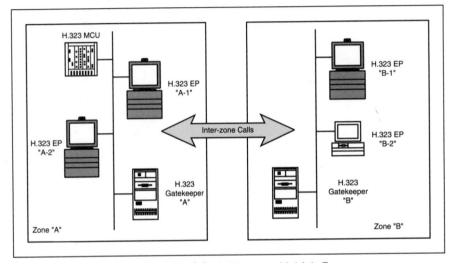

Figure 8–3d: Scenario 3: Multipoint A/V/D Call between Multiple Zones

(Courtesy of the IMTC)

Testing Scenario 4 defines a point-to-point audio/video/data call through an H.323/H.320 gateway (Figure 8-3e). In this test, an endpoint calls an ISDN number, with the call being completed via the gateway. The quality of the media transmission is evaluated, and then the endpoints terminate the call. This test is performed from both the outgoing and incoming call perspectives to test the interactions among the endpoint, gatekeeper, and gateways from both directions.

Testing Scenario 5 defines a multipoint audio/video/data call through an H.323/H.320 gateway (Figure 8-3f). In this test, two endpoints within one zone establish a conference call and evaluate the quality of the media transmission. An H.320 endpoint calls the MCU via the gateway to join the conference, and then all three endpoints evaluate the quality of the mixed audio, switched video, and shared data in the conference. The conference is terminated by the H.320 endpoint, and then the MCU calls an H.320 to invite it to join the conference. This test evaluates the endpoint, gatekeeper, and gatekeeper message handling, plus any address mapping functions that are required for the H.323-to-H.320 call establishment.

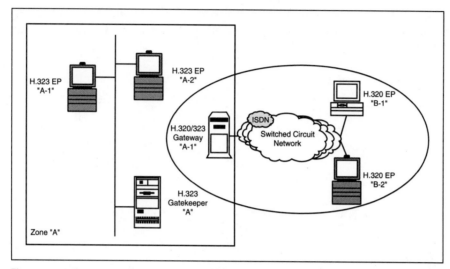

Figure 8-3e: Scenario 4: Point-to-Point A/V/D Call through H.323/H.320 Gateway
(Courtesy of the IMTC)

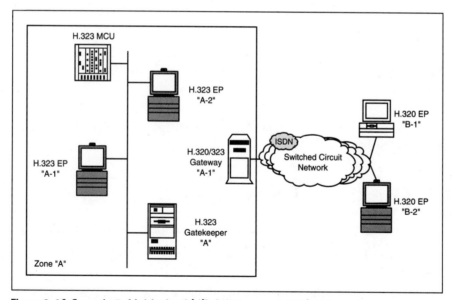

Figure 8-3f: Scenario 5: Multipoint A/V/D Call through H.323/H.320 Gateway
(Courtesy of the IMTC)

Testing Scenario 6 defines a point-to-point audio/video/data call through a Network Address Translation (NAT)/Firewall device (Figure 8-3g). In this test, an endpoint on one side of the firewall calls an endpoint on the other side; the call is established via the proxy. The quality of the media transmission is evaluated, and then the endpoints terminate the call. This test evaluates the interactions between the endpoints and the gatekeeper, plus the interactions between the proxy and the gatekeeper.

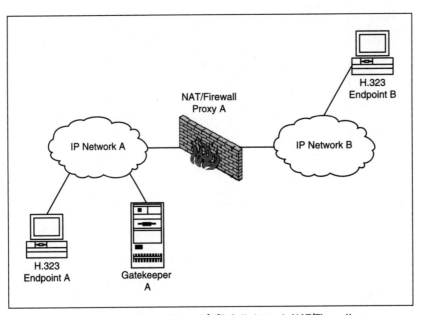

Figure 8-3g: Scenario 6: Point-to-Point A/V/D Call through NAT/Firewall

(Courtesy of the IMTC)

Additional testing scenarios have been proposed and are outlined in the H.323 Interoperability Test Plan [8-9].

8.3 Quality of Service

ITU-T Recommendation E.800 [8-10] defines Quality of Service (QoS) as follows:

> *The collective effect of service performance, which determines the degree of satisfaction of a user of the service.*

In other words, QoS will be significantly influenced by the end users and their perceptions of how well one network service performs in comparison with other network services. Almost everyone has experience with telephone calls over the PSTN and knows what level of quality to expect from that network. Therefore, one of the significant challenges that must be addressed is ensuring that the QoS the end user experiences with the converged network is on par with their previous experience with the PSTN.

Multimedia applications, such as voice and video, are connection-oriented. In contrast, IP-based internetworks are connectionless. Thus, one would expect difficulties when transmitting voice or video signals over a network that was not originally designed for that application. As is discussed in Chapter 4, the use of the Real Time Transport Protocol (RTP) and the User Datagram Protocol (UDP) provides some error and sequence control functions that IP lacks. However, other factors inherent in packet data transmission can affect the QoS that the end user perceives. And since the satisfaction of that community of end users may significantly impact the career of the network manager, a discussion of these factors is in order. But first we should discuss the measurement of QoS.

8.3.1 Measuring Quality of Service

For many years, the telephone industry has employed a very subjective rating system, known as the Mean Opinion Score, or MOS, to measure the quality of telephone connections. These measurement techniques are defined in ITU-T P.800 [8-11] and are based on the opinions of many testing volunteers who listen to a sample of voice traffic and rate the quality of that transmission. In doing so, they consider a number of factors that could degrade the quality of transmission, including loss, circuit noise, sidetone, talker echo, distortion, propagation time (or delay), and other transmission problems.

The most well-known test, described in Annex A of P.800, is called the Conversation Opinion Test. The volunteer subjects are asked to provide their opinion of the connection they have just been using, based on a five-point scale:

Quality	Rating
Excellent	5
Good	4
Fair	3
Poor	2
Bad	1

Since the test subjects are human, some variation in the scores is expected. For that reason, a large number of people are used in the test and their individual scores are averaged (hence the term *Mean* in Mean Opinion Score). A MOS of 4 is considered "toll quality" within the telephone industry.

Other tests are also defined in P.800. The listening test rates the ability of the tester to understand speech over the connection. The noise, fading, and disturbances test rates these problems from inaudible to intolerable. The comparison category rating compares a nonprocessed speech sample with a processed speech sample using ratings from "much better" to "much worse."

Readers needing further information can consult two companion standards, P.861 [8-12] and P.862 [8-13], that define other quality measurements. The first method is called Perceptual Speech Quality Measurement (PSQM) and is defined in P.861. This measurement is used for assessing the quality of voice encoders on a scale of 0 (no degradation) to 6.5 (extensive distortion). The second method is called Perceptual Evaluation of Speech Quality (PESQ) and is defined in P.862. PESQ also addresses the effects of filters, variable delay, and coding distortions, and it is thus applicable for both speech codec evaluation and end-to-end measurements. In summary, the P.800 MOS test is a subjective evaluation and somewhat dependent upon the interpretations of the humans performing the analysis, while those tests defined in P.861 and P.862 are objective measurements and are implementable in hardware for greater accuracy.

8.3.2 Factors Affecting the Quality of Service

In an ideal environment, voice and fax over IP signals move through seven steps in their journey from source to destination via the IP-based infrastructure (see Figure 8-4 and Reference [8-14]).

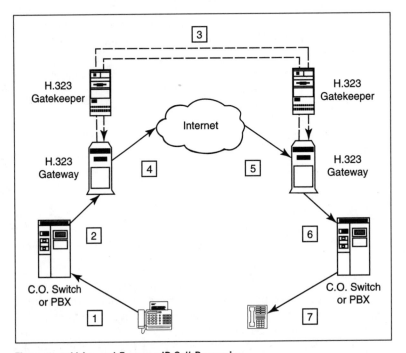

Figure 8-4: Voice and Fax over IP Call Processing

(Courtesy of U.S. Bancorp Piper Jaffray)

These seven steps include:

1. Conversion of the analog signal into a digital signal at the central office, PBX, or gateway.

2. Communication to a gateway, which may further process the signal by compressing the data, suppressing silence on the circuit, and canceling echoes.

3. The gateway may communicate with one or more gatekeepers for admission to the network, translation of telephone numbers to IP addresses, and other management-related functions.

4. The processed signal will then be placed into IP datagrams and transmitted over the IP-based network.

5. At the receiving end, the IP datagrams will be converted back into a digital bit stream at the destination gateway.

6. The digital bit stream is decompressed and sent to a receiving central office or PBX.

7. The digital signals are converted into an analog signal and sent to the intended recipient.

In an ideal case, where transmission bandwidth is either plentiful or has been reserved using some mechanism such as the Resource Reservation Protocol (RSVP), this packet-based (connectionless) transmission proceeds as if it were a connection-oriented network operation (Figure 8-5). (Packet delay, which is present even under the most ideal conditions, will have a small but measurable effect on the MOS.)

Unfortunately, not all packet transmission follows the ideal model. Some packets may be lost due to difficulties in the routing infrastructure, collisions on the local Ethernet, transmission impairments such as noisy lines, and so on. The result is a received message that is missing some of its components (Figure 8-6).

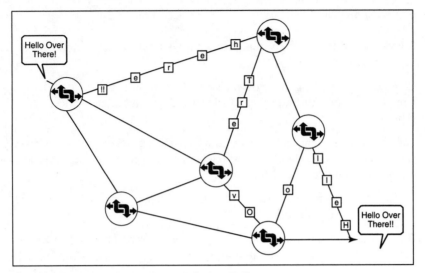

Figure 8-5: IP Telephony Transmission (with RSVP)

(Courtesy of U.S. Bancorp Piper Jaffray)

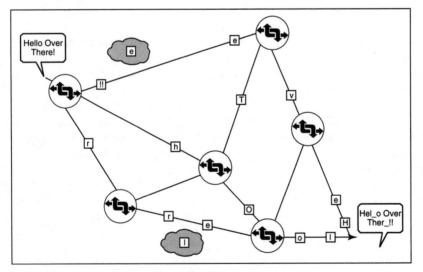

Figure 8-6: IP Telephony Transmission (with Packet Loss)

(Courtesy of U.S. Bancorp Piper Jaffray)

Delay, or latency, can also affect the quality of the transmission (Figure 8-7). The delay is the difference in time between when the signal is transmitted and when it is received. Delay is typically characterized by two components: a fixed delay and a variable delay. The fixed delays are found within the signal processing elements, such as the processing delays inherent in the voice codecs, and also within the physical transmission systems, such as the copper pairs. The variable delays result from queuing times at packet processing points, such as switches and routers, as well as transmission variables, such as the specific route that a particular packet took and any difficulties, such as congestion, that might be experienced on that route. Some of these delays can be controlled by the network manager with thoughtful network engineering decisions. For example, voice gateways containing codecs with lower processing delays could be selected, or additional bandwidth could be provisioned on the wide area network to lower the likelihood of network congestion. There are delay elements that cannot be optimized, such as the physical propagation delay. Electromagnetic signals propagate at approximately one nanosecond per foot on copper transmission facilities, while optical fiber systems, including the repeaters, have approximately ten milliseconds of delay per 1,000 miles. Both of these are principles of physics that must be dealt with.

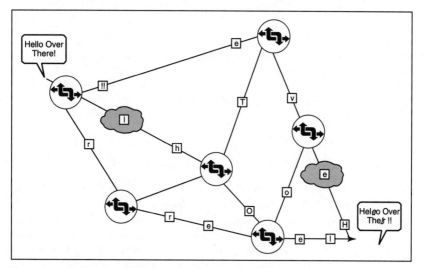

Figure 8-7: IP Telephony Transmission (with Packet Delay)

(Courtesy of U.S. Bancorp Piper Jaffray)

Packet jitter is the variation in arrival rates between individual packets (Figure 8-8). With packet networks, it is possible that a sequence of packets that enter the network at a constant rate will reach the intended destination by a number of routes. Since each of these routes may have unique delay characteristics, it is possible for the arrival rates of the packets to vary. For non-real-time signals, such as an e-mail transmission, this signal would not be an issue. However, for real-time signals such as voice, which are dependent upon a continuous flow of data, jitter affects the signal quality. To correct for jitter, the packets are buffered, or delayed, at the receiver and then played out at a continuous rate. Unfortunately, this buffering adds to the overall latency of the packet transmission.

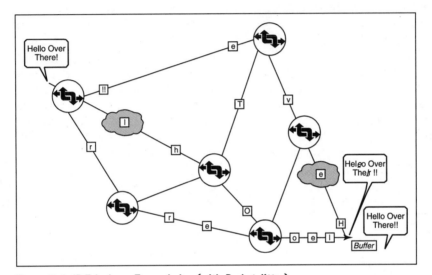

Figure 8–8: IP Telephony Transmission (with Packet Jitter)

(Courtesy of U.S. Bancorp Piper Jaffray)

8.3.3 Signal Echo and Echo Cancellation

The block diagram of a typical full-duplex hardware implementation is shown in Figure 8-9. Both the transmitter and the receiver have connections from the telephone sets to a transformer called a *hybrid*. The hybrid performs two-wire to four-wire conversions, such that the connection from the central office to your premises (two-wire) can be divided into both transmit and receive paths (total of four wires). Most transformers have some degree of inefficiency; in other words, they do not pass all of the energy that is applied to their primary winding onto the secondary winding(s). Some of that energy is reflected back to the source. That reflected energy is called an *echo*. The Echo Canceller subtracts (or cancels) out the energy that was reflected from the distant end of the connection prior to delivering that signal to the other client processes, such as the speech encoding, packet transmission, and other functions.

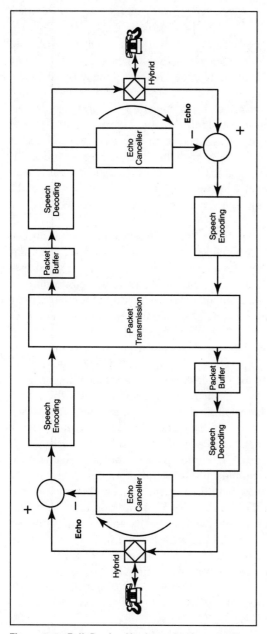

Figure 8-9: Full-Duplex Hardware Implementation

(Courtesy of the IMTC)

8.3.4 Sources of Network Delays

Three of the above transmission impairments — packet loss, packet delay, and packet jitter — impact the quality of the received signal. Since a common theme among all three of these issues is delay, or latency, this component is worthy of further exploration.

There are a number of factors that affect the application performance as perceived by the end users. Perhaps the most significant of these is the end-to-end delay. The maximum recommended one-way delay for most user applications, as specified in ITU-T G.114, is 150 milliseconds, or a round-trip delay of 300 milliseconds [8-15]. However, since voice quality is a very subjective measurement, some end users find variations above and below these standard specifications to be acceptable; therefore, round-trip objectives between 200–400 milliseconds are often quoted.

Review Figure 8-9 and note that the delays from a client implementation can come from several sources. The speech encoder incurs delays based on the algorithm used [8-16]. This encoding delay may consist of two components: a processing delay necessary to run the algorithm on the current frame of voice information, and a lookahead delay that occurs while the algorithm is looking at the next frame for correlation purposes. For example, the G.723.1 algorithm (which operates at 5.3 or 6.4 Kbps) has a processing delay of 30 milliseconds and a lookahead delay of 7.5 milliseconds, for a total coding delay of 37.5 milliseconds. In contrast, the G.729 and G.729A algorithms (which operate at 8 Kbps) have a processing delay of 10 milliseconds and a lookahead delay of 5 milliseconds, for a total coding delay of 15 milliseconds. Note the tradeoff between bit rate and coding delay — the lowest bit rate coder (G.723.1) also has a higher coding delay (37.5 milliseconds). Thus, when selecting VoIP equipment such as gateways, it behooves the network manager to ask the vendor which algorithms are available and what delays result from each one.

Other delays include switching, routing, and other packet processing delays (typically a few milliseconds); transmission delays (dependent on the speed of the transmission link, and typically less than 10 milliseconds); signal propagation delays (dependent on the physical length of the transmission link); jitter buffer delays (typically a settable parameter between 20–40 milliseconds); and decoding delays (typically half of the encoding delay, as noted in Reference [8-16]). These sources of typical delays are summarized in Figure 8-10.

References [8-17] through [8-21] provide good discussions regarding sources of network delays. Cisco Systems, Inc.'s, *IP Telephony Network Design Guide* [8-22] presents additional examples of network delay calculations and discusses configuration options for their premises equipment.

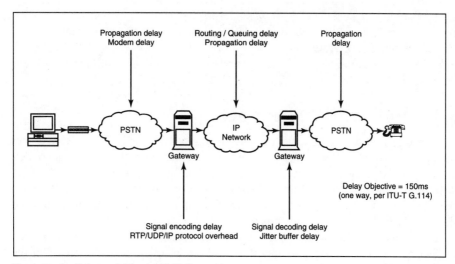

Figure 8-10: Delays within the VoIP Network

8.4 Implementing Quality of Service

Having discussed the various factors that affect QoS, such as latency within the network, packet delays and loss, and so on, the next question that must be addressed is the industry response – what steps are being taken to improve QoS within IP-based internetworks?

The traditional solution to improving service performance – throwing more bandwidth at the problem – can be expensive, especially on the WAN side of the equation. As a result, net managers are looking for ways to optimize the performance of their network infrastructures. A number of alternatives have been proposed, but at the time of this writing there is not sufficient industry experience with any one of these alternatives to declare it the leading solution. This section presents a summary of the various proposals, along with sources for additional research.

8.4.1 Integrated Services

Integrated Services (int-serv) is a model developed by the IETF and characterized by the reservation of network resources prior to the transmission of any data. The Resource Reservation Protocol (RSVP), which is defined in RFC 2205 and discussed in Chapter 4, Section 4.8, of this book, is the signaling protocol that is used to reserve the bandwidth on that transmission path. An end station that supports RSVP may request a particular level of network performance from the network, and at each downstream node the protocol attempts to reserve network resources on behalf of that end station. RSVP is designed to operate in conjunction with current routing protocols, such as the Open Shortest Path First (OSPF) and Border Gateway Protocols (BGP), and relies on these other protocols to determine where reservation requests should be sent. The int-serv model is implemented by four components: the Signaling Protocol (RSVP), an Admission Control Routine (which determines if network resources are available), a Classifier (which puts packets in specific queues), and a Packet Scheduler (which schedules packets to meet QoS requirements). Details regarding int-serv are found in RFC 1633 [8-23].

8.4.2 Differentiated Services

Differentiated Services (diff-serv) was also developed by the IETF. It distinguishes packets that require different network services into different classes. In effect, diff-serv provides a relative priority scheme, whereby the packets are handled differently based on the values of an 8-bit Differentiated Services (DS) field. That DS field replaces the IPv4 Type of Service (TOS) field or the IPv6 Traffic Class field (these fields are fortunately also 8 bits in length). Packets are classified at the network ingress node according to some Service Level Agreement (SLA) criteria established between the Internet service provider (ISP) and the customer. It is assumed that the ISP would offer different levels of service, and also different cost structures, for the various options defined by the DS field. Details regarding diff-serv are found in RFC 2474 [8-24] and are also discussed in Reference [8-25].

8.4.3 Multiprotocol Label Switching

Multiprotocol Label Switching (MPLS) is a forwarding scheme based on tag switching mechanisms developed by router vendors over the past few years. With MPLS, a 32-bit header (sometimes called the "tag") is placed between the local network and IP headers of the packet when it enters the MPLS domain. This header determines how that packet will be handled by the intervening routers. Because these routers must be able to interpret and act upon this new label, the MPLS-capable routers are called Label Switching Routers, or LSRs. The packets are classified at the ingress LSR, and only that 32-bit header is examined to determine how the packet should be handled within the network. Since the LSR only examines the MPLS header and not the entire IP header, this QoS mechanism can operate independently of the Network Layer protocol (such as IP) that is currently in use. Hence the word "multiprotocol" in the term MPLS. Details regarding MPLS are found in RFC 2702 [8-26] and are also discussed in References [8-27] and [8-28].

8.4.4 Queuing and Congestion Avoidance Mechanisms

Many router vendors have developed mechanisms to improve QoS for time-sensitive applications such as voice and video. Most of these techniques fall into two general categories: priority queuing and congestion avoidance mechanisms.

Queuing mechanisms create multiple signal queues within the router and allocate the available bandwidth to these queues according to some algorithm and/or network administrator-supplied rules. Cisco Systems' technique, called Weighted Fair

Queuing (WFQ), classifies various incoming data flows according to source/destination address, protocol in use, or application/port, and then grants each one of these flows a specific amount of outgoing bandwidth based on some fairness criteria. Reference [8-29] discusses queuing strategies.

Congestion avoidance mechanisms augment the flow control properties that exist within protocols. With many of these protocols, such as TCP, data flows are retarded only after the network becomes congested, which causes packets to be dropped. The Random Early Detection (RED) and Weighted Random Early Detection (WRED) mechanisms attempt to anticipate when these congestion points will occur and discard packets based on criteria such as buffer length or the Precedence bits within the IP header. Thus, RED or WRED minimizes the likelihood of large numbers of packets being sent to already congested queues, which would only result in further packet discard. Details regarding Cisco's use of the WFQ and RED mechanisms are found in Reference [8-22].

As might be expected, networking vendors differ in both their approaches and their recommendations regarding IP QoS issues. A trade organization, known as the QoS Forum [8-30], has been established as a central point for information exchange, interoperability testing, and education. References [8-31] through [8-33] provide additional information on QoS-related issues and implementations.

8.5 Deploying the Converged Network

Considering implementing Voice over IP? Better look before you leap – this marketplace is exploding with new vendors, products, and services. Some are ready for prime time, and some may need a little more experience. Here are some tips to get you started:

◆ **Do your homework:** For most network managers, the voice world, with its own applications and standards, is new territory. For example, are you familiar with analog and digital trunk circuits, traffic measurements, Erlang tables, and the like? If not, start learning. Many VoIP vendors and trade groups have Web sites with a wealth of information, including white papers, case studies, primers on standards, newsletters, evaluation copies of client software, and so on.

◆ **Tap your existing resources:** In many cases, the voice communication and data/networking responsibilities are handled by separate departments. Each may have a separate budget, and an empire to match. But there are likely two areas of expertise as well: circuit switching and traffic analysis for the voice side, and packet switching and IP knowledge on the networking side. Both of these skill sets are required for a successful VoIP implementation – force these two groups to collaborate, and tap into your existing resources.

◆ **Intranet versus Internet:** Voice over your corporate intranet and voice over the worldwide Internet is not the same. In the case of your intranet, you, as the network manager, can exert some control over the number of hops between two points, and the ensuing latencies. In contrast, the Internet was not designed for time-sensitive traffic that demands low delays. As a result, traffic that traverses the Internet must take whatever capacity is available at the time. Therefore, get a good handle on your objectives. Are you willing to spend the effort to redesign your intranet as required to support voice, or are you simply looking for a lower-cost alternative for voice transport? Understand the various tradeoffs between intranet and Internet transport before you begin.

◆ **Know your traffic:** Make sure that your data network can handle the increased amount of traffic before you add voice traffic to the mix. Many net managers are surprised to learn that the slow, steady growth of a few percent per month of network traffic can lead to a substantial increase when considered on an annualized basis. In other words, that T3 circuit you put in just last year may be getting close to its capacity during peak traffic periods. Make sure you really have the excess capacity that you think is available. The VoIP equipment should have mechanisms to meter the available end-to-end bandwidth and to reject additional calls when insufficient bandwidth is available. In addition, get a handle on the number of hops between selected destinations and the resulting network latency, as these delays will dramatically affect the quality of the packetized voice and video service.

Most telephone traffic is characterized using statistical models called the *Erlang tables,* which were named after A. K. Erlang, a Danish scientist who was an early pioneer in the study of telephone network design. These models are used for traffic engineering studies and can be applied to a variety of voice-based applications, including PBXs, voice mail, and interactive voice response systems. Typical applications of Erlang analysis would be to calculate the number of lines required for a particular grade of service, the number of call agents that are needed for a given call volume, and so on. An inexpensive software package, called the Westbay Traffic Calculators from Westbay Engineers Ltd. (West Sussex, U.K.), is available to ease these calculations. (A demo version of this software is available on the CD that accompanies this text.)

◆ **Measuring performance:** Your end users will likely judge the success or failure of the converged network implementation based, in part, on their current perception of the telephone industry, which is known for high-quality, reliable service. (The number of 99.999 percent — or "five nines" — of reliability is an often-quoted statistic.) Thus, in addition to managing the hardware and software elements of the network, the net architect must also consider the clients' expectations of service and reliability. To do this effectively, performance details regarding the various VoIP network elements should be measured, such as packet delay and packet loss, signal/noise ratios, and other statistics that affect voice and data transmission quality. The ability to baseline the network and identify service-affecting trends as they develop are also key ingredients for optimum performance tuning. Do you have performance tools, such as network monitors, analyzers, and management consoles, available that can give you an objective window into the operation of your converged network?

◆ **Watch your existing carrier contracts:** Many net managers have existing service contracts with their carriers that should be reviewed prior to jumping into VoIP service. A significant number of minutes may need to be diverted from existing carrier commitments to new IP services in order for the economics of the new hardware investments to be favorable. And when that diversion occurs, you may end up paying more for your existing voice services.

For example, assume that your existing service agreement specifies a rate of $0.05 per minute if you use one million minutes per month, and $0.03 per minute if you use two million minutes per month. Assume that you have recently used over two million minutes per month (at $0.03), but you estimate that you will drop substantially below this amount when you divert some of your voice traffic to data transport. In this new scenario, the existing (non-IP) voice traffic will cost you $0.05 per minute because you have dropped below a price point. In other words, while reducing costs with new IP services, you may increase costs for the remaining voice services. A word to the wise: look at the interrelated economics before you commit. In addition, a Service Level Agreement (SLA) that specifies uptime, throughput, and point-to-point latency objectives should be included in that carrier commitment.

◆ **International versus domestic long distance:** One of the early driving factors in the VoIP marketplace has been the promise of "free" or very low cost long-distance service. But before you take this promise at face value, get a good handle on your calling patterns and determine what percentage of your traffic is international versus domestic. With international rates in excess of $1.00 per minute to some destinations, VoIP rates that are only a few cents per minute look very favorable and make some compromises in quality worth it. The domestic story may paint a completely different picture, as most managers of enterprise networks are able to negotiate voice contracts that are comparable to the VoIP quotes. Clearly understand your traffic destinations so that your economic model is not unfairly biased.

◆ **Proprietary or not?** Be aware that the standards supporting multimedia networks are still relatively new, and, as a result, several generations of products are available: vendor-proprietary solutions; vendor-proprietary solutions that have been tested with other vendors for interoperability; products that claim to be compliant with standards, such as T.120 and H.323; and products that have been tested for interoperability. The International Multimedia Teleconferencing Consortium (IMTC), a nonprofit organization with over 100 members, conducts periodic interoperability tests of vendors' equipment. Become familiar with these testing efforts.

◆ **Selecting a voice codec:** The analog voice must be converted to a digital pulse stream before it can be placed into packets and sent over a corporate intranet or the Internet. A codec (short for coder/decoder) is the device that performs these voice processing functions. A variety of standards are available, including the ITU-T G.711 (64 Kbps voice), G.729 (8 Kbps), and G.723.1 (5.3–6.4 Kbps). In addition, a number of vendors have developed their own proprietary schemes. Each one of these alternatives has unique characteristics, including the quality and delay associated with the coding algorithm, which vary with the amount of voice information that is being crammed into the packet. It is therefore important to understand the characteristics of the voice to be transmitted, as well as the expectations of the end users. Do the network requirements include the ability to pass fax traffic or music-on-hold over IP? Or is voice traffic the sole need? Does the gateway product allow for multiple codec options, or is it locked into only one standard and/or algorithm? Ask some questions about the codecs to better match your network requirements.

◆ **Application priorities:** Real-time traffic, such as voice and video, should be given priority over more routine transmissions such as file transfers and e-mail. Several methods are possible: setting a priority by IP address, by protocol, or by using a reservation protocol, such as the Resource Reservation Protocol (RSVP). However, not all routers are configurable to support one or all of the above schemes. Check your existing routing infrastructure to see if prioritization capabilities exist.

◆ **Ease of use:** Remember the early days of alternative carriers, when you had to remember to dial an extra dozen access digits and account codes to complete a long distance call? Users have higher expectations now – voice gateways must be easy for the end users to operate and must work within existing dialing plans if they are going to be accepted. As you research various products, ask for a demonstration of the dialing sequence that is required to access the VoIP network, and verify that it is compatible both technically and procedurally with your existing methods of establishing, transferring, and otherwise managing voice calls.

◆ **Interoperability with existing voice systems:** What's your application? The VoIP gateway may need to interoperate with a number of existing and future voice processing systems such as your private branch exchange (PBX), automatic call director (ACD), interactive voice response (IVR) system, and others. Do the trunk circuit port types on your PBX match those that are available from your gateway vendors? Are the signaling protocols between switches compatible with the new VoIP gear? Are you planning any future expansion or applications, such as a migration to ISDN or the installation of a Web-enabled call center? Make sure that the new VoIP hardware is compatible with all other voice systems.

A related issue to examine is the number of signal processing steps from the source to the destination. In general, the voice quality degrades in proportion to the number of signal compression/decompression segments that occur on an end-to-end basis. Therefore, if such processing occurs in each of the PBX, voice mail, and VoIP gateway systems, voice quality is likely to suffer. Consider whether any of these steps can be combined, such as being integrated within the PBX system, to reduce the number of end-to-end signal processing functions.

References [8-34] through [8-37] provide additional implementation suggestions.

8.6 Looking Ahead

In this chapter, you have considered a number of issues that may arise during the implementation phase of a converged network. In the next chapter, you can dig deeper by looking into techniques of protocol analysis that can be used to resolve problems that occur in operational converged networks.

8.7 References

[8-1] Information regarding Westbay Engineers Ltd.'s network design software can be found at www.erlang.com.

[8-2] Westbay Engineers Ltd. "Network Design." White paper available at www.erlang.com/design.html.

[8-3] Westbay Engineers Ltd. "What Is an Erlang?" White paper available at www.erlang.com/whatis.html.

[8-4] Westbay Engineers Ltd. "Voice over IP Bandwidth." White paper available at www.erlang.com/bandwidth.html.

[8-5] Westbay Engineers Ltd. has a number of free traffic calculators for dimensioning telecommunications networks available at www.erlang.com/calculator/.

[8-6] Information regarding the work of the International Multimedia Teleconferencing Consortium can be found at www.imtc.org.

[8-7] The International Multimedia Teleconferencing Consortium. IMTC Voice over IP Forum Service Interoperability Agreement 1.0, December 1, 1997. Available at `ftp://ftp.imtc-files.org/imtc-site/VoIP-AG/incoming/VoIP_IA1.doc`.

[8-8] The International Multimedia Teleconferencing Consortium. iNOW! Standards–Based IP Telephony Interoperability Profile, version 2.1, September 7, 1999. Available at `ftp://ftp.imtc-files.org/imtc-site/inow/`, and then choose Profile version 2.1.

[8-9] The International Multimedia Teleconferencing Consortium, Conferencing over IP (CoIP) Activity Group. H.323 Interoperability Test Plan. Available at `ftp://ftp.imtc-files.org/imtc-site/CoIP-AG/testing/CoIP-H323TestPlan6.zip`.

[8-10] International Telecommunications Union – Telecommunication Standardization Sector. *Terms and Definitions Relating to Quality of Service and Network Performance Including Dependability.* ITU-T Recommendation E.800, August 1994.

[8-11] International Telecommunications Union – Telecommunication Standardization Sector. *Methods for Subjective Determination of Transmission Quality.* ITU-T Recommendation P.800, August 1996.

[8-12] International Telecommunications Union – Telecommunication Standardization Sector. *Objective Measurements of Telephone-band (300–3,400 Hz) Speech Codecs.* ITU-T Recommendation P.861, February 1998.

[8-13] International Telecommunications Union – Telecommunication Standardization Sector. *Perceptual Evaluation of Speech Quality (PESQ), an Objective Method for End-to-End Speech Quality Assessment of Narrow-Band Telephone Networks and Speech Codecs.* ITU-T Recommendation P.862, February 2001.

[8-14] Jackson, Edward R., and Andrew M. Schroepfer. *IP Telephony: Driving the Open Communications Revolution.* Piper Jaffray Equity Research Report, February 1999.

[8-15] International Telecommunications Union – Telecommunication Standardization Sector. *General Characteristics of International Telephone Connections and International Telephone Circuits – One-Way Transmission Time.* ITU-T Recommendation G.114, February 1996.

[8-16] Cox, Richard V., and Peter Kroon. "Low Bit-Rate Speech Coders for Multimedia Communication." *IEEE Communications Magazine* (December 1996): 34–41.

[8-17] Kostas, Thomas J., et al. "Real Time Voice over Packet Switched Networks." *IEEE Network* (January/February 1998): 18–27.

[8-18] Goodman, Bill. "Internet Telephony and Modem Delay." *IEEE Network* (May/June 1999): 8–16.

[8-19] Hassan, Mahbub, et al. "Internet Telephony: Services, Technical Challenges, and Products." *IEEE Communications Magazine* (April 2000): 96–102.

[8-20] Dickey, Clinton. "Voice and Data Convergence – Migration to an IP Telephony Network." White paper available at `www.cirilium.com/gfx/news/ip_telephony_white_paper.doc`, April 2000.

[8-21] Percy, Alan. "Understanding Latency in IP Telephony." White paper available at `www.brooktrout.com/whitepapers/pdf/iptel_latency.pdf`.

[8-22] Cisco Systems, Inc. *IP Telephony Network Design Guide.* Customer Order Number DOC-7811103, Text Part Number 78-11103-03, available at `www.cisco.com/offer/tdm_home/iptelephony/designguide.shtml`, 2001.

[8-23] Braden, R., et al. "Integrated Services in the Internet Architecture: An Overview." RFC 1633, June 1994.

[8-24] Nichols, K., et al. "Definition of the Differentiated Services Field (DS Field) in the IPv4 and IPv6 Headers." RFC 2474, December 1998.

[8-25] Forberg, Richard, and Tim Hale. "Internet Protocol Quality of Service (IP QoS) – Using DiffServ for Application-Specific Service Level Agreements." White paper available at `www.quarrytech.com/IP_QoS_Whitepaper.pdf`, 2001.

[8-26] Awduche, D., et al. "Requirements for Traffic Engineering Over MPLS." RFC 2702, September 1999.

[8-27] Woods, Darrin S. "MPLS: A New Traffic Cop for Your WAN." *Network Computing* (July 10, 2000): 98–102.

[8-28] Nortel Networks Limited provides an extensive array of resources and white papers in support of MPLS technology, which is available at `www.nortelnetworks.com/corporate/technology/mpls/doclib.html`.

[8-29] Conover, Joel. "Fine-Tuning for IP QoS." *Network Computing* (November 27, 2000): 89–101.

[8-30] Information regarding The QoS Forum is available at `www.qosforum.com`.

[8-31] Xiao, Xipeng, and Lionel M. Ni. "Internet QoS: A Big Picture." *IEEE Network* (March/April 1999): 8–18.

[8-32] Avaya, Inc. "Avaya IP Voice Quality Network Requirements." White paper available at `www1.avaya.com/enterprise/whitepapers/voicequalreqs.pdf`, 2001.

[8-33] Ortiz, Luis F. "Solving QoS in VoIP: A Formula for Explosive Growth?" White paper available at `www.brooktrout.com/news/in_the_news/0701_solve_qos.pdf`.

[8-34] Carden, Philip. "Building Voice over IP." *Network Computing TechWeb* (May 20, 2000), available at `www.nwc.com/netdesign/1109voipfull.html`.

[8-35] Hamilton, Scott, and Charles Bruno. "What You Need to Know Before You Deploy VoIP." White paper available at `www.netiq.com/Downloads/ Library/White_Papers/#CHR`, 2001.

[8-36] Polycom, Inc. "Video Communications: Building Blocks for a Simpler Deployment." White paper available at `esupport.polycom.com/ whitepapers/vc_deploy.pdf`, March 2001.

[8-37] Woods, Darrin. "Building a Video-Friendly Network." *Network Computing TechWeb* (July 9, 2001), available at `www.networkcomputing.com/ 1214/1214ws2.html`.

Chapter 9

Analyzing Converged Networks

At some point in time, you may need to use a protocol analyzer to dig deeper into the operation of your converged network and look at the bit-level protocol information from either a network optimization or network troubleshooting perspective. This chapter, illustrated with output from the Sniffer Pro Network Analyzer from Network Associates, Inc., provides an introduction into what you will see during those analysis adventures. I compare two examples: one using SIP, and the other using H.323, with both making an IP network-based telephone call. References [9-1] through [9-8] are good resources regarding voice-based network analysis. But before I jump into the analysis part, I want to review a few technical issues.

9.1 Analyzing Voice Networks

Chapter 4 examined the various protocols used within a Voice over IP network, including IP for datagram addressing; RIP, OSPF, and other protocols that keep the routing infrastructure updated, plus TCP or UDP that assure reliable end-to-end message delivery. Chapter 4 also explained that IP was developed with data transport in mind, and therefore other protocols such as RTP, RTCP, and SDP would be required to support real-time applications such as voice or video. These protocols were summarized in Figure 4-21, which is repeated below as Figure 9-1 for the convenience of the readers. Recall that some protocols use the connectionless UDP to ensure reliability, while others use the connection-oriented TCP for that function. In general, protocols that deal with the establishment, management, and termination of connections use TCP. In contrast, RTP, which is strictly used for packet transport, uses UDP. The theory behind this is that connections must be reliably established for any communication to proceed, while the loss of a voice sample here and there is not such a major issue.

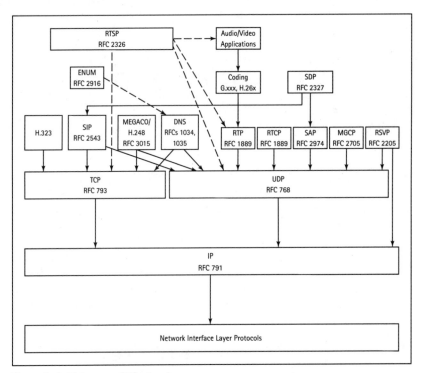

Figure 9-1: Voice over IP Protocols

The resulting Voice over IP packet format is discussed in Chapter 4 and illustrated in Figure 4-26. Note that the voice sample information is quite small – typically around 20 milliseconds long and comprising 20 octets of transmitted information (these values are noted as typical for use with the Real Time Protocol, RTP, as defined in RFC 1889). Differences between different encoding schemes may cause these numbers to vary slightly. For example, the G.723.1 encoder operating at 6.3 Kbps transmits 24 octets of audio information, as illustrated in Figure 9-2. The use of this encoder is studied in Section 9.3.

Thus, if you consider a packet format with the G.723.1 encoding shown in Figure 9-2, and assume that no additional fields, such as options and extensions, are required, the overall efficiency of the voice packet transport would be 37.5 percent (the voice sample payload (24 octets) divided by the sum of the nominal IP, UDP, and RTP headers, plus the voice sample payload (64 octets)). An obvious improvement in efficiency would be to put more than one voice sample in the payload, which is used with some encoding schemes, and another might be to compress the header information in some fashion. But when all the results were tabulated, it would be clear that the network bandwidth required to support a 6.3 Kbps G.723.1 encoder would be several times that of the encoder itself.

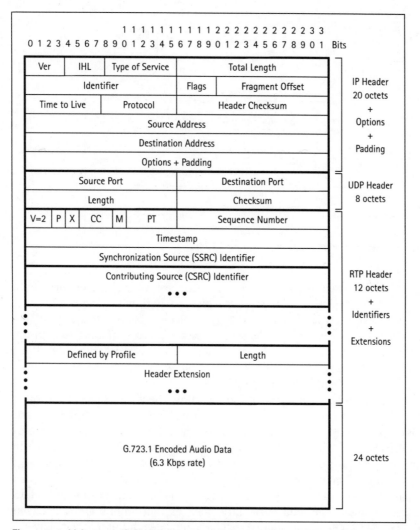

Figure 9-2: Voice over IP Packet Format with G.723.1 Encoded Audio Data (6.3 Kbps rate)

And when you take into account the bandwidth required to support the various call setup messages, plus the periodically transmitted RTCP packets, the efficiency calculations just discussed may be further degraded. Most voice or data connections require five typical operations, as illustrated in Figure 9-3: station initialization, establishment of the connection between the two endpoints, a parameter exchange between the parties, the data transfer itself, and then the termination of the connection. All of these functions add to both the overhead and the complexity of the system.

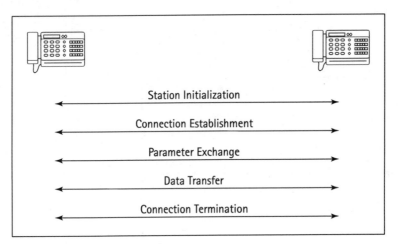

Figure 9-3: Call Establishment Processes

Therefore (as discussed in Chapter 3 on Business Case Analysis), there need to be multiple reasons to deploy a Voice over IP network. These might include the projected return from a new application, such as a voice-enabled Web site, and labor savings from consolidating separate voice and data support staffs into one. In this way, you obtain a more accurate picture of the network cost savings than if you focus all of the analysis solely on the bandwidth savings, which, in the final analysis, may not be as great as initially anticipated.

The next two sections look at the actual data flows between workstations operating in VoIP environments. The first example considers a SIP environment, and the second looks at H.323. One word of caution: both SIP and H.323 are complex protocols documented with hundreds of pages of specifications. The descriptions below are intended to provide an overview of the protocol operation with brief examples of protocol analyzer capabilities and are not intended to drill down into bit-level parameters passed between end stations. In addition, most standards allow some degree of implementation variability, such as the options and extensions shown in Figure 9-2. Therefore, another vendor's implementation that you may run across could vary from those illustrated in the following sections. Both implementations may be equally correct from a protocol standards perspective. The variances may simply illustrate one vendor's choices from a list of allowable alternatives that may not exactly match those alternatives selected by another vendor. And from a strict protocol perspective, both may be in adherence to the same standard, but implemented in a slightly different fashion. Readers needing finer details should first review Chapters 4 and 6 of this text and then consult the standards upon which these protocols are based.

9.2 SIP Phone-to-Phone Connections

This first case study considers SIP, the Session Initiation Protocol. Recall from Section 6.2 that SIP was developed by the IETF and is designed to work in conjunction with RTP and other IETF-developed multimedia protocols. The network in this example is a bus topology with three SIP devices of interest: SIP-compatible telephones manufactured by Cisco Systems, Inc. (San Jose, California), and Pingtel Corp. (Woburn, Massachusetts), plus a Proxy Server (Figure 9-4). The Proxy Server operates on behalf of the end users to facilitate the call processing. Once the call has been established via the Proxy Server, the RTP media streams flow between the end stations directly (Figure 9-5).

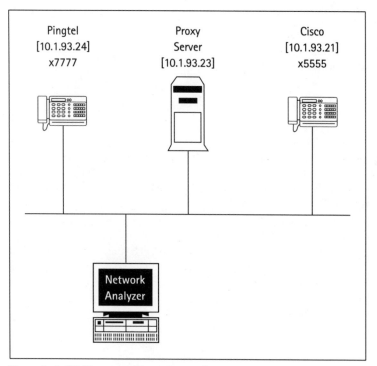

Figure 9-4: SIP Phone-to-Phone Connections

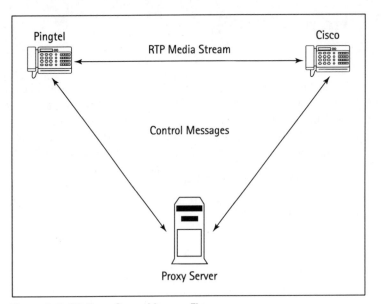

Figure 9–5: SIP Proxy Server Message Flow

A summary of these protocol interactions is shown in Figure 9-6, with the protocol details illustrated in Trace 9.2a. This trace file format from the Sniffer is called the Summary Display, as it provides a summary of the protocol interactions on a frame-by-frame basis. The fields of this display include the Frame Number (the numbers may not be consecutive if information irrelevant to this analysis has been filtered out); the Delta Time (the time, measured in seconds, between the frames); the Destination Address (the station to which the information was sent); the Source Address (the station from which the information originated); and the Summary (a brief summary of the protocol operation contained within that frame). From Trace 9.2a, note that the communication begins with a SIP INVITE message sent from the Pingtel Phone to the Proxy Server. The Proxy Server then responds with a TRYING message and also sends an INVITE message to the Cisco telephone to establish the end-to-end connection. Other messages verify the TRYING, RINGING, ACK, and other functions. These messages are considered in greater detail later in the chapter.

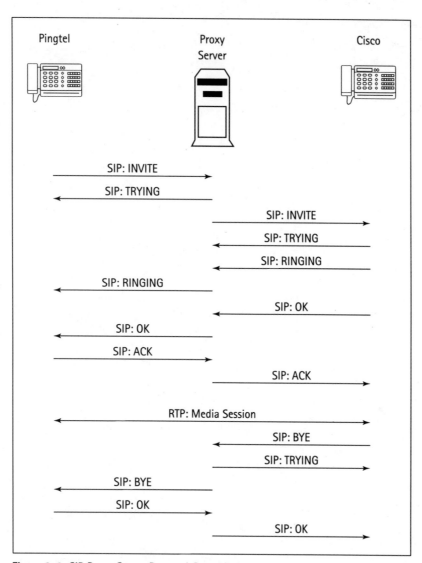

Figure 9-6: SIP Proxy Server Protocol Operations

Trace 9.2a: SIP Phone-to-Phone Summary

Frame	Delta Time	Destination	Source	Summary
13	0.839.961	Proxy Server	Pingtel	SIP C INVITE sip:5555@10.1.93.23 SIP/2.0
16	0.000.318	Pingtel	Proxy Server	SIP R SIP/2.0 100 Trying
19	0.000.780	Cisco	Proxy Server	SIP C INVITE sip:5555@10.1.93.21 SIP/2.0
20	0.026.005	Proxy Server	Cisco	SIP R SIP/2.0 100 Trying

Continued

Trace 9.2a *(Continued)*

```
21   0.012.609   Proxy Server   Cisco          SIP R SIP/2.0 180 Ringing
22   0.008.131   Pingtel        Proxy Server   SIP R SIP/2.0 180 Ringing
30   0.157.177   Proxy Server   Cisco          SIP R SIP/2.0 200 OK
31   0.007.345   Pingtel        Proxy Server   SIP R SIP/2.0 200 OK
32   0.054.162   Proxy Server   Pingtel        SIP C ACK sip:5555@10.1.93.23:5060;
                                                  maddr=10.1.93.23 SIP/2.0

33   0.026.193   Cisco          Proxy Server   SIP C ACK sip:5555@10.1.93.21:5060 SIP/2.0


    .
    .
    .


397  0.007.910   Pingtel        Cisco          RTP Payload=PCMU audio SEQ=659
                                                  SSRC=126927508
398  0.012.095   Cisco          Pingtel        RTP Payload=PCMU audio SEQ=46491
                                                  SSRC=2113934823
399  0.007.886   Pingtel        Cisco          RTP Payload=PCMU audio SEQ=660
                                                  SSRC=126927508
400  0.012.173   Cisco          Pingtel        RTP Payload=PCMU audio SEQ=46492
                                                  SSRC=2113934823
401  0.007.815   Pingtel        Cisco          RTP Payload=PCMU audio SEQ=661
                                                  SSRC=126927508
402  0.011.795   Cisco          Pingtel        RTP Payload=PCMU audio SEQ=46493
                                                  SSRC=2113934823
403  0.008.229   Pingtel        Cisco          RTP Payload=PCMU audio SEQ=662
                                                  SSRC=126927508


    .
    .
    .


744  0.009.172   Proxy Server   Cisco          SIP C BYE sip:5555@10.1.93.23:5060 SIP/2.0
746  0.006.824   Cisco          Proxy Server   SIP R SIP/2.0 100 Trying
747  0.008.823   Pingtel        Proxy Server   SIP C BYE sip:7777@10.1.93.24:5060 SIP/2.0
751  0.017.116   Proxy Server   Pingtel        SIP R SIP/2.0 200 OK
752  0.004.173   Cisco          Proxy Server   SIP R SIP/2.0 200 OK
753  0.614.982   Cisco          Proxy Server   SIP C OPTIONS sip:5555@10.1.93.21:5060 SIP/2.0
754  0.012.774   Proxy Server   Cisco          SIP R SIP/2.0 481 Invalid CallId
755  0.005.223   Pingtel        Proxy Server   SIP R SIP/2.0 481 Invalid CallId
```

To initiate the call to the user at the Cisco telephone, the user at the Pingtel telephone goes off hook and enters the extension number of the Cisco telephone (5555). These actions cause the Pingtel phone to send an INVITE message to the Proxy Server. The details of this message are found in Frame 13 and are illustrated with the Sniffer trace file output given in Trace 9.2b. Note that this new trace file format provides greater information than the previously shown Summary screen. This new format is called the Detail screen, and it provides details of every field within one particular frame. Using Frame 13 as an example, the Detail screen format begins with a timestamp and size for that frame, followed by the Source and Destination Address, plus Ethertype fields within the Data Link Control (DLC) layer. Next you see the various fields of the Internet Protocol (IP) header, then the fields within the User Datagram Protocol (UDP) header, and finally the fields within the Session Initiation Protocol (SIP) header. Within the IP header, note that this communication was between the Pingtel Telephone with IP address [10.1.93.24] and the Proxy Server with IP address [10.1.93.23]. Within the UDP header, note that the UDP Destination Port address of 5060 is used, which specifies SIP. The SIP header includes a number of fields, defined in RFC 2543, to initiate the call. For example, the INVITE line indicates the Uniform Resource Identifier (URI) of the destination that is being invited to this call (5555@10.1.93.23 – the Cisco phone at the Proxy Server's IP address), and the From line specifies the URI of the Pingtel phone. The Call-ID, also generated by the Pingtel phone, is a random number followed by the Pingtel IP address, which becomes a globally unique identifier for this call.

The lines beginning with the small letters (such as v=, o=, and so on) are part of the Session Description Protocol information, or SDP, defined in RFC 2327. Of particular interest is the media definition line (m=). This line tells us that the media for the session will be audio, that it will use Port 8766, that the Real Time Protocol Audio/Video Profile (RTP/AVP) will be used to define the audio, and that three RTP formats (0, 96, and 8) may be used. These formats are defined within the RTP document (RFC 1889). For example, the 0 format indicates PCM mu-law encoding sampled at 8 KHz. Note that this information is further specified in the rtpmap parameter on the subsequent line (a=rtpmap:0 pcmu/8000/1). (In the interest of brevity, some of the following Detail trace listings will not include all of the protocol layers, just those relevant to the discussion at hand.)

Trace 9.2b: SIP INVITE Message (from Pingtel Telephone)

```
- - - - - - - - - - - - - - - - - - - Frame 13 - - - - - - - - - - - - - - - - - - - -
DLC:  ----- DLC Header -----
     DLC:
     DLC:  Frame 13 arrived at  11:25:49.1330; frame size is 621 (026D hex) bytes.
     DLC:  Destination = Station Cmpaq2F7ACEA
     DLC:  Source      = Station 00D01E001CE9
     DLC:  Ethertype   = 0800 (IP)
     DLC:
IP: ----- IP Header -----
     IP:
     IP: Version = 4, header length = 20 bytes
     IP: Type of service = 00
```

Continued

Trace 9.2b *(Continued)*

```
        IP:      000. .... = routine
        IP:      ...0 .... = normal delay
        IP:      .... 0... = normal throughput
        IP:      .... .0.. = normal reliability
        IP:      .... ..0. = ECT bit - transport protocol will ignore the CE bit
        IP:      .... ...0 = CE bit - no congestion
        IP: Total length   = 607 bytes
        IP: Identification = 1788
        IP: Flags          = 0X
        IP:      .0.. .... = may fragment
        IP:      ..0. .... = last fragment
        IP: Fragment offset = 0 bytes
        IP: Time to live    = 64 seconds/hops
        IP: Protocol        = 17 (UDP)
        IP: Header checksum = A361 (correct)
        IP: Source address      = [10.1.93.24], Pingtel
        IP: Destination address = [10.1.93.23], Proxy Server
        IP: No options
        IP:
  UDP: ----- UDP Header -----
        UDP:
        UDP: Source port      = 1072
        UDP: Destination port = 5060 (SIP)
        UDP: Length           = 587
        UDP: Checksum         = 4090 (correct)
        UDP: [579 byte(s) of data]
        UDP:
  SIP: ----- Session Initiation Protocol -----
        SIP:
        SIP: "INVITE sip:5555@10.1.93.23 SIP/2.0.."
        SIP: "From: sip:7777@10.1.93.24;tag=1c22116.."
        SIP: "To: sip:5555@10.1.93.23.."
        SIP: "Call-Id: call-973575952-7@10.1.93.24.."
        SIP: "Cseq: 1 INVITE.."
        SIP: "Contact: sip:7777@10.1.93.24.."
        SIP: "Content-Type: application/sdp.."
        SIP: "Content-Length: 193.."
        SIP: "Accept-Language: en.."
        SIP: "Supported: sip-cc, sip-cc-01, timer.."
        SIP: "User-Agent: Pingtel/1.1.1 (VxWorks).."
        SIP: "Via: SIP/2.0/UDP 10.1.93.24.."
        SIP: ".."
        SIP: "v=0.."
        SIP: "o=Pingtel 5 5 IN IP4 10.1.93.24.."
```

```
SIP: "s=phone-call.."
SIP: "c=IN IP4 10.1.93.24.."
SIP: "t=0 0.."
SIP: "m=audio 8766 RTP/AVP 0 96 8.."
SIP: "a=rtpmap:0 pcmu/8000/1.."
SIP: "a=rtpmap:96 telephone-event/8000/1.."
SIP: "a=rtpmap:8 pcma/8000/1.."
SIP:
```

The Proxy Server then returns a TRYING message to the Pingtel telephone to indicate the processing of the INVITE request (Trace 9.2c). Note that the destination IP address for the Pingtel telephone is used [10.1.93.24], as are the SIP Destination Port address (5060) and the Call-ID (973575952-7) defined in the INVITE message.

Trace 9.2c: SIP TRYING Message (from Proxy Server)

```
- - - - - - - - - - - - - - - - - - Frame 16 - - - - - - - - - - - - - - - - - -
DLC:  ----- DLC Header -----
     DLC:
     DLC:  Frame 16 arrived at  11:25:49.1607; frame size is 242 (00F2 hex) bytes.
     DLC:  Destination = Station 00D01E001CE9
     DLC:  Source      = Station Cmpaq2F7ACEA
     DLC:  Ethertype   = 0800 (IP)
     DLC:
IP: ----- IP Header -----
     IP:
     IP: Version = 4, header length = 20 bytes
     IP: Type of service = 00
     IP:      000. ....  = routine
     IP:      ...0 .... = normal delay
     IP:      .... 0... = normal throughput
     IP:      .... .0.. = normal reliability
     IP:      .... ..0. = ECT bit - transport protocol will ignore the CE bit
     IP:      .... ...0 = CE bit - no congestion
     IP: Total length   = 228 bytes
     IP: Identification = 55220
     IP: Flags          = 0X
     IP:      .0.. .... = may fragment
     IP:      ..0. .... = last fragment
     IP: Fragment offset = 0 bytes
     IP: Time to live   = 128 seconds/hops
     IP: Protocol       = 17 (UDP)
     IP: Header checksum = 9423 (correct)
     IP: Source address    = [10.1.93.23], Proxy Server
```

Continued

Trace 9.2c *(Continued)*

```
        IP: Destination address = [10.1.93.24], Pingtel
        IP: No options
        IP:
UDP: ----- UDP Header -----
        UDP:
        UDP: Source port      = 3315
        UDP: Destination port = 5060 (SIP)
        UDP: Length           = 208
        UDP: Checksum         = B5FB (correct)
        UDP: [200 byte(s) of data]
        UDP:
SIP: ----- Session Initiation Protocol -----
        SIP:
        SIP: "SIP/2.0 100 Trying.."
        SIP: "Via: SIP/2.0/UDP 10.1.93.24.."
        SIP: "From: sip:7777@10.1.93.24;tag=1c22116.."
        SIP: "To: sip:5555@10.1.93.23.."
        SIP: "Call-ID: call-973575952-7@10.1.93.24.."
        SIP: "CSeq: 1 INVITE.."
        SIP: "Content-Length: 0.."
        SIP: ".."
        SIP:
```

Review Figure 9-6 and note that an INVITE message is passed to the Cisco telephone, which returns a TRYING message and a subsequent RINGING message (the details of these messages, which are similar to those previously discussed, are not shown). The Proxy Server then sends a RINGING message to the Pingtel telephone in Frame 22 (Trace 9.2d), which includes a date and timestamp (Thu, 06 Dec 2001 18:25:27 GMT).

Trace 9.2d: SIP RINGING Message (from Proxy Server)

```
- - - - - - - - - - - - - - - - - - - Frame 22 - - - - - - - - - - - - - - - - - - -


SIP: ----- Session Initiation Protocol -----
        SIP:
        SIP: "SIP/2.0 180 Ringing.."
        SIP: "Via: SIP/2.0/UDP 10.1.93.24:5060.."
        SIP: "From: sip:7777@10.1.93.24;tag=1c22116.."
        SIP: "To: sip:5555@10.1.93.23;tag=c2943000707905543-726.."
        SIP: "Call-ID: call-973575952-7@10.1.93.24.."
```

```
SIP: "Server:Cisco-SIP-IP-Phone/2.."
SIP: "Date:Thu, 06 Dec 2001 18:25:27 GMT.."
SIP: "CSeq: 1 INVITE.."
SIP: "Content-Length: 0.."
SIP: ".."
SIP:
```

Again review Figure 9-6 and note that the Cisco telephone sends the Proxy Server an OK message indicating that the call has been answered. This OK message is then passed to the Pingtel telephone by the Proxy Server in Frame 31 (Trace 9.2e). Note the addition of the Record-Route line that indicates that the Proxy Server will stay involved in the signaling path between the two end stations for the duration of the call.

Trace 9.2e: SIP OK Message (from Proxy Server)

```
- - - - - - - - - - - - - - - - - - - - - Frame 31 - - - - - - - - - - - - - - - - - - - -

SIP: ----- Session Initiation Protocol -----
    SIP:
    SIP: "SIP/2.0 200 OK.."
    SIP: "Via: SIP/2.0/UDP 10.1.93.24:5060.."
    SIP: "From: sip:7777@10.1.93.24;tag=1c22116.."
    SIP: "To: sip:5555@10.1.93.23;tag=c2943000707905543-726.."
    SIP: "Call-ID: call-973575952-7@10.1.93.24.."
    SIP: "Server:Cisco-SIP-IP-Phone/2.."
    SIP: "Contact:sip:5555@10.1.93.21:5060.."
    SIP: "Record-Route:<sip:5555@10.1.93.23:5060;maddr=10.1.93.23>.."
    SIP: "Date:Thu, 06 Dec 2001 18:25:31 GMT.."
    SIP: "CSeq: 1 INVITE.."
    SIP: "Content-Type:application/sdp.."
    SIP: "Content-Length: 214.."
    SIP: ".."
    SIP: "v=0.."
    SIP: "o=CiscoSystemsSIP-IPPhone-UserAgent 5313 17372 IN IP4 10.1.93.21.."
    SIP: "s=SIP Call.."
    SIP: "c=IN IP4 10.1.93.21.."
    SIP: "t=0 0.."
    SIP: "m=audio 21598 RTP/AVP 0 101.."
    SIP: "a=rtpmap:0 pcmu/8000.."
    SIP: "a=rtpmap:101 telephone-event/8000.."
    SIP: "a=fmtp:101 0-11.."
    SIP:
```

The Pingtel telephone then returns an ACK message to the Proxy Server (Trace 9.2f), which is the third leg of a three-way handshake (INVITE/OK/ACK) between the Pingtel telephone and the Proxy Server that provides the final confirmation of the SIP connection setup.

Trace 9.2f: SIP ACK Message (from Pingtel Telephone)

```
- - - - - - - - - - - - - - - - - - Frame 32 - - - - - - - - - - - - - - - - - - - -

SIP: ----- Session Initiation Protocol -----
    SIP:
    SIP: "ACK sip:5555@10.1.93.23:5060;maddr=10.1.93.23 SIP/2.0.."
    SIP: "Route: <sip:5555@10.1.93.21:5060>.."
    SIP: "Contact: sip:7777@10.1.93.24.."
    SIP: "From: sip:7777@10.1.93.24;tag=1c22116.."
    SIP: "To: sip:5555@10.1.93.23;tag=c2943000707905543-726.."
    SIP: "Call-Id: call-973575952-7@10.1.93.24.."
    SIP: "Cseq: 1 ACK.."
    SIP: "Accept-Language: en.."
    SIP: "User-Agent: Pingtel/1.1.1 (VxWorks).."
    SIP: "Via: SIP/2.0/UDP 10.1.93.24.."
    SIP: "Content-Length: 0.."
    SIP: ".."
    SIP:
```

The RTP media stream is then active between the two end stations (note from the IP addresses that the Proxy Server is not involved with this media transmission). From the Summary information (Trace 9.2a), you can see the audio streams going in both directions, and the RTP parameters incrementing accordingly from each side of the connection. The details of one RTP message are shown in Trace 9.2g, which illustrates the various parameters required in support of real-time information flows, such as the payload type (PCMU audio), timestamp (173319049 (21664881.125 ms)), and so on.

Trace 9.2g: RTP Message with PCMU Audio (from Pingtel Telephone to Cisco Telephone)

```
- - - - - - - - - - - - - - - - - - Frame 400 - - - - - - - - - - - - - - - - - - - -
DLC: ----- DLC Header -----
    DLC:
    DLC: Frame 400 arrived at  11:25:57.1497; frame size is 214 (00D6 hex) bytes.
    DLC: Destination = Station 003094C29007
    DLC: Source      = Station 00D01E001CE9
    DLC: Ethertype   = 0800 (IP)
    DLC:
```

```
IP: ----- IP Header -----
    IP:
    IP: Version = 4, header length = 20 bytes
    IP: Type of service = B8
    IP:       101. ....   = CRITIC/ECP
    IP:       ...1 .... = low delay
    IP:       .... 1... = high throughput
    IP:       .... .0.. = normal reliability
    IP:       .... ..0. = ECT bit - transport protocol will ignore the CE bit
    IP:       .... ...0 = CE bit - no congestion
    IP: Total length    = 200 bytes
    IP: Identification  = 2158
    IP: Flags           = 0X
    IP:       .0.. .... = may fragment
    IP:       ..0. .... = last fragment
    IP: Fragment offset = 0 bytes
    IP: Time to live    = 64 seconds/hops
    IP: Protocol        = 17 (UDP)
    IP: Header checksum = A2D0 (correct)
    IP: Source address      = [10.1.93.24], Pingtel
    IP: Destination address = [10.1.93.21], Cisco
    IP: No options
    IP:
UDP: ----- UDP Header -----
    UDP:
    UDP: Source port      = 8766
    UDP: Destination port = 21598
    UDP: Length           = 180
    UDP: Checksum         = 2B87 (correct)
    UDP: [172 byte(s) of data]
    UDP:
RTP: ----- Real-Time Transport Protocol -----
    RTP:
    RTP: Ver, Pad, Ext, CC:      = 80
    RTP:                10.. .... = Version = 2 (RFC 1889)
    RTP:                ..0. .... = Padding = 0 (Zero bytes of Padding at the End)
    RTP:                ...0 .... = Header Extension Bit = 0,
(No Header Extension after Fixed Header)
    RTP:                .... 0000 = Contributor Count = 0
    RTP: Marker, Payload Type: = 00
    RTP:                0... .... = Marker 0
```

Continued

Trace 9.2g *(Continued)*

```
RTP:              .000 0000 = Payload Type 0 (PCMU audio)
RTP: Sequence Number      = 46492
RTP: Time Stamp           = 173319049 (21664881.125 ms)
RTP: SSRC                 = 2113934823
RTP:
RTP:
RTP: Payload Type = 0 (PCMU audio)
RTP:
```

When the two parties have finished their conversation, a SIP BYE message is sent from the Cisco IP telephone to the Proxy Server, which returns a SIP TRYING message and then sends a BYE message to the Pingtel telephone (Frame 747 shown in Trace 9.2h). The Via: line indicates that the Proxy Server and the Cisco telephone were in this path for this BYE message. The From: and To: lines indicate the party initiating the termination (the Cisco telephone at extension 5555) and the party at the other end of the connection (the Pingtel telephone at extension 7777). Also included is a timestamp marking the end of the call.

Trace 9.2h: SIP BYE Message (from Proxy Server to Pingtel Telephone)

```
- - - - - - - - - - - - - - - - - - - Frame 747 - - - - - - - - - - - - - - - - - - - -


SIP: ----- Session Initiation Protocol -----
    SIP:
    SIP: "BYE sip:7777@10.1.93.24:5060 SIP/2.0.."
    SIP: "Via: SIP/2.0/UDP 10.1.93.23:5060;branch=1_tUROWVSf94xqQOAALvM7qog99.."
    SIP: "Via: SIP/2.0/UDP 10.1.93.21:5060.."
    SIP: "From: sip:5555@10.1.93.23;tag=c2943000707905543-726.."
    SIP: "To: sip:7777@10.1.93.24;tag=1c22116.."
    SIP: "Call-ID: call-973575952-7@10.1.93.24.."
    SIP: "Date:Thu, 06 Dec 2001 18:25:38 GMT.."
    SIP: "User-Agent:Cisco-SIP-IP-Phone/2.."
    SIP: "CSeq: 101 BYE.."
    SIP: "Content-Length: 0.."
    SIP: ".."
    SIP:
```

The Pingtel telephone then responds with an OK message (Frame 751 shown in Trace 9.2i) to confirm the receipt of the BYE message. This OK message is then passed to the Cisco telephone, and the call termination is complete (review Figure 9-6).

Trace 9.2i: SIP OK Message (from Pingtel Telephone to Proxy Server)

```
- - - - - - - - - - - - - - - - - - - Frame 751 - - - - - - - - - - - - - - - - - - -


SIP: ----- Session Initiation Protocol -----
     SIP:
     SIP: "SIP/2.0 200 OK.."
     SIP: "From: sip:5555@10.1.93.23;tag=c2943000707905543-726.."
     SIP: "To: sip:7777@10.1.93.24;tag=1c22116.."
     SIP: "Call-Id: call-973575952-7@10.1.93.24.."
     SIP: "Cseq: 101 BYE.."
     SIP: "Via: SIP/2.0/UDP 10.1.93.23:5060;branch=1_tUROWVSf94xqQOAALvM7qog99.."
     SIP: "Via: SIP/2.0/UDP 10.1.93.21:5060.."
     SIP: "Contact: sip:7777@10.1.93.24.."
     SIP: "Allow: INVITE, ACK, CANCEL, BYE, REFER, OPTIONS, NOTIFY.."
     SIP: "User-Agent: Pingtel/1.1.1 (VxWorks).."
     SIP: "Content-Length: 0.."
     SIP: ".."
     SIP:
```

This case study has illustrated the operation of SIP, the Session Initiation Protocol. The next section considers a similar operation that uses the H.323 and related protocols.

9.3 Microsoft NetMeeting Connections

Microsoft's NetMeeting application, which accompanies the Windows operating system, implements an H.323 terminal for both audio and video communication. An example of two workstations communicating using the NetMeeting application is illustrated in Figure 9-7. These two workstations are designated Station 150 and Station 180 based on their IP addresses. A summary of the protocol operations for these stations is shown in Figure 9-8. Note that the use of RSVP is optional, not mandatory, and therefore it is not included with the basic call functions (Figure 9-8). It is shown in the specific results for this case, however (Figure 9-9).

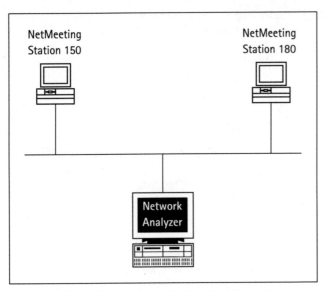

Figure 9-7: H.323 NetMeeting-to-NetMeeting Connection

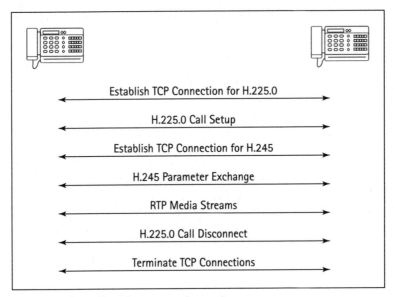

Figure 9-8: H.323 Call Management Protocols

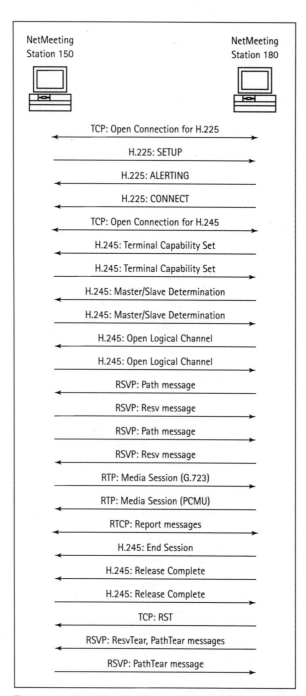

Figure 9-9: H.323 NetMeeting-to-NetMeeting Connection Protocol Operation

A number of protocols are involved in these operations, including TCP, H.225, and H.245 to manage the call, plus RTP to carry the media stream. The protocol operations can be divided into nine major sections, with the details illustrated in Figure 9-9 and detailed in Trace 9.3a: TCP connection establishment for H.225 (Frames 1–3); H.225.0 call setup (Frames 4–13); TCP connection establishment for H.245 (Frames 14–16); H.245 parameter exchange (Frames 17–35 and 38); RSVP bandwidth reservation (Frames 36–37 and 39–40); RTP media streams (Frames 41–1007); H.245 and H.225.0 call disconnect (Frames 1008–1015); RSVP bandwidth release (Frames 1018–1019 and 1022); and TCP connection termination (Frames 1016–1017, 1021, and 1023–1024).

Trace 9.3a: Microsoft NetMeeting-to-NetMeeting Protocol Operations Summary

Frame	Delta Time	Destination	Source	Summary
1	0.000.000	Station 180	Station 150	TCP D=1720 S=1474 SYN SEQ=6418137 LEN=0 WIN=8192
2	0.000.441	Station 150	Station 180	TCP D=1474 S=1720 SYN ACK=6418138 SEQ=5867490 LEN=0 WIN=8760
3	0.000.267	Station 180	Station 150	TCP D=1720 S=1474 ACK=5867491 WIN=8760
4	0.005.748	Station 180	Station 150	H225 Length = 236
5	0.160.356	Station 150	Station 180	TCP D=1474 S=1720 ACK=6418142 WIN=8756
6	0.000.457	Station 180	Station 150	H225 type=Setup-UUIE userid=0x7E length=201
7	0.034.066	Station 150	Station 180	H225 Length = 43
8	0.177.340	Station 180	Station 150	TCP D=1720 S=1474 ACK=5867495 WIN=8756
9	0.000.416	Station 150	Station 180	H225 type=Alerting-UUIE userid=0x7E length=31
10	0.199.635	Station 180	Station 150	TCP D=1720 S=1474 ACK=5867534 WIN=8717
11	1.049.728	Station 150	Station 180	H225 Length = 118
12	0.160.281	Station 180	Station 150	TCP D=1720 S=1474 ACK=5867538 WIN=8713
13	0.000.471	Station 150	Station 180	H225 type=Connect-UUIE userid=0x7E length=89
14	0.007.224	Station 180	Station 150	TCP D=1047 S=1475 SYN SEQ=6419933 LEN=0 WIN=8192
15	0.000.285	Station 150	Station 180	TCP D=1475 S=1047 SYN ACK=6419934 SEQ=5869286 LEN=0 WIN=8760
16	0.000.235	Station 180	Station 150	TCP D=1047 S=1475 ACK=5869287 WIN=8760
17	0.001.885	Station 150	Station 180	H245 Req: Terminal Capability Set, Req: Master Slave Determination
18	0.003.286	Station 180	Station 150	H245 Req: Terminal Capability Set, Req: Master Slave Determination
19	0.000.804	Station 150	Station 180	H245 of frame 17; 529 Bytes of data
20	0.000.733	Station 180	Station 150	H245 Continuation of frame 18; 529 Bytes of data

```
21   0.010.951   Station 150   Station 180   H245   Res: Terminal Capability Set Ack,
                                                     Res: Master Slave Determination Ack
22   0.003.027   Station 180   Station 150   H245   Res: Terminal Capability Set Ack,
                                                     Res: Master Slave Determination Ack
23   0.000.483   Station 150   Station 180   H245   Continuation of frame 21;
                                                     9 Bytes of data
24   0.000.265   Station 180   Station 150   H245   Continuation of frame 22;
                                                     9 Bytes of data
25   0.040.981   Station 150   Station 180   H245   Req: Open Logical Channel,
                                                     Req: Open Logical Channel
26   0.011.459   Station 180   Station 150   H245   Req: Open Logical Channel,
                                                     Req: Open Logical Channel
27   0.000.492   Station 150   Station 180   H245   Continuation of frame 25;
                                                     64 Bytes of data
28   0.000.348   Station 180   Station 150   H245   Continuation of frame 26;
                                                     53 Bytes of data
29   0.117.088   Station 180   Station 150   TCP    D=1720 S=1474    ACK=5867652 WIN=8599
30   0.078.097   Station 150   Station 180   TCP    D=1475 S=1047    ACK=6420537 WIN=8157
31   0.018.706   Station 150   Station 180   H245   Res: Open Logical Channel Reject,
                                                     Res: Open Logical Channel Ack
32   0.030.125   Station 180   Station 150   H245   Res: Open Logical Channel Ack,
                                                     Res: Open Logical Channel Ack
33   0.000.476   Station 150   Station 180   H245   Continuation of frame 31;
                                                     32 Bytes of data
34   0.000.315   Station 180   Station 150   H245   Continuation of frame 32;
                                                     38 Bytes of data
35   0.155.347   Station 150   Station 180   TCP    D=1475 S=1047 ACK=6420579 WIN=8115
36   0.103.826   Station 150   Station 180   RSVP   Type = Path
37   0.001.993   Station 180   Station 150   RSVP   Type = Resv
38   0.001.468   Station 150   Station 180   H245   Ind: OpenLogical Channel Confirm
39   0.019.201   Station 180   Station 150   RSVP   Type = Path
40   0.003.652   Station 150   Station 180   RSVP   Type = Resv


                 .
                 .
                 .


640  0.000.277   Station 150   Station 180   RTP    Payload=PCMU audio
                                                     SEQ=36793 SSRC=2058410030
641  0.062.789   Station 150   Station 180   RTP    Payload=PCMU audio
                                                     SEQ=36794 SSRC=2058410030
642  0.000.247   Station 150   Station 180   RTP    Payload=PCMU audio
                                                     SEQ=36795 SSRC=2058410030
```

Continued

Trace 9.3a *(Continued)*

```
643  0.036.850  Station 180  Station 150  RTCP  Sender Report PacketLost=0
                                                Jitter=216 Delay=2(sec)
644  0.025.805  Station 150  Station 180  RTP  Payload=PCMU audio
                                                SEQ=36796 SSRC=2058410030
645  0.000.265  Station 150  Station 180  RTP  Payload=PCMU audio
                                                SEQ=36797 SSRC=2058410030
646  0.062.880  Station 150  Station 180  RTP  Payload=PCMU audio
                                                SEQ=36798 SSRC=2058410030
647  0.000.465  Station 150  Station 180  RTP  Payload=PCMU audio
                                                SEQ=36799 SSRC=2058410030
648  0.062.543  Station 150  Station 180  RTP  Payload=PCMU audio
                                                SEQ=36800 SSRC=2058410030
649  0.000.373  Station 150  Station 180  RTP  Payload=PCMU audio
                                                SEQ=36801 SSRC=2058410030
650  0.059.814  Station 180  Station 150  RTP  Payload=G.723 audio
                                                SEQ=63219 SSRC=2244723851
651  0.002.777  Station 150  Station 180  RTP  Payload=PCMU audio
                                                SEQ=36802 SSRC=2058410030
652  0.003.544  Station 180  Station 150  RTP  Payload=G.723 audio
                                                SEQ=63220 SSRC=2244723851
653  0.005.480  Station 180  Station 150  RTP  Payload=G.723 audio
                                                SEQ=63221 SSRC=2244723851
654  0.005.344  Station 180  Station 150  RTP  Payload=G.723 audio
                                                SEQ=63222 SSRC=2244723851
655  0.005.336  Station 180  Station 150  RTP  Payload=G.723 audio
                                                SEQ=63223 SSRC=2244723851
656  0.043.019  Station 150  Station 180  RTP  Payload=PCMU audio
                                                SEQ=36803 SSRC=2058410030
657  0.000.280  Station 150  Station 180  RTP  Payload=PCMU audio
                                                SEQ=36804 SSRC=2058410030
658  0.059.110  Station 180  Station 150  RTP  Payload=G.723 audio
                                                SEQ=63224 SSRC=2244723851
659  0.003.854  Station 150  Station 180  RTP  Payload=PCMU audio
                                                SEQ=36805 SSRC=2058410030
660  0.000.257  Station 150  Station 180  RTP  Payload=PCMU audio
                                                SEQ=36806 SSRC=2058410030
661  0.002.284  Station 180  Station 150  RTP  Payload=G.723 audio
                                                SEQ=63225 SSRC=2244723851
662  0.005.912  Station 180  Station 150  RTP  Payload=G.723 audio
                                                SEQ=63226 SSRC=2244723851
663  0.006.433  Station 180  Station 150  RTP  Payload=G.723 audio
                                                SEQ=63227 SSRC=2244723851
664  0.048.250  Station 150  Station 180  RTP  Payload=PCMU audio
                                                SEQ=36807 SSRC=2058410030
```

```
665   0.000.266   Station 150   Station 180   RTP   Payload=PCMU audio
                                                    SEQ=36808 SSRC=2058410030
666   0.057.631   Station 180   Station 150   RTP   Payload=G.723 audio
                                                    SEQ=63228 SSRC=2244723851
667   0.004.957   Station 150   Station 180   RTP   Payload=PCMU audio
                                                    SEQ=36809 SSRC=2058410030
668   0.000.334   Station 150   Station 180   RTP   Payload=PCMU audio
                                                    SEQ=36810 SSRC=2058410030
669   0.000.936   Station 180   Station 150   RTP   Payload=G.723 audio
                                                    SEQ=63229 SSRC=2244723851
670   0.006.383   Station 180   Station 150   RTP   Payload=G.723 audio
                                                    SEQ=63230 SSRC=2244723851

                      .
                      .
                      .

1008  0.105.416   Station 150   Station 180   H245  Com: End Session Command
1009  0.000.382   Station 150   Station 180   H245  Continuation of frame 1008:
                                                    2 Bytes of data
1010  0.000.303   Station 180   Station 150   TCP   D=1047 S=1475
                                                    ACK=5869952 WIN=8096
1011  0.002.331   Station 150   Station 180   H225  Length = 47
1012  0.000.244   Station 150   Station 180   H225  type=ReleaseComplete-UUIE
                                                    userid=0x7E length=30
1013  0.000.217   Station 180   Station 150   TCP   D=1720 S=1474
                                                    ACK=5867700 WIN=8552
1014  0.003.077   Station 180   Station 150   H225  Length = 47
1015  0.000.387   Station 180   Station 150   H225  type=ReleaseComplete-UUIE
                                                    userid=0x7E length=30
1016  0.000.132   Station 150   Station 180   TCP   D=1474 S=1720 RST WIN=0
1017  0.000.118   Station 150   Station 180   TCP   D=1474 S=1720 RST WIN=0
1018  0.043.497   Station 150   Station 180   RSVP  Type = ResvTear
1019  0.001.833   Station 150   Station 180   RSVP  Type = PathTear
1020  0.167.084   Station 180   Station 150   H245  Length=6
1021  0.000.432   Station 150   Station 180   TCP   D=1475 S=1047 RST WIN=0
1022  0.011.692   Station 180   Station 150   RSVP  Type = PathTear
1023  0.845.877   Station 150   Station 180   TCP   D=1479 S=1503 FIN
                                                    ACK=6421502 SEQ=5870530 LEN=0 WIN=8327
1024  0.000.312   Station 180   Station 150   TCP   D=1503 S=1479
                                                    ACK=5870531 WIN=8652
```

The H.225 SETUP message is sent in Frame 6 and illustrated in Trace 9.3b. (As a point of reference, the first few trace files in this section show all protocol layers. For brevity, subsequent trace files show only the upper layer protocols.) The SETUP message is sent from a calling H.323 device to the called H.323 device to indicate its interest in setting up a connection. The originator assigns a Call Reference Value (17984) to identify this connection. Also included in this message are many parameters, which are passed between these two devices in data units known as Information Elements, or IEs. Some of the key IEs that are passed are the SETUP User-to-User IE, which carries information regarding the H.323 user's identity (Mark Miller); flags that indicate whether other devices, such as gatekeepers and gateways, are present; plus information identifying the manufacturer (Microsoft) and the product (NetMeeting).

Trace 9.3b: H.225.0 SETUP Message (from Station 150)

```
- - - - - - - - - - - - - - - - - - - - - Frame 6 - - - - - - - - - - - - - - - - - - -


DLC:  ----- DLC Header -----
    DLC:
    DLC:  Frame 6 arrived at  13:51:15.0304; frame size is 286 (011E hex) bytes.
    DLC:  Destination = Station 0050049B090F
    DLC:  Source      = Station 3Com9 195D66
    DLC:  Ethertype   = 0800 (IP)
    DLC:
IP: ----- IP Header -----
    IP:
    IP: Version = 4, header length = 20 bytes
    IP: Type of service = 00
    IP:      000. .... = routine
    IP:      ...0 .... = normal delay
    IP:      .... 0... = normal throughput
    IP:      .... .0.. = normal reliability
    IP:      .... ..0. = ECT bit - transport protocol will ignore the CE bit
    IP:      .... ...0 = CE bit - no congestion
    IP: Total length   = 272 bytes
    IP: Identification = 44046
    IP: Flags          = 4X
    IP:      .1.. .... = don't fragment
    IP:      ..0. .... = last fragment
    IP: Fragment offset = 0 bytes
    IP: Time to live    = 128 seconds/hops
    IP: Protocol        = 6 (TCP)
    IP: Header checksum = 033E (correct)
    IP: Source address      = [192.168.100.150]
    IP: Destination address = [192.168.100.180]
    IP: No options
    IP:
TCP: ----- TCP header -----
    TCP:
```

```
    TCP: Source port              = 1474
    TCP: Destination port         = 1720 (H225 Call Signaling)
    TCP: Sequence number          = 6418142
    TCP: Next expected Seq number= 6418374
    TCP: Acknowledgment number    = 5867491
    TCP: Data offset              = 20 bytes
    TCP: Flags                    = 18
    TCP:              ..0. .... = (No urgent pointer)
    TCP:              ...1 .... = Acknowledgment
    TCP:              .... 1... = Push
    TCP:              .... .0.. = (No reset)
    TCP:              .... ..0. = (No SYN)
    TCP:              .... ...0 = (No FIN)
    TCP: Window                   = 8760
    TCP: Checksum                 = 3B71 (correct)
    TCP: No TCP options
    TCP: [232 Bytes of data]
    TCP:
H225: ----- H.225 Call Signaling -----
    H225:
    H225: Protocol discriminator  = 8
    H225: Length of call reference = 2
    H225: Call reference field = 4640
    H225:  0... .... .... .... = Message from originator
    H225:  .100 0110  0100 0000 =  = 17984 (Call reference value)
    H225: Message type = 5 (Setup)
    H225:
    H225: Information element identifier   = 0x4 (Bearer capability)
    H225: Length of information element = 3
    H225: Coding and capability flags = 88
    H225:              1... .... = Extension value(s) present
    H225:              .00. .... = Coding standard = 0 (CCITT standardized coding)
    H225:              ...0 1000 = Information transfer capability = 8
    H225:                         (Unrestricted digital information)
    H225: Mode and rate flags = C0
    H225:         1... .... = Extension value(s) present
    H225:         .10. .... = Transfer mode = 2 (Packet mode)
    H225:         ...0 0000 = Information transfer rate = 0
    H225:                     (Used for packet mode calls)
    H225: Layer 1 protocol flag = A5
    H225:          1... .... = Extension value(s) present
    H225:          .01. .... = Layer 1 identification = 1
    H225:          ...0 0101 = Layer 1 protocol = 5 (H.221 and H.242)
```

Continued

Trace 9.3b *(Continued)*

```
    H225:
    H225: Information element identifier  = 0x28 (Display)
    H225: Display length = 12
    H225: Display = Mark Miller<00>
    H225:
H225: ----User-User Information----
    H225:
    H225: Information element identifier = 0x7E (User-User)
    H225: Length of user-user content = 201
    H225: Protocol discriminator = 5 (X.680 / X.691(PER)(ASN.1))
    H225:
    H225: Flags     = 10
    H225: 0... .... = No extension values present in H323-UserInformation
    H225: .0.. .... = user-data is not present
    H225: ..0. .... = No extension values present in h323-uu-pdu
    H225: ...1 .... = nonStandardData is present
    H225: .... 0... = No extension values present in h323-message-body
    H225: h323-message = 0 (Setup-UUIE)
    H225:
    H225: Flags     = A8
    H225: 1... .... = Extension value(s) present in Setup-UUIE
    H225: .0.. .... = h245Address is not present
    H225: ..1. .... = sourceAddress is present
    H225: ...0 .... = destinationAddress is not present
    H225: .... 1... = destCallSignalAddress is present
    H225: .... .0.. = destExtraCallInfo is not present
    H225: .... ..0. = destExtraCRV is not present
    H225: .... ...0 = callServices is not present
    H225:
    H225: Protocol ID = {0.0.8.2250.0.2}
    H225: H225.0 version = 2
    H225:
    H225: Number of sourceAddress = 1
    H225:
    H225: Flags     = 40
    H225: 0... .... = No extension value(s) present in AliasAddress
    H225: AliasAddress = 1 (H323-ID)
    H225: H323-ID = "Mark Miller"
    H225:
    H225: Flags     = 22
    H225: 0... .... = No extension value(s) present in EndpointType
    H225: .0.. .... = nonStandardData is not present
    H225: ..1. .... = Vendor is present
    H225: ...0 .... = Gatekeeper is not present
```

```
H225: .... 0... = Gateway is not present
H225: .... .0.. = MCU is not present
H225: .... ..1. = Terminal is present
H225:
H225: .... ...0 = No extension value(s) present in vendorIdentifier
H225: Flags     = C0
H225: 1... .... = Product ID is present
H225: .1.. .... = Version ID is present
H225:
H225: ..0. .... = No extension value(s) present in H221NonStandard
H225: T.35 country code = 0xB5 (USA)
H225: T.35 extension    = 0
H225: Manufacture code = 0x534C (Microsoft)
H225: Product Id = Microsoft. NetMeeting.<00>
H225: Version Id = 3.0<00>
H225:
H225: Flags     = 00
H225: 0... .... = No extension value(s) present in terminal
H225: .0.. .... = nonStandardData is not present
H225: ..0. .... = MC is OFF
H225: ...0 .... = Undefined node is OFF
H225:
H225: destCallSignalAddress
H225:
H225: .... 0... = No extension value(s) present in TransportAddress
H225: TransportAddress = 0 (IP address)
H225: IP   = 192.168.100.180
H225: Port = 1720
H225:
H225: Flags     = 00
H225: 0... .... = Active MC is OFF
H225:
H225: Conference id = D861DE3202E4D511B09E006097195D66
H225:
H225: Flags     = 00
H225: 0... .... = No extension value(s) present in conferenceGoal
H225: Conference goal = 0 (Create)
H225:
H225: callType
H225:
H225: ...0 .... = No extension value(s) present in callType
H225: callType = 0 (Point to point)
H225:
H225:  * Setup-UUIE - extension *
```

Continued

Trace 9.3b *(Continued)*

```
H225: .... ..0. = Extension length determinant
H225: Number of extensions = 9
H225: .... .1.. = sourceCallSignalAddress is present
H225: .... ..0. = remoteExtensionAddress is not present
H225: .... ...1 = callIdentifier is present
H225: Flags     = 0C
H225: 0... .... = h245SecurityCapability is not present
H225: .0.. .... = tokens is not present
H225: ..0. .... = cryptoTokens is not present
H225: ...0 .... = fastStart is not present
H225: .... 1... = mediaWaitForConnect is present
H225: .... .1.. = canOverlapSend is present
H225:
H225: Flags     = 00
H225: 0... .... = No extension value(s) present in sourceCallSignalAddress
H225: sourceCallSignalAddress = 0 (IP address)
H225: IP   = 192.168.100.150
H225: Port = 1474
H225:
H225: Flags     = 00
H225: 0... .... = No extension value(s) present in callIdentifier
H225: Guid = D761DE3202E4D511B09E006097195D66
H225:
H225: Flags     = 00
H225: 0... .... = Media wait for connect is OFF
H225: Flags     = 00
H225: 0... .... = Can overlap send is OFF
H225:
H225: Flags     = 40
H225: 0... .... = No extension value(s) present in NonStandardIdentifier
H225: nonStandardIdentifier = 1 (H221 non standard)
H225:
H225: ..0. .... = No extension value(s) present in H221NonStandard
H225: T.35 country code = 0xB5 (USA)
H225: T.35 extension    = 0
H225: Manufacture code = 0x534C (Microsoft)
H225:
H225: Unspecified data (60 bytes)
```

The H.225.0 ALERTING message is sent in Frame 9 by the called user (Station 180) to the calling user (Station 150) to indicate that alerting or ringing has been initiated (Trace 9.3c). This message contains the same Call Reference Value (17984) plus many of the same parameters that were sent in the SETUP message.

Trace 9.3c: H.225.0 ALERTING Message (from Station 180)

```
- - - - - - - - - - - - - - - - - - - - - Frame 9 - - - - - - - - - - - - - - - - - - -
DLC:  ----- DLC Header -----
    DLC:
    DLC:  Frame 9 arrived at  13:51:15.2423; frame size is 93 (005D hex) bytes.
    DLC:  Destination = Station 3Com9 195D66
    DLC:  Source      = Station 0050049B090F
    DLC:  Ethertype   = 0800 (IP)
    DLC:
IP:  ----- IP Header -----
    IP:
    IP: Version = 4, header length = 20 bytes
    IP: Type of service = 00
    IP:        000. .... = routine
    IP:        ...0 .... = normal delay
    IP:        .... 0... = normal throughput
    IP:        .... .0.. = normal reliability
    IP:        .... ..0. = ECT bit - transport protocol will ignore the CE bit
    IP:        .... ...0 = CE bit - no congestion
    IP: Total length   = 79 bytes
    IP: Identification = 32520
    IP: Flags          = 4X
    IP:        .1.. .... = don't fragment
    IP:        ..0. .... = last fragment
    IP: Fragment offset = 0 bytes
    IP: Time to live   = 128 seconds/hops
    IP: Protocol       = 6 (TCP)
    IP: Header checksum = 3105 (correct)
    IP: Source address      = [192.168.100.180]
    IP: Destination address = [192.168.100.150]
    IP: No options
    IP:
TCP:  ----- TCP header -----
    TCP:
    TCP: Source port           = 1720 (H225 Call Signaling)
    TCP: Destination port      = 1474
    TCP: Sequence number       = 5867495
    TCP: Next expected Seq number= 5867534
    TCP: Acknowledgment number  = 6418374
    TCP: Data offset           = 20 bytes
    TCP: Flags                 = 18
    TCP:              ..0. .... = (No urgent pointer)
    TCP:              ...1 .... = Acknowledgment
```

Continued

Trace 9.3c *(Continued)*

```
    TCP:                    .... 1... = Push
    TCP:                    .... .0.. = (No reset)
    TCP:                    .... ..0. = (No SYN)
    TCP:                    .... ...0 = (No FIN)
    TCP: Window             = 8524
    TCP: Checksum           = AD58 (correct)
    TCP: No TCP options
    TCP: [39 Bytes of data]
    TCP:
H225: ----- H.225 Call Signaling -----
    H225:
    H225: Protocol discriminator   = 8
    H225: Length of call reference = 2
    H225: Call reference field = C640
    H225: 1... .... .... .... = Message to originator
    H225: .100 0110  0100 0000 = = 17984 (Call reference value)
    H225: Message type = 1 (Alerting)
    H225:
    H225:
H225: ----User-User Information----
    H225:
    H225: Information element identifier = 0x7E (User-User)
    H225: Length of user-user content = 31
    H225: Protocol discriminator = 5 (X.680 / X.691(PER)(ASN.1))
    H225:
    H225: Flags     = 03
    H225: 0... .... = No extension values present in H323-UserInformation
    H225: .0.. .... = user-data is not present
    H225: ..0. .... = No extension values present in h323-uu-pdu
    H225: ...0 .... = nonStandardData is not present
    H225: .... 0... = No extension values present in h323-message-body
    H225: h323-message = 3 (Alerting-UUIE)
    H225:
    H225: Flags     = 80
    H225: 1... .... = Extension value(s) present in Alerting-UUIE
    H225: .0.. .... = h245Address is not present
    H225:
    H225: Protocol ID = {0.0.8.2250.0.2}
    H225: H225.0 version = 2
    H225:
    H225: Destination information
    H225:
    H225: Flags     = 02
    H225: 0... .... = No extension value(s) present in destinationInfo
```

```
H225: .0.. .... = nonStandardData is not present
H225: ..0. .... = Vendor is not present
H225: ...0 .... = Gatekeeper is not present
H225: .... 0... = Gateway is not present
H225: .... .0.. = MCU is not present
H225: .... ..1. = Terminal is present
H225:
H225: .... ...0 = No extension value(s) present in terminal
H225: Flags     = 01
H225: 0... .... = nonStandardData is not present
H225: .0.. .... = MC is OFF
H225: ..0. .... = Undefined node is OFF
H225:
H225:  * Alerting-UUIE - extension *
H225: ...0 .... = Extension length determinant
H225: Number of extensions = 5
H225: ..1. .... = callIdentifier is present
H225: ...0 .... = h245SecurityMode is not present
H225: .... 0... = tokens is not present
H225: .... .0.. = cryptoTokens is not present
H225: .... ..0. = fastStart is not present
H225:
H225:
H225: Flags     = 00
H225: 0... .... = No extension value(s) present in callIdentifier
H225: Guid = D761DE3202E4D511B09E006097195D66
H225:
```

The H.225.0 CONNECT message is sent from the called party (Station 180) to the calling party (Station 150) in Frame 13 to indicate acceptance of the call (Trace 9.3d). This message includes the name of the accepting party to be displayed at the other end of the connection (John Thompson); a Connect User-to-User IE that includes the IP address and port number to be used for the H.245 connection ([192.168.100.180], port 1047); plus other call parameters.

Trace 9.3d: H.225.0 CONNECT Message (from Station 180)

```
- - - - - - - - - - - - - - - - - - - Frame 13 - - - - - - - - - - - - - - - - - - -


H225: ----- H.225 Call Signaling -----
    H225:
    H225: Protocol discriminator  = 8
    H225: Length of call reference = 2
    H225: Call reference field = C640
```

Continued

Trace 9.3d *(Continued)*

```
        H225: 1... .... .... .... = Message to originator
        H225: .100 0110  0100 0000 = = 17984 (Call reference value)
        H225: Message type = 7 (Connect)
        H225:
        H225: Information element identifier   = 0x4 (Bearer capability)
        H225: Length of information element = 3
        H225: Coding and capability flags = 88
        H225:                    1... .... = Extension value(s) present
        H225:                    .00. .... = Coding standard = 0 (CCITT standardized coding)
        H225:                    ...0 1000 = Information transfer capability = 8
        H225:                              (Unrestricted digital information)
        H225: Mode and rate flags = C0
        H225:             1... .... = Extension value(s) present
        H225:             .10. .... = Transfer mode = 2 (Packet mode)
        H225:             ...0 0000 = Information transfer rate = 0
        H225:                       (Used for packet mode calls)
        H225: Layer 1 protocol flag = A5
        H225:             1... .... = Extension value(s) present
        H225:             .01. .... = Layer 1 identification = 1
        H225:             ...0 0101 = Layer 1 protocol = 5 (H.221 and H.242)
        H225:
        H225: Information element identifier   = 0x28 (Display)
        H225: Display length = 14
        H225: Display = John Thompson
        H225:
H225: ----User-User Information----
        H225:
        H225: Information element identifier = 0x7E (User-User)
        H225: Length of user-user content = 89
        H225: Protocol discriminator = 5 (X.680 / X.691(PER)(ASN.1))
        H225:
        H225: Flags      = 02
        H225: 0... .... = No extension values present in H323-UserInformation
        H225: .0.. .... = user-data is not present
        H225: ..0. .... = No extension values present in h323-uu-pdu
        H225: ...0 .... = nonStandardData is not present
        H225: .... 0... = No extension values present in h323-message-body
        H225: h323-message = 2 (Connect-UUIE)
        H225:
        H225: Flags      = C0
        H225: 1... .... = Extension value(s) present in Connect-UUIE
        H225: .1.. .... = h245Address is present
        H225:
        H225: Protocol ID = {0.0.8.2250.0.2}
```

```
H225: H225.0 version = 2
H225:
H225: Flags     = 00
H225: 0... .... = No extension value(s) present in TransportAddress
H225: TransportAddress = 0 (IP address)
H225: IP    = 192.168.100.180
H225: Port = 1047
H225:
H225: Destination information
H225:
H225: Flags     = 22
H225: 0... .... = No extension value(s) present in destinationInfo
H225: .0.. .... = nonStandardData is not present
H225: ..1. .... = Vendor is present
H225: ...0 .... = Gatekeeper is not present
H225: .... 0... = Gateway is not present
H225: .... .0.. = MCU is not present
H225: .... ..1. = Terminal is present
H225:
H225: .... ...0 = No extension value(s) present in vendorIdentifier
H225: Flags     = C0
H225: 1... .... = Product ID is present
H225: .1.. .... = Version ID is present
H225:
H225: ..0. .... = No extension value(s) present in H221NonStandard
H225: T.35 country code = 0xB5 (USA)
H225: T.35 extension    = 0
H225: Manufacture code = 0x534C (Microsoft)
H225: Product Id = Microsoft. NetMeeting.<00>
H225: Version Id = 3.0<00>
H225:
H225: Flags     = 00
H225: 0... .... = No extension value(s) present in terminal
H225: .0.. .... = nonStandardData is not present
H225: ..0. .... = MC is OFF
H225: ...0 .... = Undefined node is OFF
H225:
H225: Conference id = D861DE3202E4D511B09E006097195D66
H225:
H225:  * Connect-UUIE - extension *
H225: Flags     = 09
H225: 0... .... = Extension length determinant
H225: Number of extensions = 5
H225: .... ...1 = callIdentifier is present
```

Continued

Trace 9.3d *(Continued)*

```
H225: Flags    = 00
H225: 0... .... = h245SecurityMode is not present
H225: .0.. .... = tokens is not present
H225: ..0. .... = cryptoTokens is not present
H225: ...0 .... = fastStart is not present
H225:
H225: Flags    = 00
H225: 0... .... = No extension value(s) present in callIdentifier
H225: Guid = D761DE3202E4D511B09E006097195D66
H225:
```

The terminals begin the process of negotiating their respective parameters in Frame 17 (Trace 9.3e). The information sent from Station 180 includes details on a number of the terminal's functions, including Receive Multipoint Capability, Transmit Multipoint Capability, and others. Of particular interest is the Capability Table, which indicates various bit rates, protocols, and other specifications for this call.

Trace 9.3e: H.245 Terminal Capabilities Set Message (from Station 180)

```
- - - - - - - - - - - - - - - - - - - - - Frame 17 - - - - - - - - - - - - - - - - - - - -

H245:  Vector  Offset   Length    Frame
H245: ---------------------------------
H245:     0   0x0036       4       17
H245:     1   0x0036     529       19
H245: ---------------------------------
H245: 533 bytes of re-assembled data.
H245:
H245: ----- Control Protocol for Multimedia Communication -----
H245:
H245: Message length = 522
H245: Flags    = 02
H245: 0... .... = No extension value(s) present in H.245 control message
H245: H.245 call control message type = 0 (Request)
H245:
H245: ...0 .... = No extension value(s) present in request
H245: Request type = 2 (Terminal Capability Set)
H245:
H245: Flags    = 70
H245: 0... .... = No extension value(s) present in terminalCapabilitySet
H245: .1.. .... = multiplexCapability is present
H245: ..1. .... = capabilityTable is present
H245: ...1 .... = capabilityDescriptors is present
H245: Sequence number = 1
H245: Protocol id = {0.0.8.245.0.3}
```

```
H245:
H245: Flags     = 80
H245: 1... .... = Extension value(s) present in MultiplexCapability
H245: .0.. .... = Choice value is 6 bits long
H245: Multiplex capability = 0 (H2250 Capability)
H245: Flags     = 00
H245: 0... .... = No extension value(s) present in h2250Capability
H245: Maximum audio delay jitter      = 60 (ms)
H245:
H245: *** Receive Multipoint Capability ***
H245:
H245: Flags     = 00
H245: 0... .... = No extension value(s) present in receive multipoint capability
H245: .0.. .... = Multicast capability is OFF
H245: ..0. .... = Multi unicast conference is OFF
H245:
H245: Media Distribution Capability #1
H245: Flags     = 00
H245: 0... .... = No extension value(s) present in mediaDistributionCapability
H245: .0.. .... = centralizedData is not present
H245: ..0. .... = distributedData is not present
H245: ...0 .... = Centralized control is OFF
H245: .... 0... = Distributed control is OFF
H245: .... .0.. = Centralized audio is OFF
H245: .... ..0. = Distributed audio is OFF
H245: .... ...0 = Centralized video is OFF
H245: Flags     = 00
H245: 0... .... = Distributed video is OFF
H245:
H245: *** Transmit Multipoint Capability ***
H245:
H245: .0.. .... = No extension value(s) present in transmit multipoint capability
H245: ..0. .... = Multicast capability is OFF
H245: ...0 .... = Multi unicast conference is OFF
H245:
H245: Media Distribution Capability #1
H245: Flags     = 00
H245: 0... .... = No extension value(s) present in mediaDistributionCapability
H245: .0.. .... = centralizedData is not present
H245: ..0. .... = distributedData is not present
H245: ...0 .... = Centralized control is OFF
H245: .... 0... = Distributed control is OFF
H245: .... .0.. = Centralized audio is OFF
H245: .... ..0. = Distributed audio is OFF
```

Continued

Trace 9.3e *(Continued)*

```
H245: .... ...0 = Centralized video is OFF
H245: Flags    = 00
H245: 0... .... = Distributed video is OFF
H245:
H245: *** Receive and Transmit Multipoint Capability ***
H245:
H245: .0.. .... = No extension value(s) present in receive and transmit
H245:             multipoint capability
H245: ..0. .... = Multicast capability is OFF
H245: ...0 .... = Multi unicast conference is OFF
H245:
H245: Media Distribution Capability #1
H245: Flags    = 00
H245: 0... .... = No extension value(s) present in mediaDistributionCapability
H245: .0.. .... = centralizedData is not present
H245: ..0. .... = distributedData is not present
H245: ...0 .... = Centralized control is OFF
H245: .... 0... = Distributed control is OFF
H245: .... .0.. = Centralized audio is OFF
H245: .... ..0. = Distributed audio is OFF
H245: .... ...0 = Centralized video is OFF
H245: Flags    = 00
H245: 0... .... = Distributed video is OFF
H245:
H245: *** MC Capability ***
H245:
H245: .0.. .... = No extension value(s) present in mcCapability
H245: ..0. .... = Centralized Conference MC is OFF
H245: ...0 .... = Decentralized Conference MC is OFF
H245:
H245: .... 0... = RTCP video control capability is OFF
H245:
H245: *** Media Packetization Capability ***
H245:
H245: .... .0.. = No extension value(s) present in MediaPacketizationCapability
H245: .... ..0. = H261A video packetization is OFF
H245:
H245: *** Capability Table ***
H245:
H245: Number of capability table entry = 15
H245:
H245: Capability Table Entry Set #1
H245: Flags    = 80
```

```
H245: 1... .... = capability is present
H245: Capability table entry number = 32768
H245: Flags    = 04
H245: 0... .... = No extension value(s) present in Capability
H245: Capability = 0 (Non standard)
H245: nonStandardIdentifier = 1 (H221 Non Standard)
H245: T.35 country code = 0xB5 (USA)
H245: T.35 extension   = 66
H245: Manufacture code = 0x8080 (Intel)
H245: Data: 1 byte(s) of data
H245:
H245: Capability Table Entry Set #2
H245: Flags    = 80
H245: 1... .... = capability is present
H245: Capability table entry number = 15
H245: Flags    = 48
H245: 0... .... = No extension value(s) present in Capability
H245: Capability = 9 (Receive and transmit data application capability)
H245: .... .0.. = No extension value(s) present in dataApplicationCapability
H245: .... ..0. = No extension value(s) present in application
H245: Application = 1 (T120)
H245: ...1 .... = Extension value(s) present in DataProtocolCapability
H245: .... 0... = Extension index format
H245: Data protocol capability = 3 (Separate LAN stack)
H245: Maximum bit rate = 85000 (100 bit/s)
H245:
H245: Capability Table Entry Set #3
H245: Flags    = 80
H245: 1... .... = capability is present
H245: Capability table entry number = 1
H245: Flags    = 20
H245: 0... .... = No extension value(s) present in Capability
H245: Capability = 4 (Receive audio capability)
H245: .... .0.. = No extension value(s) present in AudioCapability
H245: Audio capability = 0 (Non standard)
H245: nonStandardIdentifier = 1 (H221 Non Standard)
H245: T.35 country code = 0xB5 (USA)
H245: T.35 extension   = 0
H245: Manufacture code = 0x534C (Microsoft)
H245: Data: 72 byte(s) of data
H245:
```

Station 150 then responds with its capabilities in Frame 18 (Trace 9.3f), which also includes information within the Capability Table that states its transmit and receive capabilities.

Trace 9.3f: H.245 Terminal Capabilities Set Message (from Station 150)

- - - - - - - - - - - - - - - - - Frame 18 - - - - - - - - - - - - - - - - - -

```
H245:   Vector  Offset   Length    Frame
    H245:  --------------------------------
    H245:        0  0x0036       4      18
    H245:        1  0x0036     529      20
    H245:  --------------------------------
    H245: 533 bytes of re-assembled data.
    H245:
    H245: ----- Control Protocol for Multimedia Communication -----
    H245:
    H245: Message length = 522
    H245: Flags     = 02
    H245: 0... .... = No extension value(s) present in H.245 control message
    H245: H.245 call control message type = 0 (Request)
    H245:
    H245: ...0 .... = No extension value(s) present in request
    H245: Request type = 2 (Terminal Capability Set)
    H245:
    H245: Flags     = 70
    H245: 0... .... = No extension value(s) present in terminalCapabilitySet
    H245: .1.. .... = multiplexCapability is present
    H245: ..1. .... = capabilityTable is present
    H245: ...1 .... = capabilityDescriptors is present
    H245: Sequence number = 1
    H245: Protocol id = {0.0.8.245.0.3}
    H245:
    H245: Flags     = 80
    H245: 1... .... = Extension value(s) present in MultiplexCapability
    H245: .0.. .... = Choice value is 6 bits long
    H245: Multiplex capability = 0 (H2250 Capability)
    H245: Flags     = 00
    H245: 0... .... = No extension value(s) present in h2250Capability
    H245: Maximum audio delay jitter       = 60 (ms)
    H245:
    H245: *** Receive Multipoint Capability ***
    H245:
    H245: Flags     = 00
    H245: 0... .... = No extension value(s) present in receive multipoint capability
    H245: .0.. .... = Multicast capability is OFF
    H245: ..0. .... = Multi unicast conference is OFF
    H245:
    H245: Media Distribution Capability #1
    H245: Flags     = 00
```

```
H245: 0... .... = No extension value(s) present in mediaDistributionCapability
H245: .0.. .... = centralizedData is not present
H245: ..0. .... = distributedData is not present
H245: ...0 .... = Centralized control is OFF
H245: .... 0... = Distributed control is OFF
H245: .... .0.. = Centralized audio is OFF
H245: .... ..0. = Distributed audio is OFF
H245: .... ...0 = Centralized video is OFF
H245: Flags    = 00
H245: 0... .... = Distributed video is OFF
H245:
H245: *** Transmit Multipoint Capability ***
H245:
H245: .0.. .... = No extension value(s) present in transmit multipoint capability
H245: ..0. .... = Multicast capability is OFF
H245: ...0 .... = Multi unicast conference is OFF
H245:
H245: Media Distribution Capability #1
H245: Flags    = 00
H245: 0... .... = No extension value(s) present in mediaDistributionCapability
H245: .0.. .... = centralizedData is not present
H245: ..0. .... = distributedData is not present
H245: ...0 .... = Centralized control is OFF
H245: .... 0... = Distributed control is OFF
H245: .... .0.. = Centralized audio is OFF
H245: .... ..0. = Distributed audio is OFF
H245: .... ...0 = Centralized video is OFF
H245: Flags    = 00
H245: 0... .... = Distributed video is OFF
H245:
H245: *** Receive and Transmit Multipoint Capability ***
H245:
H245: .0.. .... = No extension value(s) present in receive and transmit
H245:               multipoint capability
H245: ..0. .... = Multicast capability is OFF
H245: ...0 .... = Multi unicast conference is OFF
H245:
H245: Media Distribution Capability #1
H245: Flags    = 00
H245: 0... .... = No extension value(s) present in mediaDistributionCapability
H245: .0.. .... = centralizedData is not present
H245: ..0. .... = distributedData is not present
H245: ...0 .... = Centralized control is OFF
H245: .... 0... = Distributed control is OFF
```

Continued

Trace 9.3f *(Continued)*

```
H245: .... .0.. = Centralized audio is OFF
H245: .... ..0. = Distributed audio is OFF
H245: .... ...0 = Centralized video is OFF
H245: Flags     = 00
H245: 0... .... = Distributed video is OFF
H245:
H245: *** MC Capability ***
H245:
H245: .0.. .... = No extension value(s) present in mcCapability
H245: ..0. .... = Centralized Conference MC is OFF
H245: ...0 .... = Decentralized Conference MC is OFF
H245:
H245: .... 0... = RTCP video control capability is OFF
H245:
H245: *** Media Packetization Capability ***
H245:
H245: .... .0.. = No extension value(s) present in MediaPacketizationCapability
H245: .... ..0. = H261A video packetization is OFF
H245:
H245: *** Capability Table ***
H245:
H245: Number of capability table entry = 15
H245:
H245: Capability Table Entry Set #1
H245: Flags     = 80
H245: 1... .... = capability is present
H245: Capability table entry number = 32768
H245: Flags     = 04
H245: 0... .... = No extension value(s) present in Capability
H245: Capability = 0 (Non standard)
H245: nonStandardIdentifier = 1 (H221 Non Standard)
H245: T.35 country code = 0xB5 (USA)
H245: T.35 extension    = 66
H245: Manufacture code = 0x8080 (Intel)
H245: Data: 1 byte(s) of data
H245:
H245: Capability Table Entry Set #2
H245: Flags     = 80
H245: 1... .... = capability is present
H245: Capability table entry number = 15
H245: Flags     = 48
H245: 0... .... = No extension value(s) present in Capability
H245: Capability = 9 (Receive and transmit data application capability)
H245: .... .0.. = No extension value(s) present in dataApplicationCapability
```

```
H245: .... ..0. = No extension value(s) present in application
H245: Application = 1 (T120)
H245: ...1 .... = Extension value(s) present in DataProtocolCapability
H245: .... 0... = Extension index format
H245: Data protocol capability = 3 (Separate LAN stack)
H245: Maximum bit rate = 621700 (100 bit/s)
H245:
H245: Capability Table Entry Set #3
H245: Flags     = 80
H245: 1... .... = capability is present
H245: Capability table entry number = 1
H245: Flags     = 20
H245: 0... .... = No extension value(s) present in Capability
H245: Capability = 4 (Receive audio capability)
H245: .... .0.. = No extension value(s) present in AudioCapability
H245: Audio capability = 0 (Non standard)
H245: nonStandardIdentifier = 1 (H221 Non Standard)
H245: T.35 country code = 0xB5 (USA)
H245: T.35 extension   = 0
H245: Manufacture code = 0x534C (Microsoft)
H245: Data: 40 byte(s) of data
H245:
```

The terminals must also determine which will operate as the Master station and which will operate as the Slave. Frame 21 (Trace 9.3g) carries the information from Station 180 indicating that it will operate as the Slave.

Trace 9.3g: H.245 Master/Slave Determination Message (from Station 180)

```
- - - - - - - - - - - - - - - - - - - Frame 21 - - - - - - - - - - - - - - - - - - - -

H245:   Vector  Offset  Length   Frame
    H245: ---------------------------------
    H245:      0  0x0036     4       21
    H245:      1  0x0036     9       23
    H245: ---------------------------------
    H245: 13 bytes of re-assembled data.
    H245:
    H245: ----- Control Protocol for Multimedia Communication -----
    H245:
    H245: Message length = 7
    H245: Flags     = 21
    H245: 0... .... = No extension value(s) present in H.245 control message
    H245: H.245 call control message type = 1 (Response)
```

Continued

Trace 9.3g *(Continued)*

```
H245:
H245: ...0 .... = No extension value(s) present in ResponseMessage
H245: Response  = 3 (Terminal Capability Set Ack)
H245: .0.. .... = No extension value(s) present in TerminalCapabilitySetAck
H245: Sequence number = 1
H245:
H245: ----- Control Protocol for Multimedia Communication -----
H245:
H245: Message length = 6
H245: Flags     = 20
H245: 0... .... = No extension value(s) present in H.245 control message
H245: H.245 call control message type = 1 (Response)
H245:
H245: ...0 .... = No extension value(s) present in ResponseMessage
H245: Response  = 1 (Master Slave Determination Ack)
H245: .0.. .... = No extension value(s) present in MasterSlaveDeterminationAck
H245: Decision  = 1 (Slave)
```

Correspondingly, Station 150 responds in Frame 22 that it will operate as the Master station (Trace 9.3h).

Trace 9.3h: H.245 Master/Slave Determination Message (from Station 150)

```
- - - - - - - - - - - - - - - - - - - Frame 22 - - - - - - - - - - - - - - - - - - -


H245:   Vector  Offset  Length    Frame
  H245: -----------------------------------
  H245:      0  0x0036      4        22
  H245:      1  0x0036      9        24
  H245: -----------------------------------
  H245: 13 bytes of re-assembled data.
  H245:
  H245: ----- Control Protocol for Multimedia Communication -----
  H245:
  H245: Message length = 7
  H245: Flags     = 21
  H245: 0... .... = No extension value(s) present in H.245 control message
  H245: H.245 call control message type = 1 (Response)
  H245:
  H245: ...0 .... = No extension value(s) present in ResponseMessage
  H245: Response  = 3 (Terminal Capability Set Ack)
  H245: .0.. .... = No extension value(s) present in TerminalCapabilitySetAck
  H245: Sequence number = 1
  H245:
  H245: ----- Control Protocol for Multimedia Communication -----
```

```
H245:
H245: Message length = 6
H245: Flags     = 20
H245: 0... .... = No extension value(s) present in H.245 control message
H245: H.245 call control message type = 1 (Response)
H245:
H245: ...0 .... = No extension value(s) present in ResponseMessage
H245: Response = 1 (Master Slave Determination Ack)
H245: .0.. .... = No extension value(s) present in MasterSlaveDeterminationAck
H245: Decision = 0 (Master)
```

The two endpoints then open a logical channel for this connection, beginning with Frame 25 sent from Station 180 (Trace 9.3i). Like the previous messages, this one contains a number of parameters that request the channel number, bit rates, type of data to be transferred, and so on. Of particular interest is the Audio Capability (close to the end of the message, with a value of 3), which indicates that Station 180 would like to use G.711 Pulse Code Modulation u-law encoding operating at 64 Kbps (typically abbreviated as PCMU).

Trace 9.3i: H.245 Open Logical Channel Message (from Station 180)

```
- - - - - - - - - - - - - - - - - Frame 25 - - - - - - - - - - - - - - - - -

H245:   Vector  Offset   Length    Frame
     H245: --------------------------------
     H245:      0  0x0036       4       25
     H245:      1  0x0036      64       27
     H245: --------------------------------
     H245: 68 bytes of re-assembled data.
     H245:
     H245: ----- Control Protocol for Multimedia Communication -----
     H245:
     H245: Message length = 44
     H245: Flags     = 03
     H245: 0... .... = No extension value(s) present in H.245 control message
     H245: H.245 call control message type = 0 (Request)
     H245:
     H245: ...0 .... = No extension value(s) present in request
     H245: Request type = 3 (Open Logical Channel)
     H245:
     H245:
     H245: Flags     = C0
     H245: 1... .... = Extension value(s) present in OpenLogicalChannel
     H245: .1.. .... = reverseLogicalChannelParameters is present
     H245: Forward logical channel number = 256
```

Continued

Trace 9.3i *(Continued)*

```
H245:
H245: Flags     = 10
H245: 0... .... = No extension value(s) present in forwardLogicalChannelParameters
H245: .0.. .... = portNumber is not present
H245:
H245: ..0. .... = No extension value(s) present in dataType
H245: Data type = 4 (Data application capability)
H245: .... ..0. = No extension value(s) present in data
H245: .... ...0 = No extension value(s) present in application
H245: Application = 1 (T120)
H245: .... 1... = Extension value(s) present in DataProtocolCapability
H245: .... .0.. = Extension index format
H245: Data protocol capability = 3 (Separate LAN stack)
H245: Maximum bit rate = 0 (100 bit/s)
H245:
H245: Flags     = 80
H245: 1... .... = Extension value(s) present in MultiplexParameters
H245: .0.. .... = Extension index format
H245: Multiplex parameters = 0 (H2250 logical channel parameters)
H245:
H245: Flags     = 00
H245: 0... .... = No extension value(s) present in h2250LogicalChannelParameters
H245: .0.. .... = nonStandard is not present
H245: ..0. .... = associatedSessionID is not present
H245: ...0 .... = mediaChannel is not present
H245: .... 0... = mediaGuaranteedDelivery is not present
H245: .... .0.. = mediaControlChannel is not present
H245: .... ..0. = mediaControlGuaranteedDelivery is not present
H245: .... ...0 = silenceSuppression is not present
H245: Flags     = 00
H245: 0... .... = destination is not present
H245: .0.. .... = dynamicRTPPayloadType is not present
H245: ..0. .... = mediaPacketization is not present
H245: Session ID = 0
H245:
H245: Flags     = 50
H245: 0... .... = No extension value(s) present in reverseLogicalChannelParameters
H245: .1.. .... = multiplexParameters is present
H245:
H245: ..0. .... = No extension value(s) present in dataType
H245: Data type = 4 (Data application capability)
H245: .... ..0. = No extension value(s) present in data
H245: .... ...0 = No extension value(s) present in application
H245: Application = 1 (T120)
```

```
H245: .... 1... = Extension value(s) present in DataProtocolCapability
H245: .... .0.. = Extension index format
H245: Data protocol capability = 3 (Separate LAN stack)
H245: Maximum bit rate = 0 (100 bit/s)
H245:
H245: Flags     = 80
H245: 1... .... = Extension value(s) present in MultiplexParameters
H245: .0.. .... = Extension index format
H245: Multiplex parameters = 0 (H2250 logical channel parameters)
H245:
H245: Flags     = 00
H245: 0... .... = No extension value(s) present in h2250LogicalChannelParameters
H245: .0.. .... = nonStandard is not present
H245: ..0. .... = associatedSessionID is not present
H245: ...0 .... = mediaChannel is not present
H245: .... 0... = mediaGuaranteedDelivery is not present
H245: .... .0.. = mediaControlChannel is not present
H245: .... ..0. = mediaControlGuaranteedDelivery is not present
H245: .... ...0 = silenceSuppression is not present
H245: Flags     = 00
H245: 0... .... = destination is not present
H245: .0.. .... = dynamicRTPPayloadType is not present
H245: ..0. .... = mediaPacketization is not present
H245: Session ID = 0
H245:
H245: Flags     = 03
H245: 0... .... = Extension index format
H245: Number of extension = 2
H245: .... ...1 = separateStack is present
H245: Flags     = 00
H245: 0... .... = encryptionSync is not present
H245:
H245: Flags     = 42
H245: 0... .... = No extension value(s) present in separateStack
H245: .1.. .... = distribution is present
H245: ..0. .... = externalReference is not present
H245: ...0 .... = No extension value(s) present in Distribution
H245: Distribution = 0 (Unicast)
H245: .... .0.. = No extension value(s) present in networkAddress
H245: Network address = 2 (Local area address)
H245: Flags     = 00
H245: 0... .... = No extension value(s) present in localAreaAddress
H245: Transport Address = 0 (Unicast address)
H245: ..0. .... = No extension value(s) present in UnicastAddress
```

Continued

Trace 9.3i *(Continued)*

```
H245: Unicast address = 0 (IP address)
H245: .... ..0. = No extension value(s) present in iPAddress
H245: Network = 192.168.100.180
H245: TSAP indentifier = 1503
H245: Flags      = 00
H245: 0... .... = Associate conference is OFF
H245:
H245: ----- Control Protocol for Multimedia Communication -----
H245:
H245: Message length = 24
H245: Flags      = 03
H245: 0... .... = No extension value(s) present in H.245 control message
H245: H.245 call control message type = 0 (Request)
H245:
H245: ...0 .... = No extension value(s) present in request
H245: Request type = 3 (Open Logical Channel)
H245:
H245:
H245: Flags      = 00
H245: 0... .... = No extension value(s) present in OpenLogicalChannel
H245: .0.. .... = reverseLogicalChannelParameters is not present
H245: Forward logical channel number = 257
H245:
H245: Flags      = 0C
H245: 0... .... = No extension value(s) present in forwardLogicalChannelParameters
H245: .0.. .... = portNumber is not present
H245:
H245: ..0. .... = No extension value(s) present in dataType
H245: Data type = 3 (Audio data)
H245: .... ..0. = No extension value(s) present in audioData
H245: Audio capability = 3 (G.711 ulaw 64k)
H245: Value = 32
H245:
H245: Flags      = 80
H245: 1... .... = Extension value(s) present in MultiplexParameters
H245: .0.. .... = Extension index format
H245: Multiplex parameters = 0 (H2250 logical channel parameters)
H245:
H245: Flags      = 0F
H245: 0... .... = No extension value(s) present in h2250LogicalChannelParameters
H245: .0.. .... = nonStandard is not present
```

Station 150 returns its Open Logical Channel Request in Frame 26 (Trace 9.3j). This message also includes a number of transmission parameters, one of which specifies an Audio Capability value of 8, indicating that Station 150 will use G.723.1 encoding operating at either 5.3 or 6.4 Kbps.

Trace 9.3j: H.245 Open Logical Channel Message (from Station 150)

```
- - - - - - - - - - - - - - - - - - Frame 26 - - - - - - - - - - - - - - - - - -


H245:   Vector  Offset   Length    Frame
        H245: ---------------------------------
        H245:      0  0x0036       4       26
        H245:      1  0x0036      53       28
        H245: ---------------------------------
        H245: 57 bytes of re-assembled data.
        H245:
        H245: ----- Control Protocol for Multimedia Communication -----
        H245:
        H245: Message length = 32
        H245: Flags      = 03
        H245: 0... .... = No extension value(s) present in H.245 control message
        H245: H.245 call control message type = 0 (Request)
        H245:
        H245: ...0 .... = No extension value(s) present in request
        H245: Request type = 3 (Open Logical Channel)
        H245:
        H245:
        H245: Flags      = 40
        H245: 0... .... = No extension value(s) present in OpenLogicalChannel
        H245: .1.. .... = reverseLogicalChannelParameters is present
        H245: Forward logical channel number = 256
        H245:
        H245: Flags      = 10
        H245: 0... .... = No extension value(s) present in forwardLogicalChannelParameters
        H245: .0.. .... = portNumber is not present
        H245:
        H245: ..0. .... = No extension value(s) present in dataType
        H245: Data type = 4 (Data application capability)
        H245: .... ..0. = No extension value(s) present in data
        H245: .... ...0 = No extension value(s) present in application
        H245: Application = 1 (T120)
        H245: .... 1... = Extension value(s) present in DataProtocolCapability
        H245: .... .0.. = Extension index format
        H245: Data protocol capability = 3 (Separate LAN stack)
        H245: Maximum bit rate = 0 (100 bit/s)
        H245:
```

Continued

Trace 9.3j *(Continued)*

```
H245: Flags    = 80
H245: 1... .... = Extension value(s) present in MultiplexParameters
H245: .0.. .... = Extension index format
H245: Multiplex parameters = 0 (H2250 logical channel parameters)
H245:
H245: Flags    = 00
H245: 0... .... = No extension value(s) present in h2250LogicalChannelParameters
H245: .0.. .... = nonStandard is not present
H245: ..0. .... = associatedSessionID is not present
H245: ...0 .... = mediaChannel is not present
H245: .... 0... = mediaGuaranteedDelivery is not present
H245: .... .0.. = mediaControlChannel is not present
H245: .... ..0. = mediaControlGuaranteedDelivery is not present
H245: .... ...0 = silenceSuppression is not present
H245: Flags    = 00
H245: 0... .... = destination is not present
H245: .0.. .... = dynamicRTPPayloadType is not present
H245: ..0. .... = mediaPacketization is not present
H245: Session ID = 0
H245:
H245: Flags    = 50
H245: 0... .... = No extension value(s) present in reverseLogicalChannelParameters
H245: .1.. .... = multiplexParameters is present
H245:
H245: ..0. .... = No extension value(s) present in dataType
H245: Data type = 4 (Data application capability)
H245: .... ..0. = No extension value(s) present in data
H245: .... ...0 = No extension value(s) present in application
H245: Application = 1 (T120)
H245: .... 1... = Extension value(s) present in DataProtocolCapability
H245: .... .0.. = Extension index format
H245: Data protocol capability = 3 (Separate LAN stack)
H245: Maximum bit rate = 0 (100 bit/s)
H245:
H245: Flags    = 80
H245: 1... .... = Extension value(s) present in MultiplexParameters
H245: .0.. .... = Extension index format
H245: Multiplex parameters = 0 (H2250 logical channel parameters)
H245:
H245: Flags    = 00
H245: 0... .... = No extension value(s) present in h2250LogicalChannelParameters
H245: .0.. .... = nonStandard is not present
H245: ..0. .... = associatedSessionID is not present
H245: ...0 .... = mediaChannel is not present
```

```
H245: .... 0... = mediaGuaranteedDelivery is not present
H245: .... .0.. = mediaControlChannel is not present
H245: .... ..0. = mediaControlGuaranteedDelivery is not present
H245: .... ...0 = silenceSuppression is not present
H245: Flags      = 00
H245: 0... .... = destination is not present
H245: .0.. .... = dynamicRTPPayloadType is not present
H245: ..0. .... = mediaPacketization is not present
H245: Session ID = 0
H245:
H245: ----- Control Protocol for Multimedia Communication -----
H245:
H245: Message length = 25
H245: Flags      = 03
H245: 0... .... = No extension value(s) present in H.245 control message
H245: H.245 call control message type = 0 (Request)
H245:
H245: ...0 .... = No extension value(s) present in request
H245: Request type = 3 (Open Logical Channel)
H245:
H245:
H245: Flags      = 00
H245: 0... .... = No extension value(s) present in OpenLogicalChannel
H245: .0.. .... = reverseLogicalChannelParameters is not present
H245: Forward logical channel number = 257
H245:
H245: Flags      = 0D
H245: 0... .... = No extension value(s) present in forwardLogicalChannelParameters
H245: .0.. .... = portNumber is not present
H245:
H245: ..0. .... = No extension value(s) present in dataType
H245: Data type = 3 (Audio data)
H245: .... ..0. = No extension value(s) present in audioData
H245: Audio capability = 8 (G.7231)
H245: MaxAl-sdu audio frames = 0
H245: Flags      = 40
H245: 0... .... = Silence suppression
H245:
H245: .1.. .... = Extension value(s) present in MultiplexParameters
H245: ..0. .... = Extension index format
H245: Multiplex parameters = 0 (H2250 logical channel parameters)
H245:
H245: Flags      = 0F
H245: 0... .... = No extension value(s) present in h2250LogicalChannelParameters
```

Continued

Trace 9.3j *(Continued)*

```
H245: .0.. .... = nonStandard is not present
H245: ..0. .... = associatedSessionID is not present
H245: ...0 .... = mediaChannel is not present
H245: .... 1... = mediaGuaranteedDelivery is present
H245: .... .1.. = mediaControlChannel is present
H245: .... ..1. = mediaControlGuaranteedDelivery is present
H245: .... ...1 = silenceSuppression is present
H245: Flags     = 00
H245: 0... .... = destination is not present
H245: .0.. .... = dynamicRTPPayloadType is not present
H245: ..0. .... = mediaPacketization is not present
H245: Session ID = 1
H245: Flags     = 00
H245: 0... .... = Media guaranted delivery is OFF
H245:
H245: *** Media Control Channel ***
H245: .0.. .... = No extension value(s) present in mediaControlChannel(RTCP)
H245: Transport Address = 0 (Unicast address)
H245: ...0 .... = No extension value(s) present in UnicastAddress
H245: Unicast address = 0 (IP address)
H245: .... ...0 = No extension value(s) present in iPAddress
H245: Network = 192.168.100.150
H245: TSAP indentifier = 49599
H245: Flags     = 40
H245: 0... .... = Media control guaranted delivery is OFF
H245: .1.. .... = Silence suppression is ON
```

The Open Logical Channel Acknowledgment (Open Logical Channel Ack) message sent from Station 180 in Frame 31 indicates its IP address [192.168.100.180] and the port addresses (49598 and 49599) that will be used for this connection (Trace 9.3k).

Trace 9.3k: H.245 Open Logical Channel Ack Message (from Station 180)

```
- - - - - - - - - - - - - - - - - - Frame 31 - - - - - - - - - - - - - - - - - -

H245:   Vector  Offset   Length    Frame
   H245: --------------------------------
   H245:      0  0x0036        4       31
   H245:      1  0x0036       32       33
   H245: --------------------------------
   H245: 36 bytes of re-assembled data.
   H245:
   H245: ----- Control Protocol for Multimedia Communication -----
   H245:
```

```
H245: Message length = 9
H245: Flags     = 23
H245: 0... .... = No extension value(s) present in H.245 control message
H245: H.245 call control message type = 1 (Response)
H245:
H245: ...0 .... = No extension value(s) present in ResponseMessage
H245: Response  = 6 (Open Logical Channel Reject)
H245:
H245: .0.. .... = No extension value(s) present in openLogicalChannelReject
H245: Forward logical channel number = 256
H245: Flags     = 00
H245: 0... .... = No extension value(s) present in cause
H245: Cause = 0 (Unspecified)
H245:
H245: ----- Control Protocol for Multimedia Communication -----
H245:
H245: Message length = 27
H245: Flags     = 22
H245: 0... .... = No extension value(s) present in H.245 control message
H245: H.245 call control message type = 1 (Response)
H245:
H245: ...0 .... = No extension value(s) present in ResponseMessage
H245: Response  = 5 (Open Logical Channel Ack)
H245:
H245: .1.. .... = Extension value(s) present in openLogicalChannelAck
H245: ..0. .... = reverseLogicalChannelParameters is not present
H245: Forward logical channel number = 257
H245:
H245: Flags     = 04
H245: 0... .... = Extension index format
H245: Number of extension = 3
H245: .... ...0 = separateStack is not present
H245: Flags     = 80
H245: 1... .... = forwardMultiplexAckParameters is present
H245: .0.. .... = encryptionSync is not present
H245: Flags     = 1C
H245: 0... .... = No extension value(s) present in forwardMultiplexAckParameters
H245: .0.. .... = No extension value(s) present in H2250LogicalChannelAckParameters
H245: ..0. .... = nonStandard is not present
H245: ...1 .... = sessionID is present
H245: .... 1... = mediaChannel is present
H245: .... .1.. = mediaControlChannel is present
H245: .... ..0. = dynamicRTPPayloadType is not present
H245: .... ...0 = PortNumber is not present
```

Continued

Trace 9.3k *(Continued)*

```
H245: Session ID = 1
H245: Flags     = 00
H245: 0... .... = No extension value(s) present in mediaChannel
H245: Transport Address = 0 (Unicast address)
H245: ..0. .... = No extension value(s) present in UnicastAddress
H245: Unicast address = 0 (IP address)
H245: .... ..0. = No extension value(s) present in iPAddress
H245: Network = 192.168.100.180
H245: TSAP indentifier = 49598
H245: Flags     = 00
H245: 0... .... = No extension value(s) present in mediaControlChannel
H245:            (forward RTCP channel)
H245: Transport Address = 0 (Unicast address)
H245: ..0. .... = No extension value(s) present in UnicastAddress
H245: Unicast address = 0 (IP address)
H245: .... ..0. = No extension value(s) present in iPAddress
H245: Network = 192.168.100.180
H245: TSAP indentifier = 49599
```

Similarly, Station 150 sends an Open Logical Channel Ack message in Frame 32 that indicates its IP address [192.168.100.150] and the same port numbers to be used (49598 and 49599). In addition, many other parameters are confirmed (Trace 9.3l).

Trace 9.3l: H.245 Open Logical Channel Ack Message (from Station 150)

```
- - - - - - - - - - - - - - - - - - Frame 32 - - - - - - - - - - - - - - - - - - -

H245:   Vector  Offset   Length    Frame
    H245: ---------------------------------
    H245:      0   0x0036       4     32
    H245:      1   0x0036      38     34
    H245: ---------------------------------
    H245: 42 bytes of re-assembled data.
    H245:
    H245: ----- Control Protocol for Multimedia Communication -----
    H245:
    H245: Message length = 15
    H245: Flags     = 22
    H245: 0... .... = No extension value(s) present in H.245 control message
    H245: H.245 call control message type = 1 (Response)
    H245:
    H245: ...0 .... = No extension value(s) present in ResponseMessage
    H245: Response = 5 (Open Logical Channel Ack)
    H245:
```

```
H245: .1.. .... = Extension value(s) present in openLogicalChannelAck
H245: ..1. .... = reverseLogicalChannelParameters is present
H245: Forward logical channel number = 256
H245:
H245: Flags     = 00
H245: 0... .... = No extension value(s) present in reverseLogicalChannelParameters
H245: .0.. .... = Port number is not present
H245: ..0. .... = multiplexParameters is not present
H245: Reverse logical channel number = 258
H245:
H245: Flags     = 04
H245: 0... .... = Extension index format
H245: Number of extension = 3
H245: .... ...0 = separateStack is not present
H245: Flags     = 80
H245: 1... .... = forwardMultiplexAckParameters is present
H245: .0.. .... = encryptionSync is not present
H245: Flags     = 00
H245: 0... .... = No extension value(s) present in forwardMultiplexAckParameters
H245: .0.. .... = No extension value(s) present in H2250LogicalChannelAckParameters
H245: ..0. .... = nonStandard is not present
H245: ...0 .... = sessionID is not present
H245: .... 0... = mediaChannel is not present
H245: .... .0.. = mediaControlChannel is not present
H245: .... ..0. = dynamicRTPPayloadType is not present
H245: .... ...0 = PortNumber is not present
H245:
H245: ----- Control Protocol for Multimedia Communication -----
H245:
H245: Message length = 27
H245: Flags     = 22
H245: 0... .... = No extension value(s) present in H.245 control message
H245: H.245 call control message type = 1 (Response)
H245:
H245: ...0 .... = No extension value(s) present in ResponseMessage
H245: Response  = 5 (Open Logical Channel Ack)
H245:
H245: .1.. .... = Extension value(s) present in openLogicalChannelAck
H245: ..0. .... = reverseLogicalChannelParameters is not present
H245: Forward logical channel number = 257
H245:
H245: Flags     = 04
H245: 0... .... = Extension index format
H245: Number of extension = 3
```

Continued

Trace 9.3l *(Continued)*

```
H245: .... ...0 = separateStack is not present
H245: Flags     = 80
H245: 1... .... = forwardMultiplexAckParameters is present
H245: .0.. .... = encryptionSync is not present
H245: Flags     = 1C
H245: 0... .... = No extension value(s) present in forwardMultiplexAckParameters
H245: .0.. .... = No extension value(s) present in H2250LogicalChannelAckParameters
H245: ..0. .... = nonStandard is not present
H245: ...1 .... = sessionID is present
H245: .... 1... = mediaChannel is present
H245: .... .1.. = mediaControlChannel is present
H245: .... ..0. = dynamicRTPPayloadType is not present
H245: .... ...0 = PortNumber is not present
H245: Session ID = 1
H245: Flags     = 00
H245: 0... .... = No extension value(s) present in mediaChannel
H245: Transport Address = 0 (Unicast address)
H245: ..0. .... = No extension value(s) present in UnicastAddress
H245: Unicast address = 0 (IP address)
H245: .... ..0. = No extension value(s) present in iPAddress
H245: Network = 192.168.100.150
H245: TSAP indentifier = 49598
H245: Flags     = 00
H245: 0... .... = No extension value(s) present in mediaControlChannel
H245:             (forward RTCP channel)
H245: Transport Address = 0 (Unicast address)
H245: ..0. .... = No extension value(s) present in UnicastAddress
H245: Unicast address = 0 (IP address)
H245: .... ..0. = No extension value(s) present in iPAddress
H245: Network = 192.168.100.150
H245: TSAP indentifier = 49599
```

The next process (which is implemented with the NetMeeting product but not required for all H.323 implementations) specifies the bandwidth required on the channel between the two stations using the Resource Reservation Protocol (RSVP), as discussed in Section 4.8.4 and Figure 4-25. The first RSVP communication from Station 180 is an RSVP Path message that follows the downstream path of the data (that is, toward Station 150) and is illustrated in Trace 9.3m. The Path message carries the previous hop address [192.168.100.180]; a Sender Template, which describes the format of the data packets that the sender will originate; a Sender Tspec, which defines the characteristics of the data flow that the sender will originate; and an Adspec, which carries One Pass with Advertising (OPWA) information used for traffic flow and quality of service functions.

Trace 9.3m: H.245 RSVP Path Message (from Station 180)

- - - - - - - - - - - - - - - - - - - Frame 36 - - - - - - - - - - - - - - - - - - -

```
RSVP: ----- RSVP Header -----
      RSVP:
      RSVP: Version          = 1
      RSVP: Flags            = 0
      RSVP: Message type     = 1 (Path)
      RSVP: Checksum         = 350E (should be C5D6)
      RSVP: Send_TTL         = 63
      RSVP: Reserved         = 0x00
      RSVP: RSVP Length      = 136
      RSVP:
      RSVP: Object length    = 12
      RSVP: Object class     = 1 (SESSION)
      RSVP: C_Type           = 1 (IPv4 DestAddress)
      RSVP: IP4 DestAddress  = 192.168.100.150
      RSVP: Protocol ID      = 17 (UDP)
      RSVP: Flags            = 1 (E_Police flag)
      RSVP: Destination Port = 49598
      RSVP:
      RSVP: Object length    = 12
      RSVP: Object class     = 3 (RSVP_HOP)
      RSVP: C_Type           = 1
      RSVP: IP4 next/previous hop address = 192.168.100.180
      RSVP: Logical interface handle  = 0
      RSVP:
      RSVP: Object length    = 8
      RSVP: Object class     = 5 (TIME_VALUES)
      RSVP: C_Type           = 1
      RSVP: Refresh period R = 30000 (ms)
      RSVP:
      RSVP: Object length    = 12
      RSVP: Object class     = 11 (SENDER_TEMPLATE)
      RSVP: C_Type           = 1 (IPv4 source Address)
      RSVP: IP4 source address = 192.168.100.180
      RSVP: Reserved         = 0x0000 (must be zero)
      RSVP: Source port      = 49598
      RSVP:
      RSVP: Object length    = 36
      RSVP: Object class     = 12 (SENDER_TSPEC)
      RSVP: C_Type           = 2
      RSVP: Version          = 0
      RSVP: Overall length   = 7
```

Continued

Trace 9.3m *(Continued)*

```
RSVP: Service number      = 1 (Default/global information)
RSVP: Length of data      = 6
RSVP: Parameter id        = 127 (Token_Bucket_TSpec)
RSVP: Parameter 127 flags = 0
RSVP: Parameter 127 length= 5
RSVP: Token bucket rate   = 461EFC00
RSVP: Token bucket size   = 44940000
RSVP: Peak data rate      = 462EE000
RSVP: Minimum policed unit= 00000128
RSVP: Maximum packet size = 00000128
RSVP:
RSVP: Object length       = 48
RSVP: Object class        = 13 (ADSPEC)
RSVP: C_Type              = 2
RSVP: Error Value = 0000
RSVP:  0000 ....  .... .... = Version 0
RSVP: Overall length      = 9
RSVP: Service number      = 1 (Default/global information)
RSVP: Global break bit    = 8
RSVP: Parameter id        = 4
RSVP: Parameter 4 flag    = 0x00
RSVP: Parameter 4 length  = 1
RSVP: IS hop count        = 0
RSVP: Parameter id        = 6
RSVP: Parameter 6 flag    = 0x00
RSVP: Parameter 6 length  = 1
RSVP: Path b/w estimate   = 2139095040
RSVP: Parameter id        = 8
RSVP: Parameter 8 flag    = 0x00
RSVP: Parameter 8 length  = 1
RSVP: Minimum path latency = 0
RSVP: Parameter id        = 10
RSVP: Parameter 10 flag   = 0x00
RSVP: Parameter 10 length = 1
RSVP: Composed path MTU   = 1500
```

Station 150 then returns an RSVP Resv message in Frame 37 (Trace 9.3n), which creates and maintains the reservation state in each node toward the sender (Station 180). This Resv message includes a set of parameters called the flowspec, which specifies a desired quality of service.

Trace 9.3n: H.245 RSVP Resv Message (from Station 150)

- Frame 37 -

```
RSVP: ----- RSVP Header -----
      RSVP:
      RSVP: Version           = 1
      RSVP: Flags             = 0
      RSVP: Message type      = 2 (Resv)
      RSVP: Checksum          = 0F54 (should be C5FD)
      RSVP: Send_TTL          = 63
      RSVP: Reserved          = 0x00
      RSVP: RSVP Length       = 96
      RSVP:
      RSVP: Object length     = 12
      RSVP: Object class      = 1 (SESSION)
      RSVP: C_Type            = 1 (IPv4 DestAddress)
      RSVP: IP4 DestAddress   = 192.168.100.150
      RSVP: Protocol ID       = 17 (UDP)
      RSVP: Flags             = 0 (non E_Police)
      RSVP: Destination Port  = 49598
      RSVP:
      RSVP: Object length     = 12
      RSVP: Object class      = 3 (RSVP_HOP)
      RSVP: C_Type            = 1
      RSVP: IP4 next/previous hop address = 192.168.100.150
      RSVP: Logical interface handle  = 0
      RSVP:
      RSVP: Object length     = 8
      RSVP: Object class      = 5 (TIME_VALUES)
      RSVP: C_Type            = 1
      RSVP: Refresh period R  = 30000 (ms)
      RSVP:
      RSVP: Object length     = 8
      RSVP: Object class      = 8 (STYLE)
      RSVP: C_Type            = 1
      RSVP: Flags =  0
      RSVP: Option vector control = 11
      RSVP:             ...1 0... = Sharing control (Shared reservations)
      RSVP:             .... .001 = Sender selection control (Wildcard)
      RSVP:
      RSVP: Object length     = 48
      RSVP: Object class      = 9 (FLOWSPEC)
      RSVP: C_Type            = 2
      RSVP: Version            = 0
```

Continued

Trace 9.3n *(Continued)*

```
RSVP: Overall length      = 10
RSVP: Service number      = 2 (Guaranteed)
RSVP: Length of data      = 9
RSVP: Parameter id        = 127 (Token_Bucket_TSpec)
RSVP: Parameter 127 flags = 0
RSVP: Parameter 127 length= 5
RSVP: Token bucket rate   = 461EFC00
RSVP: Token bucket size   = 44940000
RSVP: Peak data rate      = 462EE000
RSVP: Minimum policed unit= 00000128
RSVP: Maximum packet size = 00000128
RSVP: Parameter id        = 130 (Guaranteed service RSpec)
RSVP: Parameter 130 flags = 0x 0
RSVP: Parameter 130 length = 2
RSVP: Rate                = 1176435712
RSVP: Slack term          = -1
```

Since RSVP operates along simplex (one-way) paths, Station 150 must initiate a reservation for the bandwidth that it needs for the data it will send to Station 180. The Path message in Frame 39 (Trace 9.3o) contains the Sender template, Tspec, and Adspec fields that are similar to those sent in Frame 36 from the other end of the connection.

Trace 9.3o: H.245 RSVP Path Message (from Station 150)

```
- - - - - - - - - - - - - - - - - - - Frame 39 - - - - - - - - - - - - - - - - - - -


RSVP: ----- RSVP Header -----
    RSVP:
    RSVP: Version           = 1
    RSVP: Flags             = 0
    RSVP: Message type      = 1 (Path)
    RSVP: Checksum          = 1C54 (should be C5B6)
    RSVP: Send_TTL          = 63
    RSVP: Reserved          = 0x00
    RSVP: RSVP Length       = 168
    RSVP:
    RSVP: Object length     = 12
    RSVP: Object class      = 1 (SESSION)
    RSVP: C_Type            = 1 (IPv4 DestAddress)
    RSVP: IP4 DestAddress   = 192.168.100.180
    RSVP: Protocol ID       = 17 (UDP)
    RSVP: Flags             = 1 (E_Police flag)
    RSVP: Destination Port  = 49598
    RSVP:
```

```
RSVP: Object length      = 12
RSVP: Object class       = 3 (RSVP_HOP)
RSVP: C_Type             = 1
RSVP: IP4 next/previous hop address = 192.168.100.150
RSVP: Logical interface handle  = 0
RSVP:
RSVP: Object length      = 8
RSVP: Object class       = 5 (TIME_VALUES)
RSVP: C_Type             = 1
RSVP: Refresh period R   = 30000 (ms)
RSVP:
RSVP: Object length      = 12
RSVP: Object class       = 11 (SENDER_TEMPLATE)
RSVP: C_Type             = 1 (IPv4 source Address)
RSVP: IP4 source address = 192.168.100.150
RSVP: Reserved           = 0x0000 (must be zero)
RSVP: Source port        = 49598
RSVP:
RSVP: Object length      = 36
RSVP: Object class       = 12 (SENDER_TSPEC)
RSVP: C_Type             = 2
RSVP: Version            = 0
RSVP: Overall length     = 7
RSVP: Service number     = 1 (Default/global information)
RSVP: Length of data     = 6
RSVP: Parameter id       = 127 (Token_Bucket_TSpec)
RSVP: Parameter 127 flags = 0
RSVP: Parameter 127 length= 5
RSVP: Token bucket rate  = 4512A000
RSVP: Token bucket size  = 43800000
RSVP: Peak data rate     = 45214000
RSVP: Minimum policed unit= 00000040
RSVP: Maximum packet size = 00000040
RSVP:
RSVP: Object length      = 80
RSVP: Object class       = 13 (ADSPEC)
RSVP: C_Type             = 2
RSVP: Error Value = 0000
RSVP:  0000 ....  .... .... = Version 0
RSVP: Overall length     = 17
RSVP: Service number     = 1 (Default/global information)
RSVP: Global break bit   = 8
RSVP: Parameter id       = 4
RSVP: Parameter 4 flag   = 0x00
```

Continued

Trace 9.3o *(Continued)*

```
RSVP: Parameter 4 length = 1
RSVP: IS hop count       = 0
RSVP: Parameter id       = 6
RSVP: Parameter 6 flag   = 0x00
RSVP: Parameter 6 length = 1
RSVP: Path b/w estimate  = 2139095040
RSVP: Parameter id       = 8
RSVP: Parameter 8 flag   = 0x00
RSVP: Parameter 8 length = 1
RSVP: Minimum path latency  = 0
RSVP: Parameter id        = 10
RSVP: Parameter 10 flag   = 0x00
RSVP: Parameter 10 length = 1
RSVP: Composed path MTU   = 1500
RSVP: Service number = 2 Guaranteed service
RSVP: Length of guaranteed-service data = 8
RSVP: Parameter id          = 133
RSVP: Parameter 133 flag    = 0x00
RSVP: Parameter 133 length = 1
RSVP: End-to-end composed composed value for C  = 0
RSVP: Parameter id          = 134
RSVP: Parameter 134 flag    = 0x00
RSVP: Parameter 134 length = 1
RSVP: End-to-end composed value for D = 0
RSVP: Parameter id       = 135
RSVP: Parameter flag     = 0x00
RSVP: Parameter length = 1
RSVP: Since-last-reshaping point composed for C = 0
```

In confirmation, Station 180 returns an RSVP Resv message to Station 150 (Frame 40 in Trace 9.3p), and now bandwidth is reserved in both directions along the data path.

Trace 9.3p: H.245 RSVP Resv Message (from Station 180)

```
- - - - - - - - - - - - - - - - Frame 40 - - - - - - - - - - - - - - - - - - - -


RSVP: ----- RSVP Header -----
    RSVP:
    RSVP: Version          = 1
    RSVP: Flags            = 0
    RSVP: Message type     = 2 (Resv)
    RSVP: Checksum         = 5235 (should be C5FD)
    RSVP: Send_TTL         = 63
    RSVP: Reserved         = 0x00
```

```
RSVP: RSVP Length        = 96
RSVP:
RSVP: Object length      = 12
RSVP: Object class       = 1 (SESSION)
RSVP: C_Type             = 1 (IPv4 DestAddress)
RSVP: IP4 DestAddress    = 192.168.100.180
RSVP: Protocol ID        = 17 (UDP)
RSVP: Flags              = 0 (non E_Police)
RSVP: Destination Port   = 49598
RSVP:
RSVP: Object length      = 12
RSVP: Object class       = 3 (RSVP_HOP)
RSVP: C_Type             = 1
RSVP: IP4 next/previous hop address = 192.168.100.180
RSVP: Logical interface handle  = 0
RSVP:
RSVP: Object length      = 8
RSVP: Object class       = 5 (TIME_VALUES)
RSVP: C_Type             = 1
RSVP: Refresh period R   = 30000 (ms)
RSVP:
RSVP: Object length      = 8
RSVP: Object class       = 8 (STYLE)
RSVP: C_Type             = 1
RSVP: Flags =  0
RSVP: Option vector control = 11
RSVP:              ...1 0... = Sharing control (Shared reservations)
RSVP:              .... .001 = Sender selection control (Wildcard)
RSVP:
RSVP: Object length      = 48
RSVP: Object class       = 9 (FLOWSPEC)
RSVP: C_Type             = 2
RSVP: Version             = 0
RSVP: Overall length     = 10
RSVP: Service number     = 2 (Guaranteed)
RSVP: Length of data     = 9
RSVP: Parameter id       = 127 (Token_Bucket_TSpec)
RSVP: Parameter 127 flags = 0
RSVP: Parameter 127 length= 5
RSVP: Token bucket rate   = 4512A000
RSVP: Token bucket size   = 43800000
RSVP: Peak data rate      = 45214000
RSVP: Minimum policed unit= 00000040
RSVP: Maximum packet size = 00000040
```

Continued

Trace 9.3p *(Continued)*

```
RSVP: Parameter id         = 130 (Guaranteed service RSpec)
RSVP: Parameter 130 flags  = 0x 0
RSVP: Parameter 130 length = 2
RSVP: Rate                 = 0
RSVP: Slack term           = 0
```

Once the connection has been established, the media session using RTP can proceed. An example of an RTP packet sent from Station 150 includes the 24 octets of G.723 audio, as illustrated in Trace 9.3q. (Review Figure 9-2 and recall that the amount of audio information that is carried within the RTP packet varies by encoder, with G.723 specifying 24 octets of information.) Note that RTP includes Sequence Numbers and a Time Stamp to facilitate media stream reassembly at the receiving end of the connection.

Trace 9.3q: RTP Message with G.723 Audio (from Station 150)

```
- - - - - - - - - - - - - - - - - - Frame 878 - - - - - - - - - - - - - - - - - - -


RTP: ----- Real-Time Transport Protocol -----
     RTP:
     RTP: Ver, Pad, Ext, CC:       = 80
     RTP:                10.. .... = Version = 2 (RFC 1889)
     RTP:                ..0. .... = Padding = 0 (Zero bytes of Padding at the End)
     RTP:                ...0 .... = Header Extension Bit = 0,(No Header
     RTP:                                Extension after Fixed Header)
     RTP:                .... 0000 = Contributor Count = 0
     RTP: Marker, Payload Type: = 04
     RTP:                0... .... = Marker 0
     RTP:                .000 0100 = Payload Type 4 (G.723 audio)
     RTP: Sequence Number    = 63341
     RTP: Time Stamp         = 149520 (18690.000 ms)
     RTP: SSRC               = 2244723851
     RTP:
     RTP: ----- G.723: Dual Rate Speech Coder For Multimedia Communications
     RTP:         Transmitting at 5.3 and 6.3 kbit/s -----
     RTP:
     RTP: [24 bytes of G.723 audio data]
     RTP:
```

RTCP messages are periodically transmitted by the sending stations to provide feedback regarding the quality of the information streams. Several types of RTCP messages are defined: a Sender Report (SR) containing statistics for stations that are active senders; a Receiver Report (RR) containing statistics for stations that are not active senders; a Source Description (SDES), which contains a Canonical Name

(CNAME); a Bye, which indicates the end of participation; and an App, which contains application-specific functions. Frame 879 (Trace 9.3r) illustrates an SR message, which carries a number of parameters and statistics regarding this sender (Station 180 in this case).

Trace 9.3r: RTCP Message (from Station 180)

```
- - - - - - - - - - - - - - - - - - Frame 879 - - - - - - - - - - - - - - - - -


RTCP: ----- RTP Control Protocol -----
      RTCP:
      RTCP: Ver, Pad, RC:        = 81
      RTCP:              10.. .... = Version = 2 (RFC 1889)
      RTCP:              ..0. .... = Padding = 0
      RTCP:              ...0 0001 = Reception report count = 1
      RTCP: Packet type         = 200 (Sender Report)
      RTCP: Length              = 13 (32-bit words)
      RTCP: SSRC of sender      = 2058410030
      RTCP:
      RTCP: NTP reference timestamp  = 5888.09668 sec
      RTCP: RTP timestamp            = 149168
      RTCP: Sender's packet count    = 294
      RTCP: Sender's octet count     = 75264
      RTCP:
      RTCP: SSRC                     = 2244723851
      RTCP: Fraction lost            = 0.00000
      RTCP: Cumulative packets lost  = 0
      RTCP: Extended highest sequence #  = Cycle:0, Seq:63341
      RTCP: Interarrival jitter      = 288
      RTCP: Last SR timestamp        = 421649152
      RTCP: Delay since last SR      = 4 (Sec)
      RTCP:
      RTCP: ----- RTP Control Protocol -----
      RTCP:
      RTCP: Ver, Pad, RC:        = 81
      RTCP:              10.. .... = Version = 2 (RFC 1889)
      RTCP:              ..0. .... = Padding = 0
      RTCP:              ...0 0001 = Source count = 1
      RTCP: Packet type         = 202 (Source Description)
      RTCP: Length              = 4 (32-bit words)
      RTCP:
      RTCP: SSRC/CSRC           = 2058410030
      RTCP: SDES item    = 1 (CNAME)
      RTCP:   Length     = 4
      RTCP:   User/Domain  = "BUFF"
      RTCP:
```

When the end user (a human at Station 180 in this case) has completed the conversation, he or she clicks on a button on the NetMeeting application to end the call. That button click triggers the H.245 End Session Command message transmitted in Frame 1008 and shown in Trace 9.3s.

Trace 9.3s: H.245 End Session Message (from Station 180)

```
- - - - - - - - - - - - - - - - - - - Frame 1008 - - - - - - - - - - - - - - - - - -


H245:   Vector  Offset   Length    Frame
    H245: ---------------------------------
    H245:      0  0x0036       4    1008
    H245:      1  0x0036       2    1009
    H245: ---------------------------------
    H245: 6 bytes of re-assembled data.
    H245:
    H245: ----- Control Protocol for Multimedia Communication -----
    H245:
    H245: Message length = 6
    H245: Flags      = 4A
    H245: 0... .... = No extension value(s) present in H.245 control message
    H245: H.245 call control message type = 2 (Command)
    H245:
    H245: ...0 .... = No extension value(s) present in CommandMessage
    H245: Command = 5 (End Session Command)
    H245: .... ...0 = No extension value(s) present in EndSessionCommand
    H245: End session command = 1 (Disconnect)
```

Next, an H.225.0 RELEASE COMPLETE message is transmitted from Station 180, indicating the release of the Call Reference Value (17984) that was previously established in Frame 6 with the SETUP message. Note that User-to-User information is again present (Trace 9.3t).

Trace 9.3t: H.225.0 RELEASE COMPLETE Message (from Station 180)

```
- - - - - - - - - - - - - - - - - - - Frame 1012 - - - - - - - - - - - - - - - - - -


H225: ----- H.225 Call Signaling -----
    H225:
    H225: Protocol discriminator   = 8
    H225: Length of call reference = 2
    H225: Call reference field = C640
    H225: 1... .... .... .... = Message to originator
    H225: .100 0110  0100 0000 = = 17984 (Call reference value)
    H225: Message type = 90 (Release Complete)
    H225:
```

```
       H225: Cause Information
       H225: Cause information element ID = 8
       H225: Cause contents length = 3
       H225: Coding standard and location flags = 00
       H225:                         0... .... = Continue
       H225:                         .00. .... = Coding standard = 0
       H225:                                    (CCITT standardized coding)
       H225:                         .... 0000 = Location = 0 (User)
       H225: Recommendation flags = 00
       H225:             0... .... = Continue
       H225:             .000 0000 = Recommendation = 0 (Q.931)
       H225:
H225: ----User-User Information----
       H225:
       H225: Information element identifier = 0x7E (User-User)
       H225: Length of user-user content = 30
       H225: Protocol discriminator = 5 (X.680 / X.691(PER)(ASN.1))
       H225:
       H225: Flags     = 05
       H225: 0... .... = No extension values present in H323-UserInformation
       H225: .0.. .... = user-data is not present
       H225: ..0. .... = No extension values present in h323-uu-pdu
       H225: ...0 .... = nonStandardData is not present
       H225: .... 0... = No extension values present in h323-message-body
       H225: h323-message = 5 (ReleaseComplete-UUIE)
       H225:
       H225: Flags     = C0
       H225: 1... .... = Extension value(s) present in ReleaseComplete-UUIE
       H225: .1.. .... = ReleaseCompleteReason is present
       H225: Protocol ID = {0.0.8.2250.0.2}
       H225: Flags     = 58
       H225: 0... .... = No extension values present in ReleaseCompleteReason
       H225: Reason = 11 (Undefined reason)
       H225:  * ReleaseComplete-UUIE - extension *
       H225: .... .0.. = Extension length determinant
       H225: Number of extensions = 1
       H225: .... 1... = callIdentifier is present
       H225:
       H225: Flags     = 00
       H225: 0... .... = No extension value(s) present in callIdentifier
       H225: Guid = D761DE3202E4D511B09E006097195D66
       H225:
```

A second RELEASE COMPLETE message is sent from Station 150 at the other end of the connection (Trace 9.3u).

Trace 9.3u: H.225.0 RELEASE COMPLETE Message (from Station 150)

- - - - - - - - - - - - - - - - - - Frame 1015 - - - - - - - - - - - - - - - - - - -

```
H225: ----- H.225 Call Signaling -----
      H225:
      H225: Protocol discriminator   = 8
      H225: Length of call reference = 2
      H225: Call reference field = 4640
      H225:  0... .... .... .... = Message from originator
      H225: .100 0110  0100 0000 = = 17984 (Call reference value)
      H225: Message type = 90 (Release Complete)
      H225:
      H225: Cause Information
      H225: Cause information element ID = 8
      H225: Cause contents length = 3
      H225: Coding standard and location flags = 00
      H225:                         0... .... = Continue
      H225:                         .00. .... = Coding standard = 0
      H225:                                    (CCITT standardized coding)
      H225:                         .... 0000 = Location = 0 (User)
      H225: Recommendation flags = 00
      H225:             0... .... = Continue
      H225:             .000 0000 = Recommendation = 0 (Q.931)
      H225:
H225: ----User-User Information----
      H225:
      H225: Information element identifier = 0x7E (User-User)
      H225: Length of user-user content = 30
      H225: Protocol discriminator = 5 (X.680 / X.691(PER)(ASN.1))
      H225:
      H225: Flags      = 05
      H225: 0... .... = No extension values present in H323-UserInformation
      H225: .0.. .... = user-data is not present
      H225: ..0. .... = No extension values present in h323-uu-pdu
      H225: ...0 .... = nonStandardData is not present
      H225: .... 0... = No extension values present in h323-message-body
      H225: h323-message = 5 (ReleaseComplete-UUIE)
      H225:
      H225: Flags      = C0
      H225: 1... .... = Extension value(s) present in ReleaseComplete-UUIE
      H225: .1.. .... = ReleaseCompleteReason is present
      H225: Protocol ID = {0.0.8.2250.0.2}
      H225: Flags      = 58
      H225: 0... .... = No extension values present in ReleaseCompleteReason
      H225: Reason = 11 (Undefined reason)
```

```
H225:  * ReleaseComplete-UUIE - extension *
H225: .... .0.. = Extension length determinant
H225: Number of extensions = 1
H225: .... 1... = callIdentifier is present
H225:
H225: Flags     = 00
H225: 0... .... = No extension value(s) present in callIdentifier
H225: Guid = D761DE3202E4D511B09E006097195D66
H225:
```

The final actions are for the RSVP processes to remove the bandwidth reservations along the transmission paths. This occurs when Station 180 transmits the Reservation Teardown (ResvTear) message in Frame 1018 (Trace 9.3v) and the Path Teardown (PathTear) message in Frame 1019 (Trace 9.3w). These messages delete the corresponding reservation state and path state, respectively.

Trace 9.3v: RSVP ResvTear Message (from Station 180)

```
- - - - - - - - - - - - - - - - - - - Frame 1018 - - - - - - - - - - - - - - - - - - -


RSVP: ----- RSVP Header -----
      RSVP:
      RSVP: Version          = 1
      RSVP: Flags            = 0
      RSVP: Message type     = 6 (ResvTear)
      RSVP: Checksum         = 8724 (should be C635)
      RSVP: Send_TTL         = 63
      RSVP: Reserved         = 0x00
      RSVP: RSVP Length      = 40
      RSVP:
      RSVP: Object length    = 12
      RSVP: Object class     = 1 (SESSION)
      RSVP: C_Type           = 1 (IPv4 DestAddress)
      RSVP: IP4 DestAddress  = 192.168.100.180
      RSVP: Protocol ID      = 17 (UDP)
      RSVP: Flags            = 0 (non E_Police)
      RSVP: Destination Port = 49598
      RSVP:
      RSVP: Object length    = 12
      RSVP: Object class     = 3 (RSVP_HOP)
      RSVP: C_Type           = 1
      RSVP: IP4 next/previous hop address = 192.168.100.180
      RSVP: Logical interface handle  = 0
      RSVP:
      RSVP: Object length    = 8
```

Continued

Trace 9.3v *(Continued)*

```
        RSVP: Object class      = 8 (STYLE)
        RSVP: C_Type            = 1
        RSVP: Flags =  0
        RSVP: Option vector control = 11
        RSVP:           ...1 0... = Sharing control (Shared reservations)
        RSVP:           .... .001 = Sender selection control (Wildcard)
```

Trace 9.3w: RSVP PathTear Message (from Station 180)

```
- - - - - - - - - - - - - - - - - - - Frame 1019 - - - - - - - - - - - - - - - - - -


RSVP: ----- RSVP Header -----
        RSVP:
        RSVP: Version           = 1
        RSVP: Flags             = 0
        RSVP: Message type      = 5 (PathTear)
        RSVP: Checksum          = 61A0 (should be C60E)
        RSVP: Send_TTL          = 63
        RSVP: Reserved          = 0x00
        RSVP: RSVP Length       = 80
        RSVP:
        RSVP: Object length     = 12
        RSVP: Object class      = 1 (SESSION)
        RSVP: C_Type            = 1 (IPv4 DestAddress)
        RSVP: IP4 DestAddress   = 192.168.100.150
        RSVP: Protocol ID       = 17 (UDP)
        RSVP: Flags             = 1 (E_Police flag)
        RSVP: Destination Port  = 49598
        RSVP:
        RSVP: Object length     = 12
        RSVP: Object class      = 3 (RSVP_HOP)
        RSVP: C_Type            = 1
        RSVP: IP4 next/previous hop address = 192.168.100.180
        RSVP: Logical interface handle  = 0
        RSVP:
        RSVP: Object length     = 12
        RSVP: Object class      = 11 (SENDER_TEMPLATE)
        RSVP: C_Type            = 1 (IPv4 source Address)
        RSVP: IP4 source address = 192.168.100.180
        RSVP: Reserved          = 0x0000 (must be zero)
        RSVP: Source port       = 49598
        RSVP:
        RSVP: Object length     = 36
        RSVP: Object class      = 12 (SENDER_TSPEC)
        RSVP: C_Type            = 2
```

```
RSVP: Version            = 0
RSVP: Overall length     = 7
RSVP: Service number     = 1 (Default/global information)
RSVP: Length of data     = 6
RSVP: Parameter id       = 127 (Token_Bucket_TSpec)
RSVP: Parameter 127 flags = 0
RSVP: Parameter 127 length= 5
RSVP: Token bucket rate   = 461EFC00
RSVP: Token bucket size   = 44940000
RSVP: Peak data rate      = 462EE000
RSVP: Minimum policed unit= 00000128
RSVP: Maximum packet size = 00000128
```

A concluding PathTear message is then sent from the other end of the connection (Station 150), as shown in Trace 9.3x. The communications resources along that path may then be reused for another connection.

Trace 9.3x: RSVP PathTear Message (from Station 150)

```
- - - - - - - - - - - - - - - - - - Frame 1022 - - - - - - - - - - - - - - - - - - -

RSVP: ----- RSVP Header -----
     RSVP:
     RSVP: Version            = 1
     RSVP: Flags              = 0
     RSVP: Message type       = 5 (PathTear)
     RSVP: Checksum           = 62BC (should be C60E)
     RSVP: Send_TTL           = 63
     RSVP: Reserved           = 0x00
     RSVP: RSVP Length        = 80
     RSVP:
     RSVP: Object length      = 12
     RSVP: Object class       = 1 (SESSION)
     RSVP: C_Type             = 1 (IPv4 DestAddress)
     RSVP: IP4 DestAddress    = 192.168.100.180
     RSVP: Protocol ID        = 17 (UDP)
     RSVP: Flags              = 1 (E_Police flag)
     RSVP: Destination Port   = 49598
     RSVP:
     RSVP: Object length      = 12
     RSVP: Object class       = 3 (RSVP_HOP)
     RSVP: C_Type             = 1
     RSVP: IP4 next/previous hop address = 192.168.100.150
     RSVP: Logical interface handle  = 0
     RSVP:
```

Continued

Trace 9.3x *(Continued)*

```
RSVP: Object length       = 12
RSVP: Object class        = 11 (SENDER_TEMPLATE)
RSVP: C_Type              = 1 (IPv4 source Address)
RSVP: IP4 source address = 192.168.100.150
RSVP: Reserved            = 0x0000 (must be zero)
RSVP: Source port         = 49598
RSVP:
RSVP: Object length       = 36
RSVP: Object class        = 12 (SENDER_TSPEC)
RSVP: C_Type              = 2
RSVP: Version             = 0
RSVP: Overall length      = 7
RSVP: Service number      = 1 (Default/global information)
RSVP: Length of data      = 6
RSVP: Parameter id        = 127 (Token_Bucket_TSpec)
RSVP: Parameter 127 flags = 0
RSVP: Parameter 127 length= 5
RSVP: Token bucket rate   = 4512A000
RSVP: Token bucket size   = 43800000
RSVP: Peak data rate      = 45214000
RSVP: Minimum policed unit= 00000040
RSVP: Maximum packet size = 00000040
```

As the case studies in Sections 9.2 and 9.3 have illustrated, connections involving SIP have the beauty of simplicity, while connections using H.323 can incorporate additional functionality such as bandwidth reservations along the path. At the time of this writing, both SIP-based and H.323-based products are available. Some products are implemented with capabilities for both protocols, and differ only in their firmware load. The next few years of implementation experience should determine if a clear leader emerges between these two protocols.

9.4 Looking Back

This text has taken us on a new journey, which you have hopefully found interesting. You have examined converged networks, where both voice and data applications coexist over a common, IP-based infrastructure. You have also explored some of the business, technical, and implementation aspects of these networks, and have looked at some of the current research, such as that being done by the IETF.

Now the rest is up to you. If you feel that the concepts presented here might benefit your organization, then jump in and give converged networks a try. But remember the admonitions to start small, preferably with a lab environment, and thoroughly test your applications under as controlled conditions as possible before moving these applications into a production environment. As you test, remember that you are trying to marry two vastly different architectures — connection-oriented applications with a connectionless network infrastructure — and that some professional counseling may be in order to keep that marriage running smoothly.

You will become the network marriage counselor, looking at design tradeoffs and making various adjustments so that the combined voice and data networks can live together in harmony and satisfy the toughest critics of all, the end users.

May all of your clients live happily ever after!

9.5 References

[9-1] Amoeba Telecom. "Choosing the Right H.323 Analyzer." White paper available at www.amoebatel.com/pdf/VoIP_w.pdf.

[9-2] Boger, Yuval. "Fine Tuning Voice over Packet Service." RADCOM Ltd. White paper available at www.radcom-inc.com/radcom/technlgy/pdf/finetuning_voip.pdf. 1998.

[9-3] Net Reality, Inc. "Managing and Controlling Voice, Video and Data over Wide Area Networks." White paper available at www.net-reality.com. 2000.

[9-4] Agilent Technologies. "Troubleshooting VoIP Signaling." White paper available at http://onenetworks.comms.agilent.com/whitepapers.asp, Document number, 5968-4450E. 2000.

[9-5] Pracht, Stefan. "Troubleshooting H.323 Signaling." Agilent Technologies. White paper available at http://onenetworks.comms.agilent.com/whitepapers.asp, Document number, 5968-3642E. October 2000.

[9-6] Agam, Oded. VoIP A Practical Guide. RADCOM Equipment, Inc. White paper available at www.protocols.com/papers/voip_practical_guide.pdf, 2001.

[9-7] Spirent Communications, Inc. "Voice over IP (VoIP)." White paper available at www.netcomsystems.com, Document number, PIN 340-1158-001 REV A. August 17, 2001.

[9-8] Agam, Oded. "VoIP — Guaranteeing Carrier Grade Performance." RADCOM Equipment, Inc. White paper available at www.radcom-inc.com. September 9, 2001.

Appendix A

What's on the CD-ROM

This appendix provides you with information on the contents of the CD that accompanies this book. There are three sections to this CD: one containing RFC reference documents published by the Internet Engineering Task Force, and two containing software applications. Details for the applications regarding system requirements, installation instructions, and vendor contact information for any troubleshooting needs or questions are noted in the product-specific sections below.

RFC Documents

The RFC folder includes a number of Request For Comments (RFC) documents that relate to IP-based multimedia networks. These documents are published by various Working Groups of the Internet Engineering Task Force (IETF). In addition, there is a hyperlinked RFC index file (`rfc-index.html`) that can assist in retrieving any other RFC documents you might need. For details regarding RFC documents, go to `www.rfc-editor.org`. Each RFC document published at the present time carries the following notice:

Multimedia Applications

Shareware programs are fully functional, trial versions of copyrighted programs. If you like particular programs, register with their authors for a nominal fee and receive licenses, enhanced versions, and technical support. *Freeware programs* are copyrighted games, applications, and utilities that are free for personal use. Unlike shareware, these programs do not require a fee or provide technical support. *GNU software* is governed by its own license, which is included inside the folder of the GNU product. See the GNU license for more details.

Trial, demo, or evaluation versions are usually limited either by time or functionality (such as being unable to save projects). Some trial versions are very sensitive to system date changes. If you alter your computer's date, the programs will "time out" and will no longer be functional.

itRings!

Trial version. itRings! Internet Call Waiting allows dial-up users to be notified of incoming telephone calls directly at the computer while online and to be able to choose how to handle those calls.

A copy of the software is included in the \\itRings folder of the CD-ROM accompanying this book. To install itRings!, double-click on the installation file ITRINGSINSTALLVOIP.EXE and follow the simple installation instructions. After the installation, you can start itRings!. A pop-up window will open asking you for a user ID. After you've entered the user ID of your choice, the system will recognize that you are a new user and will bring you to our Web site to fill in some information necessary for the product to work (in North America).

The software will allow you to try itRings! for a month or up to ten calls. If you like it, you can actually subscribe. Just follow the instructions on our Web site, www.itRings.com.

Our Web site includes a demo to show you how the product works and also lists the prompts that are played to the callers.

itRings! can run under Windows 95, Windows 98, Windows Me, Windows NT 4, and Windows 2000. The system requirements match those of the host operating system as recommended by Microsoft Corporation. Please note that the product will not work behind a firewall.

For further information, contact:
eRing Solutions, Inc.
245 Victoria Avenue, Suite 440
Montreal, Quebec
Canada H3Z 2M6
Tel: 514.934.0806
Fax: 514.934.0872
E-mail: info@ering.net
www.eRing.net
www.itRings.com

Westplan

Demo version. Westplan is a Voice over IP and circuit-switched voice network design software tool that can help design economical private enterprise networks or carrier voice networks.

A demonstration version of Westplan is included in the \Westbay folder of the CD-ROM accompanying this book. To install the demo, double-click on the single installation file IWESTPLANDEMO.EXE and follow the simple installation instructions. Alternatively, double-click on the INDEX.HTM file. This will open your Web browser at a page that describes Westplan in more detail and that includes the full user guide as well as a link for installing the demo.

The demonstration version included on this diskette is a time-limited version that will expire one week after it is first run. Features relating to the exporting of data and images have been disabled, but in all other respects it is an unrestricted version. Details on purchasing the full working version of Westplan are available on the screen that appears when Westplan is closed down.

Westplan includes a Guided Tour to introduce you to the most important areas of the application. The Guided Tour will open automatically when Westplan is started.

Westplan can run under Windows 95, Windows 98, Windows Me, Windows NT4 (SP3 and higher), and Windows 2000. The system requirements match those of the host operating system as recommended by Microsoft Corporation.

For further information, contact:
Westbay Engineers Ltd.
11 Langstone Close
Crawley
West Sussex
RH10 7JR
United Kingdom
Tel: +44 1293 888500
E-mail: sales@erlang.com
www.erlang.com

Troubleshooting

If you have difficulty installing or using any of the materials on the companion CD, contact the vendors at the telephone numbers listed in the sections earlier in this appendix.

If you still have trouble with the CD, please call the Hungry Minds Customer Care phone number: (800) 762-2974. Outside the United States, call 1 (317) 572-3994. You can also contact Hungry Minds Customer Service by e-mail at techsupdum@hungryminds.com. Hungry Minds will provide technical support only for installation and other general quality control items; for technical support on the applications themselves, consult the program's vendor or author.

Appendix B

Addresses of Standards Bodies

ANSI STANDARDS
American National Standards Institute
25 West 43rd Street, 4th Floor
New York, NY 10036
Tel: (212) 642-4900
www.ansi.org

ATIS PUBLICATIONS
Alliance for Telecommunications
Industry Solutions
(Formerly the Exchange Carriers
Standards Association)
1200 G Street NW, Suite 500
Washington, DC 20005
Tel: (202) 628-6380
Fax: (202) 393-5453
www.atis.org

CSA INTERNATIONAL
Canadian Standards Association
178 Rexdale Boulevard
Toronto, ONT M9W 1R3
Canada
Tel: (416) 747-4000 or (800) 463-6727
Fax: (416) 747-4149
www.csa-international.org

DOD STANDARDS
DoD Network Information Center
Science Applications
7990 Science Applications Court,
M/S CV-50
Vienna, VA 22183-7000
Tel: (703) 676-1051 or (800) 365-3642
www.nic.mil

ECMA STANDARDS
European Computer Manufacturers
Association
114 Rue de Rhone
CH-1204 Geneva
Switzerland
Tel: 41 22 849 60 00
Fax: 41 22 849 60 01
E-mail: helpdesk@ecma.ch
www.ecma.ch

EIA STANDARDS
Electronic Industries Alliance
2500 Wilson Boulevard
Arlington, VA 22201
Tel: (703) 907-7500
Fax: (703) 907-7501
www.eia.org

ETSI STANDARDS
European Telecommunications
Standards Institute
ETSI Publications Office
650, route des Lucioles
06921 Sophia Antipolis
France
Tel: 33 (0)4 92 94 42 00
Fax: 33 (0)4 93 65 47 16
www.etsi.org

**FEDERAL INFORMATION
PROCESSING STANDARDS (FIPS)**
U.S. Department of Commerce
National Technical Information
Service (NTIS)
5285 Port Royal Road
Springfield, VA 22151
Tel: (703) 605-6000 or (800) 553-6847
Fax: (703) 605-6900
www.ntis.gov

IEC STANDARDS
International Electrotechnical
Commission
IEC Central Office
3, rue de Varembé
P.O. Box 131
CH-1211 Geneva 20
Switzerland
Tel: 41 22 919 02 11
Fax: 41 22 919 03 00
E-mail: info@iec.ch
www.iec.ch

IEEE STANDARDS
Institute of Electrical and
Electronics Engineers
445 Hoes Lane
P.O. Box 1331
Piscataway, NJ 08855-1331
Tel: (732) 981-0060 or (800) 678-4333
Fax: (732) 981-9667
www.ieee.org

INTERNET STANDARDS
Internet Society
1775 Weihle Avenue, Suite 102
Reston, VA 20190-5108
Tel: (703) 326-9880
Fax: (703) 326-9881
E-mail: isoc@isoc.org
www.isoc.org

ISO STANDARDS
International Organization for
Standardization
1, rue de Varembé
Case postale 56
CH-1211 Geneva 20
Switzerland
Tel: 41 22 749 01 11
Fax: 41 22 733 34 30
E-mail: central@iso.ch
www.iso.ch

ITU STANDARDS
International
Telecommunications Union
Information Services Department
Place des Nations
CH-1211 Geneva 20
Switzerland
Tel: 41 22 730 51 11
Fax: 41 22 733 72 56
E-mail: itumail@itu.int
www.itu.ch

**NATIONAL INSTITUTE OF
STANDARDS AND TECHNOLOGY**
100 Bureau Drive, Stop 3460
Gaithersburg, MD 20899-3460
E-mail: inquiries@nist.gov
www.nist.gov/public_affairs/
pubs.htm

TELCORDIA TECHNOLOGIES
(Formerly Bell
Communications Research)
Information Management Services
8 Corporate Place
Piscataway, NJ 08854-4156
Tel: (732) 699-2000 or (800) 521-2673
www.telcordia.com

WWW STANDARDS
World Wide Web Consortium
Massachusetts Institute of Technology
Laboratory for Computer Science
200 Technology Square
Cambridge, MA 02139
E-mail: www-request@w3.org
www.w3.org

Many of the above standards may be
purchased from the following:

Global Engineering Documents
15 Inverness Way East
Englewood, CO 80112
Tel: (303) 790-7956 or (800) 854-7179
Fax: (303) 397-2740
www.global.ihs.com

PBI Media
1201 Seven Locks Road, Suite 300
Potomac, MD 20854
Tel: (301) 354-2000 or (800) 777-5006
Fax: (301) 309-3847
E-mail: clientservices@
pbimedia.com
www.pbimedia.com

Appendix C

Forums, Consortiums, and IETF Working Groups

FORUMS

ATM Forum
Worldwide Headquarters
1000 Executive Parkway, Suite 220
St. Louis, MO 63141
Tel: (314) 205-0200
Fax: (314) 576-7989
E-mail: info@atmforum.com
www.atmforum.com

ATM Forum
European Office
Av. De Tervueren 402
1150 Brussels, Belgium
Tel: 32 2 761 66 77
Fax: 32 2 761 66 79
E-mail: euroinfo@atmforum.com
www.atmforum.org

ATM Forum
Asia-Pacific Office
Hamamatsucho Suzuki Building 3F
1-2-11, Hamamatsucho, Minato-ku
Tokyo 105-0013, Japan
Tel: 81 3 3438 3694
Fax: 81 3 3438 3698
E-mail: apinfo@atmforum.com
www.atmforum.org

DSL Forum
39355 California Street, Suite 307
Fremont, CA 94538
Tel: (510) 608-5905
Fax: (510) 608-5917
E-mail: info@dslforum.org
www.dslforum.org

**Enterprise Computer
Telephony Forum**
E-mail: ectf@ectf.org
www.ectf.org

Frame Relay Forum
North American Office
39355 California Street, Suite 307
Fremont, CA 94538
Tel: (510) 608-5920
Fax: (510) 608-5917
E-mail: frf@frforum.com
ftp://frforum.com
www.frforum.com

IPv6 Forum
www.ipv6forum.com

QoS Forum
c/o Stardust.com, Inc.
15575 Los Gatos Boulevard
Los Gatos, CA 95032
Tel: (408) 402-0566
Fax: (408) 402-0567
www.qosforum.com

CONSORTIUMS

**International Multimedia
Teleconferencing Consortium**
Bishop Ranch 2
2694 Bishop Drive, Suite 275
San Ramon, CA 94583
Tel: (925) 275-6600
Fax: (925) 275-6691
www.imtc.org

IP Multicast Initiative
c/o Stardust.com, Inc.
15575 Los Gatos Boulevard
Los Gatos, CA 95032
Tel: (408) 402-0566
Fax: (408) 402-0567
www.ipmulticast.com

ISDN Users Group
www.niuf.nist.gov

IETF WORKING GROUPS

Audio Video Transport (avt)
General discussion mailing list:
avt@ietf.org
To subscribe: avt-request@ietf.org
Archive: http://www.ietf.org/
mail-archive/working-groups/avt/

Differentiated Services (diffserv)
General discussion mailing list:
diffserv@ietf.org
To subscribe: diffserv-request@
ietf.org
In body: subscribe *your_email_address*
Archive: ftp://ftp.ietf.org/ietf-
mail-archive/diffserv/

Telephone Number Mapping (enum)
General discussion mailing list:
enum@ietf.org
To subscribe: enum-request@ietf.org
In body: subscribe
Archive: ftp://ftp.ietf.org/
ietf-mail-archive/enum

IP Performance Metrics (ippm)
General discussion mailing list:
ippm@advanced.org
To subscribe: ippm-request@
advanced.org
Archive: http://www.advanced.org/
IPPM/archive/

IP Telephony (iptel)
General discussion mailing list:
iptel@lists.bell-labs.com
To subscribe: iptel-
request@lists.bell-labs.com
Archive: http://www.bell-labs.
com/mailing-lists/iptel

Media Gateway Control (megaco)
General discussion mailing list:
megaco@ietf.org
To subscribe: megaco-request@
ietf.org
In body: subscribe megaco
Archive: ftp://ftp.ietf.org/
ietf-mail-archive/megaco/

**Multiparty Multimedia Session
Control (music)**
General discussion mailing list:
confctrl@isi.edu
To subscribe: confctrl-request@
isi.edu
Archive: ftp://ftp.isi.edu/
confctrl/confctrl.mail

Signaling Transport (sigtran)
General discussion mailing list:
sigtran@standards.
nortelnetworks.com
To subscribe: lyris.
nortelnetworks.com
**In body: subscribe sigtran in the
SUBJECT field**
Archive: ftp://ftp.ietf.org/
ietf-mail-archive/sigtran/

Session Initiation Protocol (sip)
General discussion mailing list:
sip@ietf.org
To subscribe: sip-request@ietf.org
In body: subscribe
Archive: www.ietf.org/
mail-archive/working-groups/
sip/current/maillist.html

Appendix D

Multimedia Standards from the ITU-T

G.Series: Transmission Systems and Media; Digital Systems and Networks

G.114   One-way transmission time

G.165   Echo cancellers

G.168   Digital network echo cancellers

G.711   Pulse code modulation (PCM) of voice frequencies

G.722   7 KHz audio-coding within 64 Kbit/s

G.723   Speech coders

G.723.1   Dual rate speech coder for multimedia communications transmitting at 5.3 and 6.3 Kbit/s

G.724   Characteristics of a 48-channel low bit rate-encoding primary multiplex operating at 1544 Kbit/s

G.725   System aspects for the use of the 7 KHz audio codec within 64 Kbit/s

G.726   40, 32, 24, 16 Kbit/s adaptive differential pulse code modulation (ADPCM)

G.727   5-, 4-, 3-, and 2-bits/sample embedded adaptive differential pulse code modulation (ADPCM)

G.728   Coding of speech at 16 Kbit/s using low-delay code excited linear prediction

G.729   Coding of speech at 8 Kbit/s using conjugate-structure algebraic-code-excited linear-prediction (CS-ACELP)

G.729A   Annex A Reduced complexity 8 Kbit/s CS-ACELP speech codec

H.Series: Transmission of Non-Telephone Signals

H.100	Visual telephone systems
H.225.0	Call signaling protocols and media stream packetization for packet-based multimedia communication systems
H.235	Security and Encryption for H-Series multimedia terminals
H.245	Control protocol for multimedia communication
H.246	Interworking of H.Series multimedia terminals with H.Series multimedia terminals and voice/voiceband terminals on GSTN and ISDN
H.248	Gateway control protocol
H.261	Video codec for audiovisual services at $p \times 64$ Kbit/s
H.263	Video coding for low bit rate communication
H.320	Narrowband visual telephone systems and terminal equipment
H.321	Adaptation of H.320 visual telephone terminals to B-ISDN environments
H.322	Visual telephone systems and terminal equipment for local area networks that provide a guaranteed quality of service
H.323	Packet-based multimedia communications systems
H.324	Terminal for low bit rate multimedia communication
H.450.1	Generic functional protocol for the support of supplementary services in H.323
H.450.2	Call transfer supplementary service for H.323
H.450.3	Call diversion supplementary service for H.323
H.450.4	Call hold supplementary service for H.323
H.450.5	Call park and call pickup supplementary service for H.323
H.450.6	Call waiting supplementary service for H.323
H.450.7	Message waiting indication supplementary service for H.323
H.450.8	Name identification supplementary service for H.323
H.450.9	Call completion supplementary service for H.323
H.450.10	Call offer supplementary service for H.323
H.450.11	Call intrusion supplementary service for H.323
H.450.12	Common information additional network feature for H.323

I.Series: Integrated Services Digital Network

I.361   B-ISDN ATM Layer specification

I.362   B-ISDN ATM Adaptation Layer functional specification

I.363   B-ISDN ATM Adaptation Layer specification

I.363.1   B-ISDN ATM Adaptation Layer specification: Type 1 AAL

I.363.2   B-ISDN ATM Adaptation Layer specification: Type 2 AAL

I.363.3   B-ISDN ATM Adaptation Layer specification: Type 3/4 AAL

I.363.5   B-ISDN ATM Adaptation Layer specification: Type 5 AAL

I.366.1   Segmentation and Reassembly Service Specific Convergence Sublayer for the AAL type 2

I.366.2   AAL type 2 Service Specific Convergence Sublayer for trunking

Q.Series: Switching and Signaling

Q.931   Digital Subscriber Signaling System No. 1 ISDN User-Network Interface Layer 3 Specification for Basic Call Control

Q.2931   B-ISDN Layer 3 Specification for Basic Call/Connection Control

T.Series: Terminal Equipment and Protocols for Telematic Services

T.4   Standardization of Group 3 facsimile terminals for document transmission

T.6   Facsimile coding schemes and coding control functions for Group 4 facsimile apparatus

T.30   Procedures for document facsimile transmission in the general switched telephone network

T.37   Procedures for the transfer of facsimile data via store and forward on the Internet

T.38   Procedures for real-time group 3 facsimile communications over IP Networks

T.120	Data protocols for multimedia conferencing
T.121	Generic application template
T.122	Multipoint communication service – Service definition
T.123	Network specific data protocol stacks for multimedia conferencing
T.124	Generic Conference Control
T.125	Multipoint communication service protocol specification
T.126	Multipoint still image and annotation protocol
T.127	Multipoint binary file transfer protocol
T.128	Multipoint application sharing

V.Series: Data Communication over the Telephone Network

V.17	A 2-wire modem for facsimile applications with rates up to 14,400 bps
V.21	300 bits per second duplex modem standardized for use in the General Switched Telephone Network and on point-to-point 2-wire leased telephone-type circuits
V.27ter	4800/2400 bits per second modem standardized for use in the General Switched Telephone Network
V.29	9600 bits per second modem standardized for use on point-to-point 4-wire leased telephone-type circuits
V.33	14 400 bits per second modem standardized for use on point-to-point 4-wire leased telephone type circuits

Appendix E

Multimedia- and IP-Related Documents from the IETF

RFC 768	User Datagram Protocol
RFC 791	Internet Protocol
RFC 792	Internet Control Message Protocol
RFC 793	Transmission Control Protocol
RFC 826	An Ethernet Address Resolution Protocol
RFC 854	Telnet Protocol Specification
RFC 894	A Standard for the Transmission of IP Datagrams over Ethernet Networks
RFC 903	A Reverse Address Resolution Protocol
RFC 904	Exterior Gateway Protocol Formal Specification
RFC 951	Bootstrap Protocol (BOOTP)
RFC 959	File Transfer Protocol (FTP)
RFC 1034	Domain Names – Concepts and Facilities
RFC 1035	Domain Names – Implementation and Specification
RFC 1042	A Standard for the Transmission of IP Datagrams over IEEE 802 Networks
RFC 1055	A Nonstandard for Transmission of IP Datagrams over Serial Lines: SLIP
RFC 1058	Routing Information Protocol
RFC 1112	Host Extensions for IP Multicasting
RFC 1157	A Simple Network Management Protocol (SNMP)

RFC 1188   A Proposed Standard for the Transmission of IP Datagrams over FDDI Networks

RFC 1201   Transmitting IP Traffic over ARCNET Networks

RFC 1209   The Transmission of IP Datagrams over the SMDS Service

RFC 1350   The TFTP Protocol (Revision 2)

RFC 1356   Multiprotocol Interconnect on X.25 and ISDN in the Packet Mode

RFC 1438   Internet Engineering Task Force Statements Of Boredom (SOBs)

RFC 1723   RIP Version 2 – Carrying Additional Information

RFC 1771   A Border Gateway Protocol 4 (BGP-4)

RFC 1901   Introduction to Community-based SNMPv2

RFC 2032   RTP Payload for H.261 Video Streams

RFC 2131   Dynamic Host Configuration Protocol

RFC 2190   RTP Payload for H.263 Video Streams

RFC 2201   Core Based Trees (CBT) Multicast Routing Architecture

RFC 2205   Resource Reservation Protocol (RSVP)

RFC 2225   Classical IP and ARP over ATM

RFC 2236   Internet Group Management Protocol, Version 2

RFC 2250   RTP Payload for MPEG1/MPEG2 Video

RFC 2326   Real-Time Streaming Protocol (RTSP)

RFC 2327   Session Description Protocol (SDP)

RFC 2328   OSPF Version 2

RFC 2373   Internet Protocol version 6 Addressing Architecture

RFC 2390   Inverse Address Resolution Protocol

RFC 2427   Multiprotocol Interconnect over Frame Relay

RFC 2460   Internet Protocol version 6 Architecture

RFC 2474   Definition of Differentiated Services Field in IPv4 and IPv6

RFC 2475   An Architecture for Differentiated Services

RFC 2543   Session Initiation Protocol (SIP)

RFC 2547   BGP/MPLS VPNs

RFC 2570   Introduction to Version 3 of the Internet-Standard Network Management Framework

RFC 2571   An Architecture for SNMP Management Frameworks (SNMPv3)

RFC 2616   Hypertext Transfer Protocol – HTTP/1.1

RFC 2702   Requirements for Traffic Engineering over MPLS

RFC 2705   Media Gateway Control Protocol version 1.0

RFC 2719   Framework Architecture for Signaling Transport

RFC 2736   Guidelines for Writers of RTP Payload Format Specifications

RFC 2750   RSVP Extensions for Policy Control

RFC 2793   RTP Payload for Text Conversion

RFC 2805   MGCP Architecture and Requirements

RFC 2806   URLs for Telephone Calls

RFC 2821   Simple Mail Transfer Protocol (SMTP)

RFC 2833   RTP Payload for DMTF Digits, Telephony Tones and Signals

RFC 2848   PINT Service Protocol: Extensions to SIP and SDP for IP Access to Telephone Call Services

RFC 2871   A Framework for Telephony Routing over IP

RFC 2880   Internet Fax T.30 Feature Mapping

RFC 2897   MGCP Advanced Audio Package

RFC 2916   E.164 Number and DNS (ENUM)

RFC 2917   A Core MPLS IP VPN Architecture

RFC 2974   Session Announcement Protocol (SAP)

RFC 2976   SIP INFO Method

RFC 2990   Next Steps for IP QoS Architecture

RFC 3015   Megaco Protocol version 1.0

RFC 3032   MPLS Lable Stack Encoding

RFC 3035   MPLS Using LDP and ATM VC Switching

RFC 3047   RTP Payload for ITU-T G.722.1

RFC 3050   Common Gateway Interface for SIP

RFC 3054   Megaco IP Phone Media Gateway Application Profile

RFC 3063   MPLS Loop Prevention Mechanism

RFC 3064   MGCP Channel Associated Signaling Packages

RFC 3087   Control of Service Context using SIP Request-URI

RFC 3108   Conventions for the use of SDP for ATM Bearer Connections

RFC 3119   RTP Payload Format for MP3 Audio

RFC 3158   RTP Testing Strategies

RFC 3170   IP Multicast Applications: Challenges and Solutions

Appendix F

Obtaining Internet Documents

Registration Services

Verisign, Inc. (formerly Network Solutions, Inc.) maintains a listing of accredited organizations that offer domain registration services. This information is available at www.verisign.com.

Internet Organizations

A number of groups contribute to the management, operation, and proliferation of the Internet. These include (in alphabetical order):

CommerceNet
10050 North Wolfe Road, Bldg. SW2-255
Cupertino, CA 95014
Tel: (408) 446-1260
Fax: (408) 446-1268
www.commerce.net

Commercial Internet Exchange Association
1301 K Street, Northwest, Suite 325
Washington, DC 20005
Tel: (703) 709-8200
Fax: (703) 709-5249
E-mail: admin@cix.org
www.cix.org

Internet Architecture Board
E-mail: iab@isi.edu
www.iab.org

Internet Assigned Numbers Authority
4676 Admiralty Way, Suite 330
Marina del Rey, CA 90292
Tel: (310) 823-9358
Fax: (310) 823-8649
E-mail: iana@iana.org
www.iana.org

Internet Engineering Task Force
IETF Secretariat
c/o Corporation for National Research Initiatives
1895 Preston White Drive, Suite 100
Reston, VA 20191-5434
Tel: (703) 620-8990
Fax: (703) 620-9071
E-mail: ietf-info@ietf.org
www.ietf.org

Internet Service Providers' Consortium
1301 Shiloh Road, Suite 720
P.O. Box 1086
Kennesaw, GA 30144-8086
Tel: (866) 533-6990
Fax: (678) 819-1028
E-mail: office@ispc.org
www.ispc.org

Internet Society
c/o International Secretariat
1775 Wiehle Avenue, Suite 102
Reston, VA 20190-5108
Tel: (703) 326-9880
Fax: (703) 326-9881
E-mail: isoc@isoc.org
www.isoc.org

North American Network Operators Group
c/o Merit Network, Inc.
4251 Plymouth Road, Suite 2000
Ann Arbor, MI 48105-2785
Tel: (734) 764-9430
Fax: (734) 647-3185
E-mail: info@merit.edu
www.nanog.org

World Wide Web Consortium
c/o MIT Laboratory for Computer Science
200 Technology Square
Cambridge, MA 02139
Tel: (617) 253-2613
Fax: (617) 258-5999
www.w3.org

Obtaining RFCs

The following is an excerpt from the file `ftp://ftp.isi.edu/in-notes/ rfc-retrieval.txt`, which is available from many of the RFC repositories listed below. This information is subject to change; therefore, obtain the current version of this file if problems occur. Also note that each RFC site may have instructions for file retrieval (such as a particular subdirectory) that are unique to that location.

RFCs may be obtained via e-mail or FTP from many RFC repositories. The Primary Repositories will have the RFC available when it is first announced, as will many Secondary Repositories. Some Secondary Repositories may take a few days to make available the most recent RFCs.

Many of these repositories also have World Wide Web servers. Try the following URL as a starting point: `http://www.rfc-editor.org/`

Primary Repositories

RFCs can be obtained via FTP from `NIS.NSF.NET`, `FTP.RFC-EDITOR.ORG`, `WUARCHIVE.WUSTL.EDU`, `SRC.DOC.IC.AC.UK`, `FTP.NCREN.NET`, `FTP.NIC.IT`, `FTP.IMAG.FR`, `FTP.IETF.RNP.BR`, `WWW.NORMOS.ORG`, `FTP.GIGABELL.NET`, or `OASISSTUDIOS.COM`.

1. NIS.NSF.NET
To obtain RFCs from `NIS.NSF.NET` via FTP, login with username **anonymous** and password **name@host.domain**; then connect to the directory of RFCs with `cd /internet/documents`. The filename is of the form `rfcnnnn.txt` (where nnnn refers to the RFC number).

For sites without FTP capability, e-mail query is available from `NIS.NSF.NET`. Address the request to `NIS-INFO@NIS.NSF.NET` and leave the subject field of the message blank. The first text line of the message must be "send rfcnnnn.txt" with nnnn as the RFC number.

Contact: `rfc-mgr@merit.edu`

2. FTP.RFC-EDITOR.ORG
RFCs can be obtained via FTP from `FTP.RFC-EDITOR.ORG`, with the pathname `in-notes/rfcnnnn.txt` (where nnnn refers to the number of the RFC). Log in with FTP username **anonymous** and password **name@host.domain**.

RFCs can also be obtained via e-mail from FTP.RFC-EDITOR.ORG by using the RFC-INFO service. Address the request to "rfc-info@rfc-editor" with a message body of:

```
Retrieve: RFC
Doc-ID: RFCnnnn
```

where nnnn refers to the number of the RFC (always use four digits – the DOC-ID of RFC 822 is "RFC0822"). The RFC-INFO@RFC-EDITOR.ORG server provides other ways of selecting RFCs based on keywords and such; for more information send a message to rfc-info@rfc-editor.org with the message body **help: help.**

   Contact: rfc-editor@rfc-editor.org

3. WUARCHIVE.WUSTL.EDU

RFCs can also be obtained via FTP from WUARCHIVE.WUSTL.EDU, with the pathname info/rfc/rfcnnnn.txt.Z (where nnnn refers to the number of the RFC and Z indicates that the document is in compressed form).

   At WUARCHIVE.WUSTL.EDU the RFCs are in an "archive" file system and various archives can be mounted as part of an NFS file system. Please contact Chris Myers (chris@wugate.wustl.edu) if you want to mount this file system in your NFS.

   WUArchive now keeps RFCs and STDs under ftp://wuarchive.wustl.edu./doc/ or http://wuarchive.wustl.edu./doc/

   Contact: chris@wugate.wustl.edu

4. SUNSITE.ORG.UK (ALSO KNOWN AS SRC.DOC.IC.AC.UK)

RFCs can be obtained via FTP from SUNSITE.ORG.UK with the pathname rfc/rfcnnnn.txt or rfc/rfcnnnn.ps (where nnnn refers to the number of the RFC). Login with FTP username **anonymous** and password **your-email-address.** To obtain the RFC Index, use the pathname rfc/rfc-index.txt.

   For users with good, fast Internet connections, the whole archive is also available by NFS (read-only) and the RFC area can be mounted as

```
mount-r sunsite.org.uk:/public/rfc /mnt
```

   RFCs are also available via the Web at http://sunsite.org.uk/rfc/.
   Contact: wizards@sunsite.org.uk

5. FTP.NCREN.NET

To obtain RFCs from FTP.NCREN.NET via FTP, login with username **anonymous** and your Internet e-mail address as password. The RFCs can be found in the directory /rfc, with filenames of the form rfcnnnn.txt or rfcnnnn.ps where nnnn refers to the RFC number.

   This repository is also accessible via WAIS and the Internet Gopher.
   Contact: rfc-mgr@ncren.net

6. FTP.NIC.IT

RFCs can be obtained from the `FTP.NIC.IT` FTP archive with the pathname `rfc/rfcnnnn.txt` (where nnnn refers to the number of the RFC). Log in with FTP, username **anonymous** and password **name@host.domain**.

The summary of ways to get RFCs from the Italian Network Information Center is as follows:

- ◆ Via ftp: `ftp.nic.it directory rfc`

- ◆ Via e-mail: Send a message to `listserv@nic.it` whose body contains **get RFC/rfc<number>.[txt,ps]**. For receiving a full list of the existing RFCs, include in the body the command **index RFC/rfc**.

Contact: `D.Vannozzi@cnuce.cnr.it`

7. FTP.IMAG.FR

RFCs can be obtained via FTP from `FTP.IMAG.FR` with the pathname `/pub/archive/IETF/rfc/rfcnnnn.txt` (where nnnn refers to the number of the RFC).

Log in with FTP username **anonymous** and password **your-email-address**. To obtain the RFC Index, use the pathname `/pub/archive/IETF/rfc/rfc-index.txt`.

Internet drafts and other IETF-related documents are also mirrored in the `/pub/archive/IETF` directory.

Contact: `rfc-adm@imag.fr`

8. WWW.NORMOS.ORG

RFCs, STD, BCP, FYI, RTR, IEN, Internet-Drafts, RIPE, and other Internet engineering documents can be found at `http://www.normos.org` and `ftp://ftp.normos.org`.

The RFCs are available as:

```
http://www.normos.org/ietf/rfc/rfcXXXX.txt
ftp://ftp.normos.org/ietf/rfc/rfcXXXX.txt
```

STD, BCP, FYI, RTR, IEN documents are available as:

```
http://www.normos.org/ietf/[std,bcp,fyi,rtr,ien]/[std,bcp,fyi,rtr,ien]XXXX.txt
ftp://ftp.normos.org/ietf/[std,bcp,fyi,rtr,ien]/[std,bcp,fyi,rtr,ien]XXXX.txt
```

Internet-Drafts are available as:

```
http://www.normos.org/ietf/internet-drafts/draft-....txt
ftp://ftp.normos.org/ietf/internet-drafts/draft-....txt
```

Full-text search and database queries are available from the Web interface. Please send questions, comments, suggestions to `info@normos.org`.

9. FTP.IETF.RNP.BR

RFCs can be obtained via FTP from `FTP.IETF.RNP.BR` with the pathname `rfc/rfcnnnn.txt` (where nnnn refers to the number of the RFC). Log in with FTP username **anonymous** and password **your-email-address**. To obtain the RFC Index, use the pathname `rfc/rfc-index.txt`.

Internet-Drafts and other IETF related documents are also mirrored.

Contact: `rfc-admin@ietf.rnp.br`

10. FTP.GIGABELL.NET

To obtain RFCs from `FTP.GIGABELL.NET` via FTP, login with username **anonymous** and password **name@host.domain**; then connect to the directory of RFCs with `cd /pub/rfc`. The filename is of the form `rfcnnnn.txt` (where nnnn refers to the RFC number). An index can be obtained with the pathname `pub/rfc/rfc-index.txt`.

Contact: `ftpadmin@gigabell.net`

11. FTP.FCCN.PT

To obtain RFCs from `FTP.FCCN.PT` via FTP, login to `FTP.FCCN.PT` with username **anonymous** and password **name@host.domain**; then connect to the directory of RFCs with `cd /pub/IETF/RFCs`. The filename is of the form `rfcnnnn.txt` (where nnnn refers to the RFC number).

Contact: `webmaster@fccn.pt`

12. OASISSTUDIOS.COM

To obtain RFCs from Oasis Studios via FTP, login to `FTP.OASISSTUDIOS.COM` with username **anonymous** and password **name@host.domain**; then connect to the directory of RFCs with `cd /pub/RFC`. The filename is of the form `rfcnnnn.txt` (where nnnn refers to the RFC number).

For sites without FTP capability, electronic mail query is available from `oasisstudios@OASISSTUDIOS.COM`. Address the request to `oasisstudios@OASISSTUDIOS.COM` and leave the body of the message blank. The subject of the message must be **send rfcnnnn.txt** where nnnn is the RFC number.

Oasis Global, Inc., also provides an HTTP interface to the RFC archive. To browse or search the archives via a Web browser, surf to `http://www.oasisstudios.com/RFC`.

For information, send a message to `rfc-info@OASISSTUDIOS.COM` with the subject **help**.

Contact: `rfc-admin@oasisstudios.com`

Secondary Repositories

AUSTRALIA AND PACIFIC RIM

Site:	munnari
Contact:	Robert Elz <kre@munnari.oz.au>
Host:	munnari.oz.au
Directory:	rfc
Notes:	RFCs in compressed format rfc*NNNN*.Z postscript RFCs rfc*NNNN*.ps.Z

Site:	The Programmers' Society, University of Technology, Sydney
Contact:	ftp@progsoc.uts.edu.au
Host:	ftp.progsoc.uts.edu.au
Directory:	pub/internet
Notes:	Both are stored uncompressed.

CHILE

Site:	OK Internet
Host:	http://www.ok.cl/rfcs/
Directory:	http://www.ok.cl/rfcs/

DENMARK

Site:	University of Copenhagen
Host	ftp.denet.dk
Directory:	mirror/ftp.isi.edu/in-notes

FINLAND

Site:	FUNET
Host:	`nic.funet.fi`
Directory:	`index/RFC`
Directory:	`/pub/netinfo/rfc`
Notes:	RFCs in compressed format. Also provides e-mail access by sending mail to `archive-server@nic.funet.fi`.

FRANCE

Site:	Centre d'Informatique Scientifique et Medicale (CISM)
Contact:	`ftpmaint@univ-lyon1.fr`
Host:	`ftp.univ-lyon1.fr`
Directories:	`pub/rfc/*` Classified by hundreds `pub/mirrors/rfc` Mirror of Internic
Notes:	Files compressed with gzip. Online decompression done by the FTP server.

ROMANIA

Site:	SunSITE Romania at the Politehnica University of Bucharest
Contact:	`space@sunsite.pub.ro`
Host:	`sunsite.pub.ro/pub/rfc` or via `http:sunsite.pub.ro/pub/mirrors/ds.internic.net`

SOUTH AFRICA

Site:	The Internet Solution
Contact:	ftp-admin@is.co.za
Host:	ftp.is.co.za
Directory:	internet/in-notes/rfc

SWEDEN

Host:	ftp.chalmers.se
Directory:	rfc

UNITED KINGDOM

Site:	rfc.net
Contact:	Alaric Williams <webmaster@rfc.net>

UNITED STATES

Site:	uunet
Contact:	James Revell <revell@uunet.uu.net>
Host:	ftp.uu.net
Directory:	inet/rfc

UUNET Archive

The UUNET archive, which includes the RFCs, various IETF documents, and other information regarding the Internet, is available to the public via anonymous ftp (to `ftp.uu.net`) and anonymous uucp, and will be available via an anonymous kermit server soon. Get the file `/archive/inet/ls-lR.Z` for a listing of these documents.

Any site in the U.S. running UUCP may call +1 900-GOT-SRCS and use the login **uucp**. There is no password. The phone company bills you at $0.50 per minute for the call. The 900 number works only from within the U.S.

Requests for special distribution of RFCs should be addressed to either the author of the RFC in question or to `RFC-EDITOR@RFC-EDITOR.ORG`.

Submissions for Requests for Comments should be sent to `RFC-EDITOR@RFC-EDITOR.ORG`. Please consult "Instructions to RFC Authors," RFC 2223, for further information.

Requests to be added to or deleted from the RFC distribution list should be sent to `RFC-REQUEST@ISI.EDU`.

Users with `.MIL` addresses may send a request to `MAJORDOMO@NIC.DDN.MIL` with an empty Subject: line and a message: **subscribe rfc [your e-mail address]**.

Changes to this file `rfc-retrieval.txt` should be sent to `RFC-EDITOR@RFC-EDITOR.ORG`.

The RFC-Info Service

The RFC-Info Service is an Internet document and information retrieval service. The text that follows describes the service in detail; it was obtained by using **Help: Help** as discussed below.

RFC-Info is an e-mail-based service that helps in locating and retrieving RFCs, FYIs, STDs, and IMRs. Users can ask for "lists" of all RFCs, FYIs, STDs, and IMRs having certain attributes such as an ID number, keyword, title, author, issuing organization, and date.

To use the service, send e-mail to `RFC-INFO@RFC-EDITOR.ORG` with your requests in the body of the message. Feel free to put anything in the subject; the system ignores it. The body of the message is processed with case independence.

To get started you may send a message to `RFC-INFO@RFC-EDITOR.ORG` with requests such as in Table F-1 (without the explanations noted in the Explanation column):

TABLE **F-1 RFC-INFO SERVICE REQUESTS**

Request	Explanation
Help: Help	[to get this information page]
List: FYI	[list the FYI notes]

Request	Explanation
List: RFC Keywords: window	[list RFCs with window as keyword or in title]
List: FYI Keywords: window	[list FYIs about windows]
List: * Author: Cooper	[list all documents by Cooper]
List: RFC Title: ARPA*NET	[list RFCs about ARPANET, ARPA NETWORK, and so on]
List: RFC Organization: MITRE Dated-after: Jul-01-1991 Dated-before: Aug-31-1991	[list RFCs issued by MITRE, dated 7+8/1991]
List: RFC Obsoletes: RFC0010	[list RFCs obsoleting a given RFC]
List: RFC Author: Bracken* [* is a wild card matching all endings]	[list RFCs by authors starting with "Bracken"]
List: IMR Dated-after: Dec-31-1991 Dated-before: Jul-01-1992	[list the IMRs for the first 6 months of 1992]
Retrieve: RFC Doc-ID: RFC0822 [note, always 4 digits in RFC#]	[retrieve RFC 822]
Retrieve: FYI Doc-ID: FYI0004 [note, always 4 digits in FYI#]	[retrieve FYI 4]
Retrieve: STD Doc-ID: STD0001 [note, always 4 digits in STD#]	[retrieve STD 1]

Continued

TABLE F-1 RFC-INFO SERVICE REQUESTS *(Continued)*

Request	Explanation
Retrieve: IMR Doc-ID: IMR9205 [note, always 4 digits = YYMM]	[retrieve May 1992 Internet Monthly Report]
Help: Manual	[to retrieve the long user manual, 30+ pages]
Help: List	[how to use the LIST request]
Help: Retrieve	[how to use the RETRIEVE request]
Help: Topics	[list topics for which help is available]
Help: Dates	["Dates" is such a topic]
List: keywords	[list the keywords in use]
List: organizations	[list the organizations known to the system]

A useful way to test this service is to retrieve the file *Where and how to get new RFCs* (which is also the file `rfc-retrieval.txt` noted in the section "Obtaining RFCs" earlier in the appendix). Place the following in the message body:

```
Help: ways_to_get_rfcs
```

Internet Engineering Standards Repository

A search engine called NORMOS is available to retrieve information about IETF, RIPE, W3C, and IANA documents. To use the search engine, contact `http://www.normos.org`

Internet Mailing Lists

A number of mailing lists are maintained on the Internet for the purpose of soliciting information and discussions on specific subjects. In addition, a number of the Internet Engineering Task Force (IETF) working groups maintain lists for the exchange of information that is specific to those groups.

For example, the IETF maintains two lists: the IETF General Discussion list and the IETF Announcement list. To join the IETF Announcement list, send a request to:

```
ietf-announce-request@ietf.org
```

To join the IETF General Discussion, send a request to:

`ietf-request@ietf.org`

A number of other mailing lists are available. To join a mailing list, send a message to the associated request list:

`listname-request@listhost (for example, snmp-request@psi.com)`

with the following as the message body:

`subscribe listname (for example, subscribe snmp)`

A complete listing of the current IETF working groups and their respective mailing lists is available at `http://www.ietf.org/html.charters/wg-dir.html`.

Appendix G

Acronyms and Abbreviations

A

A	ampere
AARP	AppleTalk Address Resolution Protocol
ABP	alternate bipolar
ACC	audio codec capabilities
ACD	Automatic Call Distributor
ACELP	Algebraic-Code-Excited-Linear-Prediction
ACF	Admission Confirmation message
ACK	acknowledgment
ACS	asynchronous communication server
ACTLU	activate logical unit
ACTPU	activate physical unit
ADPCM	adaptive differential pulse code modulation
ADSL	asymmetric digital subscriber line
ADSP	AppleTalk Data Stream Protocol
AEP	AppleTalk Echo Protocol
AFI	authority and format identifier
AFP	AppleTalk Filing Protocol
AFRP	ARCNET Fragmentation Protocol
AGS	asynchronous gateway server
AH	authentication header
AHT	average holding time
AI	artificial intelligence

AMI	alternate mark inversion
AMT	address mapping table
ANSI	American National Standards Institute
API	applications program interface
APPC	Advanced Program-to-Program Communication
ARE	all routes explorer
ARI	address recognized indicator bit
ARJ	Admission Reject message
ARM	administrative runtime module
ARP	Address Resolution Protocol
ARPA	Advanced Research Projects Agency
ARPANET	Advanced Research Projects Agency Network
ACSE	Association Control Service Element
ASCII	American Standard Code for Information Interchange
ASIC	application-specific integrated circuits
ASN.1	Abstract Syntax Notation One
ASP	AppleTalk Session Protocol
ATM	Asynchronous Transfer Mode
ATP	AppleTalk Transaction Protocol
AUI	attachment unit interface
AUP	acceptable use policy
AUTHU	authentication option
AVM	administrative view module
AVO	audiovisual object
AVT	Audio-Video Transport

B

B8ZS	bipolar with 8 ZERO substitution
BC	block check
BER	Basic Encoding Rules

BGP	Border Gateway Protocol
BIOS	Basic Input/Output System
BITNET	Because It's Time NETwork
BIU	basic information unit
BOC	Bell Operating Company
BOF	Birds of a Feather
BOFL	Breath of Life
BOOTP	Bootstrap Protocol
BPDU	bridge protocol data unit
bps	bits per second
BPV	bipolar violations
BRI	Basic Rate Interface
BSAC	bit-sliced arithmetic coding
BSC	binary synchronous communication
BSD	Berkeley Software Distribution
BTU	basic transmission unit
BUI	browser user interface
BUS	Broadcast and Unknown Server
BW	Bandwidth

C

CAS	Channel Associated Signaling
CATNIP	Common Architecture for Next Generation Internet Protocol
CATS	Consortium for Audiographics Teleconferencing Standards
CBR	Constant Bit Rate
CCIS	common channel interoffice signaling
CCITT	International Telegraph and Telephone Consultative Committee
CCR	commitment, concurrency, and recovery
CCS	Common Channel Signaling
CD	Call Detail Records

CDV	constant delay value
CELP	Codebook excited predictive linear coding
CICS	customer information communication system
CIDR	Classless Interdomain Routing
CIF	Common Intermediate Format
CIR	Committed Information Rate
CLEC	Competitive Local Exchange Carrier
CLNP	Connectionless Layer Network Protocol
CLNS	Connectionless-mode Network Services
CLP	cell loss priority
CLR	cell loss ratio
CLTP	Connectionless Transport Protocol
CMIP	Common Management Information Protocol
CMIS	Common Management Information Service
CMISE	Common Management Information Service Element
CMOL	CMIP on IEEE 802.2 Logical Link Control
CMOT	Common Management Information Protocol over TCP/IP
Codec	coder-decoder
CONS	Connection-mode Network Services
CORBA	Common Object Request Broker Architecture
COS	Corporation for Open Systems
CO Switch	Central Office Switch
CPE	customer premises equipment
CPU	Central Processing Unit
CRC	cyclic redundancy check
CREN	The Corporation for Research and Educational Networking
CRM	customer relationship management
CRS	configuration report server
CS ACELP	Conjugate-Structure Algebraic-Code-Excited-Linear-Prediction
CSMA/CD	Carrier Sense Multiple Access with Collision Detection

CSNET	computer+science network
CSU	Channel Service Unit
CT	computer telephony
CTERM	Command Terminal Protocol
CTI	Computer Telephony Integration

D

DA	destination address
DAP	Data Access Protocol
DARPA	Defense Advanced Research Projects Agency
DAT	duplicate address test
DBMS	database management system
DCA	Defense Communications Agency
DCC	Data Country Code
DCE	data circuit-terminating equipment
DDCMP	Digital Data Communications Message Protocol
DDN	Defense Data Network
DDP	Datagram Delivery Protocol
DECmcc	DEC Management Control Center
DEMPR	DEC multiport repeater
DES	Data Encryption Standard
DFT	discrete Fourier transform
DHCP	Dynamic Host Configuration Protocol
DID	direct inward dialing
DIX	DEC, Intel, and Xerox
DL	data link
DLC	data link control
DLCI	data link connection identifier
DMA	Direct Memory Access

DMI	Desktop Management Interface
DMTF	Desktop Management Task Force
DNIC	Data Network Identification Code
DNS	domain name system
DOD	Department of Defense
DPA	demand protocol architecture
DPCM	differential pulse code modulation
DRP	DECnet Routing Protocol
DSAP	destination service access point
DSI	digital speech interpolation
DSP	digital signal processing
DSU	Data Service Unit
DSU/CSU	Data Service Unit/Channel Service Unit
DTE	data terminal equipment
DTMF	Dual Tone Multifrequency
DTR	data terminal ready
DTV	digital television
DVC	desktop videoconferencing

E

E and M	Ear and Mouth
EBCDIC	Extended Binary Coded Decimal Interchange Code
ECL	End Communication layer
ECSA	Exchange Carriers Standards Association
EDI	electronic data interchange
EFCI	explicit forward congestion indication
EGA	enhanced graphics array
EGP	Exterior Gateway Protocol
EIA	Electronic Industries Association

ELAN	emulated local area network
ELAP	EtherTalk Link Access Protocol
EOT	end-of-transmission
ERP	enterprise resource planning
ESF	extended superframe format
ES-IS	End System to Intermediate System Protocol
ESP	encapsulating security payload
ETSI	European Telecommunications Standards Institute

F

FAL	file access listener
FAS	frame alignment signal
FAT	file access table
FCC	Federal Communications Commission
FCI	frame copied indicator bit
FCS	frame check sequence
FDDI	fiber distributed data interface
FDM	frequency division multiplexing
FEC	forward error correction
FECN	forward explicit congestion notification
FID	format identifier
FIPS	Federal Information Processing Standard
FM	function management
FMD	function management data
FoIP	Fax over Internet Protocol
FT1	fractional T1
FTAM	File Transfer Access and Management
FTP	File Transfer Protocol
FXO	Foreign exchange office

G

G	giga-
GB	gigabyte
GCC	Generic Conference Control
GCF	Gatekeeper Confirmation message
GHz	gigahertz
GOSIP	Government OSI profile
GRJ	Gatekeeper Reject message
GRQ	Gatekeeper Request message
GSTN	general switched telephone network
GUI	graphical user interface

H

HA	hardware address
HDLC	High-Level Data Link Control
HDTV	high-definition TV
HEC	header error control
HEMS	high-level entity management system
HLLAPI	high-level language API
HMMO	Hypermedia Managed Object
HMMP	Hypermedia Management Protocol
HMMS	Hypermedia Management Schema
HMOM	Hypermedia Object Manager
HTML	Hypertext Markup Language
HTTP	Hypertext Transfer Protocol
Hz	hertz

I

IAB	Internet Activities Board
IANA	Internet Assigned Numbers Authority
ICD	international code designator
ICMP	Internet Control Message Protocol
ICP	Internet Control Protocol
IDI	initial domain indicator
IDP	Internetwork Datagram Protocol
IDRP	Interdomain Routing Protocol
IEEE	Institute of Electrical and Electronics Engineers
IETF	Internet Engineering Task Force
I/G	individual/group
IGMP	Internet Group Management Protocol
IGP	Interior Gateway Protocol
IGRP	Internet Gateway Routing Protocol
IMPS	interface message processors
IMTC	International Multimedia Teleconferencing Consortium
I/O	input/output
IOC	interoffice channel
IP	Internet Protocol
IPC	Interprocess Communications Protocol
IPng	Internet Protocol, next generation
IPsec	Internet Protocol security
IPv6	Internet Protocol, version 6
IPv6CP	Internet Protocol version 6 Control Protocol
IPX	Internetwork Packet Exchange Protocol
IR	Internet router

IRTF	Internet Research Task Force
ISAKMP	Internet Secure Association Key Management Protocol
ISDN	Integrated Services Digital Network
IS-IS	Intermediate System to Intermediate System Protocol
ISN	initial sequence number
ISO	International Organization for Standardization
ISOC	Internet Society
ISODE	ISO Development Environment
ISP	Internet Service Provider
ITSP	Internet Telephony Service Provider
ITU	International Telecommunication Union
ITU-D	International Telecommunication Union Development Sector
ITU-R	International Telecommunication Union Radiocommunications Sector
ITU-T	International Telecommunication Union Standardization Sector
IVR	Interactive Voice Response
IWU	internetworking unit
IXC	inter-exchange carrier

J

JDBC	Java Database Connectivity
JMAPI	Java Management Application Programming Interface
JPEG	Joint Photographic Experts Group

K

Kbps	kilobits per second
kHz	kilohertz
KLT	Karhunen-Loeve transform

L

LAA	locally administered address
LAN	local area network
LANE	LAN Emulation
LAP	link access procedure
LAPB	Link Access Procedure Balanced
LAPD	Link Access Procedure D Channel
LAT	Local Area Transport
LATA	local access transport area
LAVC	local area VAX cluster
LCP	Link Control Protocol
LDAP	Lightweight Directory Access Protocol
LD-CELP	Low delay code excited linear prediction
LEC	local exchange carrier
LEC	LAN emulation client
LECS	LAN emulation configuration server
LEN	length
LES	LAN emulation server
LF	largest frame
LLAP	LocalTalk Link Access Protocol
LLC	Logical Link Control
LME	layer management entity
LMI	layer management interface
LMMP	LAN/MAN Management Protocol
LMMPE	LAN/MAN Management Protocol Entity
LMMS	LAN/MAN Management Service
LMMU	LAN/MAN Management User
LPAS	Linear prediction analysis-by-synthesis

LPC	linear predictive coding
LPP	Lightweight Presentation Protocol
LRQ	Location Request
LSB	least significant bit
LSL	Link Support layer

M

MAC	medium access control
MAE	Metropolitan Area Exchanges
MAN	metropolitan area network
MBONE	Multicasting backbone
Mbps	megabits per second
MC	Multipoint controller
MCS	Multipoint Communication Service
MCU	Multipoint Control Unit
MDF	main distribution frame
MELP	mixed-excitation LPC
MGCP	Media Gateway Control Protocol
MHS	message handling service
MHz	megahertz
MIB	management information base
MILNET	Military Network
MILSTD	military standard
MIME	Multipurpose Internet Mail Extensions
MIOX	Multiprotocol Interconnect over X.25
MIPS	million instructions per second
MIS	management information systems
MLID	multiple link interface driver
MNP	Microcom Networking Protocol

MOP	Maintenance Operations Protocol
MOS	Mean Opinion Scores
MPEG	Motion Pictures Expert Group
MPLS	multiprotocol label switching
MP-MLQ	Multipulse Maximum Likelihood Quantization
MPOA	Multiprotocol over ATM
MSAU	multistation access unit
MSB	most significant bit
MSS	maximum segment size
MTA	message transfer agent
MTBF	mean time between failures
MTTR	mean time to repair
MTU	maximum transmission unit
MUX	multiplex, multiplexor

N

NACS	NetWare Asynchronous Communications Server
NAK	negative acknowledgment
NAPs	Network Access Points
NASI	NetWare Asynchronous Service Interface
NAT	network address translation
NAU	network addressable unit
NAUN	nearest active upstream neighbor
NBP	Name Binding Protocol
NCP	Network Control Program
NCP	Network Control Protocol
NCSI	network communications services interface
NDIS	Network Driver Interface Standard
NetBEUI	NetBIOS Extended User Interface

NetBIOS	Network Basic Input/Output System
NFS	Network File System
NIC	network information center
NICE	network information and control exchange
NIS	names information socket
N ISDN	narrowband-ISDN
NIST	National Institute of Standards and Technology
NLA	next-level aggregation identifier
NLM	NetWare loadable module
NMS	network management station
NOC	network operations center
NOS	network operating system
NSAP	Network Service Access Point
NSF	National Science Foundation
NSP	Network Services Protocol
NT	network termination
NTSC	National Television Standards Committee

O

OBASC	object-based analysis-synthesis coding
OBC	object-based coding
OC1	optical carrier, level 1
ODI	Open Data Link Interface
OID	object identifier
OIM	OSI Internet management
OSF	Open Software Foundation
OSI	Open Systems Interconnection
OSI-RM	Open Systems Interconnection Reference Model
OSPF	Open Shortest Path First

P

PA	protocol address
PABX	private automatic branch exchange
PAD	packet assembler and disassembler
PAL	Phased Alternating Line
PAP	Printer Access Protocol
PBX	Private Branch Exchange
PC	personal computer
PCI	protocol control information
PCM	pulse code modulation
PCR	peak cell rate
PDN	public data network
PDU	protocol data unit
Pel	Picture element
PEP	Packet Exchange Protocol
PIC	Primary interexchange carrier
pixel	Picture element
PLEN	protocol length
PMTU	path maximum transmission unit
POP	point of presence
POSIX	Portable Operating System Interface – UNIX
POTS	plain old telephone service
PPP	Point-to-Point Protocol
pps	packets per second
PRI	Primary Rate Interface
PSDN	packet-switched data network
PSN	packet switch node
PSP	presentation services process
PSPDN	packet-switched public data network

PSTN	Public Switched Telephone Network
PTP	point-to-point
PUC	Public Utility Commission
PVC	permanent virtual circuit

Q

QCIF	Quarter Common Intermediate Format
QoS	Quality of Service

R

RARP	Reverse Address Resolution Protocol
RAS	Registration Admissions Status
RBOC	Regional Bell Operating Company
RC	routing control
RD	route descriptor
RED	Random Early Detection
RFC	Request for Comments
RFS	remote file system
RGB	red-green-blue
RH	request/response header
RI	routing information
RII	route information indicator
RIP	Routing Information Protocol
RISV	Reference Impairment System for Video
RJE	remote job entry
RMI	Remote Method Invocation
RMON	remote monitoring
ROSE	Remote Operations Service Element
RPC	Remote Procedure Call

RPS	ring parameter server
RRJ	Registration Reject message
RRQ	Registration Request message
RSVP	Resource Reservation Protocol
RSX	Real-time Resource-Sharing Executive
RT	routing type
RTCP	Real-Time Control Protocol
RTP	Real-Time Protocol
RTSP	Real-Time Stream Protocol
RTT	round trip time
RU	request/response unit

S

SA	source address
SABME	set asynchronous balanced mode extended
SAP	service access point
SAP	Session Announcement Protocol
SAR	segmentation and reassembly
SB-ADPCM	subband adaptive differential pulse code modulation
SCS	system communication services
SDLC	Synchronous Data Link Control
SDN	software defined network
SDP	Session Description Protocol
SECAM	*Sequentiel Couleur Avec Memoire* (French), Sequential Color with Memory
SEQ	sequence
SG	Study Group
SGCP	Simple Gateway Control Protocol
SGMP	Simple Gateway Management Protocol
SIP	Session Initiation Protocol

SIPP	Simple Internet Protocol Plus
SKIP	Simple Key Management for the Internet Protocol
S/L	strict/loose bits
SLA	site-level aggregation identifier
SLIP	Serial Line IP
SMB	server message block
SMDS	Switched Multimegabit Data Service
SMI	structure of management information
SMPTE	Society of Motion Picture and Television Engineers
SMTP	Simple Mail Transfer Protocol
SNA	System Network Architecture
SNADS	System Network Architecture Distribution Services
SNAP	subnetwork access protocol
SNMP	Simple Network Management Protocol
SOH	start of header
SONET	Synchronous Optical Network
SPI	Security Parameters Index
SPP	Sequenced Packet Protocol
SPX	Sequenced Packet Exchange protocol
SQEG	speech quality experts group
SR	source routing
SRF	specifically routed frame
SRI	Stanford Research Institute
SRT	source routing transparent
SRTS	synchronous residual time stamp
SSAP	source service access point
STE	spanning tree explorer
SUA	stored upstream address
SVC	switched virtual circuit
SVGA	super visual graphics array

T

TAPI	Telephony Application Programming Interface
TASI	Time Assignment Speech Interpolation
TB	terabyte
TCP	Transmission Control Protocol
TCP/IP	Transmission Control Protocol/Internet Protocol
TDM	Time Division Multiplexing
TELNET	Telecommunications Network Protocol
TFTP	Trivial File Transfer Protocol
TH	transmission header
TLA	top-level aggregation identifier
TLAP	TokenTalk Link Access Protocol
TLI	Transport Layer Interface
TLV	Type-Length-Value encoding
TOS	Type of Service
TP	Transport Protocol
TSAG	Telecommunication Standardization Advisory Group
TSI	time slot interchange
TSR	terminate-and-stay resident
TTL	time to live
TTS	text-to-speech
TVML	television modeling language
TUBA	TCP/UDP with Bigger Addresses

U

UA	user agent
UDP	User Datagram Protocol
U/L	universal/local
ULP	Upper Layer Protocols

UNI	user-network interface
UNMA	unified network management architecture
URJ	Unregister Reject message
URQ	Unregister Request message
UT	universal time
UTP	unshielded twisted pair
UUCP	UNIX to UNIX copy program

V

V	volt
VAN	value-added network
VAP	value-added process
VARP	VINES Address Resolution Protocol
VBR	Variable Bit Rate
VC	virtual circuit
VFRP	VINES Fragmentation Protocol
VGA	video graphics array
VICP	VINES Internet Control Protocol
VINES	Virtual Networking System
VIP	VINES Internet Protocol
VIPC	VINES Interprocess Communications
VLAN	virtual local area network
VLBV	very low bit-rate video
VLC	variable length code
VLSI	very large scale integration
VLSM	variable length submask
VMS	virtual memory system
VoIP	Voice over IP

VPI/VCI	virtual path identifier/virtual channel identifier
VPN	virtual private network
VR	voice response
VRTP	VINES Routing Update Protocol
VSPP	VINES Sequenced Packet Protocol
VT	virtual terminal

W

WAN	wide area network
WBEM	Web-based Enterprise Management
WFQ	Weighted Fair Queuing
WIN	window
WRED	Weighted RED
WWW	World Wide Web

X

XDR	External data representation
XID	exchange identification
XML	extensible markup language
XMP	X/Open Management Protocol
XNS	Xerox Network System

Z

ZIP	Zone Information Protocol
ZIS	Zone Information Socket
ZIT	Zone Information Table

Appendix H

Glossary of Convergence Terms

The following Glossary of Convergence Terms is reprinted with permission from Alcatel Internetworking, Inc. This glossary is updated periodically and is available in both Adobe PDF file and Palm file formats from the following Alcatel Web site: www.ind.alcatel.com.

Alcatel builds next generation networks, delivering integrated end-to-end voice and data networking solutions to established and new carriers, as well as enterprises and consumers worldwide. With sales of $29 billion in 2000 and 110,000 employees, Alcatel operates in more than 130 countries. For more information, visit Alcatel on the Internet: www.alcatel.com. Alcatel Internetworking, Inc., does not make, sponsor, or endorse any services or products depicted herein.

10Base2 – A variant of Ethernet, connecting stations via thin coaxial cable; maximum cable distance in one nonrepeated segment is 185 meters.

10Base5 – A variant of Ethernet, connecting stations via thick coaxial cable; maximum cable distance in one nonrepeated segment is 500 meters.

10BaseFL – A variant of Ethernet, connecting stations via fiber optic cabling.

10BaseT – A variant of Ethernet, connecting stations via twisted pair cabling.

100BaseFX – A variant of Ethernet that runs on multimode or single mode fiber optic cabling at 100 Mbps. This is one version of Fast Ethernet.

100BaseTX – A variant of Ethernet that runs on Category 5 unshielded twisted pair wiring at 100 Mbps. This is one version of Fast Ethernet.

1000BaseCX – A variant of Gigabit Ethernet that runs on twin axial cable.

1000BaseLX – A variant of Gigabit Ethernet that runs on multimode and single mode fiber optic cable at a 1330 nm frequency.

1000BaseSX – A variant of Gigabit Ethernet that runs on multimode fiber optic cable at an 850 nm frequency.

1000BaseT – A variant of Gigabit Ethernet that runs on unshielded twisted pair cable.

802.x – The set of IEEE standards defining LAN protocols. A list of some common 802.x protocols can be found under IEEE in this glossary.

AAL – See "ATM adaptation layer."

ABR (available bit rate) – QoS class defined by the ATM Forum for ATM networks. ABR is used for connections that do not require timing relationships between source and destination. ABR provides no guarantees in terms of cell loss or delay, providing only best-effort service. Traffic sources adjust their transmission rate in response to information they receive describing the status of the network and its capability to successfully deliver data.

access control method – This is the main distinguishing feature between different LAN technologies. It regulates each workstation's physical access to the cable (transmission medium), and determines the order in which nodes gain access so that each user gets efficient service. Access methods include token passing, which is used in token ring and FDDI, and Carrier Sense Multiple Access with Collision Detection (CSMA/CD), which is employed by Ethernet and Fast Ethernet.

ACD (Automated Call Distributor) – A system which distributes calls to agents according to a predetermined set of rules.

active monitor – A node on a token ring network which purges the ring and generates a new token (when necessary), initiates and monitors neighbor notification, and maintains the master clock.

Adaptive Differential Pulse Code Modulation – See "ADPCM."

address mask – Used to select bits from an Internet address for subnet addressing. The mask is 32 bits long and selects the network portion of the Internet address and one or more bits of the local portion. Sometimes called *subnet mask*.

Address Resolution Protocol – See "ARP."

adjusted ring length (ARL) – Calculated to ensure that if there is a ring failure, the longest ring path is still within specifications. Generally associated with token ring, adjusted ring length ensures that the secondary ring can still function properly in the event of a failure on the shortest trunk cable.

ADPCM (adaptive differential pulse code modulation) – A form of pulse code modulation (PCM) that produces a digital signal with a lower bit rate than standard PCM. ADPCM produces a lower bit rate by recording only the difference between samples and adjusting the coding scale dynamically to accommodate large and small differences. Some applications use ADPCM to digitize a voice signal so voice and data can be transmitted simultaneously over a digital facility normally used only for one or the other.

ADSL (asymmetric digital subscriber line) – A technology that allows more data to be sent over existing copper telephone lines (POTS). ADSL supports data rates of from 1.5 to 9 Mbps when receiving data (known as the downstream rate) and from 16 to 640 Kbps when sending data (known as the upstream rate). ADSL requires a special ADSL modem. It is not currently available to the general public except in trial areas, but many believe that it will be one of the more popular choices for Internet access over the next few years. The ITU is currently defining an xDSL standard based on ADSL, called G.dmt.

agent – A person whose job is to answer calls and provide information, or to make calls to give and receive information, or sell a product or service. Sometimes also known as customer service representative or telephone advisor.

AHT – Average Holding Time.

American National Standards Institute (ANSI) – A U.S. standards body. ANSI is a member of the International Organization for Standardization (ISO).

American Standard Code for Information Interchange – See "ASCII."

ANI (automatic number identification) – Term used in USA by long distance carriers for CLI.

API (application program interface) – A set of routines, protocols, and tools for building software applications. A good API makes it easier to develop a program by providing all the building blocks. A programmer puts the blocks together. Most operating environments, such as MS-Windows, provide an API so that programmers can write applications consistent with the operating environment. Although APIs are designed for programmers, they are ultimately good for users because they guarantee that all programs using a common API will have similar interfaces. This makes it easier for users to learn new programs.

Application Generator – Proprietary software to enable a user to produce a customized voice processing system, mainly for PC based systems.

application programming interface – See "API."

ARP (Address Resolution Protocol) – A TCP/IP protocol used to convert an IP address into a physical address (called a DLC address), such as an Ethernet address. A host wishing to obtain a physical address broadcasts an ARP request onto the TCP/IP network. The host on the network that has the IP address in the request then replies with its physical hardware address. There is also Reverse ARP (RARP), which can be used by a host to discover its IP address. In this case, the host broadcasts its physical address and a RARP server replies with the host's IP address.

ARQ – See "automatic repeat request."

ASCII (American Standard Code for Information Interchange) – Pronounced *ask-ee*, ASCII is a code for representing English characters as numbers, with each letter assigned a number from 0 to 127. For example, the ASCII code for uppercase M is 77. Most computers use ASCII codes to represent text, which makes it possible to transfer data from one computer to another. Text files stored in ASCII format are sometimes called ASCII files. Text editors and word processors are usually capable of storing data in ASCII format, although ASCII format is not always the default storage format. Most data files, particularly if they contain numeric data, are not stored in ASCII format. Executable programs are never stored in ASCII format. The standard ASCII character set uses just 7 bits for each character. There are several larger character sets that use 8 bits, which gives them 128 additional characters. The extra characters are used to represent non-English characters, graphics symbols, and mathematical symbols. Several companies and organizations have proposed extensions for these 128 characters. The DOS operating system uses a superset of ASCII called extended ASCII or high ASCII. A more universal standard is the ISO Latin 1 set of characters, which is used by many operating systems, as well as Web browsers. Another set of codes that is used on large IBM computers is EBCDIC.

ASIC (Application-Specific Integrated Circuit) – A chip designed for a specific application, generally by the manufacturer of the product in which the chip is used.

asymmetric digital subscriber line – See "ADSL."

asynchronous – A method of transmitting data whereby each byte is clocked separately. One start bit is added to the beginning, and one or more stop bits to the end, of each character. Asynchronous transmission is the most rudimentary form of data communication, as the originating and recipient machines do not have to be in sync. It is commonly used for low-speed transmission, as with a PC's serial port. This meaning of the term "asynchronous" is completely different from that in the next definition.

Asynchronous Transfer Mode (ATM) – See "ATM."

ATM (Asynchronous Transfer Mode) – A network technology based on transferring data in cells or packets of a fixed size. The small, constant cell size allows ATM equipment to transmit video, audio, and computer data over the same network, and to assure that no single type of data hogs the line. ATM creates a fixed channel, or route, between two points whenever data transfer begins. This differs from TCP/IP, in which messages are divided into packets and each packet can take a different route from source to destination. This difference makes it easier to track and bill data usage across an ATM network, but it makes it less adaptable to sudden surges in network traffic.

ATM adaptation layer (AAL) – Provides a conversion function to and from ATM for various types of information, including voice, video, and data. There are several versions of AAL, each applicable to a given information type. All of them convert elements of an information stream (such as voice frame and data packets) into cells, giving ATM the versatility to carry many different types of data, from constant-rate voice data to highly bursty messages generated by LANs, all within the same cell format.

ATM Forum – An international consortium of hundreds of companies and users chartered to accelerate the use of ATM products and services by developing specifications and promoting the technology. The ATM Forum has been responsible for development of a wide range of ATM standards. It works in cooperation with standards bodies such as ANSI and ITU, submitting to them proposed standards.

ATM LAN emulation (LANE) – See "LAN emulation."

ATM-ARP – Resolves MAC to ATM address translation.

attachment unit interface (AUI) – Defined in the IEEE 802.1 specification as the interface between an Ethernet MAU and DTE. Basically, the way an Ethernet station connects to a transceiver sitting on a thick Ethernet cable.

attenuation – The progressive weakening of a signal as it travels away from its point of origin.

audiotex – Replaying selected stored information to a caller.

AUI – See "attachment unit interface."

authentication – A means to establish or prove identity; verifying eligibility of users, machines, or objects.

authorization – Privileges granted and resources available.

automated attendant (AA) – Answering incoming calls with an automatic message, and routing the call on the basis of additional input from the caller.

automated call distributor – See "ACD."

automatic call sequencer – In an ACD, a device to queue calls when all agent lines are busy.

automatic number identification (ANI) – Term used in USA by long distance carriers for CLI.

automatic repeat request (ARQ) – A type of error correction ensuring that a transmitting device automatically resends any data containing errors.

autonomous system – Internet (TCP/IP) terminology for gateways (routers) that fall under one administrative entity and cooperate using a common Interior Gateway Protocol (IGP). See also "subnet."

available bit rate – See "ABR."

average holding time – AHT.

backbone – LAN or WAN connectivity between subnets across a high-speed network. Often applied to a high-speed campus network, such as ATM OC-12 or Gigabit Ethernet, that interconnects lower-speed networks, such as ATM OC-3 or Fast Ethernet. Fiber optic cable is often used.

backplane – Describes the bus or matrix that traditionally resides at the back of a modular networking product, and into which the modules are plugged.

bandwidth – (1) The range of signal frequencies that can be carried on a communications channel. The capacity of a channel is measured in cycles per second, or hertz (Hz), between the highest and lowest frequencies. (2) Commonly, the carrying capacity of a digital translation facility, measured in bits per second (bps).

baseband – A technique whereby digital input is directly applied to transmission media without the intervention of a modulating device. Baseband is generally applied in an environment with high bandwidth over a short distance. It is generally considered easier and more cost-effective than broadband. Ethernet, token ring, FDDI, and ATM generally use baseband.

basic rate interface (BRI) – An ISDN subscriber interface which operates over a single copper cable connection, providing one control (D) channel at 16 Kbps, and one or two bearer (B) channels, at 64 Kbps each. The two B channels are sometimes combined to provide a single 128 Kbps service. BRI is the interface commonly provided to residential ISDN subscribers.

Bellcore (Bell Communications Research) — Telecommunications research and development organization currently owned by the seven U.S. regional Bell operating companies.

BGP (Border Gateway Protocol) — An Internet protocol that enables groups of routers (called autonomous systems) to share routing information so that efficient, loop-free routes can be established. BGP is commonly used within and between Internet Service Providers (ISPs). The protocol is defined in RFC 1771.

BGP4 — Interdomain policy routing protocol for communications between a router in one autonomous system (AS) and routers in other ASs.

binary digit — See "BIT."

binary term (byte) — See "byte."

biometrics — The technology associated with analyzing unique human characteristics (such as fingerprints or retinal scans). Biometric information is often used for the purpose of authentication.

BIT (binary digit) — The smallest unit of information on a machine. The term was first used in 1946 by John Tukey, a leading statistician and adviser to five presidents. A single bit can hold only one of two values: 0 or 1. More meaningful information is obtained by combining consecutive bits into larger units. For example, a byte is composed of 8 consecutive bits. Computers are sometimes classified by the number of bits they can process at one time or by the number of bits they use to represent addresses. These two values are not always the same, which leads to confusion. For example, classifying a computer as a 32-bit machine might mean that its data registers are 32 bits wide or that it uses 32 bits to identify each address in memory. Whereas larger registers make a computer faster, using more bits for addresses enables a machine to support larger programs. Graphics are also often described by the number of bits used to represent each dot. A 1-bit image is monochrome; an 8-bit image supports 256 colors or grayscales; and a 24- or 32-bit graphic supports true color.

Blowfish — A block cipher method of encryption that can be used as an alternative to DES or IDEA. It is unpatented, license-free, and free of charge.

Bluetooth — Open specification for wireless voice and data communication. The technology links devices with short-range radio links (instead of cables).

BootP (Bootstrap Protocol) — A UDP/IP-based protocol that allows a booting host to configure itself dynamically, and, more significantly, without user supervision. It provides a means to assign a host its IP address, a file from which to download a boot program from a server, that server's address, and (if present) the address of an Internet gateway.

Border Gateway Protocol — See "BGP."

bridge — See "MAC-Layer Bridge."

broadband — Characteristic of any network that multiplexes multiple, independent carrier signals onto a single cable. This is usually accomplished through frequency division multiplexing. Broadband technology allows several signals to coexist on a single cable; traffic from one signal does not interfere with traffic from another, since data is transmitted on a different frequency. Cable television uses broadband.

broadband ISDN (B-ISDN) – The new generation of Integrated Services Digital Network (ISDN), which carries digital data, voice, and video over SONET networks. B-ISDN allows Asynchronous Transfer Mode (ATM) and Synchronous Transfer Mode (STM) services to operate on the same network.

broadband LAN – A LAN that uses frequency division multiplexing (FDM) to divide a single physical channel into a number of smaller, independent frequency channels. The different channels created by FDM can be used to transfer different forms of information, such as voice, data, and video.

broadcast – A packet delivered to all workstations on a network. Broadcasts exist at layer 2 and at layer 3.

broadcast and unknown server (BUS) – An ATM LANE process that relays broadcast and multicast packets, and packets with unknown destination addresses, to all Emulated LAN clients. It can be implemented on any ATM device, including a file server, a switch, an access device, or a router.

broadcast domain – The set of end stations which receive the same broadcast packets.

broadcast storm – An overload condition in a network created by an incorrect packet broadcast onto the network that causes multiple hosts to respond all at once. Typically the response contains equally incorrect packets, which causes the storm to grow exponentially in severity.

Bus – (1) A conductor, or set of conductors (e.g., wires), that serves as the interconnection between a related set of devices. (2) A specific type of backplane in which all slots are connected to a common set of wires or traces on which they send to and receive from all other slots. (3) A network topology in which the signals sent by one device are received by all other devices. Each device then selects those transmissions addressed to it based on address information contained in the transmission.

BUS – See "broadcast and unknown server."

byte (binary term) – A unit of storage capable of holding a single character. On almost all modern computers, a byte is equal to 8 bits. Large amounts of memory are indicated in terms of kilobytes (1,024 bytes), megabytes (1,048,576 bytes), and gigabytes (1,073,741,824 bytes). A disk that can hold 1.44 megabytes, for example, is capable of storing approximately 1.4 million characters, or about 3,000 pages of information.

CAC – See "connection admission control."

cache – A special area of high-speed memory used to store addresses in a switch. Also called a forwarding table.

call – A switching function communications relationship, generally between two or more devices.

call center – A location where agents answer and originate calls.

call control – Signals used to set up, monitor, and clear down a call.

call vectoring – An alternative name used by some suppliers to describe Intelligent Dynamic Routing.

callback – Calling a caller, either at her/his request or through use of CTI on an abandoned call.

called line identification (CLI) – Number presented to an operator, agent, or application that confirms the caller's number.

caller identification – Caller identification on ISDN.

campus network – A network that covers a single customer location, such as a building, a floor of a building, or all of the buildings on a large commercial, educational, or other campus.

carrier sense multiple access/collision detection – See "CSMA/CD."

CAS (channel associated signaling) – Signaling system in which signaling information is carried within the bearer channel.

CBR (constant bit rate) – A form of ATM transmission in which a fixed bit rate is provided, with clock frequency and phase maintained end-to-end. Typical uses include emulation of a leased-line circuit and carrying traditional 64 Kbps PCM voice.

CBT (computer-based training) – A type of education in which the student learns by executing special training programs on a computer. CBT is especially effective for training people to use computer applications because the CBT program can be integrated with the applications so that students can practice using the application as they learn. Historically, CBT's growth has been hampered by the enormous resources required: human resources to create a CBT program and hardware resources needed to run it. However, the increase in PC computing power, and especially the growing prevalence of computers equipped with CD-ROMs, is making CBT a more viable option for corporations and individuals alike. Many PC applications now come with some modest form of CBT, often called a tutorial. CBT is also called computer-assisted instruction (CAI).

CE – See "circuit emulation."

cell – A fixed-length transmission unit that forms the basis of ATM. Each cell is 53 bytes in length, divided into a 48-byte payload and a 5-byte header.

cell discard – The process within an ATM switch of discarding cells when the switch's buffer capacity is exceeded.

cell loss priority (CLP) – A one-bit field in the ATM cell header that determines whether or not a given cell should be dropped by network equipment during periods of congestion. This explicit loss priority can be set by the source node or by the network. A CLP that equals zero receives high network priority while a CLP that equals one is dropped during periods of congestion.

cell loss ratio (CLR) – The ratio of discarded cells to cells that are successfully transmitted. Specifically, CLR equals the number of discarded cells divided by the number of transmitted cells.

central office (CO) – American term for a public telephone exchange.

central processing unit – See "CPU."

centrex – A PBX service providing switching at the central office instead of at the company premises. Typically, the telephone company owns and manages all the communications equipment necessary to implement the PBX and then sells various services to the company.

channel associated signaling (CAS) – Signaling system in which signaling information is carried within the bearer channel.

checksum – A computed value that is the outcome of a mathematical function applied to the contents of a packet. This value is sent along with the packet when it is transmitted. The receiving system computes a new checksum based on the received data and compares this value with the one sent with the packet. If the two values are the same, the data was received correctly.

CIR – See "committed information rate."

circuit emulation (CE) – A service provided across a public or private ATM network that emulates the characteristics of a leased-line service.

circuit switching – A communications method whereby a circuit is held open and maintained only while the sender and recipient are communicating. This is different from a dedicated circuit, which is held open regardless of whether data is being sent or not, and different from a datagram/connectionless network, in which data flows without the establishment of a connection.

CIT (computer integration telephony) – Early alternative name for CTI.

Classical IP – An IETF specification for IP connectivity on an ATM network. Classical IP resolves IP addresses directly to ATM addresses.

Classless Inter-domain Routing (CIDR) – An IAB protocol that uses variable-length subnetting techniques to distribute the allocation of Internet address space. CIDR is needed to address the exhaustion of class B network address space, the growth of Internet routing tables, and the eventual exhaustion of the 32-bit IP address space.

CLEC (competitive local exchange carrier) – A telephone company that competes with an incumbent local exchange carrier (ILEC) such as a regional bell operating company (RBOC), GTE, ALLNET, etc. With the passage of the Telecommunications Act of 1996, there has been an explosion in the number of CLECs.

CLI (called line identification) – Number presented to an operator, agent, or application that confirms the caller's number.

client – The client part of a client-server architecture. Typically, a client is an application that runs on a personal computer or workstation and relies on a server to perform some operations. For example, an e-mail client is an application that enables you to send and receive e-mail.

clip – In computer graphics, to cut off a portion of a graphic at a defined boundary. Most bit-mapped graphics utilities provide a clip feature that enables you to draw a window around an object and clip everything outside of the window.

CLP – See "cell loss priority."

CLR – See "cell loss ratio."

CO (Central Office) – American term for a public telephone exchange.

coaxial cable (coax) – Formerly common in Ethernet networks, coax comes in various types with different transmission characteristics. It is copper-based, with an inner conductor surrounded by an outer conductor, with insulation between the two, insulation around the outer conductor, and a jacket. Coax is less flexible than twisted pair cable, but more resistant to EMI and physical breakage.

codec (coder/decoder) – A device that encodes or decodes a signal. For example, telephone companies use codecs to convert binary signals transmitted on their digital networks to analog signals converted on their analog networks.

coder/decoder – See "codec."

collapsed backbone – A network architecture in which a router or switch provides a building or campus backbone using a star topology.

collision – Concurrent Ethernet transmissions from two or more devices on the same segment. A collision is sensed by the transmitting stations as an over-voltage condition, and they retransmit after waiting a random amount of time.

committed information rate (CIR) – A specified amount of guaranteed bandwidth (measured in bits per second) on a frame relay service. Typically, when purchasing a frame relay service, a company can specify the CIR level they wish. The frame relay network vendor guarantees that frames not exceeding this level will be delivered. It's possible that additional traffic may also be delivered, but it's not guaranteed. Some frame relay vendors offer inexpensive services with a CIR equal to zero. This essentially means that the network will deliver as many frames as it can, but it doesn't guarantee any bandwidth level.

Common Open Policy Service (COPS) – An IAB client/server model for supporting policy control over QoS signaling protocols with similar properties as ReSerVation Protocol (RSVP). In RSVP, the router, or network device, must respond to bandwidth reservation requests; with COPS, the router forwards the bandwidth request to the nearest COPS policy server. The server makes the end-to-end bandwidth decision; the router implements it. The result is less overhead on the router and overall lower network latency.

competitive local exchange carrier – See "CLEC."

compression – Storing data in a format that requires less space than usual. Compressing data is the same as packing data. Data compression is particularly useful in communications because it enables devices to transmit the same amount of data in fewer bits. There are a variety of data compression techniques, but only a few have been standardized. The CCITT has defined a standard data compression technique for transmitting faxes (Group 3 standard) and a compression standard for data communications through modems (CCITT V.42bis). In addition, there are file compression formats, such as ARC and ZIP. Data compression is also widely used in backup utilities, spreadsheet applications, and database management systems. Certain types of data, such as bit-mapped graphics, can be compressed to a small fraction of their normal size.

computer integrated telephony (CIT) – Early alternative name for CTI.

computer telephony integration – See "CTI."

computer-supported telephony applications – See "CSTA."

conditional routing – An alternative name for Intelligent dynamic routing.

congestion control – Mechanisms that control traffic flow so that intermediate network devices and end stations are not overwhelmed. Used in connection-oriented networks such as frame relay and ATM. More sophisticated mechanisms are needed to deal with congestion in large networks carrying different types of traffic. Sometimes referred to as flow control.

connect time – The time that a user is connected to another user or system which includes the time of setting up the call and clearing it down.

connection admission control (CAC) – The set of actions taken by the network during the call setup phase (or during call renegotiation phase) in order to determine whether a connection request can be accepted or should be rejected (or whether a request for reallocation can be accommodated).

connectionless – The model of interconnection in which communication takes place without formal connection establishment. Examples include Ethernet, Internet IP, and UDP.

connection-oriented – The model of interconnection in which communication proceeds through three well-defined phases: connection establishment, data transfer, and connection release. Examples of connection-oriented networks include ATM, frame relay, X.25, and Internet TCP.

connectivity – A computer buzzword that refers to a program or device's ability to link with other programs and devices. For example, a program that can import data from a wide variety of other programs and can export data in many different formats is said to have good connectivity. On the other hand, computers that have difficulty linking into a network (many laptop computers, for example) have poor connectivity.

constant bit rate – See "CBR."

convergence – The blurring of telecommunications, computers, and the Internet into one network. It is primarily about technology and the class of voice and data networks, but it is also a fundamental change in the way people will work and behave in the future. The public voice network will become a public multimedia network, and the Internet as it is known today will cease to exist, as every user will always be online (no dial-up required) and have ready access.

CPU (central processing unit) – Pronounced as separate letters. The CPU is the brains of the computer. Sometimes referred to simply as the processor or central processor, the CPU is where most calculations take place. In terms of computing power, the CPU is the most important element of a computer system. On large machines, CPUs require one or more printed circuit boards. On personal computers and small workstations, the CPU is housed in a single chip called a microprocessor. Two typical components of a CPU are the arithmetic logic unit (ALU), which performs arithmetic and logical operations; and the control unit, which extracts instructions from memory and decodes and executes them, calling on the ALU when necessary.

CRC – See "cyclical redundancy check."

CRM (customer relationship management) – A broad term describing business practices and hardware, software, and networking tools used for improving customer service.

CSMA/CD (carrier sense multiple access/collision detection) – A set of rules determining how network devices respond when two devices attempt to use a data channel simultaneously (called a collision). Standard Ethernet networks use CSMA/CD. This standard enables devices to detect a collision. After detecting a collision, a device waits a random delay time and then attempts to retransmit the message. If the device detects a collision again, it waits twice as long to try to retransmit the message. This is known as exponential back off. CSMA/CD is a type of contention protocol.

CSTA (computer-supported telephony applications) – An ECMA standard for commands exchanged between a PBX and host computer. Equivalent to the American ANSI standard, SCAI.

CTI (computer telephony integration) – Refers to systems that enable a computer to act as a call center, accepting incoming calls and routing them to the appropriate device or person. Today's CTI systems are quite sophisticated and can handle all sorts of incoming and outgoing communications, including phone calls, faxes, and Internet messages. Associating a call with data from a database to assist in handling an inbound call. For outbound calls, using a database to select and present outbound calls to an agent.

customer service unit (CSU) – A device used at the customer premise to connect a device, such as a PBX, to a public digital network facility, such as a T1 line. Provides repeater and control functions.

cut-through – (1) A form of switching, typically LAN switching, in which the switch begins to forward the initial portion of a packet to its destination while the remainder of the packet is still being received. This was useful when the throughput of LAN protocols was highly degraded by latency in the data path. It is uncommon today. (2) A form of switching, typically in an ATM network, in which a routing process is used to set up a connection between two devices, but the data subsequently flows directly between the two devices, without passing through the routing process. MPOA is one important example.

cyclical redundancy check (CRC) – An error-checking mechanism for layer 2 data transmissions. Polynomial calculations are performed using only the number of bits in the message. The bits are then sent along with the data to its recipient. The recipient checks the data it receives and repeats the calculation. If there are any discrepancies between the results of the two calculations, the recipient requests the originator to resend the data.

DAS – See "dual attached station."

data communications equipment (DCE) – Traditional data communications terminology for the equipment that enables a DTE to communicate over a telephone line or data circuit. The DCE establishes, maintains, and terminates a connection as well as performing the conversions necessary for communications.

data link connection identifier (DLCI) – A unique number assigned to a PVC end point in a frame relay network. Identifies a particular PVC end point within a user's access channel in a frame relay network, and has local significance only to that port.

data terminal equipment (DTE) – Traditional data communications terminology for a device receiving and/or originating data on a network. Typically a computer or dumb terminal.

database management system (DBMS) – A collection of programs that enables you to store, modify, and extract information from a database. There are many different types of DBMSs, ranging from small systems that run on personal computers to huge systems that run on mainframes. The following are examples of database applications: computerized library systems, automated teller machines, flight reservation systems, computerized parts inventory systems. From a technical standpoint, DBMSs can differ widely. The terms relational, network, flat, and hierarchical all refer to the way a DBMS organizes information internally. The internal organization can affect how quickly and flexibly you can extract information.

datagram – A self-contained, independent entity of data carrying sufficient information to be routed from its source to the destination computer without reliance on earlier exchanges between the source, the destination computer, and the transporting network.

DBMS – See "database management system."

DCE – See "data communications equipment."

DDE (dynamic data exchange) – An interprocess communication (IPC) system built into the Macintosh, Windows, and OS/2 operating systems. DDE enables two running applications to share the same data. For example, DDE makes it possible to insert a spreadsheet chart into a document created with a word processor. Whenever the spreadsheet data changes, the chart in the document changes accordingly. Although the DDE mechanism is still used by many applications, it is being supplanted by OLE, which provides greater control over shared data.

DDI (direct dial inwards) – (a) Originally the facility to dial a person connected to a PBX directly without operator intervention. (b) A service offered by network providers where the caller dials a published service number, and the call is switched by the PBX or ACD to an extension determined by the last 4 or 6 digits of the number dialed.

decryption – The inverse of "encryption."

DES (Data Encryption Standard) – A block cipher encryption algorithm published by the National Institute of Standards and Technology. A stronger alternative is Triple DES (3DES), which is DES applied to a data stream three times.

DHCP (Dynamic Host Configuration Protocol) – A protocol for assigning dynamic IP addresses to devices on a network. With dynamic addressing, a device can have a different IP address every time it connects to the network. In some systems, the device's IP address can even change while it is still connected. DHCP also supports a mix of static and dynamic IP addresses. Dynamic addressing simplifies network administration because the software keeps track of IP addresses rather than requiring an administrator to manage the task. This means that a new computer can be added to a network without the hassle of manually assigning it a unique IP address. Many ISPs use dynamic IP addressing for dial-up users. DHCP client support is built into Windows 95 and NT workstations. NT 4 server includes both client and server support.

DID (direct inward dialing) – The U.S. equivalent of DDI.

DiffServ (differentiated services) – The result of an IETF working group that is defining a new bandwidth-management scheme for IP networks. The plan redefines part of the existing Type-of-Service (ToS) byte in every IP packet header to mark the priority or service level that packet requires – see "ToS." DiffServ will work well with security protocols because the ToS byte is in the IP header and is therefore not encrypted. The DiffServ charter is defined at `www.ietf.org/html.charters/diffserv-charter.html`. Additional information is at `diffserv.lcs.mit.edu`. DiffServ has extremely widespread support among equipment vendors and service providers. It is expected to be a key element of voice over IP service. The scheme is expected to scale well because the work of making these assignments, which involves examining layer 3 or higher layers of each packet, is limited to edge routers. LDAP is the likely protocol that these routers will use for handling policies regarding how to mark each packet.

digital number identification system (DNIS) – Caller identification system used in the U.S.

digital service unit (DSU) – A device used at the customer premise to connect a data device, such as a computer, to a public digital network facility, such as a T1 line. Provides electrical translation and line coding. Technically, this is generally a DSU/CSU, combining both functions.

digital signal processing – See "DSP."

digital signature – Electronic means to ensure message integrity, typically based on a public key crypto-system.

DIMM (dual in-line memory module) – A small circuit board that holds memory chips. A single in-line memory module (SIMM) has a 32-bit path to the memory chips whereas a DIMM has a 64-bit path. Because the Pentium processor requires a 64-bit path to memory, you need to install SIMMs two at a time. With DIMMs, you can install memory one DIMM at a time.

direct dial inwards – See "DDI."

direct inward dialing – See "DID."

directory – A special kind of file used to organize other files into a hierarchical structure. Directories contain bookkeeping information about files that are, figuratively speaking, beneath them. You can think of a directory as a folder or cabinet that contains files and perhaps other folders. In fact, many graphical user interfaces use the term folder instead of directory.

Distance Vector Multicast Routing Protocol (DVMRP) – A protocol designed to support the forwarding of multicast datagrams through an internetwork. DVMRP constructs source-rooted multicast delivery trees using variants of the Reverse Path Broadcasting (RVP) algorithm. Some version of DVMRP is currently deployed in the majority of MBONE routers.

DLL (Dynamic Link Library) – A library of executable functions or data that can be used by a Windows application. Typically, a DLL provides one or more particular functions and a program accesses the functions by creating either a static or dynamic link to the DLL. A static link remains constant during program execution, while a dynamic link is created by the program as needed. DLLs can also contain just data. DLL files usually end with the extension `.dll`, `.exe`, `.drv`, or `.fon`. A DLL can be used by several applications at the same time. Some DLLs are provided with the Windows operating system and are available for any Windows application. Other DLLs are written for a particular application and are loaded with the application.

DNIS (digital number identification system) – Caller identification system used in the U.S.

DNS – See "Domain Name System."

domain – In networking, a subdivision of the hosts on a network. The division can be physical, as in separate building LANs, or logical, as in giving the hosts in a particular administrative area their own group name even though they are on the same network.

Domain Name System (DNS) – An IAB standard that provides a globally accessible table of domain names (e.g., `alcatel.com`) and their corresponding IP addresses.

DOS (disk operating system) – The term DOS can refer to any operating system, but it is most often used as a shorthand for MS-DOS (Microsoft disk operating system). Originally developed by Microsoft for IBM, MS-DOS was the standard operating system for IBM-compatible personal computers. The initial versions of DOS were very simple and resembled another operating system called CP/M. Subsequent versions have became increasingly sophisticated as they incorporated features of minicomputer operating systems. However, DOS is still a 16-bit operating system and does not support multiple users or multitasking. For some time, it has been widely acknowledged that DOS is insufficient for modern computer applications. Microsoft Windows helped alleviate some problems, but still, it sat on top of DOS and relied on DOS for many services. Even Windows 95 sat on top of DOS. Newer operating systems, such as Windows NT and OS/2 Warp, do not rely on DOS to the same extent, although they can execute DOS-based programs. It is expected that as these operating systems gain market share, DOS will eventually disappear. In the meantime, Caldera, Inc., markets a version of DOS called DR-OpenDOS that extends MS-DOS in significant ways.

DS-0 – A 64 Kbps digital channel carried within a DS-1 or E1 signal.

DS-1 – The digital signal carried on a North American high-speed facility operating at 1.544 Mbps.

DS-3 – The digital signal carried on a North American high-speed facility (T3) operating at approximately 45 Mbps.

DSP (digital signal processing) – Refers to manipulating analog information, such as sound or photographs, that has been converted into a digital form. DSP also implies the use of a data compression technique. When used as a noun, DSP stands for digital signal processor, a special type of coprocessor designed for performing the mathematics involved in DSP. Most DSPs are programmable, which means that they can be used for manipulating different types of information, including sound, images, and video.

DSU – See "digital service unit."

DTE – See "data terminal equipment."

DTMF (dual tone multi-frequency) – The system used by touch-tone telephones. DTMF assigns a specific frequency, or tone, to each key so that it can easily be identified by a microprocessor.

dual attached station (DAS) – A form of FDDI connection in which a dual counter-rotating ring is supported. Typically used for connecting concentrators and servers to a main ring.

dual in-line memory module – See "DIMM."

dual tone multi-frequency – See "DTMF."

duplex – A technique allowing bidirectional, simultaneous transmission along a channel. Generally referred to as full duplex.

DVMRP – See "Distance Vector Multicast Routing Protocol."

dynamic data exchange (DDE) – An interprocess communication (IPC) system built into the Macintosh, Windows, and OS/2 operating systems. DDE enables two running applications to share the same data. For example, DDE makes it possible to insert a spreadsheet chart into a document created with a word processor.

Whenever the spreadsheet data changes, the chart in the document changes accordingly. Although the DDE mechanism is still used by many applications, it is being supplanted by OLE, which provides greater control over shared data.

Dynamic Host Configuration Protocol – See "DHCP."

Dynamic Link Library – See "DLL."

dynamic routing – A procedure for sending messages across a network by which line failure or overload results in message rerouting.

E and M – See "ear and mouth."

E-1 – The digital signal carried on a high-speed facility operating outside of North America at 2.048 Mbps.

E-3 – The digital signal carried on a high-speed facility operating outside of North America at approximately 34 Mbps.

E-911 – Enhanced 911 for wireless services improves the reliability of wireless 911 services and provides emergency services personnel with information that enables them to locate and provide assistance to wireless 911 callers quickly without regard to validation procedures intended to identify and intercept calls from nonsubscribers. The wireless 911 rules apply to all cellular licensees, broadband personal communications service (PCS) licensees, and specific specialized mobile radio (SMR) licensees.

ear and mouth (E and M) – Trunk signaling between a PBX and a CO used to seize a line; forward digits, release the line, etc.

early packet discard (EPD) – An intelligent cell discard process that occurs within an ATM switch when its buffer capacity is exceeded. EPD discards all cells that originated as members of a single data frame, since the entire frame would have to be retransmitted if even one cell were discarded.

ECMA (European Computer Manufacturers Association) – Standards group of computer and PBX manufacturers.

ECMA 179, 180 – The first European Computer Manufacturers Association (ECMA) CTI standards.

e-commerce – A broad term that describes using an electronic medium, usually the Internet, for buying and selling goods and services.

EFCI – See "explicit forward congestion indication."

EFM (Ethernet in the First Mile) – Also called ELM (Ethernet in the Last Mile). A developing IEEE standard that will allow Ethernet networks to extend to the "first mile," which is the link between customers and their ISP, in effect reducing the number of necessary protocol translations.

EGP – See "Exterior Gateway Protocol."

EIDE (Enhanced IDE) – A newer version of the IDE mass storage device interface standard developed by Western Digital Corporation. It supports data rates of between 4 and 16.6 Mbps, about three to four times faster than the old IDE standard. In addition, it can support mass storage devices of up to 8.4 gigabytes, whereas the old standard was limited to 528MB. Because of its lower cost, enhanced EIDE has replaced SCSI in many areas. EIDE is sometimes referred to as Fast ATA or Fast IDE, which is essentially the same standard, developed and promoted by Seagate Technologies. It is also sometimes called ATA-2. There are four EIDE modes defined. The most common is Mode 4, which supports transfer rates of 16.6 Mbps. There is also a new mode, called ATA-3 or Ultra ATA, that supports transfer rates of 33 Mbps.

EISA (Extended Industry Standard Architecture) – A bus architecture designed for PCs using an Intel 80386, 80486, or Pentium microprocessor. EISA buses are 32 bits wide and support multiprocessing. The EISA bus was designed by nine IBM competitors (sometimes called the Gang of Nine): AST Research, Compaq Computer, Epson, Hewlett-Packard, NEC, Olivetti, Tandy, WYSE, and Zenith Data Systems. They designed the architecture to compete with IBM's own high-speed bus architecture called the Micro Channel architecture (MCA). The principal difference between EISA and MCA is that EISA is backward compatible with the ISA bus (also called the AT bus), while MCA is not. This means that computers with an EISA bus can use new EISA expansion cards as well as old AT expansion cards. Computers with an MCA bus can use only MCA expansion cards. EISA and MCA are not compatible with each other. This means that the type of bus in your computer determines which expansion cards you can install. Neither EISA nor MCA has been very successful. Instead, a new technology called local bus (PCI) is being used in combination with the old ISA bus.

ELAN (Emulated LAN) – See "LAN emulation."

electro-magnetic interference (EMI) – Electrical interference with the operation of an electrical device, or with a communications transmission, caused by magnetic radiation. Typically originates from another electrical device, or from a communications transmission in a nearby cable.

e-mail – Electronic message that can be distributed between computers and computer terminals. E-mail uses x.400 and x.500 standards.

encapsulation – The technique used by layered protocols in which a layer adds header information to the protocol data unit (PDU) from the layer above.

encryption – The process of converting information from an easily understandable format (plain text) into apparent random gibberish (ciphertext) by the use of well-defined rules and calculations known as algorithms or cipher. A process used to ensure the privacy and confidentiality of information. The reverse process is decryption.

ENUM – Proposed IETF standard for mapping telephone numbers to URLs using the DNS. ENUM may someday allow individuals to use just one address for all types of communication (voice, e-mail, fax, etc.).

E-Rate – Popular name for the Schools and Libraries Universal Service Fund. Part of the Telecommunications Act of 1996, E-Rate provides U.S. schools and libraries with funding for telecommunications and information services.

ERP (Enterprise Resource Planning) – Enterprise Resource Planning (ERP) is a strategic tool that helps companies gain a competitive advantage by integrating all business processes and optimizing the resources available. This allows an enterprise to deliver value added products and services in the shortest possible time.

Ethernet – The most common layer 2 protocol used in LANs. Ethernet is a 10 Mbps CSMA/CD standard originally developed by Xerox to run on thick coaxial cabling. It has evolved and now runs primarily on twisted pair cabling.

European Computer Manufacturers Association (ECMA) – Standards group of computer and PBX manufacturers.

explicit forward congestion indication (EFCI) – EFCI is an indication in the ATM cell header. A network element in an impending-congested state or a congested state may set EFCI so that this indication may be examined by the destination end-system. For example, the end-system may use this indication to implement a protocol that adaptively lowers the cell rate of the connection during congestion or impending congestion. A network element that is not in a congestion state or an impending congestion state will not modify the value of this indication. Impending congestion is the state when network equipment is operating around its engineered capacity level.

explicit rate – Explicit rate is a type of flow control mechanism defined by the ATM Forum Traffic Management 4.0 standard. With Explicit rate flow control ATM-attached sources are periodically issued resource management (RM) cells, which stipulate a maximum cell rate (measured in cells per second) at which the device can transmit and be guaranteed that traffic will not be discarded by the network.

Extended Industry Standard Architecture – See "EISA."

Extensible Markup Language – See "XML."

Exterior Gateway Protocol (EGP) – A routing protocol used by gateways in two-level Internets. EGP is used in the Internet core system.

extranet – Offers limited access to a company's intranet to outside organizations. Extranets are often designed to connect a company with its partners, suppliers, customers, etc., via a secure connection across the Internet in order to link databases, promote e-commerce, etc.

fabric blocking – The state that can exist within a switch when its internal switching fabric is not capable of handling simultaneous maximum-rate transmissions by all inputs.

Fast Ethernet – A version of Ethernet that operates at 100 Mbps. See "100BaseFX" and "100BaseTX."

fault-tolerance – The ability of a device to prevent or recover from network and internal failures. Key elements of fault tolerance include hot-swappable modules, redundant load-sharing power supplies, passive backplanes, and redundant cooling systems.

FDDI – A local area network based on a backbone of dual counter-rotating 100 Mbps fiber optic rings. One of the rings is normally designated as the primary ring; the other is the secondary ring. The dual ring is connected to single-attached "slave" rings through concentrators.

FDM – See "frequency division multiplexing."

fiber channel – A form of high-speed fiber optic transmission designed primarily for communications between mainframe computers, and between mainframe computers and high-speed peripherals such as disk drives. Sometimes used for general-purpose networking.

field programmable gate array (FPGA) – A general-purpose semiconductor component which can be customized to operate physically as though it were a chip dedicated to a specific task.

File Transfer Protocol (FTP) – The protocol within the TCP/IP protocol suite that is used to transfer files between computers.

Finder – The desktop management and file management system for Apple Macintosh computers. In addition to managing files and disks, the Finder is responsible for managing the Clipboard and Scrapbook and all desktop icons and windows.

firewall – A security mechanism that protects a server, a subnet, or an entire end user location from unauthorized access. Firewalls can be standalone devices, or they can be incorporated into routers and switches.

flooding – Transmission of a frame to all devices in a segment or ring (in routed networks) or a virtual LAN (in a virtual LAN-based network). Flooding is performed on broadcasts, multicasts, and frames whose destination address is unknown.

flow control – See "congestion control."

forwarding table – A special area of high-speed memory used to store addresses in a switch. Also called a cache.

FPGA – See "field programmable gate array."

fragmentation – The process in which a protocol data unit is broken into smaller pieces to fit the requirements of a network. The reverse process is reassembly.

frame – A unit of information in a layer 2 protocol. In LANs, a frame is a MAC-layer unit containing both control information and an entire layer 3 packet. Although the term "packet" is sometimes used to mean a frame, the term "frame" is never used to describe a layer 3 packet.

frame relay – A packet-switching protocol for connecting devices on a wide area network (WAN). Frame relay networks in the U.S. support data transfer rates at T1 (1.544 Mbps) and T3 (45 Mbps) speeds. In fact, you can think of frame relay as a way of utilizing existing T1 and T3 lines owned by a service provider. Most telephone companies now provide frame relay service for customers who want connections at 56 Kbps to T1 speeds. (In Europe, frame relay speeds vary from 64 Kbps to 2 Mbps.) In the U.S., frame relay is quite popular because it is relatively inexpensive. However, it is being replaced in some areas by faster technologies, such as ATM.

frame tagging – A process of adding a header to the front of a layer 2 frame, so that additional information needed to manage the frame through the network is provided. This information can include membership in one or more virtual LANs, priority information, and/or quality of service information.

frequency division multiplexing (FDM) – Method by which the available transmission frequency range is divided into narrower bands; each of these bands is used for a separate channel. This allows several signals to be sent over the same transmission medium.

FRF.5 – A Frame Relay Forum specification for internetworking ATM and frame relay networks. FRF.5 allows ATM networks to transparently pass frame relay data link connection identifiers over ATM virtual channel identifiers. This allows ATM networks to act as high-speed backbones for frame relay networks.

FRF.8 – A Frame Relay Forum specification for service internetworking ATM and frame relay. This allows frame relay data link connection identifiers to be directly mapped into ATM virtual channel identifiers. FRF.8 allows frame relay devices to directly communicate with ATM attached devices.

FRF.9 – A Frame Relay Forum specification for data compression within frame relay.

FTP – See "File Transfer Protocol."

full-duplex – A communications method in which a transmission path is provided in each direction, so that each end can simultaneously transmit and receive.

G723 – Audio codec for 3.1 Kbps bandwidth over 5.3 and 6.3 Kbps channels (G723 has been selected by the VoIP Forum for use with VoIP).

G728 – Audio codec for 3.1 Kbps bandwidth over 16 Kbps channels.

G729 – Audio codec for 3.1 Kbps bandwidth over 8 Kbps channels (adopted by the Frame Relay Forum for voice over frame relay).

gateway – A combination of hardware and software that interconnects otherwise incompatible networks or networking devices. The term is sometimes used to indicate a device (uncommon now) that translates between disparate protocol stacks.

Gbps – Billions of bits per second.

Gigabit Ethernet – A variant of Ethernet that operates over multimode fiber optic cable, single mode fiber optic cable, or unshielded twisted pair, at 1,000 Mbps.

graphical user interface (GUI) – See "GUI."

groupware – A class of software that helps groups of colleagues (workgroups) attached to a local area network organize their activities. Typically, groupware supports the following operations: scheduling meetings and allocating resources, e-mail, password protection for documents, telephone utilities, electronic newsletters, and file distribution. Groupware is sometimes called workgroup productivity software.

GUI (graphical user interface) – A program interface that takes advantage of the computer's graphics capabilities to make the program easier to use. Well-designed graphical user interfaces can free the user from learning complex command languages. On the other hand, many users find that they work more effectively with a command-driven interface, especially if they already know the command language.

H.323 – H.323, the important new standard for audio, video, and data communication, describes how multimedia communications occur between terminals, network equipment, and services on LANs which do not provide a guaranteed QoS (e.g., IP networks). It has had the unified support of a global coalition of personal computer and communications systems manufacturers and operating systems makers. H.323 compliance has also been promoted and accepted by Internet phone and voice–over–IP manufacturers as the standard for interoperability.

half-duplex – A communications method in which one end transmits while the other receives; then the process is reversed. This was common in wide area point-to-multipoint circuits, such as those used in many SNA networks.

head end – A central point in a broadband network that receives signals on one set of frequency bands and retransmits them on another set of frequencies. The head end is viewed as a central hub. Every transmission on a broadband network must go through the head end.

header – A portion added to the beginning of a message containing essential information such as the source address, destination address, and control information.

head-of-line blocking – The state that exists when frames or cells within a single input queue are destined for multiple outputs, and one output is congested, thus delaying all cells.

HEC (header error control) – An 8-bit Cyclic Redundancy Code (CRC) computed on all fields in an ATM header; capable of detecting single-bit and certain multiple-bit errors. HEC is used by the physical layer for cell delineation.

horizontal cabling – That portion of a building's cabling system which extends from the wiring closets to the individual workstations, servers, telephones, and other devices. This is generally copper twisted pair cable.

Hot Standby Router Protocol (HSRP) – A Cisco-driven IAB protocol that allows hosts to appear to use a single router and to maintain connectivity even if the actual first hop router fails. Multiple routers participate in this protocol by creating the illusion of a single virtual router. The protocol ensures that one and only one of the routers is forwarding packets on behalf of the virtual router. End hosts forward their packets to the virtual router. See also "Virtual Router Redundancy Protocol."

HTML (HyperText Markup Language) – The authoring language used to create documents on the World Wide Web. HTML is similar to SGML, although it is not a strict subset.

HTTP (HyperText Transfer Protocol) – The underlying protocol used by the World Wide Web. HTTP defines how messages are formatted and transmitted, and what action Web servers and browsers should take in response to various commands. For example, when you enter a URL in your browser, this actually sends an HTTP command to the Web server directing it to fetch and transmit the requested Web page. The other main standard that controls how the World Wide Web works is HTML, which covers how Web pages are formatted and displayed. HTTP is called a stateless protocol because each command is executed independently, without any knowledge of the commands that came before it. This is the main reason that it is difficult to implement Web sites that react intelligently to user input. This shortcoming of HTTP is being addressed in a number of new technologies, including ActiveX, Java, JavaScript, and cookies. Currently, most Web browsers and servers support HTTP 1.1. One of the main features of HTTP 1.1 is that it supports persistent connections. This means that once a browser connects to a Web server, it can receive multiple files through the same connection. This should improve performance by as much as 20 percent.

hub – A connection point for devices in a network. Hubs are commonly used to connect segments of a LAN. A hub contains multiple ports. When a packet arrives at one port, it is copied to the other ports so that all segments of the LAN can see all packets. A passive hub serves simply as a conduit for the data, enabling it to go from one device (or segment) to another. So-called intelligent hubs include additional features that enable an administrator to monitor the traffic passing through the hub and to configure each port in the hub. Intelligent hubs are also called manageable hubs. A third type of hub, called a switching hub, actually reads the destination address of each packet and then forwards the packet to the correct port.

hybrid network – A LAN consisting of a number of topologies and access methods, for example, a network that includes both token ring and Ethernet.

HyperText Markup Language – See "HTML."

HyperText Transfer Protocol (HTTP) – See "HTTP."

IAB – See "Internet Activities Board."

ICMP (Internet Control Message Protocol) – An extension to the Internet Protocol (IP) defined by RFC 792. ICMP supports packets containing error, control, and informational messages. The PING command, for example, uses ICMP to test an Internet connection.

ICMP router discovery – An extension of the IAB Internet Control Message Protocol (ICMP) that enables hosts attached to multicast or broadcast networks to discover the IP addresses of their neighboring routers without requiring static default route configurations.

IDE (integrated drive electronics) – An IDE interface is an interface for mass storage devices in which the controller is integrated into the disk or CD-ROM drive. Although it really refers to a general technology, most people use the term to refer to the ATA specification that uses this technology. Refer to ATA for more information.

IDEA (International Data Encryptions Algorithm) – Secret key encryption algorithm that is considered by some to be superior to DES.

IDF – See "intermediate distribution frame."

IEEE (Institute of Electrical and Electronics Engineers) – Pronounced I-triple-E. Founded in 1884, the IEEE is an organization composed of engineers, scientists, and students. The IEEE is best known for developing standards for the computer and electronics industry. In particular, the IEEE 802 standards for local area networks are widely followed.

IEEE 802.10 – The IEEE's protocol for providing security in a metropolitan area network. A variant of 802.10 has sometimes been used to provide a virtual LAN service within a campus network, although this is now generally replaced with 802.1Q.

IEEE 802.1D – See "Spanning Tree."

IEEE 802.1p – An IEEE standard for prioritizing time-critical flows and filtering multicast traffic to contain traffic in layer 2 networks. The 802.1p header includes three bits for prioritization, allowing for eight priorities to be established.

IEEE 802.1Q – An IEEE standard for providing a virtual LAN capability within a campus network, used in conjunction with IEEE LAN protocols such as Ethernet and token ring.

IEEE 802.2 – A data link standard outlining how basic data connectivity over cable should be set up. Used with the IEEE 802.3, 802.4, and 802.5 standards.

IEEE 802.3 – The IEEE's specification for Ethernet, including both physical cabling and layer 2 protocol.

IEEE 802.5 – The IEEE's specification for token ring, including both physical cabling and layer 2 protocol.

IETF (Internet Engineering Task Force) – The main standards organization for the Internet. The IETF is a large open international community of network designers, operators, vendors, and researchers concerned with the evolution of the Internet architecture and the smooth operation of the Internet. It is open to any interested individual.

IGMP – See "Internet Group Management Protocol."

IGP – See "Interior Gateway Protocol."

IISP (Interim Interswitch Signaling Protocol) – An ATM Forum specification for signaling between ATM switches, using statically defined connections. Largely replaced by PNNI.

ILMI (Interim Local Management Interface) – An interim requirements definition in ATM Forum UNI 3.1. It supports bidirectional exchange of management information between UNI management entities related to the ATM layer and physical layer parameters.

IMAP (Internet Message Access Protocol) – A protocol for retrieving e-mail messages. The latest version, IMAP4, is similar to POP3 but supports some additional features. For example, with IMAP4, you can search through your e-mail messages for keywords while the messages are still on the mail server. You can then choose which messages to download to your machine. Like POP, IMAP uses SMTP for communication between the e-mail client and server. IMAP was developed at Stanford University in 1986.

Inbound – Calls received by an organization, especially by an agent.

information superhighway – A sadly meaningless phrase, generally associated with politicians, which implies something or other having to do with the Internet.

Institute of Electrical and Electronics Engineers – See "IEEE."

integrated drive electronics – See "IDE."

integrated messaging – Voice messaging system that provides message interchange with fax and/or e-mail in a single application.

integrated services digital network – See "ISDN."

Intelligent Call Routing – An alternative name used by some suppliers to describe Intelligent Dynamic Routing.

Intelligent Dynamic Routing – Routing of a call based on call characterization, the current status of the system, and resources available.

intelligent hub – A hub that adds network management capabilities, such as maintaining port statistics, determining port status, and automatically segmenting faulty ports. Also known as a second-generation hub.

inter process communication – See "IPC."

interactive voice response – See "IVR."

Interior Gateway Protocol (IGP) – A type of protocol used to exchange routing information between collaborating routers on the Internet. RIP and OSPF are examples of IGPs.

intermediate distribution frame (IDF) – In a structured building wiring system, the gathering point for cabling from a section of a building, such as a floor or a portion of a floor. Typically, multiple IDFs located in wiring closets connect to a central MDF.

International Organization for Standardization – See "ISO."

International Telecommunications Union-Telecommunications Standards Sector (ITU-TSS) – The new name for CCITT (Comite Consultatif International Telephonique et Telegraphique), an organization that sets international communications standards. ITU-TSS has defined many important standards for data communications.

Internet – A global network connecting millions of computers. The Internet has more than 100 million users worldwide, and that number is growing rapidly. More than 100 countries are linked into exchanges of data, news, and opinions. Unlike online services, which are centrally controlled, the Internet is decentralized by design. Each Internet computer, called a host, is independent. Its operators can choose which Internet services to use and which local services to make available to the global Internet community. Remarkably, this anarchy by design works exceedingly well. There are a variety of ways to access the Internet. Most online services, such as America Online, offer access to some Internet services. It is also possible to gain access through a commercial Internet Service Provider (ISP).

Internet Activities Board (IAB) – The technical body that oversees the development of the Internet suite of protocols.

Internet Control Message Protocol (ICMP) – An extension to the Internet Protocol (IP) defined by RFC 792. ICMP supports packets containing error, control, and informational messages. The PING command, for example, uses ICMP to test an Internet connection.

Internet Engineering Task Force – See "IETF."

Internet Group Management Protocol (IGMP) – Defined in RFC 1112 as the standard for IP multicasting in the Internet. It's used to establish host memberships in particular multicast groups on a single network. The mechanisms of the protocol allow a host to inform its local router, using Host Membership Reports, that it wants to receive messages addressed to a specific multicast group. All hosts conforming to level 2 of the IP multicasting specification require IGMP.

Internet Message Access Protocol – See "IMAP."

Internet Packet Exchange Protocol – See "IPX."

Internet Protocol (IP) – The layer 3 protocol used in the TCP/IP set of protocols, which support the Internet and many private networks. IP provides a connection-less datagram delivery service for transport-layer protocols such as TCP and UDP.

Internet Protocol version 6 – See "IPv6."

Internet ReSerVation Protocol (RSVP) – See "RSVP."

Internet service provider – See "ISP."

Internet telephony (IT) – The original meaning of Internet Telephony was the ability to make voice phone calls over the Internet using a PC. It required the appropriate hardware and software. IT has grown into integrated messaging such as sending e-mail, fax, voice, video, and imaging mail/messages over the same medium.

Internet2 – A collaboration of over 180 universities, vendors, and the U.S. government to create an advanced network for the educational and research community to support the required bandwidth levels and multimedia applications.

internetwork – Two or more networks connected by bridges or routers.

Internetwork Packet Exchange – See "IPX."

internetworking – The art and science of connecting individual local area networks (LANs) to create wide area networks (WANs), and connecting WANs to form even larger WANs. Internetworking can be extremely complex because it generally involves connecting networks that use different protocols. Internetworking is accomplished with routers, bridges, and gateways.

INTERNIC – A collaborative project between AT&T and Network Solutions, Inc. (NSI), supported by the National Science Foundation. The project currently offers the following four services to users of the Internet: InterNIC Directory and Database Services – online white pages directory and directory of publicly accessible databases managed by AT&T; Registration Services – domain name and IP address assignment managed by NSI; Support Services – outreach, education, and information services for the Internet community managed by NSI; and Net Scout Services – online publications that summarize recent happenings of interest to Internet users (managed by NSI).

intranet – Network based on TCP/IP protocols (an internet belonging to an organization, usually a corporation, accessible only by the organization's members, employees, or others with authorization). An intranet's Web sites look and act just like any other Web sites, but the firewall surrounding an intranet fends off unauthorized access. Like the Internet itself, intranets are used to share information. Secure intranets are now the fastest-growing segment of the Internet because they are much less expensive to build and manage than private networks based on proprietary protocols.

inverse multiplexing – The use of multiple circuits between two devices in which the circuits are treated as a single virtual channel. Traffic is spread across the circuits, and the loss of one circuit results in reduced bandwidth rather than loss of the connection.

IP – See "Internet Protocol."

IP address – The layer 3 address of a host computer attached to a TCP/IP network. Every host must have a unique IP address. IP addresses are 32-bit values written as four sets of decimal numbers separated by periods, for example, 125.6.65.7. Each decimal number (0–255) represents 8 bits of the complete 32-bit value. The TCP/IP packet uses 32 bits to contain the IP address, which consists of a network address (netid) and a host address (hostid). The 32 bits are divided in different ways according to the class of the address, which determines the number of hosts that can be attached to the network. If more bits are used for the host addresses (such as in Class A), fewer bits are available for the network address. Network addresses are supplied to organizations by the InterNIC Registration Service.

IP datagram – The fundamental unit of information passed across the Internet at layer 3. It contains source and destination addresses along with the data, and a number of fields that define such things as the length of the datagram and the header checksum.

IP multicasting – Multipoint communication that allows one message to be distributed to multiple recipients on an IP network. A multicast message is sent to a Class D IP address, which represents the multicast group.

IP Security (IPSec) – See "IPSec."

IP switching – A form of layer 3 cut-through switching pioneered by Ipsilon Corporation, which is now a division of Nokia. In IP switching, the first packet, or packets, of each information flow are routed as in a traditional router-based network. However, if the routers detect that the flow is likely to be long-lived (as, for example, an FTP connection), then a cut-through path is set up between the end stations.

IP telephony – An emerging set of technologies that enables voice, data, and video collaboration over existing IP-based LANs, WANs, and the Internet. It uses open IETF and ITU standards to move multimedia traffic over any network that uses IP.

IPC (inter process communication) – A capability supported by some operating systems that allows one process to communicate with another process. The processes can be running on the same computer or on different computers connected through a network. IPC enables one application to control another application, and for several applications to share the same data without interfering with one another. IPC is required in all multiprocessing systems, but it is not generally supported by single-process operating systems such as DOS. OS/2 and MS-Windows support an IPC mechanism called DDE.

IPSec (IP security) – A set of protocols being developed by the IETF to support secure exchange of packets at the IP layer. Once it's completed, IPSec is expected to be deployed widely to implement virtual private networks (VPNs). IPSec supports two encryption modes: Transport and Tunnel. Transport mode encrypts only the data portion (payload) of each packet, but leaves the header untouched. The more secure Tunnel mode encrypts both the header and the payload. On the receiving side, an IPSec-compliant device decrypts each packet. For IPSec to work, the sending and receiving devices must share a public key. This is accomplished through a protocol known as Internet Security Association and Key Management Protocol/Oakley (ISAKMP/Oakley), which allows the receiver to obtain a public key and authenticate the sender using digital certificates.

IPv6 (Internet Protocol version 6) – Referred to as IPng, which is short for Internet Protocol next generation, a new version of the Internet Protocol (IP) currently being reviewed in IETF standards committees. The current version of IP is version 4, so it is sometimes referred to as IPv4. IPng is designed as an evolutionary upgrade to the Internet Protocol and will, in fact, coexist with the older IPv4 for some time. IPng is designed to allow the Internet to grow steadily, both in terms of the number of hosts connected and the total amount of data traffic transmitted.

IPX (internetwork packet exchange) – A networking protocol used by the Novell NetWare operating systems. Like UDP/IP, IPX is a datagram protocol used for connectionless communications. Higher-level protocols, such as SPX and NCP, are used for additional error recovery services. The successor to IPX is the NetWare Link Services Protocol (NLSP).

ISA (industry standard architecture) – The bus architecture used in the IBM PC/XT and PC/AT. The AT version of the bus is called the AT bus and became a de facto industry standard. Starting in the early 1990s, ISA began to be replaced by the PCI local bus architecture. Most computers made today include both an AT bus for slower devices and a PCI bus for devices that need better bus performance. In

1993, Intel and Microsoft introduced a new version of the ISA specification called Plug and Play ISA. Plug and Play ISA enables the operating system to configure expansion boards automatically so that users do not need to fiddle with DIP switches and jumpers.

ISDN (integrated services digital network) – An international communications standard for sending voice, video, and data over digital telephone lines or normal telephone wires. ISDN supports data transfer rates of 64 Kbps (64,000 bits per second). Most ISDN lines offered by telephone companies give you two lines at once, called B channels. You can use one line for voice and the other for data, or you can use both lines for data to give you data rates of 128 Kbps, three times the data rate provided by today's fastest modems. The original version of ISDN employs baseband transmission. Another version, called B-ISDN, uses broadband transmission and is able to support transmission rates of 1.5 Mbps. B-ISDN requires fiber optic cables and is not widely available.

ISO (International Organization for Standardization) – Note that ISO is not an acronym; instead, the name derives from the Greek word *iso*, which means equal. Founded in 1946, ISO is an international organization composed of national standards bodies from over 75 countries. For example, ANSI (American National Standards Institute) is a member of ISO. ISO has defined a number of important computer standards, the most significant of which is perhaps OSI (Open Systems Interconnection), a standardized architecture for designing networks.

ISO reference model for open systems interconnection (OSI) – Developed by the International Standards Organization, it is the seven-layer model describing the process of network communication. It is intended to facilitate communications among computers from different manufacturers and to provide a common basis for coordinating international standards. Most modern protocols map to the OSI model to some extent, especially at the lower layers.

Isochronous – Signals that are dependent on some uniform timing or carry their own timing information embedded as part of the signal.

ISP (Internet service provider) – A company that provides access to the Internet. For a monthly fee, the service provider gives you a software package, username, password, and access phone number. Equipped with a modem, you can then log on to the Internet and browse the World Wide Web and USENET, and send and receive e-mail. In addition to serving individuals, ISPs also serve large companies, providing a direct connection from the companies' networks to the Internet. ISPs themselves are connected to one another through Network Access Points (NAPs). ISPs are also called IAPs (Internet Access Providers).

ITU (International Telecommunications Union) – An international body of member countries whose task is to define recommendations and standards relating to the international telecommunications industry. The fundamental standards for ATM have been defined and published by the ITU (previously CCITT).

ITU-TSS – See "International Telecommunications Union-Telecommunications Standards Sector."

IVR (interactive voice response) – Voice response combined with user input (touch tone or voice) to select required options for access to data, held either on the system or in a separate computer database.

Jitter – A short-term timing deviation.

Kbps – Thousands of bits per second.

L2TP (Layer 2 Tunneling Protocol) – An extension to the PPP protocol that enables ISPs to operate virtual private networks (VPNs). L2TP merges the best features of two other tunneling protocols: PPTP from Microsoft and L2F from Cisco Systems. Like PPTP, L2TP requires that the ISP's routers support the protocol.

label swapping – Also known as label switching. A general term for a layer 3 switching mechanism that attaches a label, or tag, to each packet. The label provides intermediate switches with the information needed to forward the packet toward its destination.

LAN (local area network) – A computer network that spans a relatively small area. Most LANs are confined to a single building or group of buildings. However, one LAN can be connected to other LANs over any distance via telephone lines and radio waves. A system of LANs connected in this way is called a wide area network (WAN). Most LANs connect workstations and personal computers. Each node (individual computer) in a LAN has its own CPU with which it executes programs, but it is also able to access data and devices anywhere on the LAN. This means that many users can share expensive devices, such as laser printers, as well as data. Users can also use the LAN to communicate with each other, by sending e-mail or engaging in chat sessions. There are many different types of LANs, Ethernet being the most common for PCs. Most Apple Macintosh networks are based on Apple's AppleTalk network system, which is built into Macintosh computers. LANs are capable of transmitting data at very fast rates – much faster than data can be transmitted over a telephone line – but the distances are limited, and there is also a limit on the number of computers that can be attached to a single LAN.

LAN emulation (LANE) – A set of protocols developed by the ATM Forum that allows legacy LAN protocols, such as Ethernet and token ring, and higher-layer protocols and applications that depend on LAN protocols, to work transparently across an ATM network. LANE translates address formats, emulates the LAN broadcast function, and automatically sets up ATM connections. LAN emulation retains all Ethernet and token ring drivers and adapters; no modifications need to be made to Ethernet or token ring end stations. Multiple emulated LANs (ELANs) within the same ATM network are common. Also, single stations can belong to multiple ELANs.

LAN emulation client (LEC) – An end device in a LANE application. This can be a workstation or server with an ATM NIC, or, more commonly, a LAN switch with an ATM uplink.

LAN emulation configuration server (LECS) – A process within ATM LAN emulation that assigns individual LAN emulation clients to emulated LANs.

LAN emulation server (LES) – A process within ATM LAN emulation that translates between MAC addresses and ATM addresses.

latency – The amount of time it takes a packet to travel from source to destination. Together, latency and bandwidth define the speed and capacity of a network.

Layer 2 Tunneling Protocol – See "L2TP."

LDAP (Lightweight Directory Access Protocol) – A set of protocols for accessing information directories. LDAP is based on the standards contained within the X.500 standard, but is significantly simpler. And, unlike X.500, LDAP supports TCP/IP, which is necessary for any type of Internet access. Because it's a simpler version of X.500, LDAP is sometimes called X.500-lite. Although not yet widely implemented, LDAP should eventually make it possible for almost any application running on virtually any computer platform to obtain directory information, such as e-mail addresses and public keys. Because LDAP is an open protocol, applications need not worry about the type of server hosting the directory.

leased line – A transmission facility, which is leased by an end user from a public carrier, and which is dedicated to that user's traffic. Typically, frequency synchronization is maintained from one end of the circuit to the other. Leased line circuits are generally used less today, while public data networks are more common.

LEC – See "LAN emulation client."

LECS – See "LAN emulation configuration server."

LES – See "LAN emulation server."

Lightweight Directory Access Protocol – See "LDAP."

LLC – See "Logical Link Control."

lobe port – In token ring, a port on a MAU or hub to which the cable from a device attaches. Lobe ports must receive a specific voltage from the attached device in order to allow the device into the ring.

local area network – See "LAN."

locator services – Use of a code such as IP or telephone area code to locate local information from a database.

logical agent – Agent who is independent of the terminal at which he or she logs on.

Logical Link Control (LLC) – A sublayer of layer 2 that provides a connection between the layer 3 protocol, such as IP or IPX, and the MAC layer protocol. LLC2, one form of LLC, provides a connection-oriented service.

loopback – A testing method in which the transmitted data is looped back to the receiver.

MAC Address (media access control address) – A hardware address that uniquely identifies each node of a network. In IEEE 802 networks, the Data Link Control (DLC) layer of the OSI Reference Model is divided into two sublayers: the Logical Link Control (LLC) layer and the media access control (MAC) layer. The MAC layer interfaces directly with the network media. Consequently, each different type of network media requires a different MAC layer. On networks that do not conform to the IEEE 802 standards but do conform to the OSI Reference Model, the node address is called the Data Link Control (DLC) address.

MAC (media access control) Layer – A sublayer of layer 2 that deals with the issues specific to a particular type of LAN, e.g., Ethernet or token ring.

MAC-Layer Bridge – A device used to forward data between LANs at layer 2 by automatically filtering out traffic which is local to each LAN, while forwarding on traffic which is not local to each LAN. All broadcasts and multicasts, as well as all traffic with a destination address that has not been learned by the bridge, are forwarded.

MAC-Layer Protocol – See "media access control."

MAC-layer switching – LAN data transferred through a network based on the source and destination addresses contained in the MAC header of the frame. MAC-layer switching is essentially the same as bridging, but almost always employs dedicated hardware to perform the switching.

main distribution frame (MDF) – In a structured building wiring system, the central point for cabling throughout the building. Typically, multiple IDFs are located in wiring closets connected to a central MDF.

MAN (metropolitan area network) – A data network designed for a town or city. In terms of geographic breadth, MANs are larger than local area networks (LANs), but smaller than wide area networks (WANs). MANs are usually characterized by very high-speed connections using fiber optical cable or other digital media.

management information base – See "MIB."

MAPI (messaging application programming interface) – A system built into Microsoft Windows that enables different e-mail applications to work together to distribute mail. As long as both applications are MAPI-enabled, they can share mail messages with each other.

maximum lobe length (MLL) – The maximum allowable distance between a node and a MAU or hub on a token ring network.

maximum transfer unit (MTU) – An IAB discovery protocol that polls the network for the highest MTU possible between a source and a destination. The result is an optimized frame size that prevents fragmentation and yields better end-to-end throughput.

Mbps – Millions of bits per second.

MDF – See "main distribution frame."

media access control (MAC) – The way in which LAN workstations share access to a transmission medium. MAC-layer protocols include Ethernet, token ring, and FDDI. "MAC" in this case has absolutely nothing to do with the Apple Macintosh computer.

media access control address – See "MAC Address."

media access unit – In token ring, a hub which interconnects the devices connected to the ring, and in turn connects to other MAUs through Ring In/Ring Out connections. Generally a MAU is not managed via software.

media gateway – Data communications equipment operating at the edge of emerging multiservice packet networks. Control and management is by software programs which are known as call agents or media gateway controllers.

Megaco – Also called H.248. Megaco is a proposed standard for converged networks to be used in media gateways. It is the first standard to be developed and acknowledged by both the IETF and the ITU.

message – Auditory data placed in a voice mailbox. Messages may be left by callers, subscribers, systems, or system administrators.

metropolitan area network – A network spanning a geographical area greater than a LAN, but less than a WAN.

MGCP (Media Gateway Control Protocol) – A protocol designed to bridge between current circuit-based public switched telephone networks (PSTN) and emerging Internet Protocol (IP) technology-based networks.

MIB (management information base) – A database of objects that can be monitored by a network management system. Both SNMP and RMON use standardized MIB formats that allow any SNMP and RMON tools to monitor any device defined by a MIB.

micro-segmentation – The process of dividing up LAN segments to contain fewer users on a shared media LAN, increasing performance by reducing congestion. It is generally implemented with LAN switches.

middleware – Software that connects two otherwise separate applications. For example, there are a number of middleware products that link a database system to a Web server. This allows users to request data from the database using forms displayed on a Web browser, and it enables the Web server to return dynamic Web pages based on the user's requests and profile.

mid-level networks – The transit networks that make up the second level of the Internet hierarchy. They connect the subnetworks to the backbone networks. Also known as regional.

million instructions per second (MIPS) – See "MIPS."

MIME (Multipurpose Internet Mail Extensions) – A specification for formatting non-ASCII messages so that they can be sent over the Internet. Many e-mail clients now support MIME, which enables them to send and receive graphics, audio, and video files via the Internet mail system. In addition, MIME supports messages in character sets other than ASCII. There are many predefined MIME types, such as GIF graphics files and PostScript files. It is also possible to define your own MIME types. In addition to e-mail applications, Web browsers also support various MIME types. This enables the browser to display or output files that are not in HTML format. MIME was defined in 1992 by the Internet Engineering Task Force (IETF). A new version, called S/MIME, supports encrypted messages.

MIPS (million instructions per second) – An old measure of a computer's speed and power, MIPS measures roughly the number of machine instructions that a computer can execute in one second. However, different instructions require more or less time than others, and there is no standard method for measuring MIPS. In addition, MIPS refers only to the CPU speed, whereas real applications are generally limited by other factors, such as I/O speed. A machine with a high MIPS rating, therefore, might not run a particular application any faster than a machine with a low MIPS rating. For all these reasons, MIPS ratings are not used often anymore. In fact, some people jokingly claim that MIPS really stands for Meaningless Indicator of Performance. Despite these problems, a MIPS rating can give you a general idea of a computer's speed.

MLL – See "maximum lobe length."

modem (modulator-demodulator) – A modem is a device or program that enables a computer to transmit data over telephone lines. Computer information is stored digitally, whereas information transmitted over telephone lines is transmitted in the form of analog waves. A modem converts between these two forms. Fortunately, there is one standard interface for connecting external modems to computers called RS-232. Consequently, any external modem can be attached to any computer that has an RS-232 port, which almost all personal computers have. There are also modems that come as an expansion board that you can insert into a vacant expansion slot. These are sometimes called onboard or internal modems. While the modem interfaces are standardized, a number of different protocols for formatting data to be transmitted over telephone lines exist. Some, like CCITT V.34, are official standards, while others have been developed by private companies. Most modems have built-in support for the more common protocols – at slow data transmission speeds at least, most modems can communicate with each other. At high transmission speeds, however, the protocols are less standardized.

modulator-demodulator – See "modem."

MPLS (Multiprotocol Label Switching) – An IETF initiative that integrates layer 2 information about network links (bandwidth, latency, utilization) into layer 3 (IP) within a particular autonomous system – or ISP – in order to simplify and improve IP-packet exchange. MPLS gives network operators a great deal of flexibility to divert and route traffic around link failures, congestion, and bottlenecks. From a QoS standpoint, ISPs will better be able to manage different kinds of data streams based on priority and service plan. For instance, those who subscribe to a premium service plan, or those who receive a lot of streaming media or high-bandwidth content, can see minimal latency and packet loss. When packets enter an MPLS-based network, Label Edge Routers (LERs) give them a label (identifier). These labels not only contain information based on the routing table entry (i.e., destination, bandwidth, delay, and other metrics), but also refer to the IP header field (source IP address), layer 4 socket number information, and differentiated service. Once this classification is complete and mapped, different packets are assigned to corresponding Labeled Switch Paths (LSPs), where Label Switch Routers (LSRs) place outgoing labels on the packets. With these LSPs, network operators can divert and route traffic based on data stream type and Internet-access customer.

MPOA (Multiprotocol over ATM) – A specification that enables ATM services to be integrated with existing local area networks (LANs) that use Ethernet, token-ring, or TCP/IP protocols. The goal of MPOA is to allow different LANs to send packets to each other via an ATM backbone. Unlike other techniques, such as LAN Emulation (LANE), which operates at layer 2 of the OSI Reference Model, MPOA operates at layer 3.

MTU – See "maximum transfer unit."

multicast – A form of broadcast in which a packet is delivered to a predefined subset of all possible destinations. A specific multicast destination address is used.

multilink PPP – A form of PPP that uses inverse multiplexing of multiple wide area circuits to achieve a higher-bandwidth virtual connection.

multimode – A form of fiber optic cabling in which light is able to follow multiple paths as it traverses the cable. It is less expensive, and with a lower maximum rate and distance, than single mode fiber optic cable.

multiplex – To transmit two or more messages or message streams on a single channel, typically through the use of frequency-division multiplexing, time division multiplexing, or statistical time division multiplexing.

multiplexor – See "MUX."

Multiprotocol Label Switching (MPLS) – See "MPLS."

Multiprotocol over ATM – See "MPOA."

Multipurpose Internet Mail Extensions (MIME) – See "MIME."

Multi-station Access Unit (also abbreviated as MSAU) – A token ring network device that physically connects network computers in a star topology while retaining the logical ring structure. One of the problems with the token ring topology is that a single nonoperating node can break the ring. The MAU solves this problem because it has the ability to short out nonoperating nodes and maintain the ring structure. A MAU is a special type of hub.

Multi-Vendor Integration Protocol (MVIP) – Proprietary telephony bus standard.

MUX (multiplexor) – A communications device that multiplexes (combines several signals for transmission over a single medium). A demultiplexor completes the process by separating multiplexed signals from a transmission line. Frequently a multiplexor and demultiplexor are combined into a single device capable of processing both outgoing and incoming signals. A multiplexor is sometimes called a MUX.

MVIP (Multi-Vendor Integration Protocol) – Proprietary telephony bus standard.

NAT (Network Address Translation) – An Internet standard that enables a local area network (LAN) to use one set of IP addresses for internal traffic and a second set of addresses for external traffic. A NAT box located where the LAN meets the Internet makes all necessary IP address translations. NAT serves two main purposes: it provides a type of firewall by hiding internal IP addresses, and it enables a company to use more internal IP addresses. Since they're used internally only, there's no possibility of conflict with IP addresses used by other companies and organizations. NAT allows a company to combine multiple ISDN connections into a single Internet connection. NAT is an official IETF standard, specified in RFC 1631.

NDIS (network driver interface specification) – Developed by Microsoft for writing hardware-independent drivers. NDIS allows multiple protocol stacks (e.g., TCP/IP and NetWare) to share a single network interface module and the software which supports it.

NEBS (network equipment-building system) – Bleacher has devised a three-tier system of criteria for NEBS compliance to ensure that the telecommunications equipment that various operating companies purchase is suitable for their needs, and to reduce the time and expense for manufacturers. The main purpose of this three-tier system is to identify criteria levels and the impact of any nonconforming result. The levels cover safety, environmental, and equipment operability under increasingly rigorous conditions.

NetWare – A protocol suite developed by Novell Corporation. The second most widely used protocol in LANs, after TCP/IP.

NetWare Loadable Module (NLM) – Software that enhances or provides additional functions in a NetWare 3.x or higher server. Support for database engines, workstations, network protocols, fax and print servers are examples. The NetWare 2.x counterpart is a VAP.

Network Address Translation – See "NAT."

Network File System – See "NFS."

Network Interface Card – See "NIC."

network operating system – See "NOS."

network segment – A portion of a network set apart from other network sections by a bridge, router, or switch. Each network segment supports a single medium access protocol.

NFS (Network File System) – An open operating system designed by Sun Microsystems that allows all network users to access shared files stored on computers of different types. NFS provides access to shared files through an interface called the Virtual File System (VFS) that runs on top of TCP/IP. Users can manipulate shared files as if they were stored locally on the user's own hard disk. With NFS, computers connected to a network operate as clients while accessing remote files, and as servers while providing remote users access to local shared files. The NFS standards are publicly available and widely used.

NHRP (Next Hop Resolution Protocol) – An IAB protocol that provides a cut-through service between end stations in an ATM network.

NIC (Network Interface Card) – An expansion board you insert into a computer so the computer can be connected to a network. Most NICs are designed for a particular type of network, protocol, and media, although some can serve multiple networks.

NLM (NetWare Loadable Module) – Software that enhances or provides additional functions in a NetWare 3.*x* or higher server. Support for database engines, workstations, network protocols, fax and print servers are examples. The NetWare 2.*x* counterpart is a VAP.

node – In networks, a processing location. A node can be a computer or some other device, such as a printer. Every node has a unique network address, sometimes called a Data Link Control (DLC) address or media access control (MAC) address.

non-real time variable bit rate (nrt-VBR) – A form of ATM transmission in which clock frequency can vary, but mean variation of delay between cells is guaranteed. A typical use is transmission of stored video.

NOS (network operating system) – An operating system that includes special functions for connecting computers and devices into a local area network (LAN). Some operating systems, such as UNIX and the Mac OS, have networking functions built in. The term network operating system, however, is generally reserved for software that enhances a basic operating system by adding networking features. For example, some popular NOSs for DOS and Windows systems include Novell NetWare, Artisoft's LANtastic, Microsoft LAN Manager, and Windows NT.

object linking and embedding (OLE) – See "OLE."

OC-3 – A standard ATM/SONET rate and framing specification; approximately 155 Mbps.

OC-12 – A standard ATM/SONET rate and framing specification; approximately 622 Mbps.

ODBC (Open DataBase Connectivity) – A standard database access method developed by Microsoft Corporation. The goal of ODBC is to make it possible to access any data from any application, regardless of which database management system (DBMS) is handling the data. ODBC manages this by inserting a middle layer, called a database driver, between an application and the DBMS. The purpose of this layer is to translate the application's data queries into commands that the DBMS understands. For this to work, both the application and the DBMS must be ODBC-compliant – that is, the application must be capable of issuing ODBC commands and the DBMS must be capable of responding to them. Since version 2.0, the standard supports SAG SQL.

ODI (Open Datalink Interface) – The Novell standard for hardware-independent drivers. ODI can simultaneously support multiple protocol stacks.

OLE (object linking and embedding) – Pronounced as separate letters or as oh-leh. OLE is a compound document standard developed by Microsoft Corporation. It enables you to create objects with one application and then link or embed them in a second application. Embedded objects retain their original format and links to the application that created them. Support for OLE is built into the Windows and Macintosh operating systems. A competing compound document standard developed jointly by IBM, Apple Computer, and other computer firms is called OpenDoc.

Open DataBase Connectivity (ODBC) – See "ODBC."

Open Shortest Path First – See "OSPF."

Open System Interconnection – See "OSI."

operating system (OS) – See "OS."

optical bypass – A capability in FDDI for enhanced failure resistance. A DAS station, such as a concentrator, generates a DC voltage to an attached mechanical optical bypass unit, through which pass all optical signals between the station and the ring. If the station fails, the voltage drops, and the optical bypass unit defaults to a state in which the ring optically passes straight through the bypass unit and cuts out the station.

OS (operating system) – The most important program that runs on a computer. Every general-purpose computer must have an operating system to run other programs. Operating systems perform basic tasks, such as recognizing input from the keyboard, sending output to the display screen, keeping track of files and directories on the disk, and controlling peripheral devices such as disk drives and printers. For large systems, the operating system has even greater responsibilities and powers. It is like a traffic cop – it makes sure that different programs and users running at the same time do not interfere with each other. The operating system is also responsible for security, ensuring that unauthorized users do not access the system.

OSI (Open System Interconnection) – An ISO standard for worldwide communications that defines a networking framework for implementing protocols in seven layers. Control is passed from one layer to the next, starting at the application layer in one station, proceeding to the bottom layer, over the channel to the next station, and back up the hierarchy. At one time, most vendors agreed to support OSI in one form or another, but OSI was too loosely defined and proprietary standards were too entrenched. Except for the OSI-compliant X.400 and X.500 e-mail and directory standards, which are widely used, what was once thought to become the universal communications standard now serves as the teaching model for all other protocols. Most of the functionality in the OSI model exists in all communications systems, although two or three OSI layers may be incorporated into one. OSI is also referred to as the OSI Reference Model or just the OSI Model.

OSPF (Open Shortest Path First) – A routing protocol developed for IP networks based on the shortest path first or link-state algorithm. Routers use link-state algorithms to send routing information to all nodes in an internetwork by calculating the shortest path to each node based on a topography of the Internet constructed by each node. Each router sends that portion of the routing table (keeps track of routes to particular network destinations) that describes the state of its own links, and it also sends the complete routing structure (topography). The advantage of shortest path first algorithms is that they result in smaller more frequent updates everywhere. They converge quickly, thus preventing such problems as routing loops and Count-to-Infinity (when routers continuously increment the hop count to a particular network). This makes for a stable network. The disadvantage of shortest path first algorithms is that they require a lot of CPU power and memory. In the end, the advantages outweigh the disadvantages. OSPF Version 2 is defined in RFC 1583. It is rapidly replacing RIP on the Internet.

outbound – Making a call, usually by an agent.

packet – (1) A variable-length layer 3 protocol entity containing address and control information, plus data. Examples include IP and IPX packets. (2) A variable-length layer 2 protocol entity containing address and other control information, plus data. Examples include Ethernet and token ring packets. These are also referred to as "frames," and in this glossary the term "packet" generally refers to a layer 3 entity.

packet filtering – The ability of a bridge, router, or gateway to limit propagation of packets between two or more interconnected networks.

packet switching – A communications method in which variable-length packets are individually routed between hosts.

PAN (personal area network) – PAN is a wireless communication system that allows electronic devices on and near the human body to exchange digital information through near-field electrostatic coupling. Information is transmitted by modulating electric fields and electrostatically (capacitively) coupling picoamp currents into the body.

partial packet discard (PPD) – A process of intelligent cell discard that occurs in an ATM switch when its buffer capacity is exceeded. PPD discards traffic for whole upper-layer PDUs when congestion is encountered. This is done by identifying which cells have been segmented from an individual frame (or packet) and discarding those cells associated with that frame.

PBX (private branch exchange) – Short for private branch exchange, a private telephone network used within an enterprise. Users of the PBX share a certain number of outside lines for making telephone calls external to the PBX. Most medium-sized and larger companies use a PBX because it's much less expensive than connecting an external telephone line to every telephone in the organization. In addition, it's easier to call someone within a PBX because the number you need to dial is typically just 3 or 4 digits. A new variation on the PBX theme is the Centrex, which is a PBX with all switching occurring at a local telephone office instead of at the company's premises.

PCI (Peripheral Component Interconnect) – A local bus standard developed by Intel Corporation. Most modern PCs include a PCI bus in addition to a more general ISA expansion bus. Many analysts, however, believe that PCI will eventually supplant ISA entirely. PCI is also used on newer versions of the Macintosh computer. PCI is a 64-bit bus, though it is usually implemented as a 32-bit bus. It can run at clock speeds of 33 or 66 MHz. At 32 bits and 33 MHz, it yields a throughput rate of 133 Mbps. Although it was developed by Intel, PCI is not tied to any particular family of microprocessors.

PCM (pulse code modulation) – A sampling technique for digitizing analog signals, especially audio signals. PCM samples the signal 8,000 times a second; each sample is represented by 8 bits for a total of 64 Kbps. There are two standards for coding the sample level. The Mu-Law standard is used in North America and Japan while the A-Law standard is used in most other countries. PCM is used with T-1 and T-3 carrier systems. These carrier systems combine the PCM signals from many lines and transmit them over a single cable or other medium.

PCR – See "peak cell rate."

PCX – See "private communications exchange."

PDU – See "protocol data unit."

peak cell rate (PCR) – The maximum rate at which ATM cells can be transmitted across a virtual circuit, specified in cells per second and defined by the interval between the transmission of the last bit of one cell and the first bit of the next.

Peripheral Component Interconnect – See "PCI."

permanent virtual circuit (PVC) – See "PVC."

personal information manager (PIM) – See "PIM."

personal wireless telecommunication – See "PWT."

phase jitter – The result of repeaters regenerating a signal that has experienced envelope delay in transmission through electronics and cable. Phase jitter is removed by processing the data stream through a buffer and reclocking it.

PIM (personal information manager) – A type of software application designed to help users organize random bits of information. Although the category is fuzzy, most PIMs enable you to enter various kinds of textual notes – reminders, lists, dates – and to link these bits of information together in useful ways. Many PIMs also include calendar, scheduling, and calculator programs.

PKI (Public Key Infrastructure) – Includes all policies and procedures for sending data securely with public key encryption. A PKI uses public and private keys, digital certificates, and a certificate authority (CA).

plain old telephone service (POTS) – Refers to the standard telephone service that most homes use. In contrast, telephone services based on high-speed, digital communications lines, such as ISDN and FDDI, are not POTS. The main distinctions between POTS and non-POTS services are speed and bandwidth. POTS is generally restricted to about 52 Kbps (52,000 bits per second). The POTS network is also called the public switched telephone network (PSTN).

platform – The underlying hardware or software for a system. For example, the platform might be an Intel 80486 processor running DOS Version 6.0. The platform could also be UNIX machines on an Ethernet network. The platform defines a standard around which a system can be developed. Once the platform has been defined, software developers can produce appropriate software and managers can purchase appropriate hardware and applications. The term is often used as a synonym of operating system. The term cross-platform refers to applications, formats, or devices that work on different platforms. For example, a cross-platform programming environment enables a programmer to develop programs for many platforms at once.

PNNI (Private Network-to-Node Interface) – An advanced, dynamic routing protocol that operates between ATM switches. It is based on link-state protocols, such as OSPF, with extensions that enable switches to advertise their own capabilities, such as capacity and delay.

Point-to-Point Protocol – See "PPP."

Point-to-Point Tunneling Protocol (PPTP) – See "PPTP."

POP (Post Office Protocol) – A protocol used to retrieve e-mail from a mail server. Most e-mail applications (sometimes called an e-mail client) use the POP protocol, although some can use the newer IMAP (Internet Message Access Protocol). There are two versions of POP. The first, called POP2, became a standard in the mid-'80s and requires SMTP to send messages. The newer version, POP3, can be used with or without SMTP.

port – A communications path into or out of a voice processing system, switch, or computer.

port mirroring – A capability, typically in a switch, that allows a network manager to replicate the real-time data flow from one port at another port. Typically, the second port is attached to a protocol analyzer.

Post Office Protocol (POP) – See "POP."

POTS (plain old telephone service) – Refers to the standard telephone service that most homes use. In contrast, telephone services based on high-speed, digital communications lines, such as ISDN and FDDI, are not POTS. The main distinctions between POTS and non-POTS services are speed and bandwidth. POTS is generally restricted to about 52 Kbps (52,000 bits per second). The POTS network is also called the public switched telephone network (PSTN).

PPD – See "partial packet discard."

PPP (Point-to-Point Protocol) – The successor to SLIP, PPP is a layer 2 protocol which provides router-to-router and computer-to-network connections across a wide area circuit, generally in a TCP/IP network.

pps – Packets per second.

PPTP (Point-to-Point Tunneling Protocol) – A new technology for creating virtual private networks (VPNs), developed jointly by Microsoft Corporation, U.S. Robotics, and several remote access vendor companies, known collectively as the PPTP Forum. A VPN is a private network of computers that uses the public Internet to connect some nodes. Because the Internet is essentially an open network, the Point-to-Point Tunneling Protocol (PPTP) is used to ensure that messages transmitted from one VPN node to another are secure. With PPTP, users can dial in to their corporate network via the Internet. Although PPTP has been submitted to the IETF for standardization, it is currently available only on networks served by a Windows NT 4.0 server and Linux.

predictive dialer – A device that initiates an outbound call, to be answered by an agent, based on factors such as the number of agents, average call connect time, average successful call rate, etc.

predictive dialing — A device that displays a list of prospects to the agent, from which the agent can chose a call to be set up.

Primary Rate Interface (PRI) — An ISDN subscriber interface that operates over a copper or fiber cable connection, providing one control (D) channel at 64 Kbps, and 23 (North America) or 30 (international) bearer (B) channels, at 64 Kbps each. The B channels are sometimes combined to provide various transmission rates. PRI is the interface commonly provided to business ISDN subscribers.

private branch exchange — See "PBX."

private communications exchange (PCX) — This is an IP-based system that is now replacing PBXs. It brings together an organization's networking and information technology systems with the Internet, aligning voice communications more tightly with computer applications.

protocol — An agreed-upon format for transmitting data between two devices. The protocol determines: the type of error checking to be used, data compression method (if any), how the sending device will indicate that it has finished sending a message, and how the receiving device will indicate that it has received a message. There are a variety of standard protocols from which programmers can choose. Each has particular advantages and disadvantages; for example, some are simpler than others, some are more reliable, and some are faster. From a user's point of view, the only interesting aspect about protocols is that your computer or device must support the right ones if you want to communicate with other computers. The protocol can be implemented either in hardware or in software.

protocol converter — A device for translating the protocol of one network or device to the corresponding protocol of another network or device. A protocol converter enables equipment with different conventions to communicate with one another.

protocol data unit (PDU) — A defined data unit passed from one protocol layer to another. Each protocol layer encapsulates the PDU from the layer above within the information that it adds.

Protocol Independent Multicast (PIM) Dense Mode — An IAB multicast protocol similar to DVMRP in that it uses Reverse Path Forwarding but does not require any particular unicast protocol. It is useful when multicast senders/receivers are in close proximity to one another, there are few senders and many receivers, the volume of multicast traffic is high, and the stream of multicast traffic is constant.

Protocol Independent Multicast (PIM) Sparse Mode — An IAB multicast protocol that works by defining a rendezvous point that is common to both sender and receiver. Sender and receiver initiate communication at the rendezvous point, and when flow begins it occurs over an optimized path. This is useful when there are few receivers in a group, senders and receivers are separated by WAN links, and the traffic is intermittent.

protocol stack — Set of network protocol layers that work together. The OSI Reference Model that defines seven protocol layers is often called a stack, as is the set of TCP/IP protocols that define communication over the Internet. The term stack also refers to the actual software that processes the protocols. So, for example, programmers sometimes talk about loading a stack, which means to load the software required to use a specific set of protocols. Another common phrase is binding a stack, which refers to linking a set of network protocols to a network interface card (NIC). Every NIC must have at least one stack bound to it. In Windows, the TCP/IP stack is implemented by the Winsock DLL.

proxy – The mechanism whereby one system acts for another system in responding to protocol requests.

Proxy ARP – The technique in which one device, usually a router, answers and issues ARP requests for another device.

PSTN (Public Switched Telephone Network) – Refers to the international telephone system based on copper wires carrying analog voice data. This is in contrast to newer telephone networks based on digital technologies, such as ISDN and FDDI. Telephone service carried by the PSTN is often called plain old telephone service (POTS).

Public Switched Telephone Network – See "PSTN."

Pulse code modulation – See "PCM."

pulse dialing – A signaling method between a phone and a switch, where each digit sent by the phone is represented by a series of pulses.

PVC (permanent virtual circuit) – A virtual circuit that is permanently available. The only difference between a PVC and a switched virtual circuit (SVC) is that an SVC must be re-established each time data is to be sent. Once the data has been sent, the SVC disappears. PVCs are more efficient for connections between hosts that communicate frequently. PVCs play a central role in frame relay networks. They're also supported in some other types of networks, such as X.25.

PWT (personal wireless telecommunications) – Also known as personal wireless telephony. A U.S. cordless telephony standard for in-building wireless communications systems, PWT is a variant of the DECT (Digital European Cordless Telecommunications) standard. PWT is an air interface that operates in the unlicensed PCS (personal communications services) 1.9 GHz radio band. PWT(E) is an enhanced version that operates in the licensed PCS bands.

QoS (Quality of Service) – A networking term that specifies a guaranteed throughput level. One of the biggest advantages of ATM over competing technologies such as frame relay and Fast Ethernet is that it supports QoS levels. This allows ATM providers to guarantee to their customers that end-to-end latency will not exceed a specified level.

Quality of Service (QoS) – See "QoS."

RADIUS (Remote Access Dial-In User Service) – An IAB UDP-based protocol used for carrying authentication, authorization, accounting, and security information between a client and a server. Developed to better manage large serial line and modem pools, RADIUS leverages a single user database containing user ID/password and user authorized server types. The client/server model supports security via PAP, CHAP, UNIX login, and other authentication schemes, such as challenge/response systems.

RAID (redundant array of inexpensive disks) – A category of disk drives that employ two or more drives in combination for fault tolerance and performance. RAID disk drives are used frequently on servers but aren't generally necessary for personal computers.

RAM (random access memory) – Pronounced "ram," a type of computer memory that can be accessed randomly, that is, any byte of memory can be accessed without touching the preceding bytes. RAM is the most common type of memory found in computers and other devices, such as printers.

random access memory – See "RAM."

random early discard (RED) – A process of intelligent cell discard that occurs within an ATM switch when its buffer capacity is exceeded. RED discards cells in a round-robin fashion among affected connections.

RAS (remote access services) – A feature built into Windows NT that enables users to log into an NT-based LAN using a modem, X.25 connection, or WAN link. RAS works with several major network protocols, including TCP/IP, IPX, and Netbeui. To use RAS from a remote node, you need a RAS client program, which is built into most versions of Windows, or any PPP client software. For example, most remote control programs work with RAS.

read-only memory (ROM) – Pronounced "rahm," computer memory on which data has been prerecorded. Once data has been written onto a ROM chip, it cannot be removed and can only be read. Unlike main memory (RAM), ROM retains its contents even when the computer is turned off. ROM is referred to as being non-volatile, whereas RAM is volatile. Most personal computers contain a small amount of ROM that stores critical programs such as the program that boots the computer. In addition, ROMs are used extensively in calculators and peripheral devices such as laser printers, whose fonts are often stored in ROMs. A variation of a ROM is a PROM (programmable read-only memory). PROMs are manufactured as blank chips on which data can be written with a special device called a PROM programmer.

real time variable bit rate (rt-VBR) – A form of ATM transmission in which clock frequency can vary, but maximum delay and maximum variation of delay between cells are guaranteed. A typical use is real-time videoconferencing.

Real-Time Transport Protocol – See "RTP."

redundant array of inexpensive disks – See "RAID."

remote access services – See "RAS."

remote monitoring – See "RMON."

remote procedure call – See "RPC."

repeater – A device which propagates electrical signals from one segment to another without routing, buffering, or filtering.

Request for Comments – See "RFC."

Resource Reservation Setup Protocol – See "RSVP."

RFC (Request for Comments) – A series of notes about the Internet, started in 1969 (when the Internet was the ARPANET). An RFC can be submitted by anyone. Eventually, if it gains enough interest, it may evolve into an Internet standard. Each RFC is designated by an RFC number. Once published, an RFC never changes. Modifications to an original RFC are assigned a new RFC number.

rich text format – See "RTF."

RIF – See "routing information field."

ring – A LAN topology in which each device is connected to two other workstations, with the connections forming a ring. Data is sent from device to device around the ring in a single direction. Each device acts as a repeater by resending messages to other devices. Examples include token ring and FDDI.

ring error monitor for token ring – A ring resident function that maintains statistical records of error conditions on the ring operation.

ring in and ring out (RI/RO) – The token ring connectors on the MAU that connect it to other MAUs. Unlike lobe ports, Ring In/Ring Out ports support a "wrap" capability; if an RI/RO cable is disconnected, the ring wraps back on itself, maintaining viability.

RIP (Routing Information Protocol) – A protocol defined by RFC 1058 that specifies how routers exchange routing table information. With RIP, routers periodically exchange entire tables. Because this is inefficient, RIP is gradually being replaced by a newer protocol called Open Shortest Path First (OSPF).

riser cabling – That portion of a building's cabling system that extends from the main distribution frame to the wiring closets. For data, this is often fiber optic cable. For voice, it is fiber optic cable if the PBX is distributed, and twisted pair copper cable otherwise.

RJ-11 – A standard connector commonly used to terminate voice connections.

RJ-45 – A standard connector commonly used to terminate data connections.

RMON (remote monitoring) – A network management protocol that allows network information to be gathered at a single workstation. Whereas SNMP gathers network data from a single type of Management Information Base (MIB), RMON 1 defines nine additional MIBs that provide a much richer set of data about network usage. For RMON to work, network devices, such as hubs and switches, must be designed to support it. The newest version of RMON, RMON 2, provides data about traffic at the network layer in addition to the physical layer. This allows administrators to analyze traffic by protocol.

ROM (read-only memory) – Pronounced "rahm," computer memory on which data has been prerecorded. Once data has been written onto a ROM chip, it cannot be removed and can only be read. Unlike main memory (RAM), ROM retains its contents even when the computer is turned off. ROM is referred to as being nonvolatile, whereas RAM is volatile. Most personal computers contain a small amount of ROM that stores critical programs. A variation of a ROM is a PROM (programmable read-only memory). PROMs are manufactured as blank chips on which data can be written with a special device called a PROM programmer.

round trip delay – A measure of the delay in a network from request sent to reply received.

route – The path that network traffic takes from its source to its destination.

router – A layer 3 device responsible for making decisions regarding which of several paths network traffic will follow. To do this, it uses a routing protocol to gain information about the network, and algorithms to choose the best route based on several criteria (known as routing metrics). Routers interconnect subnets.

routing – The process of delivering a message across a network or networks via the most appropriate path.

routing domain – A set of routers exchanging routing information within administrative boundaries.

routing information field (RIF) – A field in a token ring or FDDI frame header that provides information used by source-routing bridges to move the frame through a network. The RIF specifies a series of interleaved ring numbers and bridge numbers.

Routing Information Protocol (RIP) – A protocol defined by RFC 1058 that specifies how routers exchange routing table information. With RIP, routers periodically exchange entire tables. Because this is inefficient, RIP is gradually being replaced by a newer protocol called Open Shortest Path First (OSPF).

RPC (remote procedure call) – A type of protocol that allows a program on one computer to execute a program on a server computer. Using RPC, a system developer need not develop specific procedures for the server. The client program sends a message to the server with appropriate arguments and the server returns a message containing the results of the program executed. Sun Microsystems developed the first widely used RPC protocol as part of their Open Network Computing (ONC) architecture in the early 1980s. The specification has been handed off to the Internet Engineering Task Force (IETF) as a step toward making ONC RPC an Internet standard. Two newer object-oriented methods for programs to communicate with each other, CORBA and DCOM, provide the same types of capabilities as traditional RPCs.

RSVP (Resource Reservation Setup Protocol) – A new Internet protocol being developed to enable the Internet to support specified quality of service (QoS). Using RSVP, an application will be able to reserve resources along a route from source to destination. RSVP-enabled routers will then schedule and prioritize packets to fulfill the QoS. RSVP is a chief component of a new type of Internet being developed, known broadly as an integrated services Internet. The general idea is to enhance the Internet to support transmission of real-time data.

RTF (rich text format) – A standard developed by Microsoft Corporation for specifying formatting of documents. RTF files are actually ASCII files with special commands to indicate formatting information, such as fonts and margins. Other document formatting languages include the Hypertext Markup Language (HTML), which is used to define documents on the World Wide Web, and the Standard Generalized Markup Language (SGML), which is a more robust version of HTML.

RTP (Real-Time Transport Protocol) – An Internet protocol for transmitting real-time data such as audio and video. RTP itself does not guarantee real-time delivery of data, but it does provide mechanisms for the sending and receiving applications to support streaming data. Typically, RTP runs on top of the UDP protocol, although the specification is general enough to support other transport protocols. RTP has received wide industry support. Netscape intends to base its LiveMedia technology on RTP, and Microsoft claims that its NetMeeting product support RTP.

rt-VBR – See "real time variable bit rate."

S/T Interface – A physical interface in an ISDN Basic Rate service that uses two copper pairs.

SAP – See "Service Advertising Protocol."

SAR – See "segmentation and reassembly."

SAS – See "single attached station."

SCAI – ANSI CTI standard.

SCSA (Signal Computing System Architecture) – PC telephony bus protocol promoted by Dialogic.

SCSI (Small Computer System Interface) – Pronounced "scuzzy," SCSI is a parallel interface standard used by Apple Macintosh computers, PCs, and many UNIX systems for attaching peripheral devices to computers. Nearly all Apple Macintosh computers, excluding only the earliest Macs and the recent iMac, come with a SCSI port for attaching devices such as disk drives and printers. SCSI interfaces provide for faster data transmission rates (up to 80 megabytes per second) than standard serial and parallel ports. In addition, you can attach many devices to a single SCSI port, so that SCSI is really an I/O bus rather than simply an interface. Although SCSI is an ANSI standard, there are many variations of it, so two SCSI interfaces may be incompatible. For example, SCSI supports several types of connectors. While SCSI has been the standard interface for Macintoshes, the iMac comes with IDE, a less expensive interface, in which the controller is integrated into the disk or CD-ROM drive. Other interfaces supported by PCs include enhanced IDE and ESDI for mass storage devices, and Centronics for printers. You can, however, attach SCSI devices to a PC by inserting a SCSI board in one of the expansion slots. Many high-end new PCs come with SCSI built in. Note, however, that the lack of a single SCSI standard means that some devices may not work with some SCSI boards.

Secure Shell – See "SSH."

Secure Sockets Layer – See "SSL."

segment – An electrically continuous piece of a bus-based LAN, typically Ethernet. Segments can be joined together using repeaters, switches, bridges, or routers.

segmentation – Increasing the available bandwidth per device by dividing a network with bridges, switches, or routers to decrease the number of nodes on a segment.

segmentation and reassembly (SAR) – A process that occurs within an ATM access device, such as a LAN switch, or sometimes in a LAN switch. In a SAR process, information carried in data frames, such as Ethernet, or voice frames, such as a DS-0 channel, is divided into cells. The SAR is responsible for mapping data from the AAL Convergence Sublayer into the cell payloads of an ATM cell stream.

Sequenced Packet Exchange – See "SPX."

server – A computer or device on a network that manages network resources. For example, a file server is a computer and storage device dedicated to storing files. Any user on the network can store files on the server. A print server is a computer that manages one or more printers, and a network server is a computer that manages network traffic. A database server is a computer system that processes database queries. Servers are often dedicated, meaning that they perform no other tasks besides their server tasks. On multiprocessing operating systems, however, a single computer can execute several programs at once. A server in this case could refer to the program that is managing resources rather than the entire computer.

Service Advertising Protocol (SAP) – A protocol used in Novell's NetWare protocol suite that allows servers to inform workstations of their availability, through periodic broadcast packets.

shielded twisted pair (STP) – Copper cable that includes one or more sets of cable pairs that have been molded into an insulating material and covered by a braided shielding conductor. STP offers better noise protection than unshielded twisted pair (UTP) but is much more expensive and more difficult to use. STP is commonly associated with early token ring networks.

S-HTTP – An extension to the HTTP protocol to support sending data securely over the World Wide Web. Not all Web browsers and servers support S-HTTP. Another technology for transmitting secure communications over the World Wide Web – Secure Sockets Layer (SSL) – is more prevalent. However, SSL and S-HTTP have very different designs and goals so it is possible to use the two protocols together. Whereas SSL is designed to establish a secure connection between two computers, S-HTTP is designed to send individual messages securely. Both protocols have been submitted to the Internet Engineering Task Force (IETF) for approval as a standard. S-HTTP was developed by Enterprise Integration Technologies (EIT), which was acquired by Verifone, Inc., in 1995.

Signal Computing System Architecture (SCSA) – PC telephony bus protocol promoted by Dialogic.

signaling – Communications between devices to set up calls and tear them down.

SIMMs (single in-line memory modules) – A small circuit board that can hold a group of memory chips. Typically, SIMMs hold up to 8 (on Macintoshes) or 9 (on PCs) RAM chips. On PCs, the ninth chip is often used for parity error checking. Unlike memory chips, SIMMs are measured in bytes rather than bits. SIMMs are easier to install than individual memory chips. The bus from a SIMM to the actual memory chips is 32 bits wide. A newer technology, called dual in-line memory module (DIMM), provides a 64-bit bus. For modern Pentium microprocessors that have a 64-bit bus, you must use either DIMMs or pairs of SIMMs.

Simple Mail Transfer Protocol – See "SMTP."

Simple Network Management Protocol (SNMP) – A set of protocols for managing complex networks. The first versions of SNMP were developed in the early '80s. SNMP works by sending messages, called protocol data units (PDUs), to different parts of a network. SNMP-compliant devices, called agents, store data about themselves in Management Information Bases (MIBs) and return this data to the SNMP requesters. SNMP 1 reports only whether a device is functioning properly. The industry has attempted to define a new set of protocols called SNMP 2 that would provide additional information, but the standardization efforts have not been successful. Instead, network managers have turned to a related technology called RMON that provides more detailed information about network usage.

single attached station (SAS) – A form of FDDI connection in which a single ring is supported. Typically used for connecting workstations and servers to a concentrator.

single in-line memory modules (SIMMs) – See "SIMMs."

single mode – A form of fiber optic cabling in which light follows a single path as it traverses the cable. More expensive, and with a higher maximum rate and distance, than multimode fiber optic cable.

SIP (Session Initiation Protocol) – An IETF protocol for beginning, modifying, and terminating sessions between one or more users, in which a "session" is any form of interactive multimedia communication conducted across the Internet.

Small Computer System Interface (SCSI) – See "SCSI."

SMS (Short Message Service) – Service for sending and receiving short alpha-numeric messages (up to 160 characters) to GSM mobile phones. (SMS and GSM are technologies used primarily in Europe.)

SMTP (Simple Mail Transfer Protocol) – A protocol for sending e-mail messages between servers. Most e-mail systems that send mail over the Internet use SMTP to send messages from one server to another; the messages can then be retrieved with an e-mail client using either POP or IMAP. In addition, SMTP is generally used to send messages from a mail client to a mail server. This is why you need to specify both the POP and IMAP server and the SMTP server when you config-ure your e-mail application.

SNA (Systems Network Architecture) – An important protocol suite developed by IBM Corporation beginning in the 1970s for use in both local and wide area com-munications. Pioneered many modern communications techniques. Many SNA networks are still in place at large organizations, although they are generally converting to TCP/IP.

SNMP – See "Simple Network Management Protocol."

SOCKS – A protocol for handling TCP traffic through a proxy server. It can be used with virtually any TCP application, including Web browsers and FTP clients. It provides a simple firewall because it checks incoming and outgoing packets and hides the IP addresses of client applications. There are two main versions of SOCKS – V4 and V5. V5 adds an authentication mechanism for additional security. There are many freeware implementations of both versions. One of the most common V5 implementations is SOCKS5, developed by NEC. SOCKS was recently accepted as an IETF standard and is documented in RFCs 1928, 1929, and 1961.

SONET (Synchronous Optical Network) – A set of standards for data communication over fiber optic cable at speeds of 51.84 Mbps and above.

Source Route Bridge – A bridge that is capable of processing the Routing Information Field in a token ring or FDDI frame to determine whether or not to forward that particular frame.

Source Route Transparent (SRT) – A protocol that is used in some token ring networks, which uses source routing for frames that need it, and uses transparent bridging for other frames. A variant (SRTB) translates from one type of frame to the other, so that end stations with disparate configurations can communicate.

Source Routing (SRB) – A protocol in which the end stations determine the path that frames will follow between them. An end station sends a preliminary route-finding broadcast frame, which turns into many frames, each following a separate route, and each accumulating a statement of the path it has followed. The one that arrives first is assumed to have followed the fastest path, and its path is then specified in all subsequent frames. Source routing is used in some, but not all, token ring and FDDI networks.

Spanning Tree – A protocol specified in the IEEE 802.1D standard that allows a network to have a topology that contains physical loops. Spanning Tree operates in bridges and switches. It opens certain paths to create a tree topology, thereby preventing packets from looping endlessly on the network.

Spanning Tree domain – A portion of a network in which a single Spanning Tree operates.

Speaker dependent voice recognition – Recognition of spoken words by a speaker that the system has been trained to recognize.

Speaker independent voice recognition – Recognition of words spoken by any speaker.

Speaker verification – Recognizing a speaker by his/her voice print.

SPX (Sequenced Packet Exchange) – A transport layer protocol (layer 4 of the OSI Model) used in Novell NetWare networks. The SPX layer sits on top of the IPX layer (layer 3) and provides connection-oriented services between two nodes on the network. SPX is used primarily by client/server applications. Whereas the IPX protocol is similar to IP, SPX is similar to TCP. Together, therefore, IPX/SPX provides connection services similar to TCP/IP.

SQL (structured query language) – Pronounced either "see-kwell" or as separate letters. SQL is a standardized query language for requesting information from a database. The original version called SEQUEL (structured English query language) was designed by an IBM research center in 1974 and 1975. SQL was first introduced as a commercial database system in 1979 by Oracle Corporation. Historically, SQL has been the favorite query language for database management systems running on minicomputers and mainframes. Increasingly, however, SQL is being supported by PC database systems because it supports distributed databases (databases that are spread out over several computer systems). This enables several users on a local area network to access the same database simultaneously. Although there are different dialects of SQL, it is nevertheless the closest thing to a standard query language that currently exists. In 1986, ANSI approved a rudimentary version of SQL as the official standard, but most versions of SQL since then have included many extensions to the ANSI standard. In 1991, ANSI updated the standard. The new standard is known as SAG SQL.

SS7 (Signaling System 7) – CCITT developed the Signaling System 7 specification to support the increasing number of features and integrated data services. It is a common channel signaling system. This means one channel (either analog and almost always digital) is used only for sending the signaling information whether the system has one bearer channel or multiple bearer channels. To support this architecture, a new protocol was developed and is a variation of data packet switching. This means the signaling channel uses framing words, checksums, packets for address and information packets. The packet order is well defined and flexible for the user requirements.

SSH (Secure Shell) – Developed by SSH Communications Security Ltd., Secure Shell is a program to log into another computer over a network, to execute commands in a remote machine, and to move files from one machine to another. It provides strong authentication and secure communications over insecure channels. It is a replacement for rlogin, rsh, rcp, and rdist. SSH protects a network from attacks such as IP spoofing, IP source routing, and DNS spoofing. An attacker who has managed to take over a network can only force SSH to disconnect. He or she cannot play back the traffic or hijack the connection when encryption is enabled. When using SSH's slogin (instead of rlogin), the entire login session, including transmission of password, is encrypted; therefore it is almost impossible for an outsider to collect passwords. SSH is available for Windows, UNIX, Macintosh, and OS/2, and it also works with RSA authentication.

SSL (Secure Sockets Layer) – A protocol developed by Netscape for transmitting private documents via the Internet. SSL works by using a private key to encrypt data that's transferred over the SSL connection. Both Netscape Navigator and Internet Explorer support SSL, and many Web sites use the protocol to obtain confidential user information, such as credit card numbers. By convention, Web pages that require an SSL connection start with `https:` instead of `http:`. Another protocol for transmitting data securely over the World Wide Web is

Secure HTTP (S-HTTP). Whereas SSL creates a secure connection between a client and a server, over which any amount of data can be sent securely, S-HTTP is designed to transmit individual messages securely. SSL and S-HTTP, therefore, can be seen as complementary rather than competing technologies. Both protocols have been approved by the Internet Engineering Task Force (IETF) as a standard.

standby monitor – Any 802.5 token ring adapter currently attached (active) to the ring that is not the active monitor. One standby monitor assumes the role of the active monitor if it is no longer present on the ring.

Star – A network topology in which each node is connected to a central point.

station cabling – See "horizontal cabling."

Statistical Time Division Multiplexing (STDM) – Also known as statistical multiplexing. A form of time division multiplexing in which a given data stream can obtain more or less bandwidth dynamically, based on its needs and on the demands of other data streams. Widely used in devices such as routers, LAN switches, and frame relay switches.

store and forward – A method of switching in which a message is received as a whole, buffered, and then resent. All routers and virtually all current switches work in this manner. See also "cut-through."

STP – See "shielded twisted pair." Not related to the popular engine-cleansing fuel additive.

structured query language (SQL) – Pronounced either "see-kwell" or as separate letters. SQL is a standardized query language for requesting information from a database. The original version called SEQUEL (structured English query language) was designed by an IBM research center in 1974 and 1975. SQL was first introduced as a commercial database system in 1979 by Oracle Corporation. Historically, SQL has been the favorite query language for database management systems running on minicomputers and mainframes. Increasingly, however, SQL is being supported by PC database systems because it supports distributed databases (databases that are spread out over several computer systems). This enables several users on a local area network to access the same database simultaneously. Although there are different dialects of SQL, it is nevertheless the closest thing to a standard query language that currently exists. In 1986, ANSI approved a rudimentary version of SQL as the official standard, but most versions of SQL since then have included many extensions to the ANSI standard. In 1991, ANSI updated the standard. The new standard is known as SAG SQL.

subnet – A portion of a network in which all stations share a common subnet address.

subnet address – The subnet portion of an IP address.

subnet mask – See "address mask."

subscriber – A voice messaging system user who has the capability to originate and receive voice messages and to manage stored voice data. Old name for a caller.

sustainable cell rate – The maximum throughput bursty traffic can achieve within a given virtual circuit without risking cell loss.

SVC (switched virtual circuit) – A temporary virtual circuit that is set up and used only as long as data is being transmitted. Once the communication between the two hosts is complete, the SVC disappears. In contrast, a permanent virtual circuit (PVC) remains available at all times.

switched virtual circuit (SVC) – See "SVC."

synchronous – Signals that are sourced from the same timing reference and have the same frequency. For example, in high-speed wide area digital communications, the network commonly provides a reference clocking source to which each subscriber's equipment synchronizes its transmissions.

synchronous transfer mode – B-ISDN communications method that transmits a group of different data streams synchronized to a single reference clock.

T1 – A dedicated phone connection supporting data rates of 1.544 Mbits per second. A T1 line actually consists of 24 individual channels, each of which supports 64 Kbits per second. Each 64 Kbit/second channel can be configured to carry voice or data traffic. Most telephone companies allow you to buy just some of these individual channels, which is known as fractional T1 access. T1 lines are a popular leased line option for businesses connecting to the Internet and for Internet Service Providers (ISPs) connecting to the Internet backbone. The Internet backbone itself consists of faster T3 connections. T1 lines are sometimes referred to as DS1 lines.

T3 – See "DS-3."

tagging – See "frame tagging."

TAPI (Telephony Application Programming Interface) – An API for connecting a PC running Windows to telephone services. TAPI was introduced in 1993 as the result of joint development by Microsoft and Intel. The standard supports connections by individual computers as well as LAN connections serving many computers. Within each connection type, TAPI defines standards for simple call control and for manipulating call content. The Telephony Server Application Programming Interface (TSAPI) defines similar capabilities for NetWare servers.

TAXI – An early standard for ATM transmission at 100 Mbps. Not commonly used now.

TCP – See "Transmission Control Protocol."

TCP/IP (Transmission Control Protocol/Internet Protocol) – The suite of communications protocols used to connect hosts on the Internet. TCP/IP uses several protocols, the two main ones being TCP and IP. TCP/IP is built into the UNIX operating system and is used by the Internet, making it the de facto standard for transmitting data over networks. Even network operating systems that have their own protocols, such as NetWare, also support TCP/IP.

TDM (Time Division Multiplexing) — A type of multiplexing that combines data streams by assigning each stream a different time slot in a set. TDM repeatedly transmits a fixed sequence of time slots over a single transmission channel. Within T-Carrier systems, such as T1 and T3, TDM combines Pulse Code Modulated (PCM) streams created for each conversation or data stream.

Telephony Application Programming Interface — See "TAPI."

Telephony Server Application Programming Interface — See "TSAPI."

Telnet — The protocol within the TCP/IP protocol suite that provides a terminal emulation function.

Terms of Service (TOS) — A contract specifying what a subscriber can and cannot do while using an ISP's service. Contains things like liability disclaimers, lists of actions or behaviors that will result in the termination of a customer's account, definition of terms such as "unlimited use," billing policies, SPAM clauses, etc.

TFTP (Trivial File Transfer Protocol) — A simple form of the File Transfer Protocol (FTP). TFTP uses the User Datagram Protocol (UDP) and provides no security features. It is often used by servers to boot diskless workstations, X-terminals, and routers.

Time Division Multiplexing — See "TDM."

TLS — See "Transparent LAN Service."

token — A unique packet that is passed around a token ring or FDDI LAN continuously. When a device wishes to transmit, it waits until it receives the token, attaches its message to the token, and transmits it. The device then removes its message from the ring when the token and message return to it.

token ring — A network architecture standardized in IEEE 802.5 in which the devices on a ring transmit data while they are in possession of a token which passes from node to node continuously. Token ring operates at 4 or 16 Mbps.

topology — The shape of a local area network (LAN) or other communications system. There are three principal topologies used in LANs. Bus topology: All devices are connected to a central cable, called the bus or backbone. Bus networks are relatively inexpensive and easy to install for small networks. Ethernet systems use a bus topology. Ring topology: All devices are connected to one another in the shape of a closed loop, so that each device is connected directly to two other devices, one on either side of it. Ring topologies are relatively expensive and difficult to install, but they offer high bandwidth and can span large distances. Star topology: All devices are connected to a central hub. Star networks are relatively easy to install and manage, but bottlenecks can occur because all data must pass through the hub.

ToS (Type of Service) — A field within an IP header which can be used by the device originating the packet, or by an intermediate networking device, to signal a request for a specific QoS level.

TP/PMD — See "Twisted Pair/Physical Medium Dependent."

transaction processing – Using telephone input to interrogate and update a computer database. This term has a slightly different meaning with voice processing, as opposed to data processing.

Transmission Control Protocol (TCP) – A layer 4 protocol in the set of protocols that supports the Internet and many private networks. TCP provides a guaranteed transport service.

Transmission Control Protocol/Internet Protocol (TCP/IP) – See "TCP/IP."

Transparent LAN Service (TLS) – A service provided by a common carrier in which multiple end user locations are interconnected, using layer 2 or layer 3 processes, in such a way that the entire network appears to be located on a single site. Commonly implemented today using an ATM service, with LAN switches equipped with ATM uplinks at the customer's sites.

tree – A LAN topology in which there is only one route between any two of the nodes on the network. The pattern of connections resembles a tree.

Trivial File Transfer Protocol – See "TFTP."

TSAPI (Telephony Server API) – An API developed by Novell and AT&T that enables programmers to build telephony and CTI applications. TSAPI is similar to TAPI, which was developed by Microsoft and Intel. But whereas TAPI has been implemented for the Windows operating system, TSAPI runs on NetWare platforms. Another key difference is that TAPI can be used for both client- and server-based applications whereas TSAPI is strictly a server API.

twisted pair – Insulated copper wires twisted together with the twists or lays varied in length to reduce potential signal interference between the pairs. They are usually bundled together and wrapped in a cable sheath. New data grade Unshielded Twisted Pair (Category 5) is specified for 100 Mbps transmission.

Twisted Pair/Physical Medium Dependent (TP/PMD) – A physical-level specification for FDDI which allows it to operate over unshielded twisted pair and shielded twisted pair copper cable. Sometimes referred to as "CDDI."

Type of Service – See "ToS."

U Interface – A physical interface in an ISDN Basic Rate service that uses a single copper pair.

UBR – See "unspecified bit rate."

UDP (User Datagram Protocol) – A connectionless protocol that, like TCP, runs on top of IP networks. Unlike TCP/IP, UDP/IP provides very few error recovery services, offering instead a direct way to send and receive datagrams over an IP network. It's used primarily for broadcasting messages over a network.

UNI (User-to-Network Interface) – An interface point between ATM end users and a private ATM switch, or between a private ATM switch and the public carrier ATM network; defined by physical and protocol specifications per ATM Forum UNI documents. The standard adopted by the ATM Forum to define connections between users or end stations and a local switch.

Unicast – A frame that is sent from one station to another. A unicast contains the specific MAC addresses of the source and destination devices.

Unified Messaging (UM) – Application that stores voice mail, fax mail, and e-mail in one mailbox. With UM applications, users can view and/or listen to voice, fax, and electronic mail in one Inbox, which is accessible electronically or by phone.

uniform resource locator – See "URL."

universal serial bus (USB) – See "USB."

Unshielded Twisted Pair – See "UTP."

unspecified bit rate (UBR) – A form of ATM transmission in which an information stream is supported on whatever bandwidth is available after other connection types have been satisfied. No congestion control is provided. UBR is commonly used to support information streams originating in LAN switches with ATM uplinks.

URL (uniform resource locator) – The global address of documents and other resources on the World Wide Web. The first part of the address indicates what protocol to use, and the second part specifies the IP address or the domain name where the resource is located. For example, the two URLs below point to two different files at the domain pcwebopedia.com. The first specifies an executable file that should be fetched using the FTP protocol; the second specifies a Web page that should be fetched using the HTTP protocol.

```
ftp://www.pcwebopedia.com
http://www.pcwebopedia.com
```

USB (universal serial bus) – A new external bus standard that supports data transfer rates of 12 Mbps (12 million bits per second). A single USB port can be used to connect up to 127 peripheral devices, such as mice, modems, and keyboards. USB also supports Plug-and-Play installation and hot plugging. Starting in 1996, a few computer manufacturers started including USB support in their new machines. It wasn't until the release of the best-selling iMac in 1998 that USB became widespread. It is expected to completely replace serial and parallel ports.

User Datagram Protocol (UDP) – See "UDP."

UTP (Unshielded Twisted Pair) – A popular type of cable that consists of two unshielded wires twisted around each other. Due to its low cost, UTP cabling is used extensively for local area networks (LANs) and telephone connections. UTP cabling does not offer as high bandwidth or as good protection from interference as coaxial or fiber optic cables, but it is less expensive and easier to work with.

VCI – See "virtual channel identifier."

virtual channel – A single connection across a UNI or NNI allowing the switching of various ATM cells in a virtual path to different destinations.

virtual channel identifier (VCI) – Identifier in an ATM cell of local significance across UNI or NNI which distinguishes data of one virtual channel from the data of another.

virtual circuit – A link that behaves like a dedicated point-to-point line or a system that delivers packets in sequence, as would happen on an actual point-to-point network.

virtual LAN (VLAN) – See "VLAN."

virtual path – Contains virtual circuits that are to be switched together to a common destination such as an inter-exchange carrier.

virtual path identifier (VPI) – The field in the ATM cell header that labels (identifies) a particular virtual path.

virtual private network – See "VPN."

Virtual Router Redundancy Protocol (VRRP) – A non-Cisco-driven IAB protocol that allows several routers on a multi-access link to utilize the same virtual IP address. One router will be elected as a master, with the other router(s) acting as backup(s) in case of master router failure. Host systems may be configured with a single default gateway, rather than running an active routing protocol. See also "Hot Standby Router Protocol."

VLAN (virtual LAN) – A network of computers that behave as if they are connected to the same wire even though they may actually be physically located on different segments of a LAN. VLANs are configured through software rather than hardware, which makes them extremely flexible. One of the biggest advantages of VLANs is that when a computer is physically moved to another location, it can stay on the same VLAN without any hardware reconfiguration.

VM (voice mail) – A system for storing, reviewing, and distributing voice messages.

Voice board – An interface card that handles the connection between voice input and the computer.

Voice encoding algorithm-ADPCM (G.721) – A standard for digitally encoding analog voice signals.

voice mail (VM) – See "VM."

voice message – A digitally recorded message, input from a telephone.

Voice over IP – See "VoIP."

voice processing – A broad term encompassing several voice-linked facilities. The facilities divide into two sections: treating voice calls as messages, and using a telephone as an interactive terminal to gain access to data and other message facilities.

voice recognition – Recognition of spoken words. It can be speaker dependent (see "Speaker dependent voice recognition") or speaker independent (see "Speaker independent voice recognition").

voice response (VR) – See "VR."

VoIP (Voice over IP) – VoIP is the term used to describe the hardware and software that is used to transmit voice over a data network using the Internet Protocol (IP). The data network can be either the Internet or a corporate intranet. Potential and real benefits include saving money, the ability to manage both the voice and data network as one network, easier moves of IP phones, and additional integrated new services such as integrated messaging and voice e-mails.

VPI – See "virtual path identifier."

VPN (virtual private network) – A network that is constructed by using public wires to connect nodes. For example, there are a number of systems that enable you to create networks using the Internet as the medium for transporting data. These systems use encryption and other security mechanisms to ensure that only authorized users can access the network and that the data cannot be intercepted.

VR (voice response) – Response to an incoming telephone call with synthesized speech.

WAN (wide area network) – A computer network that spans a relatively large geographical area. Typically, a WAN consists of two or more local area networks (LANs). Computers connected to a wide area network are often connected through public networks, such as the telephone system. They can also be connected through leased lines or satellites. The largest WAN in existence is the Internet.

WAP (wireless application protocol) – WAP is a carrier-independent, transaction-oriented protocol for wireless data networks. Phones that support WAP have larger screens and a rolling mouse to support visual, interactive computer telephony (the WWW) and it is also a voice response system.

Web – See "WWW."

wide area network – See "WAN."

World Wide Web – See "WWW."

WWW (World Wide Web) – A system of Internet servers that support specially formatted documents. The documents are formatted in a language called HTML (HyperText Markup Language) that supports links to other documents, as well as graphics, audio, and video files. This means you can jump from one document to another simply by clicking on hot spots. Not all Internet servers are part of the World Wide Web. There are several applications called Web browsers that make it easy to access the World Wide Web; two of the most popular are Netscape Navigator and Microsoft's Internet Explorer.

X.25 – An ITU standard for the interface to a public packet-switching network. Generally connection-oriented.

XML (extensible markup language) – A new specification being developed by the W3C. XML is a pared-down version of SGML, designed especially for Web documents. It enables designers to create their own customized tags to provide functionality not available with HTML. For example, XML supports links that point to multiple documents, as opposed to HTML links, which can reference just one destination each. Whether XML eventually supplants HTML as the standard Web formatting specification depends a lot on whether it is supported by future Web browsers. So far, the only major browser vendor to endorse XML is Microsoft, which has stated that XML will be supported in a future version of Internet Explorer.

Appendix 1

Trademarks and Copyrights

WebPhone is a trademark or registered trademark of Adir Technologies or its subsidiaries.

PostScript is a trademark or registered trademark of Adobe Systems, Inc.

The Alcatel word and the Alcatel logo are trademarks or registered trademarks of Alcatel Internetworking, Inc. (Compagnie Financière Alcatel, Paris, France).

Apple, the Apple logo, AppleTalk, EtherTalk, LocalTalk, Macintosh, and TokenTalk are trademarks or registered trademarks of Apple Computer, Inc.

Cisco is a trademark or registered trademark of Cisco Systems, Inc.

CineVideo is a trademark or registered trademark of CINECOM Corporation.

DEC, DECmcc, DECnet, Digital, Ethernet, LAT, LAVC, Micro-VAX, MOP, POLYCENTER, ThinWire, Ultrix, VAX, and VAX Cluster are trademarks or registered trademarks of Compaq Computer Corporation.

IP Library, IP Technologies Library, and DigiNet are trademarks or registered trademarks of Digital Network Corporation.

eDial is a trademark or registered trademark of eDial, Inc.

Video VoxPhone is a trademark or registered trademark of E-Tech Canada Ltd.

Eyematic iVisit is a trademark or registered trademark of Eyematic Interfaces, Inc.

CUseeMe and CUseeMe Pro are trademarks or registered trademarks of First Virtual Communications, Inc.

PhoneFree is a trademark or registered trademark of Gemini Voice Solutions, Inc.

iBasis Network is a trademark or registered trademark of iBasis, Inc.

Ethernet, Intel, and Video Phone are trademarks or registered trademarks of Intel Corporation.

AIX, AT, IBM, IBM PC LAN, NetView, PC/AT, PC/XT, PS/2, SNA, System/370, MicroChannel, NetBIOS, SAA, and System View are trademarks or registered trademarks of International Business Machines Corporation.

ClearPhone is a trademark or registered trademark of Internet Communication Technologies, Inc.

IRIS Phone is a trademark or registered trademark of IRIS Systems.

ITXC is a trademark or registered trademark of ITXC Corporation.

Net2Phone is a trademark or registered trademark of Net2Phone, Inc.

Level 3 Communications is a trademark or registered trademark of Level 3 Communications, Inc.

MediaRing and MediaRing Talk are trademarks or registered trademarks of MediaRing.com, Inc.

Mediatrix Telecom, Inc., and the Mediatrix logo are trademarks or registered trademarks of Mediatrix Telecom, Inc.

Microsoft, Microsoft NetMeeting, MS-DOS, LAN Manager, Windows, and Windows NT are trademarks or registered trademarks of Microsoft Corporation.

CoolTalk is a trademark or registered trademark of Netscape Communications Corporation.

NetVoice is a trademark or registered trademark of NetVoice Technologies Corporation.

Sniffer is a trademark or registered trademark of Network Associates, Inc.

Networks Telephony is a trademark or registered trademark of Networks Telephony Corporation.

IPX, ManageWise, NetWare, NetWare 386, Novell, and SPX are trademarks or registered trademarks of Novell, Inc.

Nuera is a trademark or registered trademark of Nuera Communications, Inc.

OnLive is a trademark or registered trademark of OnLive, Inc.

Pingtel is a trademark or registered trademark of Pingtel Corporation.

Qwest is a trademark or registered trademark of Qwest Communications International, Inc.

BSD is a trademark or registered trademark of the Regents of the University of California.

PC-Telephone and the PC-Telephone logo are trademarks or registered trademarks of SELECTRA OOD.

Java; Network File System; NFS; Sun; Sun Microsystems, Inc.; Sun Microsystems; SunNet; SunOS; and SunSoft are trademarks or registered trademarks of Sun Microsystems, Inc. SPARC is a trademark or registered trademark of SPARC International, Inc., licensed to Sun Microsystems, Inc.

Internet Phone, Communicate! Pro, and Surf&Call are trademarks or registered trademarks of VocalTec Communications Ltd.

DigiPhone is a trademark or registered trademark of Wincroft, Inc.

Ethernet and Xerox are trademarks or registered trademarks of Xerox Corporation.

UNIX is a trademark or registered trademark of X/Open Company Ltd.

Text extracted from International Telecommunication Union (ITU) material has been reproduced with the prior authorization of the ITU as copyright holder. The sole responsibility for selecting extracts for reproduction lies with the author and publisher of this text and can in no way be attributed to the ITU. The complete volume(s) of the ITU material, from which the texts reproduced are extracted, can be obtained from: International Telecommunication Union, Sales and Marketing Division, Place des Nations – CH-1211 GENEVA 20 (Switzerland); phone +41 22 730 61 41; E-mail: sales@itu.int; www.itu.int/publications.

All other trademarks are the property of their respective owners.

Index

Numerics

continued

W

WAN. *See* Wide Area Network
Weighted Fair Queuing
(WFQ), 308–309
Weighted Random Early
Detection (WRED), 309
Westbay Engineers Ltd., 280,
290, 310, 391ˑ
Westbay Traffic Calculators
(Westbay Engineers
Ltd.), 310
Westplan (Westbay
Engineers Ltd.)
demo version, CD-ROM,
391
Guided Tour, 290
link addition, 281–282
link display, 283, 286–289
node addition, 281
optimization of network,
286
Outlook Mode, 280
project property addition,
282–283
routing, 284–286
traffic parameters,
entering, 283–284
transmission medium
selection, 282
use of tool, 280–290
white board, customer service
use of, 48–49

Wide Area Network (WAN)
alternatives, 174–176
analog lines, 174–175
Asynchronous Transfer
Mode (ATM), IP over,
192–196
Asynchronous Transfer
Mode (ATM), voice
over, 196–199
carriers, list of, 204–206
cloud diagram, 173–174
digital lines, 175–176
Digital Subscriber Line
(DSL), voice over,
199–204
frame relay, IP over,
186–188
frame relay, voice over,
188–192
Integrated Services Digital
Network (ISDN),
182–183
Point-to-Point Protocol
(PPP), 184–186
Public Switched
Telephone Network
(PSTN), 174
Serial Line IP (SLIP),
183–184
signal level multiplexing
hierarchy, 177–182
T1/T3, 176–182

Window field, TCP header,
153
wireless communication,
integration with IP,
60–63
working group, IETF. *See*
Internet Engineering
Task Force working
groups
World Interactive Network,
206
World Wide Web Consortium,
395, 411
WorldCom, Inc., 206
WRED. *See* Weighted Random
Early Detection

X

X.25 protocol, 9, 186
Xerox Network Systems
(XNS) Internet
Datagram Protocol
(IDP), 186
XO Communications, 206

Y

Yankee Group, 13

Z

zone, 216, 268–269

Hungry Minds, Inc.
End-User License Agreement

5. Limited Warranty.

   (a) HMI warrants that the Software and Software Media are free from defects in materials and workmanship under normal use for a period of sixty (60) days from the date of purchase of this Book. If HMI receives notification within the warranty period of defects in materials or workmanship, HMI will replace the defective Software Media.

   (b) HMI AND THE AUTHOR OF THE BOOK DISCLAIM ALL OTHER WARRANTIES, EXPRESS OR IMPLIED, INCLUDING WITHOUT LIMITATION IMPLIED WARRANTIES OF MERCHANTABILITY AND FITNESS FOR A PARTICULAR PURPOSE, WITH RESPECT TO THE SOFTWARE, THE PROGRAMS, THE SOURCE CODE CONTAINED THEREIN, AND/OR THE TECHNIQUES DESCRIBED IN THIS BOOK. HMI DOES NOT WARRANT THAT THE FUNCTIONS CONTAINED IN THE SOFTWARE WILL MEET YOUR REQUIREMENTS OR THAT THE OPERATION OF THE SOFTWARE WILL BE ERROR FREE.

   (c) This limited warranty gives you specific legal rights, and you may have other rights that vary from jurisdiction to jurisdiction.

6. Remedies.

   (a) HMI's entire liability and your exclusive remedy for defects in materials and workmanship shall be limited to replacement of the Software Media, which may be returned to HMI with a copy of your receipt at the following address: Software Media Fulfillment Department, Attn.: *Voice over IP Technologies: Building the Converged Network*, Hungry Minds, Inc., 10475 Crosspoint Blvd., Indianapolis, IN 46256, or call 1-800-762-2974. Please allow four to six weeks for delivery. This Limited Warranty is void if failure of the Software Media has resulted from accident, abuse, or misapplication. Any replacement Software Media will be warranted for the remainder of the original warranty period or thirty (30) days, whichever is longer.

   (b) In no event shall HMI or the author be liable for any damages whatsoever (including without limitation damages for loss of business profits, business interruption, loss of business information, or any other pecuniary loss) arising from the use of or inability to use the Book or the Software, even if HMI has been advised of the possibility of such damages.

   (c) Because some jurisdictions do not allow the exclusion or limitation of liability for consequential or incidental damages, the above limitation or exclusion may not apply to you.

7. U.S. Government Restricted Rights. Use, duplication, or disclosure of the Software for or on behalf of the United States of America, its agencies and/or instrumentalities (the "U.S. Government") is subject to restrictions as stated in paragraph (c)(1)(ii) of the Rights in Technical Data and Computer Software clause of DFARS 252.227-7013, or subparagraphs (c) (1) and (2) of the Commercial Computer Software - Restricted Rights clause at FAR 52.227-19, and in similar clauses in the NASA FAR supplement, as applicable.

8. General. This Agreement constitutes the entire understanding of the parties and revokes and supersedes all prior agreements, oral or written, between them and may not be modified or amended except in a writing signed by both parties hereto that specifically refers to this Agreement. This Agreement shall take precedence over any other documents that may be in conflict herewith. If any one or more provisions contained in this Agreement are held by any court or tribunal to be invalid, illegal, or otherwise unenforceable, each and every other provision shall remain in full force and effect.